Old Glasgow: the place and the people. From the Roman occupation to the eighteenth century. L.P.

Andrew Macgeorge

Old Glasgow: the place and the people. From the Roman occupation to the eighteenth century.
L.P.
Macgeorge, Andrew
British Library, Historical Print Editions
British Library
1888
xii. 317 p. ; 8°.
10369.i.6.

The BiblioLife Network

This project was made possible in part by the BiblioLife Network (BLN), a project aimed at addressing some of the huge challenges facing book preservationists around the world. The BLN includes libraries, library networks, archives, subject matter experts, online communities and library service providers. We believe every book ever published should be available as a high-quality print reproduction; printed on- demand anywhere in the world. This insures the ongoing accessibility of the content and helps generate sustainable revenue for the libraries and organizations that work to preserve these important materials.

The following book is in the "public domain" and represents an authentic reproduction of the text as printed by the original publisher. While we have attempted to accurately maintain the integrity of the original work, there are sometimes problems with the original book or micro-film from which the books were digitized. This can result in minor errors in reproduction. Possible imperfections include missing and blurred pages, poor pictures, markings and other reproduction issues beyond our control. Because this work is culturally important, we have made it available as part of our commitment to protecting, preserving, and promoting the world's literature.

GUIDE TO FOLD-OUTS, MAPS and OVERSIZED IMAGES

In an online database, page images do not need to conform to the size restrictions found in a printed book. When converting these images back into a printed bound book, the page sizes are standardized in ways that maintain the detail of the original. For large images, such as fold-out maps, the original page image is split into two or more pages.

Guidelines used to determine the split of oversize pages:

• Some images are split vertically; large images require vertical and horizontal splits.
• For horizontal splits, the content is split left to right.
• For vertical splits, the content is split from top to bottom.
• For both vertical and horizontal splits, the image is processed from top left to bottom right.

OLD GLASGOW.

GLASGOW CATHEDRAL.

THE OLD WESTERN TOWER AND CONSISTORY HOUSE.

LOOKING NORTH-EAST.

Old Glasgow:

THE PLACE AND THE PEOPLE.

FROM THE ROMAN OCCUPATION TO
THE EIGHTEENTH CENTURY.

BY

ANDREW MACGEORGE.

THIRD EDITION.

GLASGOW: BLACKIE AND SON;
LONDON AND EDINBURGH.
1888.

PREFATORY NOTE.

The materials for a History of Glasgow are limited, and such as they are they have to be searched for through numerous books and documents—many of them not generally accessible. The present work is an attempt to bring these materials together in such a systematic form as to give a connected view of the early history of the City. I have been enabled also to add some interesting original matter.

It is not a topographical work: neither does it make any pretension to be a complete history. Its object is to give, in a popular form, some idea of the state of Scotland, and especially of the locality around Glasgow, at and subsequent to the time of Kentigern, its patron saint; of the growth of the city; of the condition of the people—their language, their habits and customs, and their municipal history; with some notices of the geology of the basin of the Clyde, and the wonderful development of the river as a means of traffic.

To friends who have supplied me with valuable information, and to the gentlemen connected with the Corporation by whose courtesy I have been afforded access to official documents and records, I return my warmest thanks.

A. M.

GLENARN, *December*, 1879.

NOTE TO THE THIRD EDITION.

The text of the present edition has been carefully revised, and in the concluding section of the work some material changes have been made so as to bring down the statistical statements as nearly as possible to the present time. The map of the city at the end, giving a comparative view of the extent of the city at the end of the last century and at the present time, has also been brought down to date.

A. M.

GLENARN, *May*, 1888.

CONTENTS.

ILLUSTRATIONS.

* This and the illustration of "The Foulis' Academy of the Fine Arts," p. 282,
are from prints, now very rare, engraved in the Academy, from drawings by David Allan,
who was himself one of the students.

The above inscription is from a stone which formed part of an old house in Back Cow Lone, believed to have been a store belonging to the Incorporation of Bakers.

The stone is now built into the back wall of the house No. 125 Candleriggs.

THE FIDDLER'S CLOSE, NO. 75 HIGH STREET.
Cleared away in the course of the City Improvements in 1878.

THE FIRST BISHOP.

AMONG the earliest, as he was one of the most celebrated, of the *Episcopi Britannorum* was Kentigern, the evangelist of the Strathclyde Britons, and the founder of the see of Glasgow. As Columba was the founder of the Christian Church among the Picts, so Kentigern was the great agent in the revolution which again, after a period of darkness, christianized Cumbria. We have his life written by Jocelin, a monk of Furness, to whom the task was intrusted by the bishop of the same name, formerly abbot of the Cistercian monastery of Melrose, and who was appointed to the see of Glasgow in 1174. The memoir by the monk contains much that is absurd—embodying as it does many legends which are evidently the invention of an age long posterior to that of Kentigern; but there is no ground for thinking, as some have supposed, that the whole history is fabulous. On the contrary, there is reason to believe that, like many others of our early authorities, it contains trustworthy fragments of authentic history, but tampered with for ecclesiastical purposes.

Jocelin informs us that, by the instructions of the bishop his patron, he visited the localities and sought out all the sources from which information could be obtained. Among others he found a missal, then, as he tells us, in use in the Cathedral; and it is curious to us, who enjoy the light of the nineteenth century, to think that in the old Cathedral of Glasgow there were read from this ancient manuscript to the early inhabitants of the city, as parts of divine service, such stories as that of the profligate Queen of Cadzow and her ring; and how Kentigern restored to life a tame robin whose head had been accidentally torn off; and how he lighted the refectory fire by breathing on a frozen twig plucked from a hedge, causing it to burst into flame; and such like fairy tales. It would be unsafe to conclude, however, that in the earlier records from which the monk of Furness drew his materials the legends appeared in the form in which he presented them, and in which they appear in the Breviary of Aberdeen. Some of them may have had their origin in very simple occurrences of easy explanation, and the form in which they have reached us is accounted for by the tendency of the Church of Rome in the middle ages to endow their adopted saints with miraculous powers. What Mr. Burton says of Adamnan's history may be applied to that of Jocelin, but making perhaps a still larger allowance for the later time in which the monk of Furness wrote. "No " doubt," says Mr. Burton, "the great bulk of the life of Columba is " occupied by vaticination and miraculous fable. But there are small " facts to be found in the telling of the large fiction, and if we disbelieve " all narratives because they have the supernatural in them it is difficult " to say at what period true ecclesiastical history commenced, or, speak- " ing strictly, is to commence."[1]

It is important as it is interesting to note that in the preface to his work, Jocelin informs us that he found in the old manuscript referred to—read in the Cathedral though it was—*quoddam sannæ doctrinæ et Catholicæ fidei adversus.* Finding, besides, as he farther states, that the style and composition were defective, he made search for some better authority, and he was rewarded by discovering another treatise *stilo scotico dictatum*—containing many solecisms, he admits, but giving a more full and accurate account of the life and acts of the saint. It is possible that this may have been the Life which the Bollandists say was written by St. Asaph, but of which no trace now remains.[2] Such as it was, Jocelin found that unfortunately it was, like the other, defiled by what he calls doctrinal error. From these statements of the monkish chronicler there can be little doubt that the two ancient records, from which he derived a portion at least, and probably the most authentic portion, of his information, belonged to the early period when the purer faith of Columba and Kentigern and Asaph was preached in Scotland. That the religious views of the earlier writers should differ very much from those held by a devoted adherent of the Church of Rome in the twelfth century is only what might be expected. By that time the greater part of what we regard as the errors of that system had come to prevail. In the tenth century corruption, both in doctrine and morals, had become general; and two centuries later, when Jocelin wrote his history, the state of matters, as regards doctrine at least, had not

---

[1] History of Scotland, vol. i. p. 256.   [2] Act. Sanct. Jan. ii. 97.

improved. It is quite natural, therefore, that Jocelin should regard as error what he would find recorded in the writings of the Irish ecclesiastics. From these materials, however, such as they were, but rejecting the " errors," the monk of Furness compiled the Life of Kentigern which we now possess; and making all due allowance for the views of the writer, it really is, what Bishop Forbes calls it, a charming piece of mediæval biography.

Every archæologist knows of course that the language in which the oldest of these records was written—*stilo scotico*—is not in any way to be confounded with what we now understand as the Scottish dialect. It was not by any means, as a recent writer has supposed, the vulgar or vernacular speech prevalent in the west of Scotland—not very different from the nascent English found in Piers Plowman and the earlier romances.[1] It is no doubt quite probable, as I shall have occasion to show afterwards, that when Jocelin wrote his history the vernacular spoken in Glasgow had already assumed very much the form of later times; but when he speaks of his authority as *stilo scotico dictatum* we may be certain it was in the Irish language. No part of Scotland was known by that name till the tenth century, and not till even after that period was Strathclyde included in the designation. The only Scotia of the time of Kentigern, and for long after, was Ireland, and the statement in Adamnan's interesting biography that Columba came *de Scotia ad Britanniam* would settle the point were there not so many other confirmations of it.

There are two accounts of the date of Kentigern's birth. One places it in the year 518, and the other in 527. The latter is, I think, the more probable. The date of his appearance on the banks of the Clyde has been generally fixed as the year 560, but it must have been ten years earlier. Jocelin states that he was consecrated a bishop at the age of twenty-five, so that (assuming his birth to have been in 527) the date of consecration must have been 552. But Jocelin also tells us that it was not till after he had been some time in Glasgow that he was made a bishop, and if we allow only two years for this previous residence, his advent to Glasgow could not have been later than 550.

He was not, however, the first missionary who had come to that district. During the Roman occupation the Christian religion had been introduced to our island under their auspices; and probably as

---

[1] The Legends of St. Kentigern, by Dr. Stevenson. Edin. 1872.

early as the second century there was a Christian church in Roman Britain. The paganism which it came to supersede has been called Druidical, but it had certainly nothing in common with the repulsive system attributed to the Druids of Gaul, with its human sacrifices and Baal worship. As little had it any connection with the singular stone erections which we find at Stonehenge and elsewhere, which were simply sepulchral monuments, and not, as is popularly supposed, temples or altars.[1] According to Mr. Skene, the paganism of Scotland was the same as what prevailed among the Picts of Ireland: "a sort of fetichism which peopled all the objects of nature with "malignant beings, to whose agency its phenomena were attributed; "while a class of persons termed Magi and Druadh or Druada exercised "great influence among the people, from a belief that they were able "through their aid to practise a species of magic or witchcraft, which "might either be used to benefit those who sought their assistance, "or to injure those to whom they were opposed."[2]

Among the earliest of the Christian missionaries was Ninian, who had been trained at Rome in the doctrine and discipline of the Western Church, and who appears to have built a cell on the banks of the Molindinar towards the end of the fourth century. All that we know of his connection with Glasgow is from the account of the monk of Furness, which bears that when Kentigern came to Strathclyde he made his settlement "near a certain cemetery which had long before "been consecrated by St. Ninian," and which, at the time when Jocelin wrote, was "encircled by a delicious density of overshadowing trees." But the probability is that Ninian did not long remain there, and this may be inferred from the fact that although he had consecrated the cemetery, no interment had ever taken place in it—the interment there by Kentigern of the old saint Fregus or Fergus, to be presently noticed, having been, according to Jocelin, "the first burial in that place where "afterwards many bodies were buried in peace." The chief labours of Ninian were among the neighbouring Picts. The southern division of that people was certainly converted to Christianity at an earlier period than the Strathclyde Britons, and probably by Ninian, who afterwards built his church at Candida Casa, or Whithorn, in Galloway, in the year 397. If Ninian made any converts at Glasgow they must have afterwards lapsed into apostasy.

---

[1] Dr. Hill Burton, in Edinburgh Review, July, 1863.   [2] Celtic Scotland, vol. ii. p. 118.

Before the end of the fourth century Christianity had also been introduced among the Scots in Ireland—whether by Ninian or at an earlier
period does not appear; but Ninian is said to have left his settlement at Candida Casa at the request of his mother and relations in
the last years of his life, and to have gone to Ireland, where, at a
beautiful place called Cluain Coner, granted him by the king, he
built a large monastery, in which he died.[1]   Soon afterwards the
dominion of the Romans in Britain, after an occupation of nearly
four hundred years, came to an end (A.D. 410), and they abandoned
the island for ever.

There now followed a long period of darkness.   Britain had practically ceased to be a part of the Roman Empire.   Her intercourse with
the Continent had been almost entirely cut off; and, with the exception
of a notice of the temporary prevalence of the Pelagian heresy in the
British Church, all is silence for a century and a half.[2]

During this period it was chiefly in the Irish Church that the
light of Christianity was preserved, and it was probably maintained
there in a comparatively pure and primitive state.   This may be inferred from the account given of himself by Columbanus or Colmanus
when, with a small band of missionaries, he appeared in Gaul in 590.
When asked who they were and whence they came, his answer was:
"We are Irish, dwelling at the very ends of the earth.   We be men
"who receive nought beyond the doctrine of the evangelists and
"apostles.   The catholic faith as it was first delivered by the successors
"of the holy apostles is still maintained among us with unchanged
"fidelity."   They did not acknowledge the supremacy of the Pope:
on the contrary, they recognized only "one head, our Lord."   They
maintained that the Pope's jurisdiction as Bishop of Rome did not
extend beyond the limits of the Roman Empire; and when opposed
by the clergy of Gaul on account of observances which were character-
ized as schismatical, Columbanus, in a letter to the Pope, said in effect:
"I am a missionary from a church of God among the barbarians, and
"though temporarily within the limits of your territorial jurisdiction,
"and bound to regard you with respect, I claim the right to follow
"the customs of our own church."[3]

As illustrating farther the separate and independent position of

[1] Round Towers of Ireland, by Dr. Petrie, p. 138.   [2] Celtic Scotland, vol. ii. p. 4.
[3] Celtic Scotland, ii. p. 11.

the church in our islands, may be mentioned the interesting fact that in the latter half of the fifth century, and for long afterwards, an old Latin version of the Scriptures peculiar to the British Isles was in use in the Scoto-Britannic churches differing largely both from the Vulgate and from the known ante-Hieronyman versions.[1] It is questionable if the Vulgate was known to St. Patrick.

The episcopal system in the form it had assumed on the Continent in the time of Columbanus, or as it now exists, was unknown in the early British churches. The monastic element prevailed: the sacerdotal was all but unknown. There was episcopacy in the church, but it was not diocesan episcopacy. The bishops were no doubt treated as a superior order. They were specially invested with functions of consecrating the elements at the communion, and of conferring the right of ordination, but practically their episcopacy was a personal more than an official dignity. They had no more jurisdiction than our ministers of parishes. Frequently they had no jurisdiction at all, and in many instances they were subject to the abbots.[2] They were very numerous. We know from Nennius that when St. Patrick founded in Ireland 365 churches he at the same time ordained 365 bishops, and it was the complaint of St. Bernard and other assailants of the Irish Church that they had a bishop for every congregation. In many instances indeed we find that a single religious community worshipping in one place had several bishops.[3]

Of this early and purer primitive church was Columba—saint, soldier, statesman—one of "the twelve apostles of Ireland" who in the year 563 sailed from Ireland to Britain and became the founder of the world-renowned island monastery, and the head of the Christian church in Scotland. Although the birth and early life of Kentigern are veiled in obscurity, there can be little doubt that his education and his religious views when he came to Strathclyde were the same as those of his great contemporary. In doctrine and matters of observance both of these eminent missionaries followed the earlier apostolic type, and opposed themselves to the differences, in matters of faith as well as practice, which had crept into the Western Church during the period when the intercourse between it and the British churches had been interrupted.

[1] Councils and Ecclesiastical Documents of Great Britain and Ireland, by A. W. Hoddan and Wm. Stubbs, vol i. p. 170.   [2] Celtic Scotland, vol. ii. p. 44.
[3] The Early Celtic Church, by the Bishop of Argyll, p. 34.

We know from Adamnan that the great instrument employed by Columba in the conversion of the pagan tribes was the simple preaching of the word of God, and the same means were no doubt followed by Kentigern.

But although a pure doctrine was preached the earliest "conversions" at the first introduction of Christianity were often of a very wholesale character. Clanship, as an eminent Celtic scholar[1] has justly said, is the true key of Irish history—political and ecclesiastical. Upon the clan Christianity was engrafted in the monastic form. When the Christian missionaries first went to Ireland they found the clans existing there as the primitive form of government, with numerous chieftains virtually independent, and one or more nominal kings. St. Patrick and his followers always addressed themselves in the first instance to the chieftain, and with his baptism followed the adhesion of the clan or sept.[2] Then followed the establishment of a monastery, and it was constituted on the model of a family. The abbot was the father: the monks his children. The society at Iona was known as "the family of Hy."

The advent of Kentigern to the banks of the Clyde occurred at a momentous period in the history of Scotland. The dominion of the Romans had come to an end more than a century before, and the light and civilization which they had brought with them had now become all but extinguished. The tribes which had, nominally at least, embraced Christianity had almost all relapsed into heathenism, and the kingdom was entering upon a long period of darkness, confusion, and anarchy. The Romans, indeed, had never practically obtained a footing in Scotland beyond the great fortified wall which they had erected between the Clyde and the Forth, and which, beginning at Bridgness near Carriden, ended at Chapelhill near West Kilpatrick on the Clyde—a distance of twenty-seven miles. But their occupation necessarily tended to diffuse a considerable amount of civilization among the tribes or nations within their lines, between whom and the barbarians to the north of the wall there must have been, in this respect, a marked contrast. When the Romans withdrew, however, a great change followed. The contest which succeeded their departure was one not merely for the possession of the Roman territory, but for the succession to her dominion in the land. "The competing parties consisted, on the one hand, of "the provincial Britons who had just emerged from under the Roman

---

[1] Dr. Todd. [2] Godkin on the Old Church of Ireland.

" rule, and on the other, of those independent tribes, partly inhabitants
" of the island and partly piratical adventurers from other regions, who
" had so frequently ravaged the Roman province, and now endeavoured
" to snatch the prize from the provincial Britons and from each other.
" The races engaged in this struggle were four—the Britons, the Picts,
" the Scots, and the Saxons or Angles. The two former were indigen-
" ous, the two latter foreign settlers."[1]

It was within this great wall that Kentigern constructed his monastery, but in his time the wall had ceased to form a barrier to the tribes
beyond, and all signs of civilization were rapidly disappearing.

The kingdom of the Britons had at this time no territorial designation, but its rulers were styled kings of Alcluith, and belonged to that
party of the Britons who bore the peculiar name of Romans, and claimed
descent from the ancient Roman rulers in Britain. The kingdom com-
prehended the greater part of Cumberland and Westmoreland, with the
counties of Dumfries, Ayr, Renfrew, Lanark, and Peebles, and part of
Dunbarton. The population embraced the two varieties of the British
race, the southern half being Cymric or Welsh and the northern being
the Damnonii, who belonged to the Cornish variety. The capital was
the Castle of Dunbarton, termed by the Britons Alcluith—the Rock of
Clyde, *Ail* being Welsh for a rock. By the Gaelic people it was called
Dunbreatan, or the Fort of the Britons. Bede, writing in the eighth
century, speaks of Dunbarton as the city called Alcluith, the chief fast-
ness of the Britons. Glasgow at that time must have been all but
unknown.

The grandfather of Kentigern is said to have been a British king, and
his mother Thaney or Tenew, the daughter of King Leudanus, a pagan
prince. She is said to have been a believer in Christianity, but not
baptized. Jocelin gives two etymologies of the name of the saint. One
is that it means *capitis dominus;* the other that it is derived from Kyen,
albanice, caput, and tigern, *dominus.* The first is the meaning in Welsh,
and the second the same meaning in Gaelic. The Welsh form Cyndeyrn
is from Cyn, chief or principal, that is, *capitalis,* and Teyrn—in composition Deyrn, *dominus.* The Gaelic form is Ceanntighearn, from Ceann, a
head, *caput,* and Tighearn, lord.[2]

Kentigern, according to Jocelin, spent his diaconate under Servanus
at the Cistercian settlement at Culross. The old bishop, he says, was

---

[1] Celtic Scotland, vol. i. p. 19.　　　　　　　　[2] Skene.

much attached to him, and was accustomed to address him by the familiar appellation of Munchu, *carus amicus.* The name is of Welsh derivation—mwyn, *clemens, urbanus,* and cu or chu, *carus.* In composition cu becomes in Welsh gu; hence Mungu. And so in process of time Kentigern came to be popularly known as St. Mungo, by which name, says his biographer, "even until the present time the common people are "frequently used to call him and to invoke him in their necessities." At an early age, according to the same account, he left Servanus and came to Strathclyde. According to Mr. Skene, however—by whose admirable work on early Scottish history so much light has been thrown on this dark period—the hitherto received accounts which connect Kentigern with Servanus must be discarded, for there are satisfactory reasons for concluding that Servanus lived two centuries later. Be that as it may, the patron saint of Glasgow did certainly not receive his consecration from Servanus and Palladius, as Professor Innes has supposed.[1] By the custom of the Scottish Church only one bishop was necessary for the consecration of another bishop, and this practice was followed in the case of Kentigern. He was ordained by a single bishop, who was invited from Ireland for that purpose.

Professor Innes points out that in the Inquisitio of David, to be afterwards noticed, it is recorded that Kentigern was ordained bishop of Cumbria; but the statement in the Inquisitio is scarcely correct. The district had no doubt come to be called Cumbria in David's time, but it was not so called in the time of Kentigern, nor for long afterwards. The diocese, if it could be so called, over which this early Christian missionary presided was probably no larger than the small territory occupied by the Christian community of which he was the head. The names Cumbri and Cumbria were not applied to any part of the territories or people of Britain prior to the tenth century. Not even in David's time, nor till long afterwards, had Scotland any recognized capital. The king's court moved from place to place, resting mostly in the great abbeys; but David had a dwelling on the castle rock of Edinburgh as a place of refuge against the surprise of an enemy.

The legend which relates the circumstances under which Kentigern is said to have come to Glasgow is interesting, connected as it is with the name of the aisle or crypt which forms the foundation of what was intended to have been the southern transept of the Cathedral. This

[1] Reg. Episc. Glasg. Preface.

portion of the building has been improperly called Blackadder's Aisle—its real name, which is inscribed on it, having, as I have pointed out elsewhere,[1] apparently escaped observation.   The legend is that on the same night on which he left Servanus Kentigern lodged in the house or cell of a holy man named Fergus, dwelling in a place called Kearnach, to whom it had been revealed that he should not die till he had seen the holy Kentigern.   He expired immediately after the saint entered his house, and Kentigern having placed the body on a car, to which were yoked two wild bulls, he commanded them to carry it to the place ordained of the Lord.   This they meekly did, and, followed by the saint and a great multitude, carried the body to Glasgow, then, as the legend says, called Cathures, where they rested beneath certain ancient trees near a forsaken cemetery, which had been hallowed by St. Ninian of Galloway.   Here the remains of the good Fergus were committed to the earth, and over what was supposed, no doubt, to be the very spot of his interment the south transept of the Cathedral was founded, and the lower aisle or crypt dedicated to Fergus.   This fact is recorded in the interesting inscription to which I have referred.   It is in long Gothic letters on a stone in the roof over the entrance, on which is also carved a rude representation of the dead saint extended on the car.   The words are, 𝔱𝔥𝔦𝔰 𝔦𝔰 𝔱𝔥𝔢 𝔦𝔩𝔢 𝔬𝔣 𝔯𝔞𝔯 𝔣𝔢𝔯𝔤𝔲𝔰.   What 𝔯𝔞𝔯 means I do not know.   The story in its main features may be true.   It is in no way improbable that Kentigern buried here one of the early Christians bearing the name recorded.   At all events as the aisle is actually dedicated to Fergus, and bears his name, it is obviously improper to call it Blackadder's Aisle.   It would appear, indeed, that it was not known by that name till a period comparatively recent, for it is called "Fergus Isle" in a minute of the Kirk-session in November 1648, recommending that it should be assigned as a burial-place for the ministers.

Some time after he had settled at "Cathures"—whatever that word may mean—Kentigern was obliged, in consequence of the persecution of an apostate British prince named Morken, to take shelter in North Wales, where, in the Vale of Clwyd, he constructed a monastery, and founded the church of Llanelwy, afterwards called St. Asaph.

It should be explained that before the advent of Kentigern to Glasgow four kings of the Britons were engaged in conflict with the Saxons. One of these kings, Rhydderch or Rederchen, was at the head of that

---

[1] Armorial Insignia of Glasgow.

party among the Britons who were, as already mentioned, termed Romans, from their supposed descent from Roman soldiers or Roman citizens, and this king appears to have embraced Christianity after its introduction by St. Ninian. The other kings belonged to a party which, though it had also embraced Christianity, had apostatized, and reverted to a semi-paganism fostered by their bards; and one of these kings having obtained an ascendency in Strathclyde opposed and persecuted Kentigern, and obliged him to fly, as I have said, to North Wales. Among these four kings the dissensions broke at last into open rupture, and a great battle took place on the river Esk near Carlisle in the year 573, which resulted in the victory of the Christian party, and the establishment of Rhydderch as king of the Cumbrian Britons. On this event Kentigern was invited to return, and having appointed Asaph, one of his monks, to be his successor, he left North Wales. On his way back he resided for a time at Hoddam in Dumfriesshire. According to one tradition he also dwelt for some years at Lockerwort, near Borthwick, and there are some historical indications that such may have been the fact. The churches of Borthwick and Pennicuik were dedicated to him, and the spring in the manse garden at Borthwick is still known as St. Mungo's well. It may have been for this reason that in the reign of David I. the bishop of St. Andrews, with consent, or more probably by command, of the king and prince, conveyed the church of Lockerwort or Borthwick to the bishop of Glasgow.

On the return of Kentigern to Strathclyde he was gladly received by the king, by whom he was protected until the death of the latter in 603. Rhydderch is mentioned by Adamnan as reigning at Alclyde or Dunbarton at the time of St. Columba, and according to Jocelin he had also a manorial residence at Partick, near Glasgow. He speaks of Rhydderch as residing shortly before his death " in the royal house " which was called Pertnech," by which no doubt Partick is meant. It is interesting to note that one of the old sculptured stones of Scotland found near Yarrow kirk, in Selkirkshire, and which attracted the attention of Sir Walter Scott, is conjectured by Dr. Wilson to have been erected in memory of the two sons of this old British king.[1]

Kentigern now took up his residence, with his colony of converts, on the banks of the then beautiful stream "vocabulo Melindonor," where he had buried Fergus, and where he and his followers maintained

[1] *Prehistoric Annals*, vol. ii. p. 211.

themselves by rural industry and by the practice of the arts of peaceful life. In this they followed the custom of the second period of the early Scottish Church, which was in its form monastic, but with a monasticism strongly mixed up with active secular life.[1] In its first and earliest form the Scottish Church exhibits a secular clergy founding churches; in its second we find a clergy observing rules and founding monasteries, of which that of Ninian at Candida Casa was perhaps the first. In these communities the elders gave themselves up to devotion and the service of the church, and to transcribing the Scriptures and works of devotion, while the remainder were occupied in the labours of the field and mechanical work. Of such a community Jocelin no doubt gives a correct account when he is describing the arrangements of the monastery constructed by Kentigern at St. Asaph's. Of the multitude who came to the saint there, and brought their children for instruction, Kentigern, he says, appointed a portion who were unlettered to the duty of agriculture, the care of the cattle, and other necessary duties outside the monastery. Another portion he assigned to duties within the inclosure, such as preparing food, erecting workshops, and doing other ordinary work; and the remainder who were lettered he appointed to the celebration of divine service in the church by day and by night. The same arrangement appears to have prevailed at Iona, and the description which we possess of that monastery by Adamnan, and of the habits of the community, may be accepted as applicable to the settlement of Kentigern at Glasgow. At Iona the erections included a church with an altar, and a *hospitium*, or house of entertainment for strangers; a space including the separate huts or bothies of the monks; a dwelling-place for Columba himself, styled *domus;* offices for laying up the produce of their fields, and a place or plateau surrounded by the various portions of the monastery. No vestige remains of these old erections. The buildings now on the island are the remains of the Benedictine monastery and nunnery founded by Reginald, Lord of the Isles, in 1203. The Abbey Church was built shortly before. The first buildings were constructed entirely of timber and wicker-work. The monks were employed in reading and prayer, in the rearing and repairing of the buildings, in the cultivation of the ground, and in the tending of cattle. They were summoned to their devotions by a bell. They were not barefooted, but substantially shod with some kind of *calceus* or sandals. They possessed

[1] Burton's Hist. of Scotland, vol. i. p. 242.

wheeled vehicles, and they used sailing vessels made of hides stretched on wicker-work, which are thus alluded to in an old stanza:—

> "With their curachs across the sea
> And for rowing threescore men." [1]

The monks of later times lived much like these old communities. As a rule they held a great part of their lands in their own hands, and cultivated them by their serfs or villains in their several granges. The grange itself, the chief house of each of the abbey baronies, must have been a spacious farm steading. In it were gathered the cattle, implements, and stores, needed for the cultivation of their demesne lands, and the serfs or carles who cultivated it lived there, with their women and families. A monk or lay brother superintended the whole. [2] I am not aware than any remains of these exist in Scotland, with the exception of an old tower at Huntlaw, near Hassendean, in Roxburgh, still called the Monks Tower, where there was a grange belonging to the Abbey of Paisley. [3] But there is yet to be seen at Torquay, in the present farm steading of Ilsham, a grange which exactly corresponds with the description of Mr. Innes. It was the home farm of Tor Abbey, a very ancient foundation. The massive farm buildings still in use there, remain as they were in the time of the monks, and in the centre is a square tower divided into three stories, in which lived the monk who superintended the farm. The lower part was appropriated to stores. The centre, approached by a massive flight of steps, was his oratory or chapel, and above was his dormitory. In the farm buildings can still be seen the loft, with its fire-place, in which the *nativi* or serfs were accommodated. Outside of the grange dwelt the *cottarii* or cottars, a class higher than what are now called cottars, as each occupant was the tenant of from one to nine acres of land, for which they rendered certain services as well as a money payment. [4]

In like manner as lived the monks at Iona lived Kentigern and his followers at Glasgow under the shade of the trees of St. Ninian, and here he was visited by his celebrated contemporary Columba, who came from Iona with a great following, *multa discipulorum turba et aliorum.* On this occasion it is recorded by Jocelin that the Irish saint presented Kentigern with a crozier, *virga de simplice ligno.* This crozier or staff

[1] Dr. Reeves and Professor Innes, quoted by the Bishop of Argyll. Iona, p. 32.
[2] Scotland in the Middle Ages, p. 138.   [3] The Abbey of Paisley, by Dr. Lees, p. 161.
[4] Scotch Legal Antiquities, p. 244.

appears to have found its way to Ripon, originally a monastery founded for a branch of the Scottish Church, which owned Hi, or Iona, for its head; and Fordun, who wrote at the beginning of the fifteenth century, and who, however doubtful his authority when he deals with ancient history, may be trusted for contemporary events, says that in his time it was still to be seen in the church of St. Wilfrid at Ripon, where it was held in great veneration, and preserved in a case inlaid with gold and pearls. In form it was in all probability similar to the "Bachal More," or pastoral staff of St. Moloch, represented in the sub-

joined cut, and now in the possession of the Duke of Argyll. It is a black thorn stick with traces of a metal covering—the latter, no doubt, the addition of a more recent period. Like other ancient croziers, it is very short, measuring only two feet ten inches in length. Such was probably the pastoral staff of Kentigern.

His costume is thus given by the monk of Furness, who may have found the description in the ancient Irish record which he had discovered. "He wore," says Jocelin, "a shirt of roughest haircloth "next his skin, and over it a garment made of the skins of goats, "and a close hood like that of a fisherman. Above this garment, "concealed by a white alb, he wore over his neck a long stole. He "had a pastoral staff, not rounded, or gilt, or gemmed, as is now "seen with those in high places, but of plain wood, yet curved back, "*tamen reflexum.* He carried in his hand a manual, always ready "for the exercise of his ministry whenever necessity or cause demanded. "Thus," adds his biographer, "by the whiteness of his dress he ex-"pressed the piety of the inner man and avoided vainglory." He is described as tall of stature, of a robust constitution, and capable of enduring great fatigue both of body and mind. He was of a mild and gentle temperament, had the spirit of a true missionary, and was indefatigable in the exercise of his ministry. Such was the first bishop of Glasgow. He died in the year 603, full of years, leaving a name which has come down to us as a bright light out of an age when a very profound darkness prevailed in Scotland.

The monastic settlement formed by Kentigern and his followers was no doubt a very simple affair—nothing more, indeed, than a rude village of huts, constructed probably of wood and wattles. The huts at Iona, as we have seen, were so constructed, and this was, in all likelihood, the case with most of the monastic houses and oratories down to the twelfth or thirteenth centuries.[1] In the life of Columba we read that when he went to the monastery of Mobhi Clairenach, on the banks of the river Finglass, where no fewer than fifty scholars were assembled, he found their "huts or bothies," *botha*, by the water or river; and it is told of Mochasi, abbot of Nendrum, that on one occasion he went with seven score young men "to cut wattles to "make the church." The so-called cathedral of Lindisfarne, built by disciples of Columba, was merely an edifice of wood thatched with reeds "after the manner of the Scots," that is, of the Irish.[2]

But even at that early time it is certain that, so far as the churches were concerned, some of them were built of stone, and in a few cases the whole of the monastic buildings were constructed of that material. A monastery established by Columba in one of the Gaveloch islands was constructed entirely of stone, and remains of it, consisting of two beehive-shaped cells, still exist.[3] There is another interesting example of a stone cell adjoining the ruins of the beautiful old church of St. Blane in Bute, and which is supposed to have been erected by St. Chattan, or Cathan, the uncle of St. Blane, before the middle of the sixth century. It is a circular building, constructed of irregular-shaped blocks of stone, not dressed, but chosen so as to fit each other, and some of them of great size. There are no small stones for packing, but probably the interstices were filled with turf and mud. It is thirty-three feet six inches in diameter, and the walls are eight feet six inches thick. This is not unlike the cell constructed by St. Cuthbert on the island of Farne in the year 670, as described by Bede. It was "nearly circular, constructed not of hewn stone nor of brick "and mortar, but of unwrought stones *and turf.* Of these stones "some were of such a size that it seemed scarcely possible for four "men to lift them. It was divided into two parts—an oratory, namely, "and another dwelling suited for common uses."

[1] Dr. Petrie's Round Towers of Ireland, p. 138. [2] Bede. [3] Reeve's Adamnan, Appendix No. 1.

In Ireland there are many such remains, but there is every reason to believe that stone churches existed in Scotland before they were known in Ireland. According to Dr. Petrie, a very reliable authority, there were no stone churches in Ireland before the time of St. Patrick; and he is of opinion that the very earliest church in Ireland built of that material was built by Patrick at Daimhliag, now Duleek, in Meath. That St. Patrick was the first to erect stone churches there is confirmed by an ancient poem quoted by Dr. Petrie,[1] and which he accepts as authentic, in which the various persons who constituted the household of Patrick are enumerated, and among them the names of his three stone-masons, with the remark that they were the first builders of Daimhliags or stone churches in Ireland. The passage is as follows:—

> " His three masons, good was their intelligence,
> Caeman, Cruithnec, Luchraed strong:
> They made damliags first
> In Erin: eminent their history."[2]

This was certainly not earlier than the middle of the fifth century. But the church at Candida Casa, which we know was built of stone in the Roman style—*insolito Britonnibus more*, as Bede expresses it —was erected by Ninian in 397, at least half a century earlier than the church at Duleek. Ninian, as I have said, afterwards left Candida Casa and passed over to Ireland, where he built the large monastery in which he died; and as this was the first introduction of monachism into Ireland, so it is not improbable that Ninian was the first to introduce there the building of stone churches, the knowledge of which he had acquired at Tours on his return from Rome, although the first actual erections may have been made under the directions of Patrick.

If the first church at Glasgow was of stone, the probability is that it was similar in form to those interesting erections combining church and cell, of which examples known to have been constructed at that very time still remain in Ireland, and of which another example exists in the little island of Inchcolm, in the Firth of Forth. The latter is described in Dr. Wilson's Prehistoric Annals as "an irregular quad-"rangle, measuring externally only 21½ feet in greatest length. Inter-"nally it is little more than 6 feet in breadth at the east end, where "probably the stone altar table stood under its small window; while

---

[1] The Poem of Flann, preserved in the Book of Lecan, fol. 44.   [2] Eccles. Arch. Ireland, p. 138.

" it diminishes to 4 feet 9 inches at the west end. The vaulted ceil-
" ing is constructed of rude masonry, with a triangular wedge for the
" key-stone; and over this it is roofed with square stones laid in regular
" courses."[1] Dr. Petrie was of opinion that this was one of the cells

belonging to the period of Columba, erected in all probability by one
of Columba's disciples who had made his way from Iona to the eastern
territories of the Picts.

The first church or oratory at Glasgow may have been constructed
in the same way. Such as they were, these early erections—the church
and the adjoining dwelling-places—were the origin of the city of
Glasgow.

THE BELL AND THE MIRACLES.

It is not within my purpose to write the life of Kentigern, or to
detail all the stories of his acts and miracles as related by his historian
Jocelin. But familiar as we all are with the devices or emblems on
our city arms—the tree, the bird, the fish, and the bell—it will not
be out of place to notice here the legends which relate to these.

[1] Prehistoric Annals, vol. ii. p. 370. I am indebted to the courtesy of the publishers, Messrs.
Macmillan & Co., for the illustration. See also Proceedings of the Society of Antiquaries of Scotland,
vol. ii. p. 497.

As regards the bell, however, which appears on the sinister side of the shield, the story is not a legend, for it has an authentic history. It represents a real bell, which, although its origin cannot be traced, is known to have been in existence in Glasgow from a very early period till so late as the middle of the seventeenth century.

Jocelin says that the bell was brought to Glasgow by St. Kentigern among certain "sanctorum pignora et ecclesiæ ornamenta quæ "ad decorem domus Dei pertinaverunt," which he had received from the hands of the pope; but upon this légend no reliance can be placed. The popes in early times did, no doubt, in certain cases, give bells to bishops, and an instance is recorded in the Breviary of Aberdeen of a bell which Pope Gregory the Great presented to St. Ternan, the apostle of the Picts; but it is most improbable that the pope ever gave one to Kentigern, for the early Scottish Church had no connection with Rome, and did not recognize the supremacy of the Roman bishops.

Bells were held in great reverence in the ancient church. They were baptized, and anointed *oleo chrismatis*, and there is a ritual for these ceremonies in the Roman Pontifical. They were, indeed, among the articles which appear to have been necessary to the episcopal function. It is so stated by Dr. Petrie, than whom there can be no higher authority; and he mentions as an instance the presents given to Fiac, bishop of Sletty, near Carlow, when St. Patrick conferred on him the episcopal dignity. The passage in the Book of Armagh which Dr. Petrie refers to as his authority is as follows:—"He (Patrick) con- "ferred the degree of bishop upon him (Fiac), so that he was the "first bishop that was ordained among the Lagenians; and Patrick "gave a box to Fiac containing *a bell*, and a menstir (reliquary) and "a crozier, and a poolire." The poolire was a leather case for holding sacred books and reliquaries.

According to Jocelin Kentigern visited Rome seven times, and he adds that it was on the last of these occasions that he received from the pope "what was wanting to his ordination," including the bell. This supposed visit is referred to in a hymn believed to be of the 15th century:—

> "Romam visit septies: papa quem honorat
> Ut serviret præsuli: avi se decorat
> Et campanum sustinet que sonos dulcorat."

But that Kentigern ever received anything from the pope, or that he was ever at Rome at all, is, as I have said, in the highest degree improbable. The same story is told of Columba in the later legends of that saint, but in the authentic Life there is not a word of it, and the bishop of Rome is not even mentioned.

The probability is that Kentigern's bell was made at home—perhaps in Ireland—and it is quite possible it may have been given to Kentigern at the time of his ordination by the bishop who came from Ireland to perform that office. We have unquestionable evidence, at least, that bells of the same form as Kentigern's, and of which the form is preserved on our ecclesiastical seals, were made in Ireland at quite as early a period. Dr. Petrie says—I quote from his work on the Round Tours:—"We have not only abundant historical evidence "to show that many of the ecclesiastics in those early times obtained "celebrity as artificers and makers of the "sacred implements necessary for the "Church, and as illuminators of books, "but we have also still remaining the "most indisputable evidences of their skill "in these arts in ancient croziers, bells, "shrines, &c., and in manuscripts not in-"ferior in splendour to any extant in "Europe." Some of these old bells are of the same shape as that of Kentigern, and many of them are most elaborately ornamented. In an ancient but authentic

life of the celebrated artificer Saint Dageus, who lived in the early part of the sixth century, as quoted by Colgan, it is stated that "he "fabricated bells, croziers, and crosses, and though some of these im-"plements were without ornament, others were covered with gold silver, "and precious stones, in an ingenious and admirable manner." Some of these bells are still preserved in Ireland, and among others the bell of St. Mura of the early part of the ninth century—a representation of which is given in the Ulster Journal of Archæology—exhibits a wonderful richness of ornamentation.

The bell appearing on the early seals of our bishops, and also, as we shall find, on one of the early seals of the community, is undoubtedly a representation of a bell then in existence in Glasgow, and believed to have belonged to Kentigern. It is a quadrangular bell—a form which indicates a very high antiquity. The seal on which it is here shown (page 19) is that of the Chapter of Glasgow "for Causes," which was in use 1488–1540.

Dr. Petrie, in the learned work to which I have referred, gives a representation of a sculptured stone which formed the pediment of one of the oldest of the Irish churches, and on which there is a figure holding a bell of the same form as that which appears on this seal. Referring to that stone Dr. Petrie says: " The quadrangular-shaped bell which "appears in the hand of one of the figures exhibits that peculiar form "which characterizes all the consecrated bells which have been preserved "in Ireland as having belonged to the celebrated saints of the primitive "Irish Church, and there is every reason to believe that this quadrangular "form gave place to the circular one now in use previous to the twelfth "century. Indeed (Dr. Petrie adds) we see a remarkable example of the "transition to the latter form in a bell formerly in the collection of the "Dean of St. Patrick's, and now in the Museum of the Academy, which, "as an inscription in the Irish character carved upon it clearly shows, is "undoubtedly of the close of the ninth century."

Some fine specimens of these quadrangular-shaped bells will also be found in the Museum of the Society of Antiquaries in Edinburgh. The workmanship of them may be classed among the earliest efforts of art in connection with the introduction of Christianity into the British Isles. Their base is usually malleable iron longitudinally riveted on either end. A coating of bronze envelops the iron, and over all there is, in some cases, a coating of gold.

A curious illustration of the great reverence in which consecrated bells were held is given in the great national work of Ireland, the Annals of the Four Masters. It is there recorded, under date 1261, that in that year "Donnell O'Hara committed a depredation upon the clann Feoraes "[Mac Ioris or Bermingham, Barons of Athenry] in revenge for their "having slain Cathal O'Hara and desecrated the church of Saint Feich-"inn; he also killed Sefin Mac Feorais, who, while being killed, had "upon his head the bell which he had taken from the church of Ballysa-"dare." In a note to this passage the learned editor, Dr. O'Donovan, explains that " Sefin had on his head a blessed bell which he had taken "away from the church of Ballysadare, thinking that O'Hara would not "attempt to strike him while he had so sacred a helmet on his head, "even though he had obtained it by robbery."

We find another illustration of the importance and value of the bells of the old saints in a notice which has been preserved of the bell of St. Medan, the patron saint of the parish of Airlie. It had been assigned to the care of a hereditary keeper, who in the year 1447 resigned it into the hands of Sir John Ogilvy, and Sir John thereupon, by a formal deed, conferred on Lady Margaret Ogilvy, his wife, the bell "with its pertinents" for her liferent use.[1]

It does not appear whether the bell of St. Kentigern was adorned with any of those rich ornaments which are found on some of the contemporary bells. We know, however, that it was held in great veneration in Glasgow, and it forms the subject of various minutes of the corporation. It is also mentioned more than once in the ancient offices for the festival of the saint. I need hardly say it was not a church bell for calling the people to worship, nor of such a size as would have made a helmet for the sacrilegious scion of the house of Athenry. Neither is it to be confounded with that kind of bell called a *skellat*, such as was used in old times by the town-criers in Glasgow and other towns, and of which we find repeated mention in our burgh records. It was one of those small tinkling bells, called a sacryn bell, which among other uses was employed in the altar services of the Cathedral. In size it was probably less than that of the beautiful bell of St. Mura, already referred to, which was 4½ inches high exclusive of the handle, and 3 inches broad at the bottom. That bell was made of bronze, and that of St. Kentigern was probably of the same material.

These bells were not used exclusively at the altar services. They were also rung through the streets by the friars for the repose of the souls of the departed, especially of those who had been benefactors to the church; and we know that to this use Saint Mungo's bell—as it was familiarly called—was put in Glasgow. There is preserved an indenture executed at Glasgow "the xviij day of the moneth of December in the "yher of our Lord a thousand four hundreth fyftie and four yheris," between "ane honorabyll man Johne Steuart the first provost that was "in the citie of Glasgu on the ta part, and discreyt religious men frieris "of Glasgu, and the covent of the samyn, on the tother part," by which, in consideration of certain lands and tenements conveyed by Provost Steuart, "the saydis priour, covent, and their successouris" undertake to say certain masses at St. Katherine's altar in the Cathedral for the

---

[1] Second Parliamentary Report on Historical Manuscripts, p. 187.

soul of the donor, "and alsua, on the day of the discesse of the said
"Johne Steuart yherely, tyll ger Sant Mongouse bell be rungen throw
"the toun for the said Johnes sawle." There are other deeds to the
same effect preserved, and among them a "foundatioune donatione and
"legatione" by "Schir Archibald Crawfurd vicar of Cadder," bearing
date 28th November, 1509, which contains the following among other
burdens on the property:—"Item I leif to Sanct Mongowes bell to pas
"throwe the toune one salmes day eftyre noune, and one the morne for-
"roure nyne, to gar praye for mye faderis saule, mye moderis saule, my
"awin saule, and all Christyne saulis, aucht peneis of annuale of the said
"place."

After the spoliation of the Cathedral which took place at the Reformation this interesting relic appears to have fallen into the hands of two
of the citizens, by whom, a few years later, it was brought to the magistrates, who, with good taste, and apparently with a true sense of its
archæological value, secured it for the community. On the 19th of
November, 1577, there occurs in the records of the council the following
interesting entry:—"SANCT MONGOWIS BELL. The quhilk day the
"provest baillies and counsall with dekeins, coft [purchased] fra John
"Mr. sone to umquhile James Mr. and Andro Laing þe auld bell that
"ȝed throw the toune of auld at þe buriall of þe deid for þe soume of
"ten pundis money quhilk thai ordainit Patrick Glen thair thesaurare to
"pay to thaim and also grantit þe said Andro to be maid burges gratis;
"quhilk bell thai ordainit in all tymes to remane as comone bell to gang
"for þe burial of þe deid and to be gevin ȝeirlie to sic persoun as thai
"appoynt for anys in þe ȝeir takand caution for keping and delyvering
"thairof the ȝeiris end. And the said Andro Laing, as sone to umquhile
"Mr. Robert Layng, is maid instantlie burges, as ane burges sone, gratis,
"for þe said caus of þe bell."

The liberal terms accorded to those who had thus rescued the bell,
and the anxious provision made for its safety by taking security from
the person intrusted with it for its careful preservation, shows the value
attached to it, and the veneration in which it was held as a relic dating
from the foundation of the city. In October of the following year the
treasurer's accounts contain a charge of two shillings "for ane tong to
"St. Mongowis bell." And under date 4th June, 1590, there occurs the
following entry:—"The quhilk day the provest baillies and counsall hes
"gevin thair twa commoun bells viz the Mort and Skellat bells togedder

"with the office of pwnterschipe to George Johnstoune for ane zeir to "cum bund for the soume of thrie scoir pundis to be payit in maner "following:" and then follow the terms of payment and names of sureties.

A few years later the presbytery claimed to have the custody of the bell and the nomination of the party intrusted with the ringing of it, as being more within their province than that of the magistrates, and on 5th November, 1594, there is the following entry in the records of the presbytery:—"Quhilk day the presbiterie declairis the office of the ring-"ing of the bell to the buriall of the deid to be ecclesiastical and that "the electioun of the persone to the ringing of the said bell belongis to "the kirk, according to the ancient canonis and discipline of the reformit "kirk." Whether anything followed on this resolution does not appear. In 1631 the bell was still preserved, as we learn from Camerarius, in whose work "De Scotorum Fortudine Doctrine et Pietate," printed in that year, it is stated that Glasgow "has for its achievment a salmon and "also a bell which was used by the man of God [Kentigern] and which "is preserved in Glasgow at the present day."

But at the time when Camerarius wrote the ancient bell was probably almost worn out, and in 1640 we find an order by the town council directing a new one to be made. The order is as follows:—"Anent ane deid bell: The said daye ye "deid bell delyverit to Patrick forsyth, qᵐ· "ordaines to give ye half of ye pryces "[emoluments] of his part of ye bell to "William Bogle during his lyfetime. And "ordaines ye Dean of gild to caus mak ane "new deid bell to be runge for and before "ye deid under hand."[1] The new bell then made, after having been in use for many years, disappeared, but in 1867 it was dis-covered and restored to the corporation, in whose possession it now is.

It is 4½ inches in height, exclusive of the handle, and bears the date 1641, the year after the order by the council to have it made. It is in-teresting as having upon it a variety of the city arms not found on any of the other examples—the fish not being on the shield at all, but below

[1] Council Records, 23d October, 1640.

it, just as it appears below the shield of Bishop Blackader on the base-
ment of the rood screen in the Cathedral.   But what is still more interesting is that the bell represented on the shield is not a round bell, such
as were by that time exclusively in use, but an ancient square bell, the
same as appears on the seal of the Chapter of Glasgow "for Causes,"
and none of which were manufactured later than the beginning of the
ninth century.   There is every probability, therefore, that the sculptor of
the shield on this "new deid bell" had before him and copied the ancient
bell of St. Kentigern, then still preserved and used in Glasgow.   It is
possible that, notwithstanding the manufacture of the new bell of 1641,
the old bell of the saint may have still continued to be used occasionally,
because Ray, when he wrote his account of the city in 1661, says: "Their
"manner of burial is, when one dies the sexton or bellman goeth about
"the streets with a *small* bell, which he *tinkleth* all along as he goeth,
"and now and then he makes a stand and proclaims who is dead, and
"invites the people to come to the funeral at such an hour."   This
description would be very applicable to the old bell of the saint, though
it may possibly refer to the other.   At all events, subsequently to this
all trace of the saint's bell, so long known to the inhabitants, and the
affectionate veneration for which had survived the levelling storm of the
Reformation, is unfortunately lost.

The salmon with the ring, appearing on the seals of the bishopric
and on the city arms, refers to the story of the recovery by St. Kentigern of the lost ring of the Queen of Cadzow.   The story is thus given
in the office for the saint's day in the Breviary of Aberdeen: "It
"happened that the Queen of Cadzow had laid herself open to the
"suspicion of an intrigue with a certain knight, whom the king had
"taken with him in hunting.   And the knight being asleep, the king
"abstracted from his scrip[1] a ring which the queen had given him, and
"flung it into the river called Clyde (*Cludam*).   Returning home he
"demanded the ring of the queen, threatening her with death if she
"did not produce it.   She having sent her maid to the knight, and not
"receiving the ring, despatched a messenger to Kentigern, telling him
"everything, and promising the most condign penance.   St. Kentigern,
"taking compassion on her, sent one of his people to the river to angle
"with a hook, directing him to bring alive the first fish he might take;
"which being done, the saint took from its mouth the ring, and sent it

---

[1] *Mercipio* in the Breviary, being monks' Latin for *marsupio*.

"to the queen, who restored it to the king, and so saved her life." The whole scene is well represented on the counter seal of Bishop Robert Wyschard, made about the year 1271. In the upper portion of this interesting old seal St. Kentigern is represented seated, to whom a monk kneeling presents the fish with the ring in its mouth. In the middle compartment are two niches. On the dexter side appears the king, with a drawn sword in his hand, prepared to slay his frail lady unless she shall produce the abstracted ring; and on the sinister side is the lady

triumphantly presenting the missing pledge. In a niche occupying the lower part of the seal the saint is again represented in the act of prayer, kneeling on a lion couchant, and on each side are heads of saints crowned with the nimbus. The legend round this fine and very curious example of ancient art tells in few and pithy words what the sculpture so well represents—REX FURIT: HÆC PLORAT: PATET AURUM: DUM SACER ORAT. The hymn appointed for the more solemn altar service of the saint's day thus sums up the story:—

> "Mœcha mœrens[1] confortatur
> Regi reconciliatur
> Dum in fluctu qui jactatur
> Piscis profert annulum."

What has recently grown into an oak tree, covering a large portion of the escutcheon, was at first only a twig or branch. It is properly so expressed in all the early seals, and it appears in that form on the seal of the chapter given above. It was introduced to commemorate a frozen bough which St. Kentigern miraculously kindled into flame. The saint, then a boy, had, according to the legend, been appointed by his master Servanus to maintain in the refectory the holy fire which had been sent to Servanus from heaven. Having fallen asleep, some of his companions,

---

[1] I have corrected these words from the version hitherto given by all the writers, who (following the monkish Latin of the Breviary) write them "mecha" and "merens." The first word would be quite unmeaning, and the latter would convey a meaning the very opposite of what it was intended to express, for the lady was anything but a deserving character.

out of envy, extinguished the fire, whereupon Kentigern when he awoke broke off a frozen branch from a neighbouring hazel, and, breathing on it in the name of the holy Trinity, it immediately burst into flame. This story forms the subject of the third lesson for the saint's day, and is commemorated in the lines of the hymn—

"Ardent rami congelati
Sacro flatu inflammati."

It is interesting to observe, in passing, that the constant maintenance of the fire referred to in this legend appears to have been one of the customs introduced by the Asiatic ancestors of the ancient British population. In prehistoric times the sacred fire of the Aryans was kept perpetually burning on the family hearth. It was regarded in some sort, indeed, as a living household deity who watched over the family, and when the members met at meals a portion was always first offered to the fire.[1]

The legend of the bird is also curious. In most of the verbal descriptions of the city arms it is called "a bird" merely. One writer calls it a raven, and in the "Additions," by Dr. Brown and others, to the third edition, published in 1718, of Captain Slezer's interesting work, the *Theatrum Scotiæ*, it is stated that on the arms of Glasgow "there is an "oak with a red bird on it." This is nearer the truth. The bird was a redbreast, and it is so described in the office of the saint in the Breviary of Aberdeen. The second lesson for the day in that ancient office consists of the story which tells how the saint miraculously restored to life " quodam avicula que rubesca[2] dicitur." A tame robin, the favourite of St. Serf, was by chance killed by his disciples, who, to screen themselves, laid the blame on Kentigern. That youthful confessor, taking the bird in his hand, made over it the sign of the cross, whereupon it was restored to life, and flew chirping to its master. Mr. Robertson, in his preface to the *Liber Collegiæ*, says, "The bird is obviously the little favourite of "Saint Serf—the *avicula quæ vulgo ob ruborem corpusculi rubesca non-*"cupatur*—the tale of whose miraculous restoration to life by Saint Ken-"tigern fills the fifth chapter of his Acts by Jocelin." And he adds, "Long after this legend was wholly forgotten it was remembered that "the bird exhibited in the arms of the city was a redbreast, as we learn "from the inscription which Dr. Robert Magnus has prefixed to his

---

[1] Dawn of History, p. 89.   [2] *Rubesca* is mediæval Latin for *Rubecula.*

"epigram on the Insignia Civitatis Glasguæ: Salmo, quercus, cui insidet
"*rubecula avis*, campana, et annulus aureus salmonis ore exortus."

It appears to have been a common thing for these old saints to tame
wild animals and make pets of them, as St. Serf did of his robin. We
read in an ancient Life of the Irish Saint Kiaran of Saigher, that he had
a fox, a badger, a wolf, and a fawn, who became tame and lived with him
in the desert; and another Irish legend of the sixth century, contained
in the Book of Ballymote, tells that Saint Carnech, who was son of the
King of Alban, kept a pet fawn. And many other instances might be
cited of the same kind.

THE NAME OF THE CITY.

The name of the city founded by Kentigern has been differently spelt
at different times. In the manuscript of the Life by Jocelin in the British
Museum—the one which Pinkerton followed—the original name is said
to have been "deschu." The first church, the manuscript bears, was
established "in villa dicta *deschu* quæ nunc vocatur *glaschu*." What this
word *deschu* could mean has given rise to much conjecture, and has
puzzled many archæologists. None of the writers have attempted to
explain it, and, indeed, it is meaningless. I mentioned it to Mr. Whitley
Stokes, one of our best Celtic authorities, and with the instinct of a true
archæologist, he made it clear at once. He suggested that what had
taken the form of the letter *d* in the word was nothing more than the
letters *c* and *l* placed too close together in the original manuscript; that
the monk, copying only by the eye, had mistaken them for the letter *d*
(which is just *c* and *l* joined), and that the word is *cleschu*, pure Welsh,
the same as the *glaschu* which Jocelin says the place was called in his
time. That this is the true explanation I have no doubt, and it is an
instructive example of the manner in which names become unintelligible
by the carelessness of copyists. Since I obtained that explanation my
attention has been called to another example, mentioned by Mr. Skene,
of the very same mistake made by the transcriber of the history written
by Asser in the end of the ninth century. In narrating the subjugation,
by the Danes, of the Picts and the Strathclyde Welsh or Britons, the
names of these nations are written Pictos and Strathduttenses. The last

word should be Strathcluttenses, the *d*, as in the case of deschu, being put for *c l.*

In the earliest of the charters the name is written Glasgu, but on the oldest of the city seals, of which impressions exist as early as 1325, the legend is "Sigillum comune de Glagu." How it came to be so written I do not know. I suppose it was intended for a contraction, but if so it is an unusual one. It was certainly not a mere error of the artist who cut the seal, in omitting the *s* by mistake, as I have found the same spelling in documents under the hand of the accomplished prelate Wyschard, written while he was a prisoner in England, shortly before the battle of Bannockburn. One of these is a petition addressed by the bishop to Edward II., in which he prays the king "pur Dieu et pur charite et pr "salvacion de sa alme," to allow him to dwell in England within certain bounds, and in this document he styles himself "le Evesque de Glagu." The petition appears to have received no attention, and again the unfortunate prelate, in a second appeal, prays, "a nre seignr le rey et a son "conseyl voyle fere grace de sa deliveraunce a demorer deinz Engleterre "denz certynz boundes al volonte le roy;" and here also Wyschard designs himself "le Evesque de Glagu." In other documents of the time the name of the city appears in different forms. On the seal of the chapter used in 1180 it is called *Glesgu.* In a letter by the Earl of Warrenne and Surrey to the English king, in 1297, he makes mention of the "evesque de *glasgcu.*" In another letter addressed by the same nobleman to his sovereign he speaks of "Sire le evesk de *Glascu.*" In a letter by Hugh de Cressingham to the King of England, written in the same year (1297), the name appears in one place as *Glasgu* and in another as *Glasgou*—very much its present form. In a charter by Robert III. in 1324 it is written *Glasgw.* In a charter by John Stewart, lord of Darnley, in 1419, it is written *Gleschow;* and in the will of Archbishop Betoun he designs himself Archevesque de *Glasco.*

The local historians have interpreted the name as meaning "grey "smith." This is a mistake, and it has arisen from their seeking its origin in the Gaelic of the Scottish Highlands. An archæological friend and an excellent Gaelic scholar, looking for the origin of the name in the same direction, suggests "clais," a ravine or hollow, and "dhu," dark. But this part of Clydesdale was a Welsh settlement, and the origin of the name is to be sought in the British branch of the Celtic language. It means, I think, the beloved green place—"glas," *viridis,* and "cu" or "gu," *carus*, as in Munchu; and it probably took its origin from the spot where Kentigern and Columba met, and where the first church was erected.

THE EARLY CHURCH.

Of the early church and of the local history of Glasgow during the long dark period between the time of Kentigern's patron, King Rydderch, and the accession of David in the beginning of the twelfth century, during which the kingdom was passing through so many changes, we have almost no record. It was a period of great confusion and change. For some time the district fell under the dominion of the Angles. Then the Britons regained their liberty. Towards the middle of the eighth century we find the Picts and Angles in alliance against the Britons and Scots, and in 756 the Britons of Alclyde passed a second time under subjection to the Angles. Early in the ninth century Kenneth, king of the Dalriad Scots, taking advantage of the weakened state of the Picts, caused by an invasion of the Norwegians and Danes, invaded Pictavia and subdued it, and became its king. After various vicissitudes, and after the death of the last of the kings called of Alclyde, the district re-appears as an independent kingdom under the designation of the Britons of Strathclyde, and then, for the first time, the people appear under the name of Cumbri or Cumbrians. In the year 900 the greater part of the kingdom north of the Forth and the Clyde became established in the male line of the Scottish descendants of Kenneth Macalpine, and became known as the kingdom of Alban or Albania—Orkney and Shetland, with the Isle of Man, being claimed by the Norwegians. South of those provinces there were, on the east coast, the northern district of Northumbria, and on the west the district occupied by the Britons of Strathclyde, including the site of Glasgow. The kingdom of Northumbria came to an end in 954, when it was incorporated into the kingdom of the Angles. About the same time Edmund, king of the Angles, subdued Cumbria, and gave it to Malcolm, king of the Scots. The mixed population of Picts and Scots now became to a great extent amalgamated, and under the influence of the Scots, now the dominant race, became identified with them in name. Early in the following century Lothian was ceded to the Scots after a great battle with the English, and the Tweed became on that side the boundary of the Scottish kingdom. Scotia, as a territorial designation, first appears in the year 1034, superseding the previous name of Alba, but in the year 1092 Cumbria south of the Solway Firth was wrested from the Scots. After this the name of Cumbria or Cumberland was transferred to the English portion—the Scottish part, including the districts extending from the Solway to the Clyde, being comprised under the name of Gallovidia or Galloway. On the death of Malcolm Cænmore, in 1093, he left the kingdom for the first time with the same southern frontier which it ever after retained.

In the beginning of the twelfth century the bishops of St. Andrews were the sole bishops in Scotland. There was no bishop then in Glasgow. Of the immediate successors of Kentigern in the church we have no record, and of the state of religion in that district during the dark period which preceded the restoration of the see by David I. we have little information. The Britons of Strathclyde, on regaining their freedom from the domination of the Angles, obtained from Ireland, about the year 720, a bishop named Sedulius. Previous to this nearly the whole, probably, of the Strathclyde Britons, as well as the entire nation of the Picts, had conformed to Rome, and there is evidence of Sedulius having been at Rome in 721. But the movement towards Rome was resisted by the Columban community till the year 717, when they were expelled from Iona. They were the last to disappear of the Celtic communities, and they were replaced by monks who adopted the canonical observance of Easter, and the coronal mode of tonsure. The breaking up of the monastic church and the introduction of a secular clergy followed. Early in the ninth century the supremacy exercised from Iona came to an end. In Ireland it was transferred to Kells, and in Scotland to Dunkeld, but the supremacy of the Columban Church remained, and the Abbot of Dunkeld was placed at the head of the Pictish Church.

To the early part of the eighth century may be ascribed the introduction of the *Deicolæ*, otherwise *Keledei*, or God-worshippers, who came to be called Culdees. They were an ascetic order, who led a solitary life of devotion and self-mortification, and who became associated in communities of anchorites or hermits. Jocelin of Furness, in his Life of Kentigern, relates that the saint joined to himself a great many disciples, whom he trained in the sacred literature of the divine law, and educated to sanctity of life by his word and example. He says they were content with spare diet and dress—possessing nothing of their own, and living in separate huts or cottages. "These solitary clerics," he adds, "were called in common speech Calledei." But, as Mr. Skene points out, in assigning the Kallidei of Glasgow to the time of Kentigern, Jocelin is guilty of as great an anachronism as when he assigned to him Servanus as a teacher. When Jocelin wrote, however, there did exist bodies of Keledei in Scotland, and in his description of the characteristics of the Culdean clergy, before they became canons, he is no doubt reporting a genuine tradition. The Kaledei of Glasgow really belong to the time of Servanus and Sedulius, bishop of the Britons, and this connection with the real Servanus may have led to the history of this period being drawn back, and both the Kaledei and Servanus associated in popular tradition with the great apostle of Glasgow.[1] These Kaledei or Culdees were in the ninth century brought under the canonical rule along with the secular clergy.

The "Scottish Church" first appears under that name in the end of the ninth century, when it became amalgamated into one body. At this time the kingdom of the Picts still existed, and by a king of that dynasty the church with its possessions was "freed from servitude under Pictish "law and custom"—freed, that is, from all secular exactions. The supremacy, after Iona had been deprived of it, had been, as I have said, transferred to Dunkeld, and now it was transferred to St. Andrews, and the church placed under one head, who was designated Bishop of Alban.[2] The last of the bishops of Alban was Tuthald. He died in 1107, when the old Celtic Church came to an end, and the see of St. Andrews, then the only bishopric in Scotland, remained for a considerable time vacant. The old church was superseded by the bishoprics founded in the earlier years of King David's reign, and by the establishment of the ordinary cathedral staff of canons, deans, and other functionaries. The process of assimilating the native church to that of Rome was begun by Queen Margaret, and resumed by her sons Alexander and David. Alexander filled up the vacancy in St. Andrews, under the bishops of which were placed all the Culdee establishments which remained in the kingdom, including that of Glasgow. Alexander also created the bishopric of Moray, and revived that of Dunkeld.

In the southern districts David, who ruled as earl, was carrying out the same policy, and among others he reconstituted the bishopric of

---

[1] Celtic Scotland, ii. p. 260. [2] Ibid. ii. p. 320.

Glasgow, at which place, as stated in his "Notitia," "the confusions and "revolutions in the country" had destroyed all traces of the church. A record of the proceedings for the restoration of the see, and for ascertaining the possessions of the church, is contained in this Notitia—a remarkable document, of which a copy is preserved in the Chartulary of Glasgow. A Notitia such as this was the admitted and approved mode at that time of establishing the property and privileges of churches before charters came into general use. The date of the document is fixed by Father Innes as circa 1116, but Mr. Skene—probably with more accuracy—places it in 1120 or 1121. It records an investigation by the good men of the country, directed to be made by David, who is designed in it as Prince of the Cumbrian region—*regione quadam inter Angliam et Scotiam sita.* It relates the foundation of the church and the ordination of Kentigern as bishop of Cumbria. It mentions the death of the saint, and that he was succeeded by many bishops in the see, but that the confusions and revolutions in the country had at length destroyed all traces of the church and almost of Christianity. The restoration of the bishopric by David is then stated, and the election and consecration of John, who had been tutor and afterwards chancellor to the prince, and who has been commonly called the first bishop of Glasgow. This is followed by a record of the possessions of the church "in all the pro-"vinces of Cumbria which are under his [David's] dominion and power." The district thus designated extended from the Clyde on the north to the Solway Firth and the march with England on the south, and from the western boundary of Lothian on the east to the river Urr on the west, and it included Teviotdale, which had remained a part of the diocese of Durham while the Lothian churches north of the Tweed were transferred to St. Andrews, but which was now reclaimed as properly belonging to Glasgow.[1]

Professor Innes truly observes that there is no more instructive record for ecclesiastical antiquities than this Inquisition regarding the possessions of the church of Glasgow. Some people talk loosely of the Scottish Church having been endowed by the state, or at least by the crown, but such was not the case. With certain trifling exceptions in our own day—so small as not to be worth mentioning—the church in Scotland has never received any endowment either from the crown or from the state. If David was a "sair saunt for the crown," the see of Glasgow

---

[1] Celtic Scotland, vol. ii. p. 375.

certainly experienced little of his bounty. It was endowed, as all the other parishes both in England and Scotland were endowed, by the private voluntary liberality of the great landowners, and it is a remnant of these grants, and that a very small one, which now forms the endowment of the Church of Scotland—a church whose doctrine has been from time to time modified or reformed, but which, in historical continuity, and in a strictly legal sense, is identically the same church as that on which the endowments were first bestowed. In the case of Glasgow the probability is that the valuable possessions with which the Inquest of David dealt consisted of donations which had been made to the first bishops and their early successors, for it is extremely improbable that during the long dark periods of confusion and anarchy which preceded the reign of David the church received any accession of property.[1] And these possessions consisted not of mere tithes, nor of the dues of churches only, but of broad lands and numerous manors, scattered all over the south of Scotland. The object of the Notitia, accordingly, was not to confer on the see of Glasgow any new possession, but to ascertain, by careful investigation, and by the verdict of the Inquest, what were the properties which at the time legally belonged to the church, and to confirm the title by a royal charter.

Previous to the Reformation the see of Glasgow possessed the baronies of Glasgow, Carstairs, Ancrum, Lilliesleaf, Ashkirk, and Stobo, besides Eddleston, called in the Inquisition Penteiacob. What came to be called the Regality of Glasgow embraced the city and a large district adjoining, comprising the Barony Parish, the parishes of Cadder and Govan, and a large portion of the parish of Old Monkland. But under the benignant rule of the church the lands were let for small returns. At the Reformation the whole money rental of the archbishops, as given up in the Book of the Assumption of Thirds (1561), amounted to only £987, 8s. 7d. Scots, which, according to the value of money at that time, was equal to about only £200. Besides this there were of meal 32 chalders 8 bolls; of malt, 28 chalders 6 bolls; of bear, 8 bolls; of horse corn, 12 chalders 13 bolls; and lastly of "salmond," 14 dozen.

Before leaving the Inquisitio—that important old document by which, to use the words of Professor Innes, "the full light of history first falls "on Glasgow," it may be interesting to give a short account of the Register in which it is preserved. When Beton, the last of the arch-

---

[1] Professor Innes, Preface to Origines Parochiales, p. xxiv.

bishops, fled from Glasgow he took with him the ancient muniments and Registers of the diocese, including two volumes of the original Chartulary. These two volumes, with many other papers now lost, were deposited by him in the Scots College at Paris. At the French Revolution they were removed for safety, and eventually they were brought to Scotland by the Abbé Paul Macpherson, who left them in the hands of Bishop Cameron, by whom again they were transferred to the custody of Bishop Kyle in Aberdeenshire. There exist several copies of the Glasgow Chartulary, but the first in importance is the ancient Register—one of the volumes referred to—which is quoted by Father Innes and other antiquarians as the *Registrum vetus Ecclesiæ Cathedralis Glasguensis.* It is an octavo volume of vellum, and the early portion of it, consisting of 67 leaves—the portion which contains the Inquisitio of David—is undoubtedly in a handwriting of the twelfth century. It is valuable, therefore, as being a contemporary copy.[1] I have given a facsimile of the commencement of the Inquisitio, which, apart from its intrinsic value, is interesting as a specimen of the handwriting of the period.

THE EARLY INHABITANTS.

Of the condition and habits of the early inhabitants of the district now occupied by Glasgow there are few materials from which to obtain authentic information. At the time of Kentigern, it may well be believed, they were in a very rude state. Even within the Roman wall, as I have said, neither the language nor the civilization of the Romans appears to have made any great impression on the ancient population; and when the forces of the Empire were finally withdrawn, the people returned in a great measure to their primitive barbarism.[2]

The Roman historians describe the barbarians or hostile tribes in Scotland with whom they came in contact as two nations, bearing the names of Caledonii and Mæatæ. The latter occupied the territory next the Roman wall. They had neither walls nor cities. The historian Dio, as abridged by Xiphiline, describes them as living on the milk of their

---

[1] Professor Innes, Pref. to Reg. Epis. Glasg. p. xii.
[2] Hudson Turner's Domestic Architecture, Introd. p. i.

FACSIMILE OF FIRST PAGE OF THE INQUISITIO OF DAVID I., CIRCA 1120.

FROM THE COPY PRESERVED IN THE ANCIENT CHARTULARY OF GLASGOW

flocks and wild fruits, and on what they could get by hunting. They had, he says, no houses properly so called, but tents or huts, where they lived almost entirely naked, and they painted or punctured their bodies, so as, by a process of tattooing, to produce the representations of animals. As regards their houses, however, this was no doubt their condition only at the period of the year, namely summer, when the Romans saw them. That they had houses better fitted to protect them in winter is certain. Remains of these have been found in various parts of Scotland, and they are almost invariably found in groups. The rudest of them consisted simply of shallow excavations in the soil, of a circular or oblong form; they rarely exceeded 7 or 8 feet in diameter, and they were generally surrounded by a raised rim of earth, in which a slight break indicated the door. On digging within the area charred wood or ashes, mixed with fragments of decayed bones or vegetable earth, are generally found.[1] An interesting group of these huts or "weems" was discovered not many years ago near Busby, in the vicinity of Glasgow. They were of the most primitive kind, being mere semicircular pits cut out of the hill side, with a passage to the door, also dug out of the slope on a level with the floor. Each consisted of one small apartment, about 12 feet square and 5 feet high, and faced with stone. The floors were neatly paved with thin flagstones. In the centre was a hole for a fireplace, in which ashes were still visible. Near the fireplace were small piles of water-worn stones, 2 or 3 inches in diameter, probably for cooking food by placing heated stones round it, as is still done by some of the islanders in the Pacific. Several hand querns of stone for grinding grain were also found in these houses. At a short distance a grave was discovered, lined with stone, and containing rude urns filled with ashes, indicating that the inhabitants had disposed of their dead by cremation. Unfortunately, the whole of these curious pit houses were destroyed.[2]

In the country lying north of the Forth, the ancient Pictland, the remains of underground weems or "eirde houses" are very abundant, while on the south of that river they are rare, and in Galloway they seem to be unknown.[3] In these weems, querns, deers' horns, and bones have been found. They agree very much with the description by Tacitus of the winter dwellings of the Germans. Another group of these weems was found within a few miles of Aberdeen, which Professor Stuart sug-

[1] Wilson's Prehistoric Annals, vol. i. p. 104.   [2] Dr. John Buchanan.
[3] Progress of Archæology, by Dr. Stuart. Glasgow, 1866.

gested might mark the site of the capital of Taixali when the Roman eagles passed the river Dee in the second century.[1] They show a slight advance in constructive skill in the strengthening of the inclosure with stone.

Remains have also been found of another class of ancient Scottish dwellings. In some parts of Argyleshire there have been found rough oval pavements of stone, bearing marks of fire, and in many instances covered with charred ashes. They are usually found to measure 6 feet in greatest diameter, and they are sometimes surrounded with the remains of pointed hazel sticks or posts, the relics, doubtless, of the upright supports with which the walls and tapering roofs, probably of straw, were framed.[2] Julius Cæsar describes the dwellings of the Britons as similar to those of the Gauls, and these, we know, were constructed of wood, in a circular form, and with tapering roofs of straw. Some of these ancient Caledonian hearths have been discovered beneath an accumulation of 8 to 10 feet of moss, with a stratum below of a foot deep of vegetable mould, resting on an alluvial bed of gravel and sand; and Dr. Wilson conjectures from these accumulations that the dwellings point to an era more remote than that of the Romans. But I think there are reasons for concluding that geologists have been too hasty in assigning such very long periods of time for deposits of this kind, and the discoveries recently made in the neighbourhood of Glasgow, of a pavement, apparently Roman, under deposits to which an equally long period might be assigned, and to which I shall afterwards have occasion to refer, confirm me in this opinion.

Other ancient Scottish dwellings have been found constructed of huge masses of granite frequently over 6 feet in length. Some of these have been found 30 feet long and from 8 to 9 feet wide. The walls are made to converge towards the top, and the whole is roofed in by means of the primitive substitute for the arch which characterizes the cyclopean structures of infant Greece, and the vast temples and palaces of Mexico and Yucatan.[3]

What are called the bee-hive houses were circular in form, with dome-shaped roofs, and walls of great thickness, which were built without mortar. They were called by the Irish clochans. When used for solitary retirement by hermits or anchorites they were called carcair or

---

[1] Archæolog. Scot. vol. ii. p. 54.　　　[2] Prehistoric Annals, vol. i. p. 106.
[3] Prehistoric Annals, vol. i. p 109.

prison cells. Examples of these ancient houses are still frequently to be met with along the remote coasts, and on the islands, of the western and south-western parts of Ireland; and in Scotland the bothans or bee-hive houses of Lewis and Harris, which are occupied to the present day as the summer sheilings of the Hebrideans, are of the same description. The cut represents one of these interesting structures at Aird in Lewis. In form it is almost identical with one in Ireland described by Dr. Petrie, and of which he gives a drawing in his work on the Round Towers. It is—or was when Dr. Petrie sketched it—situated on the north side of the

great island of Aran in the Bay of Galway, and was known by the peasantry as the Clochan-na-Carraige, or the stone house of the rock. Dr. Petrie ascribes it to a period before the introduction of Christianity, when the use of lime was unknown.[1]

There is every reason to believe that in the time of Kentigern, and even in times far more remote, the country around what is now Glasgow, and, indeed, the whole face of Scotland, was covered with immense forests, chiefly of oak; and it is interesting to note that in the oldest of the canoes dug up from under the streets of Glasgow, we possess portions of the wood grown in these ancient forests, not later, and probably earlier, than the time of Abraham. By waste, and want of care in replanting, much of this wood disappeared, but many of the forests continued to exist long after the time of Kentigern; and when Edward I. overran the country, he was in the practice of repaying the services of those who submitted, or whom he desired to win to his authority, by presents of so many oaks and stags from the forests which he found in possession of

[1] Round Towers, p. 126.

the crown. Thus, on the 18th of August, 1291, the king directed the keeper of the forest of Selkirk to deliver thirty stags to the Archbishop of St. Andrews; twenty stags and sixty oaks to the Bishop of Glasgow; and six oaks to Brother Bryan, Preceptor of the order of the Knights Templars in Scotland. Among these old forests was that of Glasgow, but, like all the others, it gradually disappeared, partly, no doubt, from waste, and partly that the ground might be brought under cultivation, but also as a measure of safety, for the wolf and other savage animals abounded in them to an extent which must have proved troublesome, and, indeed, dangerous. But while the forests existed the game was, as a rule, scrupulously preserved, and many of the old charters relate to these rights. There is preserved a composition or settlement, in the reign of Alexander II., between the Avenals, Lords of Eskdale, and the monks of Melrose, regarding disputed game rights in their forests. The Avenals were to have the great game, viz., "hart and hind, wild boar and "sow, buck and doe; also eyrie of falcons and sparrowhawks." The monks were to have the other game, but were forbidden to hunt with dogs and nets, or to set traps, except for wolves.

Another striking peculiarity in the aspect of the country was the prevalence of those marshes or fens which Herodianus describes as forming places of refuge for the early Britons when pressed by their enemies. They existed all over Scotland, occupying those now fertile and beautiful districts which, by clearing and drainage, have been brought under cultivation. Within these inaccessible morasses, which came to be intersected by paths known only to the inhabitants, Wallace and Bruce often defended themselves, and were able to defy the heavily-armed English soldiery. It is said that by lying out amid their damp and unhealthy exhalations Bruce caught the disease of which he died.[1]

In the midst of these morasses, in very old times, the natives were accustomed to construct fortified dwellings and strongholds. Cæsar describes the ancient Britons as living in palisaded strengths and marshes; and quite recently many fortified islands or "crannogs" have been discovered, in marshy grounds and in lakes, which are no doubt what Cæsar referred to, and which correspond with the pile buildings of the Swiss lakes. An interesting group of these was discovered in Dowalton Loch, in Galloway, in 1863. They were all constructed on

[1] Tytler's History of Scotland, vol. ii. p. 112.

the same principle. Masses of fern and heather were laid on the bottom of the loch, and above this layers of brushwood, consisting of hazel and birch, mixed with occasional large boulders. On this rested a flooring of sawed trees, and above all a surface of stones. The whole of the mass was penetrated by vertical piles formed of young oak trees, and the islands were surrounded by numerous rows of these piles. Strong beams of oak, with large morticed holes, seemed to have been part of a framework surrounding the edge of the islands for keeping them compact. Bones of the ox, deer, and other animals were found in them. In the same loch were found canoes of a size exceeding any of those discovered in the Clyde, to which I shall afterwards have occasion to refer, and several articles of bronze were found—one a beautiful specimen of Roman workmanship. Another of these crannogs, formed of masses of stones resting on the moss, was discovered in a marsh in the parish of Culter. It was penetrated by many oak piles, and connected with the firm ground by a causeway. The old name of the place is the Cranney Moss, which may have been derived from the crannog erected in its centre. Similar constructions have been found in Loch Doon and other localities. Among others, an interesting example was found quite recently at the farm called Lochlea, of which the father of Robert Burns was tenant; but there is no loch there now. In some instances these crannogs were approached by a causeway, but more generally they must have been reached by the canoes which are almost invariably found in their neighbourhood.[1]

The period of the introduction of these lake dwellings in Scotland is uncertain, but in Switzerland the earliest of them may be assigned to a period 2000 years before Christ.

Of the people who, in the time of the Romans, inhabited these and the other primitive dwellings I have been describing, there have come down to us more than one interesting representation. In the museum of the College of Glasgow there is preserved a sculptured stone of the period of the Roman occupation, having on it a Latin inscription, and the figures of three natives seated on the ground as prisoners, with their hands tied behind their backs, and guarded by a cavalry soldier armed with shield and spear. Behind him is a figure of Victory holding a wreath, and on another part of the stone is the Roman eagle. The prisoners are represented naked. The sculpture is considerably oblit-

[1] Dr. Stuart, Recent Progress of Archæology. Glasgow, 1866.

erated by the wearing of the stone, but the face of one of the figures is pretty well preserved. He wears a cap or bonnet, and has a beard and moustache. The head is massive, and the expression of the face is grave and shows determination. This interesting slab was discovered in the Roman fort at Castlehill, in the wall of Antoninus near Kilpatrick. It represents, no doubt, three of the captives taken by the Romans from the tribes outside of the wall.[1]

Another example in better preservation was found in 1868, at another part of the same wall at Arniebog, a mile west from Castlecarry. The stone had been broken, but the two pieces fitted exactly, and they had evidently formed part of a larger slab which had probably been broken by the Romans themselves, and hid when they finally retreated from the district. On one of the portions was a representation of Neptune, and on the other that of a captive Briton. The latter is thus described by Dr. Buchanan, who visited the spot on hearing of the discovery:—" The figure of the captive is particularly interesting, for " it affords a portrait by Roman hands of a native Briton. He is " naked, on one knee, with his hands tied behind his back. The coun- " tenance is that of a young man of about twenty-two years of age; " the features not at all savage; the nose good, slightly aquiline; no " beard or moustache; the hair rather short and apparently plaited " round the brow; the body plump and muscular, the whole figure " exhibiting a strong, well-built man."[2]

A third slab, also representing British captives, was discovered in the same year, 1868, at Bridgness, near Carriden, and it is particularly interesting from the fact that one of the captives is a woman—verifying and illustrating what we read in history, that in the battles with the Roman troops the British women fought side by side with the men. On this stone a mounted Roman soldier is represented galloping among and slaying the captives. The attitude of the woman is that of shrinking modesty. Her hair is arranged in two bands plaited round the forehead. It would have been interesting had there been also preserved a representation of the celebrated British dogs—the ferocious mastiffs which, along with the women, took part in the battles against the invaders.

[1] A representation of the stone, but badly executed, is given in Stuart's Caledonia Romana, plate ix. fig. 1.

[2] Paper read at meeting of Society of Antiquaries, Edinburgh, by John Buchanan, Esq., LL.D. 1868.

From historical accounts we know that the native Britons were exceptional in stature, and that the Romans greatly admired the beauty of the females—their commanding forms, their fine complexions, their small and delicate eyebrows, and their pearly teeth.[1] Of the men, Herodianus, writing about the year 245, says: "They swim through " the fens, or run through them up to the waist in mud. They wear " iron about their loins and necks, esteeming this as fine and rich an " ornament as others do gold. They make on their bodies the figures " of divers animals, and use no clothing that these may be exposed to " view. They are a very bloody and warlike people, using a little shield " or target and a spear." Another writer, Xiphiline, describes the inhabitants, both those near the great wall and those beyond it, as living " upon barren uncultivated mountains, or in desert marshy plains, where " they have neither walls nor towns nor manured lands, but feed on the " milk of their flocks and what they get by hunting, and some wild " fruits. They never eat fish, though they have great plenty of them. " They have no houses, but tents, where they live naked. They fight " upon chariots; their horses are low but swift. They have great agility " of body, and tread very surely. The arms they make use of are a " buckler, a poniard, and a short lance, at the lower end of which is a " piece of brass, in the form of an apple. They are accustomed to " fatigue, to bear hunger and cold, and all manner of hardships. They " run into the morasses up to the neck, and live there several days " without eating. When they are in the woods they live upon roots " and leaves."

These descriptions must be taken with reserve, as the Romans perhaps never saw the inhabitants outside of the wall except during the summer season and when they met them in combat. The habits and mode of living of those within the great rampart would of course be greatly modified by their intercourse with the Romans, but the account is interesting as giving a description, no doubt correct in the main, of the inhabitants in the neighbourhood of Glasgow before Kentigern entered on his Christian mission in Strathclyde.

It is not difficult to conjecture on what food these early inhabitants of our district subsisted, but we possess some real evidence on the subject in the state of the teeth in various crania which have been from time to time discovered. Dr. Thurnham, after describing

[1] Athenæus, quoted by Logan.

one of the earliest of these, says: "Altogether the condition is such "as we must attribute to a rude people subsisting in great measure "on the products of the chase and other animal food, ill provided "with instruments for its division, and bestowing little care on its "preparation, rather than to an agricultural tribe living chiefly on corn "and fruits."[1] In the remains of the older settlements by far the larger number of the bones of animals found are those belonging to wild species, showing that the principal food of the people was obtained by hunting. After the introduction of bronze the reverse is the case,. and in the later remains the bones of domestic animals become much more common, and those of wild animals rare.

Dr. Wilson observes that a decided change took place in the common food of the country, from the era when the native of the primeval period pursued the chase with the flint lance and arrow, and the spear of deer's horn, to that recent one when Saxon and Scandinavian marauders began to effect settlements and build houses on the scenes where they had ravaged the villages of the older British natives. "The "first class, we may infer," Dr. Wilson says, "attempted little culti- "vation of the soil, though within their narrow insular limits only a "very thinly scattered population could long subsist on the spoils of "the chase, and the combined labours of the megalithic builders were "doubtless expended on other works besides their chambered barrows. "Improving on the precarious chances of a mere nomadic or hunter "life, we are led to suppose from other evidence that the ancient islander "introduced the rudiments of a pastoral life while yet his dwelling "was only the slight circular earth pit incovered with overhanging "boughs and skins. To the spoils of the chase he would then add "the milk of his flock of goats or sheep, probably with no other ad- "dition than such wild esculents, mast, or fruits, as might be gathered "without labour in the glades of the neighbouring forest."[2] This is exactly the state in which Xiphiline, in the passage just quoted, says he found the natives in Scotland in the year 245.

But the habits of the people were to undergo a change, as the natives themselves were to be in a great measure dominated or displaced by a new people now rapidly and steadily spreading over the lowlands of Scotland. It has been commonly considered that the marriage of Malcolm Cean Moir with the Saxon princess Margaret

---

[1] Crania Britannia, Table I. No. 13.   [2] Prehistoric Annals, vol. i. p. 295.

gave a great impetus to this immigration of Southerns, and no doubt it did; but it had begun much earlier. The character of the movement, as described by a high authority, was peculiar. It was not the bursting forth of an overcrowded population seeking wider room. The new colonists were what we should call of the upper classes— of great Anglian families, and Normans of the highest blood and names. They were men of the sword, above all servile and mechanical employment. They were fit for the society of a court, and many became the chosen companions of our princes, and the old native people gave way before them. These new settlers were of the progressive party —friends to civilization and the church. In many cases they found churches on their manors—for the endowments made for the benefit of the people date from a very early period—or if not already there they erected them.[1] As a rule they respected the existing endowments, and they themselves made liberal grants from their private estates, and the districts so endowed eventually became parishes.

When we come to mediæval times we find what remained of the native population in a state of serfdom under the dominion of these Saxon invaders, and it is not easy for us who live in the light and liberty of the nineteenth century to form an adequate idea of the degraded state of the great bulk of the population at that time. Professor Innes, writing of the district around Melrose—and that district was not by any means exceptional—says: "The original inhabitants "had either removed to districts not yet coveted by the southern "colonists, or were reduced to the condition of serfs, then appropri- "ately termed *nativi*, who were transferred by sale or gift along with "the soil which they cultivated." In the reign of Alexander II. there is a charter by which Osulf the Red, with his son Walter, are sold for ten merks (£6, 13s. 4d.). By another charter of the same period one Patrick de Prendergast, burgess of Berwick, purchases the freedom of Renaldus, a Neyf or slave, with all his followers, "so that "his wife and children and all descendants from him may go and "return and stay wherever they please like other freemen."[2] What is curious in this case is that the Neyf or native whose freedom is purchased is styled in the deed *præpositus*, or bailie, of the town of Berwick. The price paid is twenty merks (£13, 6s. 8d.), a high sum

---

[1] Professor Innes, Preface to Origines Parochiales, p. xxvii.
[2] Parliamentary Report on National MSS., part i. p. 3.

compared with the usual price of serfs at that time, but this may be
accounted for by the higher position held by the subject of the transaction. At Brackley, in the beginning of the thirteenth century, a serf
was sold for three merks, and in the end of the same century another,
with all his family and chattels, was sold for twenty shillings.[1]

In the old chartularies there are many other interesting notices
of this state of serfdom. In the LIBER DE MELROS is a charter dated
towards the end of the thirteenth century, in which John de Vesey
conveys and confirms to the abbey certain lands, and along with
them assigns the "bondos cum nativis, sequeles, et catalles eorundum."
Sequeles means the followers, the children of the native, just as a
horse-dealer sells a mare with her followers.[2] There is another charter,
granted in the year 1820 by one Andrew Fraser, by which he conveys
to the abbey of Kelso two crofts occupied by Adam of the Hog and
John the son of Lethe, together with "Adam of the Hog himself my
"native with all his following;" and the charter contains a clause of
warrandice of the subjects conveyed, which are enumerated as "the
"said lands, meadows, *men*, and pastures." And to come nearer home
we find a charter of King William (*circa* 1180), by which he conveys
to Jocelin, bishop of Glasgow, one Gilmachoi de Conglud, "with his
"children and all his descendants." This was an exceptional case,
for as a rule the Neyf or serf was conveyed or sold only along with
the land on which he resided. There appears, however, to have been
an exception to this rule when the sale was made to provide for the
necessities of the granter. Among the national manuscripts of the
twelfth century is a deed by which Bertram, son of Adam of Lesser
Reston, sells to the prior and convent of Coldingham "Turkil Hog
"and his sons and his daughters for three merks of silver which in
"my great want they gave me of the house of Coldingham."[3] Other
charters occur about the same time of serfs sold apart from the land,
but in each case it is for sums paid to the granters "in their great
"necessity;" and Professor Innes conjectures, I have no doubt correctly,
that the villains of an estate might not be sold off the lands except
in such circumstances.[4]

In England also there are many other examples of the sale of serfs.

---

[1] MSS. of Magdalene College, Oxford—Report on National MSS., part iv. p. 458.
[2] Scottish Legal Antiquities, p. 51.   [3] National MSS., No. liv.
[4] Introduction to National MSS., p. xii.

By a deed in the beginning of the thirteenth century John de Parles grants to the monks of St. Mary of Lancaster his naif John son of John son of Hamo, with his issue and chattels, for the yearly payment of one pound of cummin—no land being conveyed. In some cases the bondman purchased his freedom, the price being commuted into a yearly payment. By a charter granted by the John de Parles just mentioned he enfranchises his naif William—the newly made freeman undertaking to pay yearly to the prior and monks of Lancaster the sum of two pence.[1]

Even where the native continued in a state of serfdom his labour was occasionally commuted into a stated tax in money. In the earliest times it was the custom to extort from the serfs the largest possible amount of manual labour, and their condition must have been miserable in the extreme; but this became gradually relaxed, and they acquired some few privileges, one of these being that the lord accepted an annual money payment instead of labour, and the serf, if he was industrious, was enabled in this way to earn something for himself, and even to acquire cattle and to rent a piece of land from his master. An example of this, by which certain land held by a serf was sold along with the serf himself, occurs among the papers of Queen's College, Oxford. It is a charter granted in the reign of Richard I. by Nicholas de Pentiz, by which he conveys to the Hospital of Hamtone "illam virgatam terræ in Gersiz *quam Turstinus tenuit* cum ipso "Turstino et tota sequela sua."[2]

Sometimes the son of a bondman might, without the knowledge of his overlord, leave the land and rise to a better position, but if his birth could be traced he could at any time be reclaimed. An example of such reclamation occurs in one of the old deeds belonging to the corporation of Axbridge, in the county of Somerset, granted in the thirty-fourth year of Edward III. (1361), but in this case the owner of the serf, after asserting his right, had the generosity to give him his freedom. The deed (in Latin) by which he did so is worth quoting as an example of these curious old writs. It is as follows:—"To all the faithful in "Christ to whom this present writing shall come, John de Cleveden, "knight, Lord of Alre, greeting in the Lord: Whereas Thomas Salamon "was lately claimed in my court as being a bondman born by blood,

---

[1] MSS. of Thurnham Hall—Third Report on Historical MSS., p. 305.
[2] Fourth Report on Historical MSS., p. 453.

"yet do I, the said John, will and grant for myself and my heirs that
"the said Thomas shall be quit in future of all servitude and neifty,
"together with all his following and his issue: granting that he shall
"be free, and of free condition, without any claim by me or my heirs for
"ever."[1]   In England we find frequent examples of natives or bondmen
so improving their condition as to become burgesses; and in the city of
York, in the fourteenth century, this appears to have prevailed to such
an extent that the corporation had their attention called to it, and the
practice was prohibited.   In an old MS. book of "Memoranda touching
"the City of York," there occurs, in the year 1394, an ordinance that no
nativus or born bondman shall be admitted to the freedom of the city.[2]
Probably in consequence of this resolution the archbishop—Scrope—
was encouraged to insist on a claim "to the person of William de
"Wystowe, as being his nativus or bondman;" but either his claim was
unfounded, or for some reason the corporation saw fit to resist it, for it
is recorded that the mayor and others "protested personally and openly
"in the chamber of the archbishop, within his palace at York, that he
"is not such bondman, but a free man born."[3]   The result is not stated.

The great proprietors kept genealogies, or stud books, as we might
call them, of their serfs, to enable them to trace and reclaim them,
and numerous examples of these are to be found in the Dunfermline
Chartulary.

Among the mass of the common people, indeed, there was at that
time no real personal liberty.   With the exception of the "king's bur-
"gesses," every man was under one lord or another, to whom he owed
allegiance and personal service.   There is a law of King David which
provides that "gif any man," other than a freeman of course, "be funden
"in the kyngis land that has na propir lord he sal haf the space of
"xv dayes to get him a lord; and gif that he wythin the saed term
"fyndes na lord, the kyngis justice sal tak of hym to the kyngis oise
"viii ky and kepe his body to the kyngis behuffe quhill he get him a
"lord."

There was, however, another kind of serfdom, that of a freeman
finding it necessary to seek the protection afforded by that condition,
and for that purpose voluntarily rendering himself a bondman to a
feudal lord.[4]

---

[1] Third Report on Historical MSS., p. 305.   [2] First Report on Hist. MSS., p. 109.
[3] Ibid. p. 109.   [4] Quoniam Attachementa.

Of course those who entered the church became free from the conditions of compulsory servitude, but this applied only to those in orders, and it was so from the earliest times. The *familia* of a monastery included every one attached to it, and every individual down to the lowest grade of those who occupied the church lands was a monk, but it was only those on whom church orders were conferred who acquired the valued privilege of freedom from slavery.[1]

The practice of selling serfs along with the land continued in England till the end of the sixteenth century. Among the Oxford manuscripts is a deed recording the manumission of a serf in Lincolnshire so late as 1562.[2] Professor Innes says that the last claim of neyfship or serfdom proved in a Scotch court was in 1364, and he adds that in that or the following century the institution must have died out.[3] I doubt this. The probability is that it continued as long in Scotland as in England. There is a charter by James VI. (1584) granting the lands of Bandeith, in Stirlingshire, to Alexander Rannald, son of John Rannald and Elizabeth Alschinder, *veteri nativo et tenenti nostro.*[4]

Certain it is, incredible as it may appear, that the institution of slavery continued to exist in Scotland among certain classes down almost to our own day. Such was the condition of every person employed in a colliery or salt work, including women as well as men. These, by the mere operation of law, and without any paction, by entering the employment became the property of the owner, and bound to perpetual servitude in that particular work. The master could not sell him off the land to another, but if the owner sold or alienated the ground on which the works were, the collier or salter passed over to the new owner as *fundo annexum*, and if he made his escape the master could follow him and bring him back—exercising this power, to use the words of our great institutional writer Erskine, in virtue of "his right of property in "the deserter." This state of matters continued to a period within the memory of some still living. It was not till the year 1799 that it was put an end to by the act 39 Geo. III., which declared colliers to be "free from their servitude." One of these slaves, an old man called Moss Nook, was living in 1820. He had been originally on the estate of Mr. M'Nair of Greenfield, near Glasgow, but in the year mentioned

[1] Brechon Laws, vol. iii. p. 31.
[2] MSS. of Magdalene Coll., Fourth Report on National MSS., p. 458.
[3] Scotch Legal Antiquities, p. 159.   [4] R. M. S. xxxvj. 193.

D

he was in the service of Mr. Dunlop, of Clyde Iron Works, to whom, as he himself told the gentleman who relates the story, he had been many years before transferred by Mr. M'Nair in exchange for a pony.[1] But this was an illegal transaction, as colliers, although they could not leave the land and were sold with it, could not, as the law then stood, be transferred to another estate. I may add that so late as 1843 the late Dr. Norman Macleod had among his parishioners at Dalkeith a woman who had been in this state of slavery.[2]

The records of the ancient "lawting" courts of Orkney and Shetland contain decrees which, in a somewhat similar way, controlled the personal liberty of the cultivators of the soil. One of these, dated in 1602, proceeds on a complaint made by "ane greit number of the gentilmen "and utheris the commonis of the contrie," that permission had been given to "a great number of servandis and wtheris indwellars within "the land to pas afe the contrie to wther partis quharbe a great part of "the landis of the contrie are likelie to ly ley." It is therefore ordained that "na skippair, merchand, or awner carie away or transport afe the "contrie ony persoun or personis in ther schipis bottis, great or small, "without my lordis licence or his deputis," under penalties. "My lord" here referred to is "Patrik, Earl of Orkney, Lord Zetland."[3]

In Scotland, for a long time, a very different class of the community were made the subjects of sale, namely, thieves and other malefactors. Among the Argyll papers is a charter, granted (circa 1350) by John of Menteith, lord of Knapdale and Arran, in favour of Archibald Campbell, lord of Lochow, by which is given to the said Archibald and his heirs the power "of *selling* and dismissing of thieves as they please; and if "they be condemned to death with power to hang them on the gallows."[4] By an act of the Scottish Parliament in 1606 power is given to the owners of Coalheughs and Saltpans to apprehend and put to labour in their works all vagabonds and sturdy beggars.[5]

I do not know what exact amount of liberty the inhabitants of Glasgow enjoyed in the old times of which I have been speaking, for the subject is involved in considerable obscurity. In the earlier part of their history they were most of them, no doubt, the native bondmen of the bishop; and I find no reason for supposing that they were exempt from

---

[1] Domestic Annals of Scotland, vol. iii. p. 250.   [2] Old Country Houses of Glasgow.
[3] Maitland Club Miscellany, vol. ii. p. 147.
[4] Fourth Report on Historical Manuscripts, p. 476.   [5] Act Parl. Scot., vol. iv. p. 286.

the law to which I have referred, which entitled the bishop, as their feudal lord, to prevent them from leaving his jurisdiction. The *homines episcopi* were, however, of a higher grade than the natives or serfs, and they might, by acquiring a "toft," become burgesses. In 1242 we find a grant by King Alexander to the Bishop of Glasgow, "ut burgenses *et* "*homines* sui," should be free to buy and sell in Argyll and Lennox "without disturbance from our bailies of Dumbarton." But whatever was their status, it was higher than that of the neyfs. The latter, there is every reason to believe, were, as their name, *nativi*, indicates, the original native population who had been brought under subjection by the invaders. They were mere chattels, over whose persons the bishop had a power, or rather a right of property, which entitled him, if the bondsman escaped, to pursue him and bring him back. And the greater part of the rural population—called churles, thrylls, and upland men, and also natives and serfs—were in the same condition.

But the ancient burgh laws provided certain limitations to the power of the bishop. If one of his native bondsmen could escape to a royal burgh—to Rutherglen or Dunbarton, for example—and there "remain "quietlie the space of ane yeir and ane day" without being challenged and reclaimed by his lord, "in that case he shall be free and delyvered "fra bondage." Such was the law when the bishops got the grant of a burgh at Glasgow, and it applied to every native bondsman in the kingdom "whais bond that ever he be."[1]

Another limitation of the power of the bishops and other feudal lords over the persons of their bondmen was, that at all fairs the liberty of the bondman was assured during his presence there. By one of the old burgh laws it was provided that if a serf (*nativus*) had fled from his master, and the latter found him at a fair, he could not take or attach him while the fair lasted.[2] Neither could any one, serf or freeman, be taken at a fair for debt.

In Glasgow, perhaps, as was the case at one time in the English burghs, the "masters" of certain crafts enjoyed greater privileges than others, and those who were able to buy a "toft" in the burgh, and who thereby became burgesses, would acquire a higher status; but it is certain that none of the inhabitants enjoyed the rights and immunities peculiar to royal burghs, and out of the royal burghs there was at that time no real liberty. In the case of all mere burghs of barony the

[1] Regiam Majestatem, lib. ii. c. ix.   [2] Leges Burg. 83.

property of the community continued as truly a part and parcel of the barony as if it were the property of a single vassal. The bishop was accordingly the feudal as well as the spiritual lord of the community, and of every individual composing it. For his own interest, and in order to promote the prosperity of his diocese, he permitted them to go and come in trading; but, without his permission, they could not permanently leave the district. One of the *Leges Quatuor Burgorum* provides that it shall be "lachful and lefull till ilk burges to geyff or sell his " lands the quhilk he has gotten of purchas or of conquest *in the kyngis* " *burgh* to quham sa evyr hym likes, and may frelie pass and gang quhar " he wyl"—a privilege which, limited as it is to the royal burghs, would seem to imply that at that early time no other, neither the "homo epis- " copi" nor any one else, could leave the territory where he was settled and "gang quhar he wyl" without his lord's permission. Even in the royal burghs personal freedom was not enjoyed by every class of the traders and burgesses. We find an example of this in the case of the wool- combers, in regard to whom it is provided that "gif ony kemistaris levis " the burgh to dwell with uplandys men, having sufficient work to occupie " thaim within burgh, thai aw to be takyn and prisonyt." And so late as the year 1369 it was enacted by the parliament of David II., held in Perth in February of that year, "that na burgisis nor marchands tran- " sport thaim out of the realme withoutyne leave of our lord the king " or his chalmerlan soucht and obtenit." If such was the case with the king's freemen we may conceive what must have been the powers of the bishop over those *homines ejus*, as well as over the *nativi et servi*, of whom he was the feudal lord.

The king's burgess, again, had the right of battle, *potest habere duellum*, with the burgess of an earl, baron, or churchman, but the latter was denied that privilege against the king's burgess. The royal burghs, from the outset, enjoyed complete self-government. The magistrates were appointed "thruch the counsals of the guid men of the toun," but in Glasgow they were named by the bishop, and could be removed by him at his pleasure. In Glasgow there were no "freemen burgesses" and no guildry or convenery—these being the two incorporated classes into which burgesses of royal burghs alone were divided. Again, no citizen of Glasgow could, in the time of these laws, have an oven, that being a privilege confined, by stringent enactment, to the king's burgess. Such were some of the ancient burgh laws of Scotland, and there were many others in which the freedom which the "burgenses domini regis" enjoyed stands out in striking contrast with the state of dependence and vassalage of the "burgenses abbatis prioris comitis et baronis." In process of time, no doubt, many of the privileges and immunities of the royal burghs came in practice to be conceded to the burghs of barony and regality; but the change must have been very gradual, and it is probable that for a long time none but the royal burghs enjoyed the benefit of those *leges burgorum* which placed them so high above the burghs which held only of subject superiors.

But on the whole the people of Glasgow appear to have been fortunate in their ecclesiastical rulers, and their condition was greatly superior to that of the communities who were under the sway of lay barons. From the time of David the city was ruled by bishops till 1491, when Robert Blackader, who then filled the see, was at the instance of James IV. (who, like James II., was a canon of the cathedral) promoted by the pope to the dignity of archbishop, with metropolitan, primatical, and legislative dignity, and until the Reformation the archbishops were the lords temporal as well as spiritual of the community. But farther on I shall have occasion to refer again to the condition of the citizens, and their municipal rights under the rule of the bishops.

THE EARLY LANGUAGE.

Another interesting subject of inquiry is the language spoken by the early inhabitants of Glasgow. In remote times it was undoubtedly that of the Celts or Kelts, the first of the many divisions of the Aryans which found its way to our country. At first inhabiting the greater part of Europe, and either exterminating or partly mingling with the Stone Age men whom they found there, we find this people inhabiting the British Isles—for the ancient Britons belonged to that family, as did also the old Gaelic population, until they were ousted by another branch of the same Aryan race, the Teutons, from whom the English are descended. This early Celtic language, in the form in which we first have any knowledge of it, was Irish or Welsh, and with it the language now spoken in the Scottish Lowlands has little or no affinity. When we read of the early

"language of the Scots," it was undoubtedly, Mr. Skene says, "the Irish
"language still spoken there, and which is identic with the Gaelic of the
"Scottish Highlands and the Manx of the Isle of Man.   They form
"indeed but one language, which may be called Gaelic, and show no
"greater variety among each other than those which characterize the ver-
"nacular speech of different provinces of the same nation."[1]   The common
belief is that the Western Highlands were peopled from Ireland, but there
can be little doubt that this Irish or Dalriadic tradition was an invention
of the Scottish monks, and that the Highland clans are, with very few
exceptions, descended from the northern Picts, and formed one peculiar
and distinct Gaelic nation, who have inhabited the same country from
time immemorial.[2]   But it is equally true that it is to the Columban
Church, issuing from Ireland, that the northern Picts owed the introduction of letters and a written language.   To it we owe the standard of the
written Irish, and in that most interesting old manuscript, the Book of
the Columbite Abbey of Deir, there is preserved a specimen of it.   The
portion of this MS. which contains an imperfect copy of the Gospels in
Latin, is in a character which may be ascribed to the ninth century.   The
other portions—written on what had been the blank pages—which contain legends of the foundation of the church and memoranda of grants of
land, are in Gaelic, in the Irish character, in a handwriting of the early
part of the reign of David I.   It is identic with the written Irish of the
period, and it was in this language no doubt that the "little volume" of
the Life of Kentigern found by Jocelin, the monk of Furness, was written.
It was then called Scottish, the Lowland Scotch being termed English, as
indeed it was.   In the beginning of the sixteenth century the spoken
language of the Highlands began to be called Irish, and the Anglican
dialect of the Lowlands came to be called Scotch.   In course of time the
language spoken in the Highlands came to be different from its written
form, but after the Reformation the first literature introduced in the
Highlands, consisting of some religious books and the Bible, were all in
the written Irish language.   The version of the Bible read in our parish
churches in the Highlands was, till within quite a recent period, Bishop
Bedel's translation into Irish.   The general use of written Scottish Gaelic
is comparatively recent.   The only charter of Scotch lands in Celtic
speech extant is one by M'Donald, lord of the Isles, which is dated on
"the sixth day of the month of Beltaine," 1408.

[1] Celtic Scotland, vol. i. p. 193.   [2] The Highlands of Scotland, by W. F. Skene, vol. ii. p. 16.

The British language—that which was spoken in Clydesdale in the time of Kentigern—must have been very much the same as what is still spoken in Wales, though not now in Cornwall, though a variety of it lingered there till the middle of the last century.[1] The Gaelic spoken by the Picts who peopled the Highlands and Islands, and the Irish spoken by the Scots, were displaced by the language of the Angles, except in localities where each of them continued to exist to a greater or less extent in its own country—these localities being in each case the maritime and mountainous parts.[2]

This language of the Angles—Anglo-Saxon, as it is often called—is known to have been, in its early forms, the national speech of the same race since at least the end of the fifth century, when the first settlers by whom it was spoken came to our island. It is interesting to find the roots of it—to find, indeed, many of our English words themselves—in the Gothic, the oldest representative of the Teutonic branch of the Aryan or Indo-Germanic family of languages as it was written so early as the fourth century. All that remains to us of this old language is a portion of a translation of the New Testament from the Greek, written about A.D. 370 by Ulfilas, a Gothic prince, who had been converted to Christianity, and afterwards preached to his countrymen in the region of the Lower Danube. From this precious fragment a few words as examples cannot fail to be interesting. In Mat. v. 35 footstool is rendered *fotubaurd*, *i.e.* footboard. The same phonetic resemblance in our language between sun and son is found in this old Gothic. Sun is *sunna*, and son *sunns*—both being derived from the Sanskrit *su*, to beget. Our word steal is the representative of the Gothic *stelan*. Gate and door are rendered by the word *daur*. The term used for woman or wife is *qino* or *quens*, from which two words of very opposite meaning with us, queen and quean, have their common origin. The mysteries of the kingdom of heaven are, in Gothic, its runes, *runa:* hence our runic. The word for millstone, *asiluquairnus*, is the relic of a time when the mill was worked by asses. The second half of the word survives in our word quern, the rude handmill till quite recently used so much in the Highlands. When our Lord is described as twelve years old it is rendered twelve winters— *tvalib vintruns.* When the disciples are told that they shall tread on serpents the old Gothic is *trudan ufaro vaurme, i.e.* tread on worms. Dust is rendered *mulda*, mould. When St. Paul calls himself the least

---

[1] Celtic Scotland, vol. i. p. 193.   [2] Craik's English Literature, vol. i. p. 320.

of the apostles the rendering is the smallest, *smallista*. Thrones are rendered *sitlos*, *i.e.* settles. Such are a few specimens of English words used by the Goths fifteen hundred years ago.[1]

Since the introduction of the Anglo-Saxon language into our country it has been moving—now faster, now slower—throughout the twelve or thirteen centuries over which our knowledge of it extends, and it appears to have at an early period come northwards to Scotland, and to have continued to make the same progress there as in England. Many causes conduced to the establishment of the English tongue over that of the Normans. Among others, as Professor Innes observes, the Anglo-Saxon language had been cultivated in prose and poetry. It was endeared to the people from having been written by their great Alfred and by the fathers of the Church before any of the vernacular tongues of Europe had been studied by the learned; and the cultivated and written language prevailed over the rude and unwritten.[2]

King Alfred left a collection of " Proverbs," one of which, taken from an early version, shows that the matrimonial experiences of some in his time were not different from many in our own:—

> Monymon singeþ
> Þat wif hom bryngeþ
> Wiste he hwat he broughte
> Wepen he myghte.[3]

That is,

> Many a man singeth
> That a wife home bringeth,
> If he knew what he brought
> Weep he might.

Among the MSS. of Sir William W. E. Wynne at Poniarth is a gift of land made in the year 942, in which occur the words, "nou is thisses " landes feourtie hyde."[4]

The English of the eighth century differed nearly as much from that of the nineteenth as Latin differs from Italian.[5] But the change after that was rapid, and by the beginning of the eleventh century the language was fast assuming its present form. An interesting example of

---

[1] The Gothic Fragments of Ulfilas, by Professor Stanley Leathes.
[2] Scotland in the Middle Ages, p. 75.   [3] Old English Miscellany, London, 1872, p. 118.
[4] Second Report on Historical MSS., p. 105.   [5] Craik's English Literature, p. 36.

the English of that period is preserved in the fragment of a song composed by Canute. It refers to the music which came floating from the choir of Ely as the king was rowing on the Nen:—

> Merie sungen the muneches binnen Ely
> Tha Cnut ching rew there by
> Roweth cnichtes noer the lant
> And here we these muneches saeng.

That is,

> Merry (sweetly) sang the monks within Ely
> That (when) Cnute king rowed thereby.
> Row, knights, near the land,
> And hear we these monks' song.

The lines are recorded by a monk of Ely who wrote about 1166, and being in verse and in rhyme it is, with reason, conjectured by Dr. Craik that the words are reported in their original form.

The English of Canute's song was—making allowance for ordinary provincial differences—the same language that was spoken at that time in the little fishing village founded by Kentigern on the banks of the Clyde.

Passing over a period of more than two hundred years it is the same language which we find in Chaucer, only advancing farther to its present form. The writings of Chaucer can be read now with little assistance from a glossary, and the same is to be said of the vernacular of Glasgow and of the rest of the Lowlands of Scotland at the same time. The language spoken in the Lowlands at that period (circa 1370) sprang from the same sources and had been affected by the same influences as the language of England. In fact it was the same language. What we are accustomed to call the Scottish dialect differs less from that of England than do the dialects of different counties in the latter kingdom at the present day. Divested of the cumbrous spelling of the old manuscripts, the verses of Barbour are quite as intelligible to an English reader as are those of Chaucer; and, indeed, Barbour's great poem of Bruce, though earlier in date than the Canterbury Tales, is, in some of the grammatical forms, even more modern than those which we find in the poetry of Chaucer. For example, Barbour uses our present *they*, *them*, and *there* (thai, thaim, and thar), while Chaucer and his countrymen were still adhering to the Saxon *hey* or *hi*, *hem*, and *hir* or *her*.

The language of Wycliffe—whose translation of the New Testament was made in 1380—is, although subsequent to Barbour, still less modern than the language of that writer. It is proper to add, however, that the earliest manuscripts of Barbour extant must have been transcribed fully a century later than the time when he wrote the poem, and the language, therefore, cannot be absolutely relied on as that of the writer. The change after Wycliffe was very rapid, and the language of Tyndale's Testament—the first printed in English, and which appeared in 1525, only forty-five years after Wycliffe—differs little from that of our own day.

Of the vernacular language used in Scotland in legal writs Professor Innes has given, as the earliest known example, a writ of the year 1389;[1] but there exists an example still older in a document preserved among the family papers of Sir Patrick Keith Murray of Auchtertyre, which, apart from the language, is curious as a record of early judicial proceedings. In early times the local courts of the great barons were held on a hill or mound called the Moot-hill, and the document to which I have referred shows that these courts survived till towards the end of the fourteenth century. It is peculiarly interesting as a record of probably one of the last of these early baron courts, and it is perhaps the only example in existence. The proceedings took place in the year 1385, and had reference to a disputed right to certain lands. The record bears that the court was held on a Moot-hill called the hill of Longforgund, and that the baron was attended by the same officers as figure in the courts of the sovereign, while the special character of the proceedings is their strict adherence to legal formalities. The locality is away from our city, but it will not be without interest to quote the final decree as a specimen of the same vernacular which was spoken in Glasgow in an age contemporary with Barbour's great poem.

It is recorded that at the final court, held at the Hund hill on the 21st of April, 1385, "throw Sir Patrick Gray lorde of the chefe barony " of Langforgande, mony nobilles thare beande, with consale of tha " nobillis and of his curt, he wele awisit that the forsayde personaris " contenyt in his prosces souch hym nother with grace lufe na with " lauch to delay his dome na his proces, with consale of the forsayde " curt and noblis that thare was, throw the moutht of Robert Louranson " than dempstare of oure lord the kingis curt and of his, it was giffyn for

[1] Scotland in the Middle Ages, p. 260.

"dome that the Lytilton and Lourandston of Ouchtercomane suld
"dwell in the handis of the forsayde Sir Patrick and his ayeris quhill
"the tyme that all the forsaydis personaris, and all thaire namys
"nemmyt, suld recouir the landys othir be grace, trety, or prosces of
"law: and thus endyt the proces."[1]

But if Professor Innes is right in supposing that the interlined
glossings which occur in a *conventio*, or lease, between the Abbot of
Scone and the Hays of Leys, in the year 1312, are contemporary
with the deed itself, we have in these interlineations a specimen of
the Scots language more early still—perhaps, with the exception of
local names and terms, the earliest in existence. It is possible these
glossings may have been introduced at a later period, but after carefully examining the facsimile of the deed which is given in the
Chartulary of Scon,[2] I am disposed to think that they are, within
a very few years at least, as old as the text. The following are a few
of them. I give the Latin words first, adding the gloss or translation
(which is written over them) in italics:—Triginta, *thretti;* Annuatim,
iere bi iere; quod motent pro sustacione sua, *y* *yai sal grind for
yair fode;* in circuitu, *abute thaime;* percipiunt focale, *sal take fuayl;*
et eorum successoribus, *tha y* *comis in thair stede;* (Abbatis) dominio,
y *laurdscape;* residenti, *dwelland;* revocare, *cal again;* demittat
edificata, *sal leve biggit;* exorte fuerint, *haf gruyn;* solebant, *war
wont;* (sigilla) appensa, *hingand;* rectis divisis, *richtwis divisis;* cyro-
graphi, *hand chartir;* construi facient, *sal ger be made.*

One of the most interesting of the glosses is that over the word
nativi. It is *inbornmen*, confirming the hypothesis that these were
the remains of the native-born population compelled by the invaders
to become their serfs. The date of the deed is two years before
Bannockburn and nearly fifty years before Chaucer, and it shows
that the language was very little different then from what it was
a century afterwards. And it was the same in England. In a Latin
document in the reign of Edward II. among the papers of the corporation of Bridport, there occur various English glosses over the
Latin terms; for example, *vebbis* (webs), *vedercoc* (weathercock), *stokes*
(stocks), *bordis* (boards), &c.[3]

---

[1] Third Report of Royal Commission on Historical MSS., App., p. 410.
[2] Liber Eccles. de Scon, Maitland Club, p. 104.
[3] Sixth Report on Historical MSS., p. 490.

Of the vernacular language of Glasgow in local writs, one of the earliest examples is to be found in a deed which I have referred to elsewhere—an agreement between "Frer Oswald Priour of the Freris "of Glasgow and the Convent of the Samyn on the ta part and "John Flemyn of the Covglen on the tother part," bearing date 22d January, 1433.[1] It is a curious document apart from its interest as an example of what the language in Glasgow was four hundred and fifty years ago. It bears that "the said Johne has set in to feferm "tyll the said Priour and the Convent, or quha sa be Priour in that "said Convent, a rud of lands lyand on the gat at strekis fra the "Markat Cors tyll the he kyrk Glasgu . . the said priour and con- "vent payit thar for yherly tyll the said Johne hys ayris or assignyis "ten schylling of vsuale mone of the kynryk of Scotland . . and "stabylling for twa hors in that samyn place or ellis within the Freris "tyll the said John Flemyn qwhen hym lykis tyll cum tyll do hys "erandis or mak residens within the toun / And attour gyf it lykis "the said Johne Flemyn tyll cum and dwell and mak residens within "Glasgu / the said priour and convent, or qwha sa be priour in the "tym, sall byg tyll the said Johne an honest hall chamir and butler, "with a yard to set cale in, sic as effeiris in thir thyngis, till the "said Johne Flemyn till be herberӱt in / the said Johne ressavand "nan annuell of the said plase sall lang as he maynures it in the "maner as is beforsaid but fraud or gyle / To be haldyn and had "the said landis with thair appertenans fra me myn ayris executoris "and assignyis tyll the priour and the convent of the said freris in "fourme and maner as is befor spokyn . . with all profitis commoditeis "and eysmentis and als frely as ony land is broukyt or possedyt in "fe and heritayge within the burgh of Glasgu."

We have a specimen of the language spoken in Scotland of an earlier date than this—although much later than the Scone frag- ments—which is interesting from the curious circumstance in connec- tion with which it has been preserved. Thomas of Walsingham tells that when the Scots of the Borders were making inroads on the English territory in the fourteenth century, they found a pestilence prevailing, and on inquiry were told by the inhabitants that it had come on them "by the special grace of God." The Scots did not quite appreciate a "grace" that came in this fashion, and in their

[1] Lib. Coll., p. 166.

inroads they used as an invocation, Walsingham says—and he gives it in the vernacular, instead of the Latin in which his work is written —"Gode and Sainct Mungo Sainct Romayn and Sainct Andrew "schield us this day fro Goddis grace and the foule death that Englisch "men dien upon." This was in 1379, five hundred years ago.[1]

Among the papers in the Glasgow Chartulary is a curious and, so far as I am aware, a unique document, which is also worthy of notice not only as another specimen of the vernacular language of the period (1477), but as the record of a peculiar process of law observed at that time in Glasgow, which cannot fail to be interesting to the legal antiquary.

The vicars of the choir of the Cathedral were in right, it appears, of "a certain annual yearly"—what we would now call a ground annual—payable from a tenement in the Rottenrow. The "annual" had ceased to be paid, and the vicars were unable to recover it from the property in consequence of the tenement having fallen into disrepair—being, indeed, in an utterly dilapidated state. The proprietor had died, and his heirs having failed to pay the arrears, the vicars took proceedings to obtain possession of the ground in satisfaction of the debt. With this view the following process is adopted. The document from which I quote is an instrument under the hand of a notary, entitled "Adjudicatio curie civitatis Glasguensis vasti tene-"menti in favorem Vicariorum chori Glasg. pro solutione annuo "reditus vicariis ex eo tenemento debiti." The notary, after the usual commencement in Latin, proceeds to embody in his instrument the proceedings from the records of the court "in wlgare"—that is, in the vernacular tongue—as follows. I avoid the old contractions of words:—

"The hed court of the burgh and cite of Glasgw haldyn in the "Tolboth of the samyn be Johne Stewart provest James Stewart and "Johne Robynson Bailzies of Glasgw the xxij day of the moneth of "January in the ȝere of God a thousande four hundreth lxx and sevyn "yers. the soyts (suits) callit, the court affermyt &c. the quhilk day "in presens of the said hed court and al the members thereof planly "comperit Sir Thomas of Bargille ane vicar ministrand in the queyr "of Glasgw and procuratour til al the vicars of the said queir as his "power was thair sufficiently knawin And openly said that ane tene-

[1] Chronica Thomæ Walsyngham, Edit. Carndeni 1602, p. 228.

"ment within the said cite lyand within the Ratonraw and on the
"south side of the samyn, betwyx ane tenement of Master Gilbert
"Reryk archiden of Glasgw on the est syde and the tenement of
"Schir Johne Browne vicar of the quehyr of Glasgw on the west syde
"the quhilk acht [owed] the vicars forsaid certane annuel ȝerly as
"was noterly knawin to al the membrs of that court was destitut of
"all bigging and reparacion in al parts at [that] it mycht not be
"strenzeit be thaim for the payment of the annwell bot alanarly the
"groonde remanande wast and wnhabit. Quarfor he besoch the juge
"and court forsaid til deliver hym erd and stane in falt of payment
"of the grund annuell accordand to the kyngis lawis maid tharupon
"And that considerit to be consonande to ressone thai assignit to
"the said Sir Thomas procurator Johne of Monfode sergeand to pass
"to the said tenement and deliver to the said procurator erd and stane
"of the samyn befor witnes. the quhilk sergeand at comand as said
"is passed to the grunde and fand wast and uninhabit and not strenze-
"able and therfor deliverit to the said Sir Thomas procurator erd
"and stan closit efter the consuetude of the cite in sik things as for
"the first court of recognicioun befor thir witnes George Robynsoun
"and Johne M'clelane citenars of the samyn and therof the said Sir
"Thos Bargylle procurator askit ane rowment and tuk the court to
"witnes et sic finit rotulament."

This, which is called, it will be observed, "the first court of recogni-
"tion," takes place on the 27th of January. Then the instrument goes
on to record a proceeding of precisely the same kind—verbatim, indeed
—on the 7th of April following. This is called "the second court of
"recognition." And once more the whole proceeding is again repeated
and recorded word for word at a head court held on the 13th of October,
thus completing what the notary calls "rotulamentum tercie curie."

Earth and stone having been thus delivered to the vicars on three
several occasions, the instrument proceeds to narrate the conclusion of
the process by which the vicars were invested in the absolute property
of the tenement. It states that on the 26th of January following, at
another head court of the burgh, the previous procedure was referred
to, adding that proclamation had been also made at the market cross
"openly warnand the lochful heritars or Ayrs of xl dais to cum and pay
"the said annuell acht of the said tenement efter the forme of the lawis
"of the burgh the quhilk payment was not maid." The instrument

then proceeds thus:—"And therfor continuand the said Sir Alexander
"procurator present, erd and stane of fortyme deliverit as said is after
"the forme of the lawis, and askyt in plan court ward and dome of the
"said wast tenement as it was lachfully recoverit in full of payment of
"the annuel acht of the samyn efter the forme forsaid and effect of the
"rowments maid tharupon at the thre hed courts And this beand said,
"the foresaid Sir Alexander procurator remouyt, the court wardit and
"ryply and weil avisit, and therefter the said Sir Alexander called in
"againe, Sir John Michelson borow clerc at the special command of the
"provest and bailzeis forsed judicialy informyt the demestar John
"Nerlson the quhilk gaif for dome at [that] the said procurator to the
"vicars of the queir of Glasgw had lachfully wonnyn and obtenyt the
"foresaid tenement with the pertinents in defalt of the payment acht of
"the samyn. The quhilk dome the said Sir Alexander procurator askit
"to be rowit and therof ane instrument of the samyn." The instrument
concludes with the usual attestation by the notary in Latin.

It is interesting to note that in the proceedings preparatory to and
after giving judgment the same forms are here observed which still
prevail in our ecclesiastical courts. Before the court proceeds to
deliberate the party is "removed," and he is "called in again" to hear
the sentence.

Of early examples of local names in the vernacular tongue as early
as the Inquisition of David (1116) we have "Aschchyrc" (Ashkirk) and
"Drivesdale." In a charter in 1130 we have "Strevelinschire."[1] In
1179 "Kirkpatric," "Cludesdale," "Annansdale," "Glenkarn." In 1189
"Neuton." In 1283 "le Weynde."[2] In 1304 "Meduwell" (Meadow
well). "The Bromilaw" (broomy law) occurs in 1325; "Gallowgate,"
of the same date; "Bogtoune" in 1336.[3] In a Latin charter of a tenement in Rutherglen in 1405 the subject conveyed is described as called
"*vulgariter* Thendehows" (the end house), in the street called "la
"Watryraw" (the watery row). In a charter of a property in Roxburgh
in 1309 it is described as situated "in vico qui vocatur Kyngstret."[4] In
other charters as early as the reign of William the Lion (1190) we have
specimens of Lowland Scotch, such as "standand stane," "stane cross,"
and others. From these and various other names and terms occurring
in the earliest writs which exist there is every reason to believe that

[1] Lib. Cart. Sancti crucis, p. 8.   [2] Reg. de Passelet, p. 385.
[3] Lib. Coll., pp. 156, 158.   [4] Reg. Epis. Glasg., No. 280.

from the beginning of the twelfth century, and probably earlier, a genuine Teutonic language was spoken in Scotland, and that the vernacular language of Glasgow was very much then what it was down to a comparatively recent period.

In later times the intimate relations which prevailed between Scotland and France were the cause of the introduction into the Scottish language of many words which are still retained, and which are unknown in the vernacular of England; such as jigot, ashet (assiette), caraffe, and many others; and in the sixteenth and seventeenth centuries we have frequent examples, in stating sums or dates, of the use of French idiom. For example there is mention in our burgh records of a head court held at Glasgow on "the xix day of Januare, the ʒeir of God IMVᶜlx "threttene yeirs"—the *soixante treize* of the French. In an entry in the council records (13th August, 1660) a sum is written "thrie scoir twelfe "pounds." In another minute mention is made of the occasion when the tanners "paises" their hides—that is, weighs them—from *peser;* and there are many other similar examples.

To save recurring to the subject I may mention here that the same close relations with France were the cause of the introduction into Glasgow of great quantities of inferior French coin. The expression that something useless is "not worth a doyt" is still in use among us. The doyt was a French copper coin of the value of the twelfth part of a penny sterling, and under date 19th March, 1660, there is an entry in the burgh records bearing "that the toune and country is lyke to be "abused be the frequent inbringing and passing of French doyts," and strictly prohibiting the introduction "of all sort of such bais capper "coyne." Another French coin with which the town council had also to deal because of its large circulation in Glasgow was "dinnaries," as they are called in the minute.[1] This was the French *denier*, the tenth part of a sous.

THE EARLY HOUSES.

Of the houses of the ancient inhabitants of Clydesdale and other parts of Scotland I have referred only to those of very early times—the weems and earth-houses and the fortified crannogs used by the natives

[1] 7th Sept. 1667.

at and preceding the time of the Roman occupation. Buildings of a better kind were, of course, used by the Romans themselves, and by the limited number of colonists who accompanied them from Belgium and Gaul, and by the few of the chief inhabitants who had obtained the honour of citizenship. These houses would no doubt exhibit, in a greater or less degree, the peculiar features of the Roman style of building, but after the Romans withdrew they fell into ruin, and the houses, or rather huts, occupied by the native population generally—not only by the peasantry and labourers, but by the chiefs and leaders—must have been for a long time of the rudest description. The first cluster of houses in Glasgow were no doubt mere hovels built of wattles and mud, and thatched with reeds or coarse grass or turf. As a rule they had no second room, and the single apartment served as a chamber in which all the family slept promiscuously.[1] A description of such a house is given by Longland in "Piers the Ploughman's Crede." When such was the case in England we may be sure matters would be no better in Glasgow—probably worse. But no doubt in the first Glasgow houses stone might be also partially employed; for in the middle ages the materials used for building were always those which were cheapest and which came most readily to hand—none being brought from a distance when it could possibly be avoided, and as stone as well as wood was to be had at Glasgow, both of these materials would probably be employed—the stones being, in the oldest constructions, left unwrought, and the interstices filled in with mud.

An incidental mention of an old wattled house not far from Glasgow occurs in an interesting document of the year 1233, relating to certain lands which the abbot and monks of Paisley averred to have been unjustly alienated from their abbey. The document is entitled *Litera examinationis de terra Monochkenneran injuste alienata*, and consists of a recorded declaration, *intentio*, of the abbot's claim in a suit depending before certain judges delegated by the pope to decide between the abbot and convent and one Gilbert, son of Samuel of Renfrew, the party in possession of the disputed lands. The writ records the evidence adduced by the abbot, and one of the witnesses testifies that sixty years before— which would take back the date to about the year 1170—he recollected a person named Bede Ferdan in possession of the land, and "habitantem " in quadam domo magna fabricata de virgis juxta ecclesiam de Kylpat-

---

[1] Domestic Architecture of England, part i. p. 17.

E

" rik." The decision of the delegates follows, in a separate writ, adjudging the land to the monks, and finding Gilbert liable in expenses, which are taxed at thirty pounds, "videlicet in triginta libris a parte monachorum "juratis et a nobis taxatis et moderatis." Other writs follow, recording the restoration of the lands with the large house made of wands upon it. They form altogether a most interesting record of a mediæval lawsuit conducted with as much attention to the forms of strict justice as would be done in our own day.[1]

It is highly probable that most of the earliest houses in Glasgow were constructed in a similar way to that at Kilpatrick, and that it was not till after the bishop got a grant of a burgh that buildings of a more substantial kind began to be erected, if indeed the proper building of the city was commenced at all before that time. In the Chartulary of Melrose there is a grant (circa 1195) by Bishop Joceline, who had formerly been abbot of Melrose, in favour of his old abbey, of a house in Glasgow, which he describes as that toft which Ranulphus de Hadintune built "in the first building of the burgh"—expressions which seem to imply that it was only after the date of the charter by King William, in 1175, in favour of this same bishop, that any houses within the burgh other than mere huts began to be built. There is another early notice of buildings and a garden in Glasgow in a charter of the year 1260 granted by the bishop to William de Cadihow, which conveys "aream " illam de gardino nostro apud Glasgu," with trees and buildings.

It is extremely improbable indeed that in the then unsettled state of the country any substantial erections would be made, except under the walls of the feudal lords or in territories protected by burgal rights; and even these were very different from what would be called substantial in our days. It is necessary to keep this in mind when reading of the damage caused by the destruction of towns and villages by fire in these early times. A fire in Edinburgh or Glasgow is a very serious thing nowadays, but in the thirteenth or fourteenth centuries, when the houses were chiefly constructed of wood, although such a calamity must have no doubt caused much temporary distress, it was comparatively easy to repair it. When Richard II., in revenge of an inroad made by the Scots into the northern parts of England in 1385, advanced towards Edinburgh he resided there for a few days, and then consigned the town to destruction. Froissart tells us that "the kyng of Englande came and lodged

---

[1] Reg. de Passelet, pp. 166–168.

" in Edenborrowe the chefe towne in all Scotlande and there taryed fyve
" dayes; and at his departyng it was set a fyre and brent up clene." Only
the castle escaped, "for it was strong ynough and well kept."[1] Another
passage from Froissart is also interesting as showing how unsubstantial
were the dwellings of the people generally in those times. After describing the wildness of the country and the poverty and rudeness of the people
whom the French had come to assist, he mentions the uncourteous reception his countrymen had met with—the Scots complaining that "they
" (the French) wyll ryffle and eat up alle that evir we have in this coun-
" trey. They shall doo us more dispytes and damages than thoughe the
" Englysshemen shulde fyght with us: for though the Englysshe men
" brinne our houses we care lytell therefore; we shall make them agayne
" chepe ynough: we axe but thre dayes to make them agayne, if we
" may gete four or fyve stakes and bowes to cover them."[2]

It no doubt took more trouble than this to rebuild Edinburgh after
King Richard burned it, but probably a great part of what had been
flimsy wooden erections covered with straw was then replaced by more
substantial stone buildings, so that the actual loss to the inhabitants
would be comparatively small. In 1544 Edinburgh was burned again
by the English under the Earl of Hertford. The author of a contemporary account says—"Settynge fyer in thre or iiii partes of the toune
" we repayred for that night unto our campe. And the next mornynge
" very erly we began where we lefte and continued burnynge all that
" daye and the two dayes nexte ensuinge contynually, so that neither
" within the wawles nor in the suburbes was lefte any one house unbrent.
" Also we brent thabbey called Holy Rodehouse and the pallice adjon-
" ynge to the same." The stone walls of the houses remained, however,
and the city would appear to have been again speedily repaired. The
burning of the Abbey and Palace could only have been partial, as Queen
Mary was residing in the Palace in 1561, and she was married to Darnley
in the Abbey Church five years afterwards.

The description by Froissart of the dwellings of the people is confirmed by that of Eneo Silvio, afterwards Pope Pius II., who, writing of
Scotland in the time of James I., describes the towns as unwalled, the
houses commonly built without lime, and in villages, roofed with turf,
while a cow's hide supplied the place of a door.[3]

---

[1] Froissart's Chronicles, by Lord Berners, vol. ii. fol. iii.

[2] Bannatyne Miscellany, vol. i. p. 180; Froissart vol. ii. p. 170, edit. 1518.

[3] Pii II., Comment. rerum mem. sui temporis, Francfurt, 1614.

Even in England, during the Saxon dominion, the best of the habitations of the common people were wooden huts of small dimensions, with rarely more than one room, in the centre of which the fire was kindled, and this was the case even in the towns.[1]   The walls were constructed of wattles plastered with mud, and sometimes of wood with twigs and mud over it.   The roofs were mostly of thatch, but occasionally slates were used in districts where they could be easily had.   London itself continued to be a town mainly of wood and plaster almost to a period so late as the great fire in the seventeenth century.   Among the papers of Queen's College, Oxford, there is a curious and highly interesting account, dated 1306, containing the whole disbursements for the erection in the town of what must have been one of the better class of these ancient houses.   The materials employed are all given in detail, even to the quantities of nails used, with the cost, and also the wages of the workmen.   The house was entirely of wood, and it is curious to note that among the materials for constructing the front were the staves of ten "tun-casks."   Twigs were placed on the walls over the wood, and these were covered with plaster.   The roof was covered with "sclattes," and the windows appear to have been of wooden "trellis."[2]   In none of these houses were there chimneys.   In another of the accounts of the same college, relating also to the erection of a house about the same period, there is a charge indicating that chimneys were only then coming into use. The charge is for "a wooden construction in the roof for the smoke to "escape by,"[3] and items of the same description occur in other accounts of the period.   The floors were of clay, and instead of carpets they were strewed with rushes, and many entries for "claying" floors and of the purchase of rushes to cover them occur in the old accounts both in England and Scotland.   The fuel used was chiefly peat and furze, and payments for the cutting of these are also frequent.   Occasionally coke was used.

In Glasgow, houses of this description, combined with more or less of stone work, remained to a comparatively recent period.   Glass was seldom used in the old houses.   It is found in our ecclesiastical buildings as early as the twelfth century, and there is evidence of its being used in the houses of some of the ecclesiastics in Glasgow in the beginning of the sixteenth century;[4] but for a long time it was a luxury seldom known in

---

[1] Hudson Turner.   Introduction, p. xi.   [2] Sixth Report on Historical MSS., p. 561.
[3] Ibid. p. 557.   [4] Liber Protocollorum, Grampian Club, No. 307.

private houses, the windows of which, when closed at all, were either, like the Oxford house, of trellis, or protected by wooden shutters only. In some instances we know that canvas was used to fill in windows, and in England there is evidence of this being resorted to, even in the case of churches, so late as the thirteenth century. In houses in Scotland where glass was used the casements appear to have been frequently made so as not only to fit different windows in the same house, but even those in different houses to which they might be removed.[1]

It is probable that in Glasgow, and in other towns in Scotland, the partial use of stone in the construction of houses was introduced sooner than in England, and it was certainly used in our towns at an earlier period than in the rural districts. An English traveller who visited Scotland in the beginning of the eighteenth century, and who passed through Glasgow and a considerable part of Lanarkshire, gives an interesting account of the poor state in which he found the rural districts, although it was probably much the same in England at that time. Of Crawfordjohn he says: "The houses here are of much such building as "those of Dulwich Wells, near London. The walls are either of earth "or loose stones, or are raddled. The roofes are of turfe and the floors "of the bare ground. They are but one storey high, and the chimney is "a hole in the roof and the fire place is in the middle of the floor. Their "seats and beds are of earth turfed over and raddled up, near the fire "place, and serve for both uses." Coming to a village not far from Moffat, early in the morning, he could obtain no admittance at any of the houses. To make himself heard, he says, he would have broken their windows, "*but could not find a pane of glass in the town.* I shall never," he adds, "go into such a country again. I had heard much talk of it, "and had a mind to see it for variety, and indeed it was so to me, for I "thank my God I never saw such another, and must conclude with the "poet Cleveland that

"Had Cain been Scot God sure had changed his doom,
Not made him wander, but confined him home."[2]

Probably the first houses of any importance which were erected in Glasgow were the manses which Bishop Cameron caused the thirty-two

[1] Accounts of Lord High Treasurer, p. ccii.
[2] North of England and Scotland in MDCCIV. Printed in Edinburgh from an original MS. 1818.

rectors of the Cathedral to build near the church, some of which remained till a recent period. This would be about the year 1440. In Edinburgh the introduction of stone-built houses was earlier—probably after the burning of the ancient city by King Richard, and by the end of the fifteenth century they were very common. The Spanish ambassador at the court of Scotland, in his report to Ferdinand and Isabella, written in 1497, says: "The houses are good, all built of hewn stone, and provided " with excellent doors, glass windows, and a great number of chimneys."[1] But this account must, as regards the glass windows, be taken with reserve. The walls inside, even in the case of the king's palaces, were only very roughly plastered, and when the apartments were occupied they were hung with cloth or arras. Even in the best houses there were no carpets, the floors being, as I have said, strewn with bent-grass or rushes mingled with sweet herbs.

But in Glasgow, although the manses of the rectors and a few others were built of stone, the great majority of the houses were, till the middle of the seventeenth century, constructed chiefly of timber and covered with thatch. Even where the houses were in part constructed of stone, the fronts to the streets were mostly composed of timber, and it was the same in other towns. Sir William Brereton, a gentleman of Cheshire, who visited Scotland in 1634, and who wrote an account of his travels, says of the High Street in Edinburgh: "If the houses, which are very " high and substantially built of stone, were not lined to the outside and " faced with boards, it were the most stately and graceful street that I " ever saw in my life, but this face of boards, which is towards the street, " doth much blemish it and derogate from glory and beauty; as also the " want of fair glass windows, whereof few or none are to be discovered " towards the street. This lining with boards, wherein are round holes " shaped to the proportion of men's heads, and this encroachment into " the street, about two yards, is a mighty disgrace unto it."[2]

To the same effect Ray, who wrote in 1661, says that in the towns in Scotland "they make up the fronts of their houses with fir boards nailed " one over another, in which are often made round holes or windows to " put out their heads. Instead of ceiling, even in the best houses in great " towns they cover the chambers with fir boards nailed on the roof within " side." Such were most of the houses in Glasgow, and, as might be ex-

---

[1] Calendar of Spanish Papers, quoted by Mr. Dickson. Preface to Accounts of Lord High Treasurer, p. cc.   [2] Brereton's Travels.

pected in such circumstances, the town more than once suffered severely by the ravages of fire. By a great conflagration which occurred in 1652 nearly a third of the town was destroyed, and many families were obliged to betake themselves to huts hastily erected in the adjoining fields. A minute of the town council of 22d June in that year, after enumerating the closes and tenements destroyed, thus sums up the loss: "Whereby " after compt it is fund that there will be neir fourscoir closses all burnt, " estimat to about ane thousand families so that unless spidie remedie be " vseit and help soght out fra such as hes power and whois harte God " sall move it is lyklie the toune sall come to outer ruein." On this occasion the magistrates ordered the church doors to be opened, not for shelter, but for the benefit of people who "now want chalmberis and " other places to reteir to for making of their devotioune." A collection was made throughout the kingdom to assist those who had suffered by the fire—the funds being distributed by a committee of the town council. In making grants to assist in rebuilding a limited sum only was allowed if the windows were to be " built with dealls," and a larger amount if they were built of stone.

But the old mode of construction appears to have been very much adhered to, and fifteen years afterwards another great fire occurred, by which 136 houses and shops were destroyed. On this occasion the heat was so great at the Cross that it set fire to the clock of the tolbooth, and the people broke open the doors and liberated the prisoners, who were in danger of perishing—among them being the laird of Kersland, who had been confined on account of the part he had taken at the Pentland rising.[1] By this fire between six and seven hundred families were rendered houseless. The distress was very great, and it engaged the anxious consideration of the magistrates. Their minute on the occasion, under date 4th December, 1677, is curious. It commences by noticing " the great impoverishment this burgh is reduced to throw the sad and " lamentable wo occasioned by fyre on the secund of Novr. last that God " in his justice hath suffered this burgh to fall under, and lykwayes the " most pairt of the said burgh being eye-witnesses twyse to this just " punishment for our iniquities by this rod which we pray him to make " us sensible of that we may turn from the evill of our wayes to himselfe " that so his wraith may be averted and we preserved from the lyk in " tyme to come." And then, feeling satisfied, no doubt, that providence

[1] Memorials by Law.

helps those who help themselves, they proceed to practical measures—first stating the obvious cause of the calamity and then providing against its recurrence. This part of the minute is valuable, as containing a contemporary description of how the houses in Glasgow were at that time constructed. Such calamities, it bears, "are mor incident to burghs " and incorporatiounes be reasone of their joyning houss to houssis, and " on being inflamed is reddie to inflame ane uthir, especiallie being con-" tiguouslie joyned and reared wp of timber and deall boards without so " much as the windskew of stone." To remedy this it is provided "that " each persone building *de novo* on the Hie Street, or repairing, sall be " obleiged to doe it by stone work from head to foot back and foir with-" out any timber or daill except in the insett thereof, quhilk is understood " to be partitions, doors, windows, presses, and such lyk." This is ordered to be done "not only for their probable security, but also for decoring of " the said burgh."

But till far on in the eighteenth century there was little improvement in the construction of the houses of the middle classes in Scotland. Captain Burt, writing in 1725, speaking of towns so considerable as Inverness, says, "The houses were neither sashed nor slated before the " Union, and to this day the ceilings are rarely plastered. Nothing but " the single boards serve for floor and ceiling, and the partitions being " often composed of upright boards only, and they are sometimes shrunk, " anybody may not only hear but see what passes in the room adjoining. " The houses that are not sashed have two shutters that turn upon hinges " for the low part of the window, and only the upper part is glazed, so " that there is no seeing anything in the street in bad weather without " great inconvenience."[1] Such were, no doubt, a large number of the houses in Glasgow at that time.

With the exceptions mentioned, there were in these early times few instances where the magistrates interfered with the mode of erection of houses, and those possessing tofts put down their buildings very much according to their own fancy. It is interesting to notice, however, that, in the division of land and the fixing of boundaries, certain officials, then as afterwards called Liners, exercised at a very early date the functions now performed by the Dean of Guild Court. There is preserved an instrument in 1512 relating to the transfer of certain lands adjoining the church and cemetery of Saint Roche, in which

[1] Burt's Letters, vol. ii. pp. 59–61.

it is stated that seisin was given of the lands as equally divided *per lineatores civitatis Glasguensis.*[1]

After the first great fire the city procured a fire-engine. The magistrates had heard that Edinburgh possessed one—probably the first that was in Scotland—and they sent a person to ascertain what sort of a thing it was—in the words of their minute, "to visit the "engyne thair for slockening of fyre;"[2] and being satisfied with the report they had one made for themselves. But it must have been a very primitive machine, and practically useless in such a conflagration as that which so soon again overtook them. The first proper engine which they got was in 1725, and it was made in London.[3] After the two great fires the houses erected within the burgh were more carefully constructed, and the magistrates appear to have again given premiums to encourage a better kind of building. A fund had been raised to assist those whose houses were burned, called at the time "the brunt moneye," and we find a grant made to one John Dainziell, the amount being limited to 400 pounds Scots, "if he build his win-"dowes with daills in Saltmercat," but he is to have 600 pounds "if he build them with stone."[4] And again, a grant of 500 merks is paid to Mr. John Bell, "more than what he gote formerly, for build-"ing his land in a decent way and decoring Bell's Wynd."[5] But some of the old tenements "reared up of timber and deall boards," which had escaped the fire, remained to our own day. The woodcut on following page represents a characteristic example of one of these, which stood in the close No. 77 Saltmarket. It is from a drawing made by Mr. Thomas Fairbairn in 1849.[6]

In 1684 a great fire occurred in Gallowgate, and in the absence of any efficient fire-engine the device was resorted to of taking wet hides and spreading them over the sides and thatched roofs of the adjacent houses to prevent the spread of the conflagration. Under date 26th September, 1684, there is a minute of council ordering reparation to be made "to John Woddrop for the loss of his hides that "was taken out of his holes" for this purpose.

But imperfect in their construction as the houses in Glasgow and

---

[1] Protocolla Diocesis Glasguensis, No. 606.   [2] 23d August, 1656.
[3] Minute of Council, 25th September, 1725.   [4] 4th November, 1671.   [5] 28th September, 1682.
[6] Relics of Ancient Architecture, from Water-colour Drawings by T. Fairbairn. Lithographed by Miller & Buchanan, 1849.

in the other towns in Scotland unquestionably were, till a comparatively recent period, they were undoubtedly, as I have already said, greatly superior to those in the rural districts. And this was what in the nature of things was to be expected. Many of the "bishop's men," as they acquired means by trading, would be able to buy a toft, and so become a burgess and to build a good house; but others of a higher

grade than the bishop's vassals came also to hold property in the burgh, and these no doubt set the example of building superior tenements. Among others we find ecclesiastics in other localities acquiring property in the town, and thereby becoming burgesses. For example, the monks of Kilwinning and of Paisley held land in the burgh at a very early period, and in some of the old deeds the distinction between ecclesiastics and other burgesses is noted by the latter being termed "laic burgesses."[1]

[1] Lib. Coll. N.D., p. 246.

It is interesting also to notice that the great military fraternity of the Knights Templars were among the very first holders of property in the infant city. There is a charter, executed circa 1180, by which " brother Raan Corbeht, Master of the Temple in the territory of " the King of Scotland, with advice and consent of our brethren of " Plentidoc," grants and confirms to William Gley of Glasgow, *homini nostro*, a plenary toft which Jocelin, bishop of Glasgow, had given to the Templars and " which the said William held before the bishop " gave it to us." It will be observed—and it illustrates the independence and power of this great fraternity—that William Gley, the disponee, is designed neither a burgess of Glasgow nor one of the *homines episcopi*, but " our man," and the property is to be held not of the bishop, but of the military order of the Temple—*domo militie Templi*—the reddendo being the payment of twelve pence annually at the feast of St. Michael. This is one of the very earliest transferences of property after the grant to the bishop of a burgh.

The Templars at this time held vast possessions in almost every part of Europe, and in Scotland they had several preceptories dependent on the Temple in London. The annual income of the order has been roughly estimated at the enormous sum of six millions sterling. Besides the larger grants which they obtained in land and money, they enjoyed, under various Papal bulls, immunities and advantages which ultimately gave great umbrage to the clergy. Their fall was as rapid as their rise. The Master of the Temple in London, and his vicegerent the Preceptor of Scotland, both fell in the battle of Falkirk in 1298. The order was thereafter subjected to persecution, and, after suffering repeated acts of spoliation, it was abolished by the pope in 1313. The real cause of their downfall was their wealth, which fell a prey chiefly to King Philip and the pope and the European sovereigns.[1]

TENURE OF PROPERTY.

Any one who acquired a toft in Glasgow was at liberty to sell it, but this privilege was limited. If he acquired it " by conquest or " purchase " he could dispose of it as he thought proper; but if it

[1] Addison's History of the Knights Templars.

came to him by inheritance from a father or mother he could not
voluntarily dispose of it except in the case of extreme poverty.   In
that case, and it was the same in the royal burghs, he was bound
first to offer it to the nearest heir, and this was done by a peculiar
judicial process at three several head courts of the burgh.   If the
heir availed himself of the offer he was bound to provide the seller in
food and clothing—"the clothing to be of a hew grysande or quhyte."[1]
If again the property was seized for debt the creditor was bound to
hold it for a year and a day, and within that time to offer it to the
nearest heirs; and only if they declined to buy it, or to pay the
debt, was he at liberty to sell the land—returning, in that case, the
surplus of the price, if any, to the debtor.[2]

One of the earliest examples of a sale of land in Glasgow on account
of poverty occurs in the deed already referred to, granted in 1280 by
Robert de Mithyngby to Reginald de Jrewyn, Archdeacon of Glasgow.   It proceeds on the narrative of the granter being compelled to
make the sale in consequence of his extreme poverty and necessity—
the fact of his poverty having been certified "by men worthy and
"sufficient."   It bears that the land had been offered to the granter's
nearest relatives and friends, at three principal head courts, and at
other courts of Glasgow, "according to the law and custom of the
"burgh," and it acknowledges receipt of a sum of money "paid to
"me in my urgent necessity."   The granter gives warrandice "against
"all men *and women.*"[3]

Besides the possession of a toft, residence was necessary to confer the
privileges of a burgess, and every burgess was bound to render the services of watch and ward.   He might, however, become free from these
and from other burgal obligations by renouncing his freedom and the
privileges of a burgess, and this was occasionally done.[4]   After selling
his property the granter in all cases ceased to be a burgess, and in the
royal burghs, as I have already mentioned, he was at liberty "to go where
"he will."

Among the oldest transferences of property in the Glasgow Chartulary
is one which is interesting from the circumstance that the land is conveyed not to any individual, but direct to one of the lights in the Cathedral.
It is dated in 1293, and bears that Odardus, son of the deceased Richard

[1] Leg. Burg. 42.   [2] Ibid. 90.   [3] Reg. Episc. Glasg. No. 236.
[4] Burgh Records of Aberdeen, 7th June, 1596.

Hangpudyng, had *pro salute anime sue, predecessorum et successorum suorum ac ceterorum Christi fidelium*, given, granted, and confirmed "to " the Light of the blessed Mary in the great church of Glasgow," a certain piece of land—seisin being given to John of Boyewyl, vicar of the choir of Glasgow, "then procurator of the said Light, *per intol et uttol.*" Another peculiarity of this old deed is, that it does not proceed in name of the real granter. It proceeds in the name of " Oliverus et Ricardus " Smalhy prepositi, et ceteri prepositi ac cives, congregati in placitis burgi " que tenebantur apud Glasgu," and it is they who certify, through the said Oliver, that Odardus has made the gift. Other examples occur of deeds of the same kind where the property is transferred without the signature of the granter, and without the deed proceeding in his name, there being only the declaration of a notary that the transfer had been made. In one of the deeds the notary declares that the transaction had taken place in the church of Glasgow, in presence of the sub-dean, the vicar of Kilpatrick, and two burgesses of Glasgow;[1] and another bears that the transfer had been made in presence of the notary and twelve of the citizens and two of the town's officers—*ville servientibus.*[2]

The old records contain also some curious notices as to infeftments. The usual mode was by earth and stone, and by hesp and staple,[3] but an instance occurs where, in addition to this, the bailie, in token of possession, shut up the procurator of the purchaser in the principal house of the lands—*in signum possessionis inclausit dictum Willelmum Small in principali domo sive messuagio dictarum terrarum.*[4]

The rural properties belonging to the see were held by a very simple tenure. They were to a large extent possessed by a class—generally poor—called rentallers, who, although technically holding only by will of the bishop, were, as a rule, treated as proprietors, and allowed to transmit the possession to their descendants, or, if held by a female, to her husband, and in some cases to transfer it to a third party. The rents which they paid were small, and in some instances the returns were in service instead of money. Thus a possession called Columby in the barony of Carstairs is given to James Livingston and William his son, and to Isable his wife after his death, on condition of the said James, William, and Isable "resevand the Archebischop of Glasgow present and " to cwm als aft tymes he pleises til repair to the said place of Columby

---

[1] 1418. Lib. Coll. N.D.
[2] Reg. Episc. Glasg. No. 248.
[3] Liber Protocollorum, No. 603.
[4] Ibid. No. 262.

" til hospitality on the said archebischops expenss: the said James, Wil-
" liam and Isable and their successours fyndant fyre weschelle and tyn
" with sax furnist beddis, stable for viii horss with hay feirand tharto,
" and fewale, vpon thair expenss."[1] The barony of Carstairs was one of
the earliest possessions of the see, and it is known that Wyschard, the
warrior-bishop, built a castle there towards the end of the thirteenth century. No trace of it remains, but it is not improbable that it was at this
place of Columby.

When the right to one of these rental possessions came by succession,
there was always a reservation of the liferent of the new rentaller's father
and mother. There was also in the diocese a peculiar custom known
as that of "Sanct Mungo's Wedo," by virtue of which the widow of a
rentaller was entitled, while she remained single, to possess the lands
during her life.[2]

The rentallers possessed no written title. Their names, with the different transmissions of the possession, were merely entered in the rental
book of the diocese, and this appears to have been always done by the
archbishop himself. The record, which has been preserved, extends from
1509 to 1570, and the volume is holograph of the three prelates respect-
ively, the period of whose possession of the see it embraces.

THE RULE OF THE BISHOPS.

But I must now return to the ecclesiastical and municipal history of
the city from the time of the restoration of the see by David in 1120.
After the famous Charter or Notitia by that prince, the see of Glasgow
received many rights and privileges from popes and kings. In the reign
of Malcolm IV. (1172), there is a writ by the pope confirming a Constitution of the Dean and Chapter of Glasgow which had been introduced
after the model of Sarum by Herbert, elected bishop in 1147.[3] The
Archbishop of York claimed at first a supremacy over Glasgow, but this
was resisted, and the non-dependence of the diocese on any metropolitan
bishop was established.

---

[1] Rental Book of the Diocese. Grampian Club, vol. i. p. 195.
[2] Chalmers: Caledonia.   [3] Reg. Epis. Glasg. No. 28.

In 1175 the bishops of Glasgow obtained from William the Lion the grant of a burgh, which was confirmed by Pope Lucius in 1181; and King Alexander, by a charter in 1189, granted to the bishop the right of a fair *cum firma et plenaria pace,* and this important privilege of "the "king's peace" to every one frequenting the fair was confirmed by a subsequent royal charter in 1210. The right of a fair was a very valuable privilege in those days, and without it the trade which the bishops coveted could not have been attracted to their burgh. A considerable commerce was in this way established in Glasgow, including trade from foreign countries, particularly from France, with which, from a very early period, Glasgow had much intercourse. An incidental notice of this occurs in one of the Argyll charters of the fourteenth century, from which we learn that French gloves were among the articles then sold at the fair of Glasgow. By this charter, which is dated in 1363, Mary, Countess of Menteith, grants to her kinsman Archibald, the son of Colin Campbell of Lochow, the lands of Kilmun on Cowal, and the reddendo is the yearly payment of a pair of Paris gloves at Glasgow fair.[1] The bishops had also grants at different times of tofts in other burghs, *e.g.* in Forfar, Stirling, and Dumfries.

Originally the district in which Glasgow is situated was included in the territory over which the rights of the royal burgh of Rutherglen extended—for the territory of the latter, as defined in its charter, extended "de Garin usque ad Kelvin"—and Rutherglen exacted toll in Glasgow itself, at that time, no doubt, a very insignificant village. From this toll the bishops obtained an early exemption for themselves and their people, but only for their own chattels. This was renewed in the reign of Alexander II. (1235), but it brought them into collision with Rutherglen, and also with Dunbarton. Against the latter the bishops, as I have already stated, succeeded in securing for their vassals a free trade in Argyll and Lennox; but as regards the more powerful burgh of Rutherglen, all that could for some time be obtained was a protection against its levying toll and custom within the town of Glasgow itself, or nearer than "the cross of Schedenistoun" (Shettleston).[2]

I have already referred to the dependence of the inhabitants on the bishops as their feudal lords, and the whole history of the city shows how small was the amount of liberty which they enjoyed compared with the king's burgesses. For the government of his burgh, the Bishop of

---

[1] Orig. Paroch. vol. ii. p. 72.   [2] Cosmo Innes, pref. to Reg. Epis. Glasg.

Glasgow appointed magistrates, but they had no independent power. Whatever were their functions, they were the mere nominees and instruments of their lord paramount. Gibson, in his History of Glasgow, has gone far wrong on this subject. He says that so early as the year 1268 Glasgow was governed "by provosts, aldermen or wardens, and " bailies, who seem to have been independent of the bishop, and were " possessed of a common seal distinct from the one made use of by the " bishop and chapter," and in this Gibson has been followed by other local historians. It is true that at that early period the community had a seal, but in other respects there is no foundation for the statement, if it means that Glasgow was at that time presided over by a provost. Gibson cites as his authority the terms of the charter by Robert de Mithyngby in 1280, but that deed does not prove that there was a provost as we now understand that term. The statement is that seisin of the lands conveyed was given, not coram *præposito* et ballivis, but coram *præpositis* et ballivis—terms which appear to have been at that time synonymous, and to indicate nothing more than officers entrusted by the bishop with the management of the civil affairs of his burgh, and who acted, I have no doubt, under his instructions, as it is beyond question they were nominated by him. I am confirmed in this by the terms of the charter of 1293 already referred to, which bears that seisin was given in presence of " Oliverus et Ricardus præpositi *et ceteri præpo-* "*siti* ac cives Glasguensis." The seal of the community was appended to this document, as it was to the one cited by Gibson, but it is not unimportant to observe that that seal was not considered sufficient to attest the writ. It required also to be attested by the ecclesiastical seal, and accordingly there are added the words, "et ad majorem rei gesti " securitatem sigillum officialitis Glasguensis eidem est appensum." And this appending of the seal of the bishop in all writings of importance continues in the later charters.

In England, in the old times, the term *præpositus* was equivalent to reve or bailiff. A deed of conveyance of a property in Bridgewater in the second year of Henry II. is certified by the seal of the provostship —*præpositatus*—and two persons designed as provosts set their seal to the deed at the request of the granter, "because his seal is unknown to " most persons."[1]

I would just add as a farther proof that there was no provost in

1 Third Parliamentary Report on Historical Documents, App. p. 310.

Glasgow in those days, that a Transumpt in 1322—professing to proceed in name of the magistrates of Glasgow—of a charter by Gilaspac Maclachlan, dated from his castle on Loch Fyne, commences in these terms: "Noverint universi quos nosse fuerit opportunum, quod *nos bal-* "*livi ceterique burgenses* de communitate civitatis Glasguensis vidimus, "&c." The word *præpositus* does not occur at all. Indeed there was no provost in Glasgow, as we understand the term, till the middle of the fifteenth century—the first who filled that office being John Steuart, to whom I had occasion to refer in connection with the story of St. Mungo's bell.

There has been much misunderstanding in other respects on the part of our local historians in regard to the early history and constitution of the city. We find M'Ure complacently telling how Glasgow was created a royal burgh by the charter from King William the Lion, and the same statement is repeated by such respectable historians as Gibson and Brown, and later still by Dr. Cleland. For this I need not say there is no ground. But it may be interesting to trace shortly the early history of the burgh in order to see how very small was the amount of civic liberty enjoyed by the inhabitants or burgesses in the olden time.

Glasgow was at first a mere bishop's burgh—a constitution which, while it increased the power and importance of the bishop, implied no real independence on the part of the inhabitants. On this subject it is with diffidence that I differ from an authority so deservedly high as Professor Innes. He was quite aware, as may be supposed, that Glasgow was not at first a royal burgh, but he says that at the early period to which I am referring, the citizens "obtained privileges of the same "nature as those of the free burghs." Elsewhere he says: "Such bishops' "cities in later times were scarcely distinguishable from royal burghs "as to privileges of trade, as to bearing public burdens, and even as to "representation in Parliament."[1] In "later times" this in a great measure was so, but at the earlier period to which I am referring it was certainly not the case. The object of the sovereign in creating the royal burghs was to raise up a class of freemen between himself and his powerful barons, of whom, therefore, the burgesses were to be entirely independent. It was the essential peculiarity of their position, therefore, that they held, not of any subject superior, but directly of the king himself, and under the obligation of doing service to the king only.

[1] Preface to Ancient Laws and Customs of the Burghs of Scotland, p. 42.

F

One of the old burgh laws was that " na man may be the kyngis burges
" bot gif he may do service to the king of als mekyl as fallys til ane rude
" of land at the leste;" and he was also required first of all to be faithful
and true " to the king, his bailies and communitie of that burgh in the
" quhilk he is made burges." Having thus qualified himself, the " king's
" burgess" became a free man, and owed allegiance to no subject superior
whatever. But such was by no means the position or status of the inhabitant of a mere burgh of barony. It was not the object, as it could
not possibly be the policy, of the bishop in acquiring right " to have a
" burgh at Glasgow," to give freedom to his vassals, or to render them
in any respect independent of his powers and jurisdiction over them.
What he desired, and what he obtained by the grant, was to secure for
his infant city the protective privileges of a market, so as to induce
dealers to come and trade there, and also to acquire for his vassals those
rights of burgal trade which were so essential to his own prosperity.
But this was all. The inhabitants continued, after the town became
a burgh as before, to be what they are called in the charters, mere
" homines episcopi," with a lower grade of native bondsmen—" nativi
" et servi." They continued to hold not of the sovereign, like " the
" king's freemen," but of the bishop, and to be subject to his power as
their feudal lord. They acquired the advantages of fairs and markets
no doubt, and protection in going from and returning to the city—" in
" eundo et redeundo "—when engaged in trading; but as between them
and the bishop, their overlord, the relations which previously subsisted
remained unchanged. The terms of a charter constituting a royal
burgh, and of that which was granted to the Bishop of Glasgow, were
essentially different. The charter, for example, by Alexander II. erecting Dunbarton into a burgh, bears that the king had made a burgh
" ad novum castellum meum apud Dunbritan," and the grant is " eidem
" burgo *et burgensibus meis* in eo manentibus omnes libertates, &c."
But the charter of William the Lion, to which M'Ure refers with so
much pride, so far from conferring any right on the inhabitants, or on
Glasgow the status or independence of a free burgh, bears that the
king had " granted, and by this my charter confirmed to God and St.
" Kentigern, and Joceline, bishop of Glasgow, and all his successors
" for ever, *that they* shall have a burgh at Glasgow with a weekly market,
" &c."

In the same way the charter by William, conferring the right to hold a fair, grants and confirms "to God and St. Kentigern, *to the church of* "*Glasgow, and Joceline, the bishop of that place,* and to all his successors "for ever, a fair to be kept at Glasgow, and to be held every year for "ever from the 8th of the Apostles Peter and Paul for the space of eight "days complete, with my full protection, &c."

Again, in the charter by Alexander II. in 1235, granting a charter of exemption from toll—sixty years after the date of the grant which made Glasgow a burgh—the exemption is not in favour of the citizens or burgesses as such, but to the bishop, that he and his successors, et eorum homines, nativi et servi, should be free from toll.

Again, in a precept by James II. in 1449, addressed to the royal burghs of Renfrew and Rutherglen, and which the Bishop of Glasgow had obtained in order to check certain alleged encroachments by these domineering corporations on his own territory and jurisdiction, in the matter of fairs and markets, the narrative bears that complaint had been made—not by the citizens or magistrates—for they had no say or voice in the matter—but "by Wylӡam Bischop of Glasgu that ӡe mak "disturblans and impediment tyll our leiges and communities of burgh "and land that bryng ony guds to the mercat of Glasgu to sell or by, "doing tharthrow hurtyng and prejudice *to the privileges and custom* "*granted to the kyrk of Glasgu* of auld tym." The refractory burghs are accordingly prohibited "to mak ony minwsing prejudice or lattyng "to the fredom and kyrk of Glasgu or the mercat of it." In this precept Glasgow is not called a burgh at all, but only "the barony of "Glasgow."

In like manner the charter of James II. of 20th April, 1450, which raised the city from the rank of a burgh of barony to that of a burgh of regality, was in reality nothing more than an increase of power and dignity to the bishop. It is granted in favour of Bishop Turnbull, the founder of the university, and it confirms, not to the citizens, but to the bishop and his successors, "the city of Glasgow, barony of Glasgow, and "lands commonly called Bishop forest, to be held by them of us in free "pure and mere regality in fee and heritage for ever."

In all this there is no recognition of the inhabitants as a separate or independent community. The whole power over the temporalities of the city, and of the lands embraced in the charter, remained centred in the bishop, with all the rights of a feudal lord over the inhabitants as his vassals. The charter last quoted contains a provision giving power to the bishop to appoint a sergeant for executing the edicts of his court, who was to have a silver staff or mace having the royal arms blazoned on the upper part and those of the bishop on the lower. Of the arms of the city no mention is made, nor had it any at that time. The community, indeed, is not mentioned or recognized in the charter at all. The bishop, in whom alone any power is vested, appointed civic officers to manage the affairs of his city, and he may have called them "pro- "vosts" or "bailies," for, as we have seen, even a native or serf might hold the position or office of *præpositus*, but this implied no freedom. The status of the inhabitants, no doubt, came gradually in time to be of a higher grade than at the date of the charter of Alexander II. They bought and sold and traded, and those of them who acquired heritable property were burgesses, and they must have possessed many advantages which were not shared by the landward inhabitants "ututh the burgh." But the privileges of the royal burghs they certainly did not possess; and as the magistrates, by whatever name they were called, were the mere creatures of the bishop, the entire power and control in everything relating to the affairs of the community centred in his person, and he "did what he liked with his own."

Even when the town had to vindicate its rights at law the process proceeded in name of the bishop as the principal party. Thus so late as the parliament of 1469 a decree is recorded "in the actioun and caus "pursuat *be a reverend fader in Christ Andro bischop of Glasgu*, and the "provost, bailies, and communitie *of his cite* of Glasgu, against the "provost, bailies, and communitie of the burgh of Dumbartane." The complaint was that the burgh of Dunbarton "has wrangit and injured "the said reverend fader and the said provost, bailies, and communitie "of Glasgu in the stopping of them in bying of certane wyne frae Pevis "Copate, Fransch man, out of his schip in the water of Clide." The decree, it is satisfactory to know, was in favour of the bishop and the bailies, who got their wine—no doubt good claret, such as that to the more general use of which we have returned.

In the following year, namely in 1470, there is a charter by James III. in favour of the Bishop of Glasgow, John Laing, afterwards lord high chancellor, by which, *inter alia*, there is confirmed to the bishop full powers "to constitute and appoint provosts, bailies, sergeants, and other "officers within the said city, for the management and government of "the same, as often as to him shall seem expedient, and to appoint

"and remove to and from these offices such persons as he shall think
"proper." In favour of the inhabitants as an independent community
there is no grant.

I need hardly say that the community was not represented in the
early parliaments of Scotland, as the royal burghs were. It was not till
the parliament of Queen Mary, held in August, 1546, on the very eve of
the Reformation, that Glasgow first appears among the "commisarii
"burgorum" who sat as part of the third estate, and it is only after that
period that I find the city mentioned in any state document along with
the other burghs. The first example of this which I have noticed—and
even that was only in a matter of trade—is in the act of Mary, 1555,
where it is declared that "the haill burrowis of the west cuntrie, sic as
"Irwin, Air, Dunbertane, Glasgow, and other burrowis at the west parts,"
shall be free from the exactions which "certain cuntrie men adjacent
"and dwelland besyde Loch Fyne" had been enforcing "on every last
"of maid hering that are tane in the said loch." It is somewhat curious
that the first time in which Glasgow found mention as a burgh in an act
of parliament should be on the occasion of its contending for freedom of
trade in salt herrings.

Down to that time, or rather till 1560, Glasgow as a city had not even
the appearance of independence. If a Seal of Cause was to be granted
incorporating one of the trades, it could only be done by consent and
with the concurrence of the bishop; and the fees payable for the "upsett"
of a freeman, with the fines for the infringement of the rules of the
society, were to be applied for the benefit, not of the craft itself, or even
of the community as in the royal burghs, but of the church. Thus the
charter in 1516 in favour of "the kirkmasters and the laife of the maisters
"of the skinner craft and furrier craft" of Glasgow, is granted by the
magistrates "with the consent approbatioune and ratificatioune of our
"maist reverend fadir in God James Archbishop in Glasgow, Chancellor
"of Scotland and Commendatour of the Abbey of Kilwinning." The
fees for the "upsett" are to be applied "to the reparatioune and up-
"holding of divine service at our said altar." One of the penalties is
"ane pund candle of wax thairfor als aft as the fault happens;" and "ilk
"maister haulding buith within the said burgh and citie, of the said craft,
"shall pay his wouklie pennie to the reparatioune of the adornments of
"the said altar, and to susteine the priests; and that na falss stuff be
"sauld to the kingis leidges under the paine of ane halfe pund candle of

"wax to the altar;" while power is given "to poynd and distrenzie gif "need be for the takeing raising and inbringing of these dhewes forsaid "to the sustentatioune and uphalding of God's fabric foresaid."

In like manner the seal of cause in favour of the cordiners, dated more than forty years later (1558), bears to be granted by the magistrates "with þe consent, assent, approbatioune, and ratificatioune of "me maist reverend fadir James by the mercie of God Archbishop of "Glasgow." And "the reverend fadir, our lorde and prelat, in verifi-"catioune of his consent and approbatioune," appends his seal before that of the community.

If, again, a provost had to be elected, he was nominated by the bishop, and when bailies fell to be appointed a list was prepared by the provost, who, along with the council, proceeded to the castle and presented it to the bishop, who chose from the list any two names he thought proper, and these were elected to the vacant offices. There is preserved a curious instrument under the hand of John Hamilton, notary, bearing date 3d October, 1553, in which one of these transactions is recited. The instrument bears how "an honourable man, Andrew "Hamilton of Cochnay, provost, and all the rest of the council of the "said city" came into "the inner flower garden, near the palace in Glas-"gow, of the most reverend father in Christ, James, by divine mercy "Archbishop of Glasgow, having in their possession a certain schedule "of paper in which the names of some of the most respectable and sub-"stantial men of the said city were inserted, which they reached out, "desiring the most reverend father that he would admit two of them to "be consuls or bailies for the ensuing year . . . out of which the said "most reverend elected two by pointing out the names of those on the "schedule to be proclaimed by the said provost and council," which, being done, the instrument bears, "the provost and council promised "faithfully to the most reverend" to elect the parties named "by saying "these words: We will satisfy the desire of your lordship; and having "so said they repaired to the town hall."

It is an interesting picture of the olden time which is disclosed in this record of the Glasgow notary. The whole council, composed of the most respectable and substantial of the citizens, headed by their aristocratic provost, wending their way up the High Street, the palace of the archbishop with its then beautiful surroundings, and the prelate himself in his inner flower garden under the shadow of the grand old cathedral, receiving his vassal burghers. It was one of the closing scenes in the ecclesiastical greatness of the city. The prelate who figures in the picture was Betoun, the last of the archbishops. Troublous times were at hand—were even now upon him. Within a short time and his beautiful garden was trodden down by armed men; the walls of his castle, then occupied by Lennox, were being battered by the guns of the Regent Arran; a very short time later and the archbishop was a fugitive, and the palace, and the garden, and the glory of the old hierarchy had all passed away for ever.

On the flight of Betoun in 1560 there was no one to nominate the magistrates as formerly, and the expedient resorted to in these circumstances is recorded in a notarial instrument which bears date September, 1561. In this document the notary declares that search had been made for the archbishop in order to the election of magistrates, and not being found, he protests that the council there, who had been nominated by his lordship, may themselves elect, which they accordingly did.

But this was but an isolated act of independence, as the Protestant archbishops, or the feudal lords who had obtained grants of the temporalities, continued to nominate the provost and bailies, and to interfere as before, and this, there is every reason to believe, in a manner much more oppressive than their Roman Catholic predecessors. The Reformation, too, was followed by anything but a state of tranquillity, and for some time after that event the community had other matters to think of. The constant troubles, civil and ecclesiastical, which followed the arrival of Mary: English invasions and civil wars at home—some of the latter, such as that of 1570, unexampled in exasperation and ferocity; the efforts made by the Romish party to recover their ascendency; and then the obstinate struggle which took place between Episcopacy and Presbyterianism—all these kept the kingdom in a continued state of agitation, and distracted men's minds from all but the stern realities and exigencies of the moment. Glasgow, too, was in a state of transition. Though steadily advancing in importance, however, it was as yet but of insignificant extent. So late as 1556 it held only the eleventh place among the towns of Scotland, and at that time the population did not exceed 4500.

Not till 1636 did Glasgow take its place among the royal burghs under the charter of Charles I. granted in that year. Yet even this did not bring independence. Certain rights were still reserved, and the archbishop not only claimed but exercised the right to appoint the provost and magistrates, under the charter granted by James VI. and Charles I.;[1] and when the power of nomination fell from the hands of the archbishop, it was taken up and exercised by a temporal baron. In 1641 Glasgow was erected, upon a royal signature, confirmed by the Parliament of that year, into a temporal lordship in favour of the Duke of Lennox, one of the nearest collateral male heirs of James VI. By this act there is ratified and confirmed to the duke "the lands and "barony of Glasgow, castel citie and regality thereof, with the right "of nomination of the bailies and magistrates of the said burgh." The corporation was thus still very far from real freedom.

It is probable that in the earlier history of the city the rule of the bishops sat lightly on the community, and the absence of civic privileges would be less felt in presence of the substantial advantages derived from the residence among them of the bishop and his clergy. The rule of the Church was notoriously more benignant than that of the feudal barons, and the saying, "better under the crozier than "under the lance," was applicable to the vassals of all the spiritual lords. The see of Glasgow formed no exception to this state of matters. In early times, before the spoliation of its possessions, it was one of the most opulent in the kingdom. Its prelates lived in a style of great splendour, and exercised a powerful influence, not only locally, but in the affairs of the kingdom. Their court was the resort of influential members of the aristocracy, and they but followed the practice of the other dignitaries of the Church in dispensing a liberal and generous hospitality; while the residence of the thirty-two rectors, first enforced by the princely Bishop Cameron, who required each of them to build a manse near the cathedral, added to the importance and wealth of the city. To all this is to be added the great influx of suitors to the bishop's court, attracted by the high character and reputation of the chapter, and the large amount of civil business which resulted from the extension of the privileges and civil jurisdiction of the bishop conferred by James IV. The temporal advantages which would necessarily result to the community from this state of matters must have been great, and —considering the limited ideas of freedom which then prevailed—more than sufficient to reconcile them to the absence of those civic privileges

---

[1] Burgh Records, 3d October, 1637.

which were enjoyed by their less favoured neighbours of Rutherglen, Renfrew, and Dunbarton.

It is not surprising, therefore, to find that in Glasgow there was an influential party by no means favourable to that great movement which resulted in the reformation of religion and the subsequent ab-juration of Episcopacy. It was no doubt under the influence of such sentiments that, after the long vacancy in the see caused by the flight of Betoun, we find a large body of the citizens taking the part of even so notorious a character as Montgomery, the nominee or "tulchan bishop" of the Duke d'Aubigné, when the question concerned the resettlement of a resident archbishop. We read in Calderwood how in 1582 the Laird of Minto, the provost, with one of the bailies, and a number of the citizens, invaded the presbytery-house, and because the presbytery, then sitting in judgment with a view to the deposition of Montgomery, re-fused to stay proceedings, "put violent hands on the moderator, Mr. "John Howsone, smote him on the face, pulled him by the beard, knocked out one of his teeth, and put him in the Tolbooth."

The effect of the Reformation was at first indeed very injurious to the prosperity of Glasgow. The seizure by the crown and the great barons of property which had been originally gifted by private liberality for the benefit of the people, and which belonged to the Church, after as before it was reformed, by a title as indefeasible as that by which the lords held their own lands, was an act of unjustifiable spoliation. And it was rendered still more oppressive by the mode in which the lords exercised their usurped rights. All the lands within St. Mungo's hali-dom which were not in the actual possession of the bishops them-selves, were held, like other church lands, by tenures of the most mild and liberal character; but now the possessors of these lands— the rentallers, who, as we have seen, were practically proprietors—were threatened with ejection if they did not feudalize or enfranchise their titles by heavy payments, amounting in many cases to confiscation. In the case of Glasgow, the greater part of the church lands seized by the crown were disponed to Walter Stewart, commendator of Blantyre,[1] from whom the poor proprietors were compelled to take new charters, and this although in a crown charter quoted by Mr. Hill, confirming one

[1] 1587. Act. Parl. iii. 431. The baronies of Stobo and Eddleston were excepted, these being granted to Maitland of Thurlstane. What remained of the other large possessions were erected into a temporal lordship called the barony of Glasgow, for payment to the crown of a feu-duty amounting to only £50 of our money.

of these titles, it is admitted on the face of the charter itself that the titles of the previous possessors of the church lands—styled in the charter *antiquæ nativi, pauperes tenentes, et rentallarii*—had "for times " past memory of man been estimated and reputed as equally sufficient " to the said rentallers for their lands as if the lands had been disposed " to them in feu"—that is in perpetuity.[1]

The Reformation was injurious also at first to the trade of the city; and it is curious to observe that the change from the palmy days when so many ecclesiastics were "in residence," seems to have been felt most severely by the inhabitants who lived in the upper part of the town —those who lived towards the foot of the High Street, and about the Cross, finding a compensation in the pursuits of trade, for which their fellow-citizens higher up the street possessed fewer facilities. In the year 1587 there was presented to Parliament a supplication "be " the fremen and vtheris induellaris of the citie of Glasgw abone the " gray frier wynde," setting forth "that q^r that p^t of the said citie that " afoir the reformatioun of the religioun was intertenyt and uphalden " be the resort of the bischop, parsonis, vicaris, and vtheris of clergie, " for the tyme, is now becum ruinous, and for the maist part altogidder " decayit, and the heritouris and possessouris therof greitly depauperit, " wanting the moyane to vphald the samen." It is then set forth that this state of matters might be greatly remedied were "the grite con- " fusion and multitude of mercattis togedder in ane place about the " croce" to be divided, and some of them appointed to be holden in the upper portion of the city; and they feelingly put it that "as thai " ar ane pairt of the bodie and memberis subject to the payment of " taxt stent, watcheing, warding, and all uther precable charges, even " sa al the commodities of the said cietie suld be commoun to thame " all." As a crowning reason why the supplication should be granted, it is added that "that part of the said cietie abone the said gray frier " wynde is the onlie ornament and decoratioun thereof, be ressone of " the grite and sumptuous buildingis of grite antiquitie, varie propir " and meit for the ressait of his hienes and nobilitie at sic tymes as " thai sall repair thereto; and that it wer to be lamentit to sie sic " gorgeous policie to decay." The Parliament ordered some changes to be made, but it does not appear that the petitioners succeeded in getting any of the "mercattis" permanently moved above the wynd.

[1] Huchesoniana, by Laurence Hill, Esq., p. 13.

It soon came to be understood, however, that in whatever way matters were to be mended, this was not to be attained by the maintenance of Episcopacy. The splendid court of the Roman Catholic archbishops, and the advantages derived from the resident clergy, had become things of the past. The Protestant archbishops, who were in most cases the mere nominees of the party in power, were poor, and their status had become contemptible. The archbishop, indeed, was nothing more than the *locum tenens* of a non-resident baron who held the temporalities, and who exacted everything he could wring out of them, caring nothing for the interests of the community when his own were in question. To this the amiable Leighton was certainly an exception. Although he filled the see but a short time, he quite won the affections of the people of Glasgow; and when it was known that he had gone to London to resign his charge, a deputation of the citizens waited on the magistrates " entreating and desiring them," as the minute of council bears, to endeavour to prevent his demission, alleging " that the whoill citie and incorporatiouns therin hes lived peaceably " and quietlie since the said archbishop his coming to this burgh, throw " his christian cariage and behaviour towards them, and by his govern- " ment with great discretioune and moderatioune."[1] But as a rule the archbishops, enjoying but a miserable pittance out of the once ample revenues of the see, were tempted, perhaps obliged, to exercise all the power that was left to them, and to enforce their exactions, in a manner very different from that which had prevailed in former times; while the magistrates imposed on the community were those, of course, who would prove most subservient to the interests of those who appointed them.

Under this state of "tyranny and avarice," as the new magistrates soon after had occasion to describe it, Glasgow, which by means of the extension of trade had been growing in importance and prosperity, appears to have declined considerably.[2] The community also, under the more general diffusion of liberty and expression of thought which was now beginning to prevail, must have felt more keenly the inferiority of their status to that of their smaller neighbours who enjoyed the full privileges of the royal burghs, while their subjection to the archbishops

---

[1] Burgh Records, 2d May, 1673.

[2] The population, which at the restoration of Charles II. in 1660 amounted to 14,600, had in 1688 fallen to 11,900. No doubt the great fire of 1677 accounted in part for this.

and to the temporal lords, in the nomination of their provost and magistrates, as well as in other matters relating to the city, must have become intolerably irksome. We are prepared, therefore, to find the community now taking a prominent part in those events which resulted in the Revolution. We know that they took an active share in promoting the cause of the Prince of Orange, and as they were among the first of the burghs to congratulate the prince and the queen on their accession, so the services which the city had rendered towards bringing about that event were early recognized by the new sovereigns. By royal charter dated 4th January, 1690, the city was declared free; and in the "humble "and thankful address" which "the provost, bailiffs, town council and "other citizens" presented in the following month, the feelings of the community on the contrast between the past and present state of matters found energetic expression. "As your citie of Glasgow," the address bears, "hath shared in the common benefit, so hath she tasted of your "royal bounty and favour, in particular by giving your high commis- "sioner a special instruction for our freedom by act of parliament. And "now by your royal grant, given at Kingsintown the 4th of Januar last, "wherein your majestie is graciously pleased to notice and putt ane value "upon the zeal for the Protestant religion and loyal affections of your "citie of Glasgow, and to give to her a full right and libertie for electing "her own magistrates in all tyme comeing, als frelie as the royal bor- "rowes of this your majesties ancient kingdom, by which being emanci- "pated from the slaverie of ane imposed magistracie, the instruments of "our bishops, their tyrannie and avarice, the public interest of this once "flourishing corporation being thereby recovered, we are delivered from "the fears and secured from the dangers of a future relapse into what "has been the source of our past miserie." This address was presented on the 1st of February 1690, and by the act of William and Mary of that year the city and town council acquired for the first time "the power "and privilege to choose their own magistrates, provost, bailies, and other "officers within the burgh, als fully and als freely as the city of Edinburgh "or any other royal burgh within the kingdom enjoys the same." Then, and not till then, may Glasgow be said to have acquired an independent political existence.

THE ARMORIAL INSIGNIA AND CITY SEALS.

The armorial insignia of the city, and the corporation seals, may be briefly referred to as part of our municipal history.

Towards the end of the sixteenth century Glasgow, then growing in importance, began to use armorial bearings: whether under the authority of the Lord Lyon does not appear. The probability is it was done without any official sanction, and certainly the authorities adhered to no fixed blazon. On the contrary, it appears to have been left very much to the caprice of stone-masons and seal engravers to represent the arms from time to time as they thought fit, and this loose practice continued down to a very recent period. The first example, of which I am aware, in which the devices now borne by the corporation appear on a shield, occurs on a stone built into the wall over the entrance to the Tron Church, and which bears the date 1592; and the first mention which is made of "the tounes armes" is in an entry in the council records under date 17th July, 1630. From 1592 down to 1866 the arms appeared at intervals on stones and seals and medals, official and non-official, in every variety of combination, each differing from the other in points which in heraldry are essential. In the year last mentioned the whole subject was investigated by order of the magistrates and council, and a report was prepared, which resulted in the blazon being authoritatively settled by a patent from the Lyon office in the form in which it is now borne. Lyon at the same time granted to the city supporters and a crest.[1]

The history of the arms is detailed very fully in the report just mentioned. I shall therefore only give here the verbal blazon as contained in the patent: "Argent, on a mount in base vert an oak tree proper, "the stem at the base thereof surmounted by a salmon on its back, also "proper, with a signet ring in its mouth, or; on the top of the tree a "redbreast, and on the sinister fess point an ancient hand bell, both also "proper: Above the shield is to be placed a suitable helmet, with a "mantling gules, doubled argent, and issuing out of a wreath of the "proper liveries is to be set for crest the half length figure of St. Kenti- "gern, affronté, vested and mitred, his right hand raised in the act of "benediction, and having in his left hand a crozier, all proper: On a

[1] Enquiry as to the Armorial Insignia of Glasgow. Printed for Private Circulation. 1866.

"compartment below the shield are to be placed for supporters two
"salmon proper, each holding in its mouth a signet ring, or; and in
"the escrol entwined with the compartment this motto, 'Let Glasgow
"Flourish.'"

I have already given the history of the bell and the legends which
gave rise to the other "charges" on the shield. In regard to the mount,
out of which the tree is represented as growing, Dr. Stevenson says[1] that
it represents the mound which elevated itself beneath the feet of Kentigern on the occasion related by his biographer, when he was preaching,
so as to enable him to be better seen and heard. This is a mistake.
The mound is quite a modern addition. The original "branch" of the
legend having been expanded into a tree, it was natural to introduce the
mound for it to rest on. The first example in which it is thus represented is on the bell of the Tron Church, which was made in 1631, but
the mound did not appear on the seal of the corporation till so late as
the end of the last century (1789).

Although Glasgow had no armorial bearings, properly so called, till
towards the end of the sixteenth century, it had, from a very early period,
a common seal, which the bishop, acting through the magistrates whom
he appointed to rule the city for him, caused to be appended to public
documents. As I have already mentioned, however, it was never used
except in subserviency to the bishop, whose own seal, in all important
matters of civic administration, was also appended, and which always
took precedence of that of the city. The bishops, as we have seen, obtained their grant of a burgh in 1175, and so early as the century following, there is evidence that the community was using a common seal. In
the charter granted by Robert de Methyngby in 1280, the notary states
that, besides his own seal, "sigillum commune de Glasgu huic scripto
"est appensum." This seal has unfortunately been lost, but we have a
description of it by Father Innes, who saw it. His note, appended to a
manuscript copy of the charter, is as follows: "Huic carta appensa erant
"dua sigilla, quorum unum [that of Methyngby the granter] amissum
"est: alterum, sigillum commune Glasguensæ, remanet, fere integrum, ex
"cera alba, exhibens caput episcopi cum mitra, scilicet S. Kentigern."

There can be no doubt that the designs on the seals of the community were adopted from the seals of the bishops. The one just
described contained the head of St. Kentigern only. In like manner,

---

[1] Legends of St. Kentigern, p. 145.

on the earliest examples which we have of the seals of the bishops—such as those of Florence in 1200, of Walter in 1208, and of William de Bondington in 1233, there is nothing but the figure of the saint in the act of benediction. The first of the bishops who added to his seal any of the emblems of the miracles was William Wyschard, who was elected to the see in 1270, and immediately afterwards we find the civic seal altered, and to the head of the saint there is added a representation of his bell, which was then, as it continued for a long time afterwards, in use in the Cathedral services. In the beginning of the fourteenth century the city seal was again altered, and to the head of Kentigern and his bell were added the fish, the bird, and the branch. In this also the civic seal was copied from the ecclesiastical, for these emblems were at that time represented on the seal of the prelate who then filled the see. This was Wyschart, the grand old warrior-bishop, who, in the crisis of his country's liberties, exchanged the crozier for a sword, and buckled on his armour in defence of the cause for which Wallace and Bruce were at that time contending against such terrible odds.

This old seal of the corporation must have continued in use for a very long time. A representation of it is given in the *Liber Sancte Marie de Melros*, in which the document to which it is appended is printed, being the return or certificate of a service and infeftment of one Thomas de Aula. It is addressed to the Abbot of Melrose, and bears date 8th October, 1325. But I have found in the archives of our own city several impressions of the same seal, attached to charters and seals of cause, in more perfect condition—one in 1445; another, nearly a hundred years after, in 1551; another in 1605, appended to a deed of agreement among the incorporated trades of Glasgow for the support of St. Nicholas' Hospital, with a ratification by the provost and magistrates; and another relating to the same hospital in 1606. I subjoin a copy of the last-mentioned impression.

This ancient seal continued in use till 1647, so that even assuming that it was not made earlier than 1325, the date of the first document to which it has been found appended, it must have been in use for the long period of three hundred and twenty-two years. I have carefully compared the different examples, and I am satisfied that the one attached to the charter of 1606 is impressed from the same die that was used in 1325.

In 1647 this seal ceased to be used, and a new one of a totally different design was adopted in its place. The change is so complete, indeed, that the two seals have hardly a single feature in common.

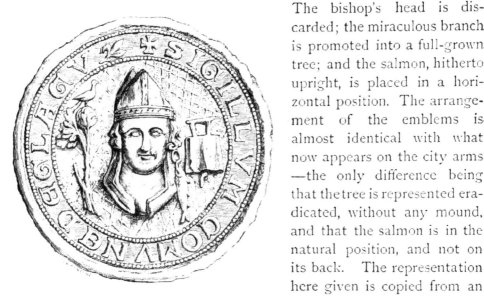

The bishop's head is discarded; the miraculous branch is promoted into a full-grown tree; and the salmon, hitherto upright, is placed in a horizontal position. The arrangement of the emblems is almost identical with what now appears on the city arms —the only difference being that the tree is represented eradicated, without any mound, and that the salmon is in the natural position, and not on its back. The representation here given is copied from an impression appended to a charter in favour of the incorporation of Hammermen in Glasgow, dated 16th July, 1650. This seal continued

in use for one hundred and forty-three years—a long period also —longer in proportion, perhaps, than that of the previous seal, if judged by the greater number of impressions which must have been taken from it. It was replaced, for what reason I cannot conceive, by a seal in which again the position of the emblems is changed. There is no precedent for it, and the whole arrangement is in the worst possible taste. The field is parted per fess argent and gules; the bell is placed on the wrong side, and the fish is raised up and placed across the centre of the stem of the tree. This seal continued in use till the form of the arms was finally settled by the Lord Lyon in 1866, when the seal now in use was made, showing the city arms as then adopted.

In regard to the "arms of the bishopric" so often spoken of in our local histories, I am satisfied that neither the see of Glasgow nor any other of the bishoprics of Scotland ever had any. Nisbet speaks of the see of Glasgow as having arms, and in the register of the Lyon office there are arms registered which are erroneously called those of the see of St. Andrews. But in both instances the arms blazoned are only those personal to the bishop who filled the office at the time. The first, those referred to by Nisbet, are the arms of Archbishop Cairn-

cross, and the second are those of Archbishop Sharp; and I believe the same will be found in regard to the so-called arms of all the Scottish bishoprics. None of the sees had even a permanent seal. Each bishop varied the devices on the seal according to his taste. Sometimes heraldic bearings occur on them and sometimes not, but in every instance where they are found they are the family arms of the incumbent.

Before leaving the seals and armorial bearings, I must mention the origin of the peculiar motto of the city—"Let "Glasgow flourish"—about which there has been a good deal of controversy. It forms part of an old inscription on the bell of the steeple of the Tron Church which bears the date 1592. The entire inscription is "Lord let Glasgow "flourish through the preaching of the word and praising thy name." This certainly never was intended as a heraldic motto, and at no time was it used as such. The city arms no doubt appear on the bell, but the inscription has reference not to them but to the bell itself. It is an invocation in short,—an ecclesiastical inscription, or dedication, or prayer,— examples of which are so common on the bells of churches. In subsequent examples it is curtailed, and reads thus: "Lord let Glasgow

G

"flourish by the preaching of thy word." In 1699 it appeared for the first time occupying the place of a heraldic motto in connection with the city arms over the entrance to Blackfriars church, and here it is still further shortened to the words, "Let Glasgow flourish." In this form alone was it ever used heraldically. It continued to be so used in all the subsequent examples, and it was approved and confirmed by the Lord Lyon, as what had become, by usage, the motto of the city. When the patent was obtained, some members of the Town Council suggested whether we should not adopt one of the earlier forms of the inscription —"Let Glasgow flourish by the preaching of the word"—but it was answered that if we went back to the original, the whole invocation should be adopted, and that the "praising of God" should be included, as a practice calculated to promote the prosperity of the city as well as "preaching." And the motto as it stands was adopted by the corporation.

THE CATHEDRAL.

It is not my purpose, nor would my limits permit me, to write a topographical history of Glasgow. I must confine myself to a few notices of its principal buildings in the olden time, and of the wonderful progress of the city.

As originally built after the restoration of the see, Glasgow consisted of only a small cluster of residences near the Cathedral and the bishop's castle. All around was muirland and forest. At first the only access from the south side of the river was by a ford, but at a very early period a bridge was constructed, probably of wood, on or near the site of the old Stockwell Bridge. It has been supposed by some of our local historians that this last-mentioned bridge, which was constructed by Bishop Rae in 1345, was the first ever erected over the Clyde at Glasgow; but this was certainly not the case, as in a charter dated sixty years earlier —namely in 1285—mention is made of the *pons de clud*. The following view of Bishop Rae's Bridge is from an engraving published by the Foulises in 1761.

From a very early period—long anterior to the present Cathedral— there must have been a church at or near the spot where Kentigern resided. The first church no doubt was a very humble structure, but we have no record of what it was previous to the twelfth century. David having refounded the see and appointed John to be bishop, that prelate proceeded to rebuild the old church which he found there, and the new structure was dedicated on the nones of July, 1136. A great part of it was probably of wood, and not long afterwards it was destroyed by

fire. Bishop Jocelin, who was consecrated in 1174, probably repaired this original structure. He certainly added to it, and he founded a society to collect funds for the purpose. For this he obtained the royal sanction and protection, by a charter granted by William the Lion in 1190, in which the king states that the original erection had been destroyed by fire "in these our days." In the year 1197 the new Cathedral was dedicated.

Professor Innes speaks of the church thus erected as the present Cathedral, although not completed at the date of the dedication, and this has been for a long time the general belief, but I have become satisfied that it was not so. There is, I think, every reason to believe that the present magnificent structure was only commenced to be built by Bishop Bondington, who was consecrated in 1233, and this is the result arrived at, after a critical investigation, by Mr. Honeyman, whose eminence as an architect, and attainments as an archæologist, entitle his opinion to the greatest respect.[1] Mr. Honeyman made a more careful

[1] The Age of Glasgow Cathedral, &c., by John Honeyman, Architect, Glasgow.

examination of the structure, and a more strict comparison of its styles of architecture than appears to have been done before, and the conclusion at which he arrived was that the only portion which remains of the building consecrated in 1197 is a small pillar and part of the vaulting in the south-west corner of the crypt. This, as Mr. Honeyman points out, belongs to the transitional style. At the supposed time of the building of the present Cathedral the style in which it is erected was not even in existence. The architecture of the present building is early English, of a fully developed type, and the very oldest examples of that style, even in England, were not erected till after 1190.[1] Apart from this, there is no reason to doubt that the church which was dedicated in 1197 was, at that date, a completed structure. It is described as a building which Bishop Jocelin "ipse novam construxerat"—terms which could not properly be applied to a building then, as Mr. Innes supposes, still only in the course of erection.

All the probabilities indeed go to show that the building so dedicated by Jocelin in 1197 was of a temporary character, to be superseded by a grander structure, and that sometime after the year 1238 the erection of the present Cathedral was commenced by Bishop Bondington. In all probability the crypt and choir were completed in his time. That he was engaged in extensive building operations, and not in mere additions, is rendered probable by the fact that in 1242—forty-five years after the dedication of Jocelin's Church—there is an ordinance for a national collection annually during Lent, in aid of the new building, then in progress; and more than thirty years later, namely in 1277, under the episcopate of Robert Wyschard, there is evidence that the work was still unfinished. In that year we find among the Glasgow charters a deed by the Lord of Luss, by which, in consideration of a sum of money paid to him, he makes a grant of timber from his forests in Dumbartonshire for building a steeple and treasury, *campanile et thesauraria;* and later still there is a grant by King Edward to Bishop Wyschard for the same purpose. The wooden spire erected with the timber from Luss was, in the year 1400, struck by lightning and totally consumed. The erection of a stone structure to supply its place was immediately projected, and the work was begun and carried at least as far as the first battlement by Bishop Lauder, who died in 1425. It was continued and probably completed by his successor, Bishop Cameron, whose episcopate lasted till the year 1446.[2]

[1] Sir Gilbert Scott's Lectures on Mediæval Architecture, 1879, vol. i. p. 126.   [2] Billings.

THE CRYPT, GLASGOW CATHEDRAL.

The crypt is the finest in the kingdom. The annexed view of a portion of it is from an original drawing by the late Mr. Kemp, the architect of the Scott monument in Edinburgh.

The nave was no doubt added subsequently to the crypt and choir, although there appears to be no means for determining the date; and the massive and imposing square tower, which till recently stood at the north-west end of the Cathedral, must have been commenced and finished immediately afterwards. Mr. Billings, indeed, is of opinion that the west doorway of the nave, and the lower stage of that tower, were the oldest portions of the Cathedral.[1] Be that as it may, the tower was undoubtedly of great antiquity. It was 120 feet high, and on each side near the top were two fine windows with rounded arches. In the upper part of the tower were some curious grotesque sculptures. These are now lying in the crypt below the chapter-house. On the opposite or south-west corner of the nave stood also, till recently, another important erection in all probability coeval with the tower. This was the Consistory house. It had no doubt been intended for a tower, but it was not carried up, having been finished with gables. In the ancient records it is called the library house of the Cathedral. It was a highly picturesque building, supported by buttresses, and lighted on the south side by a variety of windows, square headed and pointed; and it was specially interesting as the place where the bishops held their ecclesiastical courts, and where the records of the diocese were preserved. Both buildings, apart from their antiquity, were valuable as adding greatly to the beauty of the Cathedral, and the tower was really essential to the proper balance of the structure.

Yet, incredible as it may appear, these two interesting and important parts of the Cathedral—the tower and the Consistory house—both at the time in the most perfect state of preservation, were, within the last forty years, pulled down by order of Her Majesty's First Commissioner of Works, in the course of certain operations professing to have for their object the improvement and restoration of the Cathedral! This was done at the instigation of certain individuals in Glasgow whose want of taste was only equalled by their ignorance, and among them, with shame be it told, were the then Lord Provost and magistrates of the city. Mr. Billings condemns the removal of the tower as an act of barbarism, and I have never met an artist or an archæologist, or any other person having

---

[1] Baronial and Ecclesiastical Antiquities of Scotland.

a reputation for good taste, who did not share his opinion. A remonstrance against the outrage was presented to the magistrates at the
time, subscribed by a number of gentlemen, comprising probably every
one in the city competent to form an opinion on the subject—ten of
them being architects—but it was of no avail. The late Mr. M'Lellan,
who wrote an account of the Cathedral, and who was one of those who
instigated the act of sacrilege, sought to excuse the removal of the tower
on the ground that it was of a date later than the nave, yet he himself
ascribes it to the time of Bishop Bondington—that is to the thirteenth
century—a period sufficiently remote surely to have saved it from the
profane hands of modern empirics.

The evidences of the great antiquity both of the tower and the Consistory house or library, are abundant. At the time of the Reformation
the whole structure, as is well known, was saved by the spirit and good
sense of the trades of Glasgow, from the violence incited by the ministers,
which, under the pretext of putting down idolatry, would have made it
share the fate of the other grand old ecclesiastical monuments of Scotland. But although thus saved, the building had, during the troublous
times which preceded and accompanied the Reformation, been allowed
to fall into a state of disrepair, and one of the first acts of the magistrates,
when quieter times came, was to save it from falling into ruin. The
minutes of the town council, towards the end of the sixteenth century,
and in the beginning of the seventeenth, are full of entries recording the
efforts made in this direction by the magistrates in conjunction with the
citizens, and it will be found that the western tower and the Consistory
house shared their attention, as ancient portions of the fabric, deserving
their care equally with the nave and choir. This is so important as to
deserve more than a passing notice.

It was not the duty of the magistrates to uphold the church; but,
as true archæologists, they had a reverence for it as a great national
monument—in this respect presenting a contrast to their degenerate
successors of the nineteenth century. Very soon after the Reformation,
accordingly, we find them summoning the representatives of the crafts,
and some of the leading citizens, to consult with them on the subject,
and under date 21st August, 1574, the following interesting minute
occurs in their records. I quote from the volume of extracts so well
edited by Dr. Marwick: "The provest baillies and counsale with the
" dekynnis of the crafts, and divers wtheris honest men of the toun, con-

" venand in the counsal hous, and haveand respect and consideratio unto
" the greit dekaye and ruyne that the hie kirk of Glasgw is cum to
" throuch taking awaye of the leid, sclait, and wther grayth thairof in
" thir trublus tyme bygane, sua that sick ane greit monument will
" alluterlie fall doun and dekey without it be remedit, and becaus the
" helping thairof is so greit, and will extend to mair nor thai may spair,
" and that they are nocht addettit to the vphalding and repairing thairof
" be the law, yit of thair awin fre willis vncompellit, and for the zele thai
" beir to the kirk, of meir almous and liberalite, sua that induce na
" practik nor preparative in tymes cuming, conforme to ane writting
" to be maid thairanent, all in ane voce has consentit to ane taxt and
" impositioun of twa hundredtht pundis money to be taxt and payit be
" the tounschip and fremen thairof for helping to repair the said kirk
" and haldyng it wattirfast."

On a subsequent date, 10th December, 1581, the magistrates are
joined by " the superintendent, with the deyne of facultie, principall of
" the college, and others members of the kirk," and there is farther
discussion as to the " rwyng and decay of the kirk."

A later minute, 26th July, 1589, records that complaint had been
made by " the ministers, elderis, deaconis and vtheris of the toun for
" non-repairing of the Hie Kirk according to the charges and ordinances
" maid thairanent," and arrangements are made for raising money for
the repair of " the queir." On the same occasion it is recorded that
Lord Blantyre attended and offered to contribute 400 merks towards
the expense.

The funds thus raised appear to have been altogether inadequate for
the purpose, as a still later minute, 29th April, 1609, bears that " Maister
" John Bell and Robert Scot, ordiner ministeris of this burgh and citie,"
attended the council " to deploir the present hurt of the High Kirk and
" metropolitan of this diocie, and apperand rowen thairof;" and it is
resolved to ask help of the king, besides promoting a voluntary subscription. In this way more funds were raised and the work was proceeded with.

The choir would probably be first repaired, but the western tower is
specially treated as part of the structure which had fallen into decay.
Under date 15th May, 1624, there is a minute in these terms:—" The
" provest, baillies, and counsall ordanis that the laich steple of the Heich
" Kirk [the western tower] be theikit with leid." On a subsequent date,

16th August, 1628, the treasurer is ordained to have a warrant for the balance of £178, 15s. "debursed for poynting the tua stipillis of the "Metropolitan Kirk"—that is, the centre spire and the western tower. And again on 18th October, 1628, a warrant is granted to the treasurer for forty merks for "beitting and repairing the laich stipill of the "Metropolitan Kirk."

The Consistory house, which, as I have said, was probably coeval with the tower, had, through age, fallen into still greater decay, and it required a more extensive repair. A minute of the town council of date 5th April, 1628, bears that "the proveist, bailyeis, and counsell has "condescendit and aggreit that James Colquhoun, wricht, and John "Boyid, masoun, build and repair the dekayet pairtis of the Librarie "hous of the Hie Kirk, putt the ruiff thairon, geist and loft the samyn, "and theik the samyn with leid, and do all thingis necessar thairto for "3100 merk."

All this shows that the western tower and the Consistory house were, so far back as nearly three hundred years ago, regarded then as part of the ancient structure, and deserving of preservation equally with the other parts of the Cathedral. I have already stated that there is every reason for believing that the western tower was erected immediately after the nave. Indeed it may be said to have been coeval with it. Of this there is proof in a piece of real evidence which has been communicated to me by Mr. Honeyman. "I was told," he writes me, "by "one who examined it at the time, that the jambs of the west window of "the north aisle, which was covered up by the tower, were found when "exposed to be quite fresh. *There was no chase cut for glazing*, and "evidently the window had never been used before the erection of the "tower." The inference from this is obvious. If the tower did not form part of the original design, its erection must have been resolved on before the nave was completed, and it was built before even the window of the north aisle required to be glazed.

Such were the portions of our grand old minster which were pulled down in the middle of the nineteenth century. Every archæologist —every person with any taste or knowledge of architecture has condemned it. Dr. Wilson, after referring to "the rich groining spring-"ing from large half figures of angels bearing shields and scrolls of "the west tower," observes truly that its removal, "for the purpose of "restoring the west front to a uniformity, but poorly repays the idea

THE LADY CHAPEL, GLASGOW CATHEDRAL

" of size and elevation formerly conveyed by the contrast between the
" central and west towers."[1]

One excuse put forward for the removal of the tower and the Consistory house was that they were to be replaced by two finer towers,
as if anything modern could supply the loss of such venerable relics
of a past age. It is said that a fund was partly raised, and a government grant promised towards the erection of these towers, but if so,
nothing came of it, and the mutilated building remains, a disgrace to the
city, and a monument of bad taste and ignorance.

To my friend Mr. W. L. Leitch, the eminent water-colour painter,
and himself a Glasgow man, and one who deplores the outrage by which
the Cathedral was mutilated, I am indebted for the beautiful drawing
of the western tower and Consistory house which is prefixed to the
present volume.[2] The annexed view of the Lady Chapel is from an
original drawing by the late Mr. George M. Kemp, architect.

The see of Glasgow was one of great dignity and influence, and
its cathedral was held in very high reputation. The general jubilee
proclaimed in 1450 on the termination of the great papal schism was
extended to Scotland, and penitential visits and offerings at the Cathedral of Glasgow were declared equally meritorious with those at Rome.[3]

As might be inferred from the importance of the see, and the extent
of its possessions and endowments, the church was richly furnished with
ornaments, jewels, and vestments, and its "library house" contained
what would then be considered a pretty extensive collection of books.
A catalogue of these and of the ornaments, vestments, and other items
belonging to the cathedral has been preserved.[4] But none of the
religious houses possessed extensive libraries. A catalogue exists of
the books of the priory of Lochleven, and it comprises only seventeen
volumes, and among them there is not one complete copy of the Bible.
In the list, however, which we have of the books of the Cathedral of
Glasgow 165 volumes are particularized, many of them distinguished
as being *solennes, auro illuminati, magni voluminis*, &c., indicating that
they were rare and expensive books. Among them were some fine
Bibles—one of them *pulcra bene illuminata*. There were also Con-
cordances and Psalters, several lives of the saints, including a life of
St. Kentigern and one of Servanus, several costly missals, a number

---

[1] Prehistoric Annals, vol. ii. p. 428.   [2] Mr. Leitch died April 25, 1883.
[3] Professor Innes, Pref. to Reg. Epis. Glasg. p. xlvii.
[4] Printed by the Maitland Club, from a copy made by Mr. Dillon from the ancient Chartulary.

of works in theology and philosophy, but very few of the classics.   One exceptionally important work there was, a *Catholicon*, or Great Dictionary of the Latin Tongue, compiled by Johannes Balbus Januensis, described as *valde preciosum et solenne*.   There are two manuscript copies of this work in the Hunterian Museum at Glasgow, each in two immense volumes.   The collection did not contain a single book in the Greek language.   All these books were distinguished in the catalogue by their colours, size, number of volumes, or the place where they were deposited, some being chained, and others preserved in chests and presses.   In the same old catalogue one of the breviaries is described as being outside of the choir—chained, no doubt, for the use of the general public, few of whom probably were capable of taking advantage of it.   Other books are mentioned as chained both in the choir and in the library.   This collection is all now lost or scattered. In a minute of the town council of 20th September, 1660, Bailie Pollock reports "that he had gottin in from James Porter the thrie great Bybilles "belongs to the kirks, and that they are now lying in the clarkes "chamber."   But these were in all likelihood English versions belonging to a much later period—probably the first large folio of 1611, or other folio editions of the version now in use.

The Cathedral possessed, besides its books and vestments, many relics.   In an inventory of these, and of the vestments and ornaments which was made by order of the bishop and chapter in 1432, we find, among other items, two linen bags containing part of the bones of St Kentigern and St. Thomas of Canterbury; a small phial of silver-gilt containing a portion of the girdle of the blessed Virgin Mary, and a piece of the crib of our Lord.   To these and the other relics many offerings were made.   In the accounts of the Lord High Treasurer in 1495 there is a charge of xiiij*s.* given to James IV. "to offir "to the reliquis in Glasgw."[1]   The vestments and ornaments would appear from the inventory to have been of more than usual magnificence.

The interior of the Cathedral was enriched with many beautiful altars and sculptures.   There were also many richly decorated altars in the crypt.   In 1290 Robert, a burgess of Glasgow, and Elizabeth his wife, give a tenement for the augmentation of the Light of St. Mary the Virgin in "le crudes"—the crypt.[2]   And in 1460 David Hynde, a burgess, gives an annual of twelve pence to sustain the lights of

---

[1] Annals L. H. Treasurer, p. 242.   [2] Regist. Glasg. p. 298.

St. Mary and St. Kentigern in the crypt.[1]   The altars in the choir and nave were very numerous, and each of them had a separate endowment.   There were besides endowments for the general services of the Cathedral.[2]

The windows were no doubt filled with painted glass, and the stalls were richly decorated.   There is preserved a contract, in the year 1506, between the dean and chapter and one Mychall Waghorn, wright, for the repair of five of the stalls, and making a covering for them of carved work, the details of which are given in a separate schedule, in the vernacular.   It includes " schorne and kerset work, and colums, and " anglis, and frontellis fiellis with knoppis, and four lefis about ilk knop, " sik lik as is in the chapell of Striviling," with other details.   Michael was to have for the work 40 merks, a considerable sum for that time, considering that the dean and chapter were besides to do the sawing of the larger "burdis and treis," and also to find the stuff for the scaffolding.[3]

All this beautiful work, with the altars and their ornaments, the sculptures and the painted glass, disappeared at the Reformation.   Indeed the whole structure, as already mentioned, very narrowly escaped destruction at that time.   The magistrates, probably against their own judgment, but instigated by Andrew Melville and others of the ministers, agreed to demolish the Cathedral, and workmen were actually convened for a particular day to commence the work.   But the crafts of the city assembled with arms in their hands "swearing with many " oaths that he who did cast doun the first stone should be buried under " it."   The magistrates were compelled to yield, but they cited the leaders, and threatened them with punishment.   The young king, however, on being appealed to, took the part of the crafts, and prohibited the ministers, who were the complainers, "to meddle any more in that " business, saying that too many churches had already been destroyed, " and that he would not tolerate more abuses of that kind."[4]

But the crafts were unable to save what would have been so dear to the archæologist—the altars and ornaments.   An order by the Lords for the destruction of the images and altars was obtained, but it was granted with the proviso that " ʒe tak guid heyd that neither the dasks,

---

[1] Regist. Glasg. p. 412.   [2] Orig. Paroch. pp. 4-6.

[3] Reg. Episc. Glasg., vol. ii. p. 612.   There is also a copy of this curious contract—probably the original—inserted in the Lib. Protocollorum, lately brought to light by the Grampian Club, No. 198.

[4] Spottiswoode.

"windocks, nor durris be ony wise hurt or broken—either glassin wark
"or iron wark."   Nevertheless, all the painted glass was destroyed,[1]
with many other decorations, and some of the beautiful windows of
the choir were roughly built up with stone, to save the expense of
putting other glass in them.   The nave also fell into complete disrepair.   I have told how much had been accomplished by the citizens
to remedy this state of matters, but in 1638 a great deal remained to
be done.   In the prospect of the famous General Assembly which was
held in Glasgow in that year, the magistrates—ashamed no doubt of
the state into which the church had fallen—made an effort to put it
into better order.   It was the only place in which the Assembly could
meet, and in view of so many distinguished strangers coming to the
city they were naturally anxious to make both the church, and the
city generally, look respectable.   With this object they ordered that
all poor people should be kept off the streets and confined to their
houses; stringent orders were issued to keep the streets clean, and
the inhabitants were directed to "put out candells and bowattis" at
night during the sitting of the Assembly.   As regards the Cathedral,
it was resolved by the town council that "grate paines be takin by
" making of the sait for the assemblie; repairing of the flure of the
" uter kirk; taking doun certain windous in the inner kirk biggit up
" with stane, and putting glass thairin; and other warks thair incum-
" bent as occasion sall offer."[2]   The repairs then and previously made
prevented the fabric from falling to ruin, but it continued in a sadly
neglected state down to the period of its restoration in the present
century—a noble work if it had not been marred by the act of vandalism
which I have referred to.

[1] The disregard of the fine painted glass of our old churches which was shown till quite recently is
incredible.   There is among the MSS. of Miss Conway Griffith at Carreglwyd, a letter dated so late
as 1786, addressed by a glazier at Hornham, near Salisbury, to a Mr. Lloyd in London, sending him
a box full of old painted glass.   "It is the best," the glazier says, "I can get at present, but I expect
" to beat to pieces a good deal very soon, as it is of no use to us *and we do it for the lead*.   If you
" want any more of the same sort you may have what there is, if it will pay for taking out, as it is a
" deal of trouble to what breaking to pieces is."   This letter is endorsed " Berry the glazier, about
" beating to pieces the fine painted glass window at Sarum to save the lead."—*Fifth Report on Hist.
MSS.*, p. 415.
[2] 20th October, 1638.

THE CASTLE, AND THE MANOR HOUSES OF THE BISHOPS.

Another of the old landmarks of Glasgow—of which unhappily no trace now remains—was the bishop's castle or palace, which stood near the western entrance of the Cathedral, and the ruins of which remained till the end of the last century. It is mentioned in an old charter as early as 1290. At first a mere place of strength, it was extended into a palace with gardens and courts, and we have already seen that it was in "the inner flower garden" that the archbishop, in 1553, received the provost and council of the city, when they waited upon him for the purpose of his nominating the bailies for the year. Of its early history we have no record. A great tower and some other portions of the structure are known to have been built by Bishop Cameron towards the middle of the fifteenth century. A smaller tower was built by Archbishop Beton, a short time before the battle of Flodden, and by the same prelate the castle was surrounded by a protecting wall, on several places of which, Nisbet tells us, were "the arms of Beton "quartered with Balfour, and below "the arms a salmon with a ring in its mouth."[1] When the castle was demolished the greater part of the architectural ornaments were no doubt destroyed, but a few sculptured stones were saved. One of these, evidently one of those described by Nisbet, was till recently to be seen built into the front wall of an old house in North Woodside Road which was pulled down in 1869. This stone is now, or was recently, in the possession of the clergymen of the Roman Catholic church of St. Joseph. The arms, it will be observed, are those of the archbishop as described by Nisbet: Quarterly, 1st and 4th azure a fess between 3 mascles, or, for Beton; 2d and 3d argent, on a chevron

---

[1] Nisbet's Heraldry, iii. 2, p 41.

sable an otter's head erased of the first, for Balfour—the archbishop
having been descended from the heiress of Sir John Balfour of that ilk.

A handsome gatehouse and arched gateway were added to the castle

by Beton's successor,
Bishop Dunbar—the
last but one of the
Roman Catholic pre-
lates who occupied
the see, and who died
in 1547. Over this
gateway was an ela-
borate sculpture, or
rather series of sculp-
tures, on two separate
stones, the one over
the other. These
stones have also for-
tunately been pre-
served. Like the
one already men-
tioned they were re-
moved by one of the
citizens, and about
the year 1760 they
were built into the
back part of the
tenement No. 22
High Street, where
they remained till
quite recently. On
the upper stone are
the arms of Scotland
with the supporting
unicorns; and this

portion I have no doubt was erected by Dunbar himself, for it bears the
initial of the reigning sovereign—" I. 5 "—(James V.), who died in 1542
while the archbishop was still living. On the lower stone are two shields.
On the one is sculptured the paternal arms of Dunbar. He was of the

family of Mochrum, descended from Randolf, Earl of Moray, and the arms are those of that noble family:—or, three cushions within a double tressure flory and counter-flory gules, with a mullet for difference. Underneath this shield is the salmon with the ring in its mouth. On the lower shield are the arms of James Houston, sub-dean of Glasgow, being those of Houston of that ilk, viz., or, a chevron chequé sable and argent between three martlets of the second, with a rose in chief for difference. On each side of these shields is an ornamental pillar. The sub-dean was a friend of the archbishop, and a person of great influence in Glasgow, and the probability is that this part of the sculpture was erected by him after Dunbar's death. These interesting sculptures were recently presented by Bailie Millar, the proprietor of the tenement, to Sir William Dunbar, the lineal descendant of the Dunbars of Mochrum, for the purpose of being built into his new mansion in Wigtonshire—a fitter resting-place, perhaps, for the old stones than the back tenement in High Street, though it is to be regretted they were not retained in the city. The engraving is from a photograph taken immediately before their removal. These stones, and an oak panel in the possession of the Archæological Society of Glasgow, are, so far as I know, all that remain of the old castle.

Within this castle of Glasgow the bishops, in the palmy days of the see, kept a splendid court, and entertaining, as they did, princes and other visitors of rank, their expenditure must have been considerable. After the Reformation the castle presented a very different aspect. Yet, although the building was ruinous, and the archbishops poor, they still exercised a limited hospitality, but it was little they could afford to do in that way. We have one interesting peep into the interior towards the middle of the seventeenth century—Sir William Brereton being our informant. "Going into the hall of the castle," he says, "which is a poor " and mean place, the archbishop's daughter, a handsome and well-bred " proper gentlewoman, entertained me with much civil respect, and would " not suffer me to depart until I had drank Scotch ale, which was the " best I had tasted in Scotland."[1] This was in 1634. The archbishop was Patrick Lindsay, a descendant of an old branch of the Earls of Crawford—a quiet gentlemanly man by all accounts. In 1638, when matters came to a crisis, he was deposed and excommunicated with the other bishops by the General Assembly, when he left the castle and withdrew

[1] Brereton's Travels, p. 117.

into England, where he died in poverty.   But it is pleasant to know that his handsome and hospitable daughter was well married.

Before the Reformation the meetings of the town council appear to have been held in the castle, but after the flight of Beton they were removed to the old Tolbooth at the Cross.   Under date 28th September, 1576, there is an entry in the burgh accounts of a payment "for " bringing doun of the counsal hous burds furth of the castell;" and another for the bringing of "furmes, coilles, and peittis fra the castell." After this the building fell into disrepair.   It was partially restored in 1611 by Archbishop Spottiswoode, who made it his residence.   Ray, writing in 1681, speaks of it as "a goodly building," and still in good preservation; but Morer, who wrote his "Short Account of Scotland" in 1689, speaks of it as a building "formerly without doubt a very magni- " ficent structure, but now in ruins."   For some time after this, however, it was occasionally used as a prison.

In the beginning of the eighteenth century a praiseworthy, but apparently fruitless attempt, was made by one of the burgesses to save the building from further dilapidation.   Among the scattered leaves saved from the fire at the Exchequer in Edinburgh, is a representation to the barons by "Robert Thomson, merchant in Glasgow," dated 1720, which sets forth that "the castle formerly possest by the archbishops is, " throw its not being inhabited thes many years past, become wholly " ruinous.   And also that some bad men are become so barbarous and " unjust as to carry of the stones timber sklates and other materials " belonging thereunto, and apply the same to their own particular use, " to the shame and disgrace of the Christian religion—which the said " Robert Thomson as living neer to the said castle thought it his duty " to represent to your Lops."[1]   About forty years afterwards, when the Saracen's Head Inn was erected in the Gallowgate, the magistrates, who actively promoted that undertaking, by way of encouragement to the contractor allowed him to take the stones for building it from the castle.   All that remained of it in 1789 was removed in that year when the present Royal Infirmary was erected.   Even at that time, however, judging from drawings of it which are preserved, it must have been a picturesque building and the ruins of considerable extent.   The annexed view is from an engraving published in 1783, after a drawing by a Mr. Hearne.

[1] Preface to Reg. Epis. Glasg. p. lviii.

There is a tradition that the bishops had, not very far from the castle, a rural manor in a locality which was then a part of the old Bishop's Forest, but is now almost in the heart of Glasgow, and which is traversed by the street in Anderston called Bishop Street; but of this I have not been able to find any positive confirmation. An elderly woman, who had all her life resided in Bishop Street, informed me recently that when she was a child she was told by a person, then a very old woman, that the bishop's house was situated in the midst of gardens on the west side of the street; and she described a narrow lane existing in her day, and running northwards from the main street of Anderston, on the east of Bishop Street, as what had been the bishop's entry to his house. It was called the Bishop's Walk. The name of the present street, and the name of the corn-mills on the west side of it—Bishop's Garden Mills— give countenance to this tradition.

It is certain, however, that the bishops had, from very early times, a manor at Partick. Mention is made of it as early as the twelfth century in a charter by King David (1136), giving lands in "Perdeyc" to the church of Kentigern in Glasgow. In 1277 the grant already mentioned, by Maurice, Lord of Luss, of wood for the repair of the church, is dated at Partick, where he was no doubt at the time on a visit to the bishop; and a notarial instrument executed in 1362, entitled *Compromisso in Arbitros inter Episcopum et capitulum*, bears to be dated "apud manerium "dicti domini Glasguensis episcopi de Perthik." It may have been from a tradition of this residence that an old house, the ruins of which stood till recently on the right bank of the Kelvin, not far from the junction of that river with the Clyde, came to be called the bishop's castle. But it was certainly not built by a bishop of Glasgow. Chalmers, in his *Caledonia*, referring to this house, says that Archbishop Spottiswood, who repaired the Cathedral and the archiepiscopal palace, built also in 1611 a castle at Partick as a country seat for the archbishops; and elsewhere he speaks of it as situated "on an elevated site on the west bank of the "Kelvin, the ruins being called the bishop's castle." By this name it was no doubt known for nearly a century, but it is certain that the house referred to was built by George Hutcheson, one of the founders of the hospital of that name, as a residence for himself, and the contract for building it, dated in 1611, is still extant.[1] The view which I have given on p. 114 of this well-known old landmark is from a drawing made

---

[1] History of Partick Castle, by Laurence Hill, Esq., LL.B. Glasgow: privately printed.

H

in 1828. Of the old manor-house erected by the bishops, there remains no trace, but it is not improbable that Mr. Hutcheson may have built his house on the site of the bishop's residence, and that, indeed, he may have used in its construction some of the stones of the old castle.

While mentioning Partick, it is interesting to note that in one of the

earliest charters, granted by Bishop Herbert in 1152, mention is made of lands in Partick "with the adjacent islands between Guvan and Perthic." Of these islands no trace now remains. But there were till a comparatively recent period several islands in the Clyde below the mouth of the Kelvin, some of which may be recognized although now joined to the land. They are shown on Blaeu's map, which was published in 1654. The cut on p. 115 is a fac-simile of the portion of that map containing the islands. One was the Water Inch, lying immediately west of the mouth of the Kelvin. Another, farther down and much larger, was the White Inch, comprising the district which still bears that name. Still farther down was the Sand Inch, and below the mouth of the river Cart was the New-shot Isle. There were other islands in the Clyde above the harbour. One, according to the map, was below the bridge, and another, called the Point Isle, was opposite the Green, a little below the Arns Well, but this does not appear on Blaeu's map. It was in 1730 upwards of an acre in extent, and at that time it formed one of the principal salmon shots of the river. No trace of it now remains.

At a period still earlier than that of the manor at Partick the Bishops of Glasgow had a rural palace at their barony of Ancrum. Of this manor and barony they were the earliest possessors on record, and the lands are mentioned as belonging to the see as early as the Notitia of David in 1121. Here the bishops often resided, and from here they dated many of their charters. In a letter from Lord Dacres to Henry VIII. in October, 1513, shortly after the battle of Flodden, the bishop's

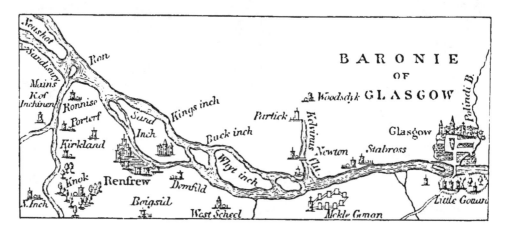

house is styled the Castle of Ancrum. Its remains form part of the present mansion of the Scotts of Ancrum.[1]

Besides these, the bishops possessed from the beginning of the four-teenth century another residence at Lochwood, about six miles eastward from Glasgow. The castle stood on the south side of a small lake called the Bishop's Loch, and in the old charter it is called *Manerium de lacu juxta Glasgu.* It contained a chapel, and many of the episcopal charters are dated from this place. It is mentioned also in a curious instrument of protest, taken during the episcopate of Bishop Lindsay, which bears that while the bishop was residing at his Manor of the Lake, his seal had been lost by Robert del Barkour near the chapel of St. Mary of Dunbretan, and found and restored to him by James of

[1] Orig. Paroch. vol. i. p. 304.

Irwyn, a monk of Paselet. After the flight of Beton, the last Roman Catholic archbishop, Lochwood was taken possession of by the Duke of Chatelherault, from whom Robert Boyd of Bannheith obtained a grant of the lands, but his right appears to have been disputed. The archbishop was then at the court of France, as ambassador of Queen Mary, and one of his adherents in Scotland writes to him, under date 7th March, 1588: "Quhat sall becum of the Lochwood God knawis, for the "Laird of Bannheith and the gudeman of Orbiston are contendand for "it, althocht the best richt be ʒours."[1] By an act of parliament in 1600 Beton, in consideration of his services as ambassador, was restored to his archbishopric, notwithstanding his never having acknowledged the reformed religion. This restitution was made, however, without prejudice to certain feus which had been made of the episcopal lands, and under reservation of the stipends of the ministers, and of certain rents and duties which had been given to the college. There was exempted also from the restitution "the castell of Glasgow and cheising of the "provest and bailleis of Glasgow, and provestrie and baillierie thereof."[2] But the bishop got back his Manor of the Lake, the rents of which he enjoyed for the remainder of his life. He did not return to Scotland, however, and died at Paris in 1603. The castle of Lochwood was afterwards demolished, and no trace of it now remains. In later times the place became the property of Mr. John Baird, of the Gartsherrie family.

The Bishops of Glasgow had still another residence—Castel Tarras, or Castel Staris, a locality now known as Carstairs, where, as I have already mentioned, Wyschard, the zealous supporter of Bruce, built a castle. He was called to account by Edward I. for having done so without his permission, but was afterwards allowed to complete it.

OLD STREETS AND BUILDINGS.

To the south of the castle was the Stable Green, so called from its being near the castle stables, and from which one of the ports of the city took its name. It is described in an instrument in 1510 as "the "Stablegreyn beyond the city gates."[3] It was in the Stable Green that

---

[1] Miscellaneous Papers, Maitland Club, p. 44.　　[2] Munimenta Universitatis, vol. i. p. 155.
[3] Liber Protocollorum, No. 434.

the family of Lennox acquired their first residence in the city, by the purchase of a house in 1509 by Earl Matthew, afterwards provost of Glasgow, from the rector of Stobo. It was in this house that the earl's widow, the granddaughter of James II., resided after her husband had been killed at Flodden. Here also her descendant, the unfortunate Darnley, resided with his father during his recovery from the effects of poison; and it was here that Queen Mary visited him not long before his murder. There has been preserved a stone on which are sculptured arms, as shown in the cut, which formed part of that house. The arms are those of Sir John Stewart, second son of Alexander, high-steward of Scotland, from whom the family of

Lennox was descended.[1] The house which formerly stood to the south-west of the Cathedral, called Darnley's Cottage, was a comparatively modern building.[2]

The "Place of the Vicars" was on the north side of the Cathedral. We learn this from an instrument in 1508, in which a tenement with garden and pertinents is described as "lying on the north side of the "church of Glasgow between the great garden of the archbishop and the "place of the vicars."[3]

Near the Stable Green, on the west side of Castle Street, stood St. Nicholas Hospital, founded by Bishop Muirhead about the year 1460, the revenues of which, though very small, are still, after the lapse of four hundred years, administered by the Magistrates and Town Council of Glasgow. The original endowment was for twelve indigent old men, and a priest to perform divine service in the hours of canonical devotion. Archbishop Leighton in 1677 left to it £150 as a further endowment. The other revenues which still remain were derived from some small ground rents bequeathed by Martin, chancellor of the Cathedral, in 1501. In 1795, when Brown wrote his History, the hall and chapel of the

---

[1] The Earls of Lennox carried buckles on a border gules, and a progenitor carried roses. The stone is curious as showing both buckles and roses as ornaments exterior to the shield.

[2] Liber Protocoll. preface, p. 19.   [3] Ibid. No. 307.

hospital still existed, but were in ruins and used as a cow-house. Nisbet in his Heraldry describes the chapel as "of fine aisler work of a Gothic "form, and the windows supported by a buttress between each of them." He adds that over the door were the arms of Bishop Muirhead—three acorns on a bend, surmounted by the salmon, and a crozier behind the shield. This chapel remained till so late as 1808, when it was pulled down. Nisbet also notices a manse opposite the hospital, built by the bishop as a residence for the priest, on which also were the bishop's arms. Farther to the north, and near the Stable Green port, stood another hospital, known as the Back Almshouse. It was founded by Roland Blackadder, sub-dean of Glasgow, for the benefit of indigent persons coming casually to the city. This hospital appears to have become united to the foundation of Bishop Muirhead. In 1590 there is a deed of bequest by which John Painter, master of the Sang school, leaves three pounds "to the twelve poor men in the free almshouse called St. "Nicholas Hospital, and twenty shillings to the four poor men of the "back almshouse." And in a minute of council in 1606 the two hospitals are called "the Bishop of Glasgow Almshouses situat besyde the castell "of Glasgow." From one of the minutes of the Presbytery of Glasgow, 25th November, 1595, we learn that at that time these almshouses were surrounded with trees. By this minute the presbytery ordains the four ministers of Glasgow, with the master of work, and others, "to sicht the "treis at the almoushous gif it be expedient for the weal of the almous- "hous that the samin be cuttit and gif swa be fund that the same be "applyit to sum wse of the said almoushous." The presbytery also appears to have had the nomination of the parties to be admitted to the benefit of the foundation.[1]

In a minute of council in 1589 is preserved a description of this "hospitall besyde the stabil grene," which is interesting as a portrait of one of our old houses, now that so much of the ancient city has dis- appeared. The minute records a visit of inspection by "the bailleis." It first mentions "the ȝaird dyk, the north syd therof, weill dykit and "kaipit with stane, and ane haill hedge on the south syd thereof." The "hcich chalmer of the said hospitall" is described as "well loftit and "jestit, twa windois within the samyn, staincherit with irne; ane stand "bed fixit in the wall of the said chalmer, weill burdeit; ane pantrie "dure and ane saig dure . . . without has ane sufficient gude dure, and

---

[1] Presbytery Records, 12th Feb. 1606.

" foir ʒett, weill wallit and lokit, with ane raill galrie stair, and ane
" turlies upon the northmost windo thereof. Item fand the laich hous
" thereof with sex stand beddis of aik sufficient, with ane paintrie lokfast,
" and ane mekill kist standand within the same claspit with irne on every
" nook. Item fand the coilhous dure sufficientlie lockit and bandit, weill
" wallit, and kapit round about. Item the haill hous of the said hospitall
" sufficient in ruiff, tymmer, sklait, and waterfast. Item fand ane doubill
" foir ʒett bandit, without ane lok, with the walls of the clois weill kapit
" about."[1]

All that has been saved of the endowments of these ancient foundations is a capital of £380 and about £15 yearly from grain rents and old
houses.

Immediately contiguous to St. Nicholas Hospital stood the manse of
the prebendary of Morebattle, which after the Reformation was acquired
by the Incorporated Trades of Glasgow, and became the Trades House.
On the other side of the Hospital stood the manse of the prebendary of
Barlanark and lord of Provan. These manses, which remained till quite
recently, were in all probability two of those which were erected by order
of Bishop Cameron as residences for his canons. James IV. was a canon
of the Cathedral, and held the appointments of prebendary of Barlanark
and lord of Provan.

Besides the hospitals just mentioned there was an hospital for lepers
on the south side of the river. In 1494 it was called "hospitale lepro-
" sorum degentium prope pontem;" and in 1555 it is described as "the
" Leper house of St. Ninian beyond the bridge of Glasgow." It is said
to have been founded by a lady of the family of Lochow about 1350. It
had a burying ground and chapel near it. An entry in the burgh records
supplies a graphic picture of these poor lepers—describing their peculiar
enforced costume, and the precautions prescribed against contact with
them. It is as follows:—"It is statut and ordainit that the lipper of the
" Hospital sall gang only upon the calsie syde, near the gutter, and sal
" haif clapperis, and ane claith upon thair mouth and face, and sall stand
" afar of qll they resaif almous, or answer, under the payne of banisching
" thame the toun and Hospitall."[2]

So terrible does this disease appear to have been, and so much
dreaded, that when a member of a family was stricken the others sought
to have them separated from the family circle. An example of this

[1] Council Records, 30th December, 1589.   [2] 6th October, 1610.

occurs in the records of the Presbytery of Glasgow, where a husband denounced his leper wife, requiring, apparently, the sanction of the church in order to effect the separation. The entry in the presbytery books is very curious: "Anent yᵉ *lamenting* gevin in be James Mitchell in baluvin, " twiching yᵉ disease of marioun Layng his spous in Leprosie, to his " great grief qʳ throw nether he nor his servands can have with hir, swa " diseasit, sic familiaritie and pleasantnes as is requirit." The presbytery refers "the tryal thereof to the minister of Campsie, and neighbours to "the said marioun," and to report.[1] The result is not stated; but no doubt, if it confirmed the "lament" of the husband, the poor woman would be ordered to the almshouse beyond the bridge. This leper-house was an old foundation. We find James IV., during a visit to Glasgow in 1491, giving alms to the unfortunate inmates. In his household accounts there is this entry: "Item to the sick folk at the brig of Glasgw be the kings command ij s."

While the temporal wants of the inmates of the several hospitals were no doubt well attended to, the presbytery was careful of their spiritual interests. By a minute of 5th June, 1593, they "ordaine the puir folk of "the Almshouse to be summoned to this daye viii dayes to compeir be- " fore them to give the confessioune of their faithe."

In process of time houses extended from the Cathedral along the Rottenrow—called in the old charters *via Rattonum*—and eastward along the Drygate. In early times there was a mint in Glasgow, and it is supposed to have been in the Drygate, though no trace of it remains. It existed as early as the reign of Alexander II., as appears from coins of that reign which have been preserved;[2] and from the minute description given by M'Ure of coins of Robert III., of which, he says, specimens existed in his day, there can be no doubt that in that reign also coins were struck in Glasgow; but of these last none are now known to exist.

From the Drygate and Rottenrow houses gradually extended down the east side of the steep part of the High Street, but till a comparatively recent period there is no record of houses on the west side of that street. The houses on the east side had most of them gardens with fields ex- tending down to the Molendinar Burn—then an open limpid stream— which acquired its name from the mill of the bishop's manor. One of these possessions in the High Street is described in a charter of 1463 as

---

[1] Presbytery Records, 19th Nov. 1606.
[2] Records of the Coinage of Scotland, by R. W. Cochrane Patrick, Esq., vol. i. p. xliii.

the tenement of John Wilson, with a garden and fields extending to the burn—"cum orto et aggeribus tendentibus ad rivolum de Malyndoner "jacen. in civitate Glasguen. in publico vico principale."

At the foot of the New Vennel was a bleaching green, so large that it came to be used for pasturing horses and cattle. But to this abuse the magistrates put a stop, ordaining that "all hors or kyne that beis "fund thereon be poyndit."[1]

To almost all the old houses gardens were attached. Gardening was much cultivated in Scotland. It was a favourite amusement of James I., as it had been of David I., and the monasteries, as well as most lands near cathedrals, were distinguished for good gardens and orchards. And the gardens in Glasgow were not mere "kail yards," for they were of such extent and importance as to be the subject of a special teind duty. "The tiends of the yairds of Glasgow" were those which were exigible from the gardens attached to the houses of the ancient city, and some of these gardens were not deemed unfit for even a king to walk in. There is a charter in 1649 by Charles II., to Janet and John Cleland, of a tenement on the south side of the Drygate, with the gardens, upper and lower, attached to it—the conveyance being burdened with the payment of a certain yearly sum to the rector and other members of the Academy and College of Glasgow; and in this charter the king reserves to himself and his successors the right to one chamber and a stable in the back part of the tenement, with the liberty of walking and recreation in the gardens whenever they resided in Glasgow. The words are, "Cum potestate spaciandi, "ambulandi, et nos delectandi in horto sive hortis, vocatis *gairdenes*, "durantibus nostrorum residentiis in dicto burgo Glasguensi."

Buildings gradually extended down the High Street to the Cross—at first a thin line of houses with probably frequent spaces between, and nothing behind them but fields and gardens, and the open country beyond. In an old charter this street is called "magnus vicus tendens "ab ecclesia cathedrali ad crucem fori;"[2] and in a later deed (1433) it is called "the gat at strekis fra the mercat cors tyll the He kirk "of Glascu."[3] The first cross of the burgh stood at the junction of the Rottenrow with Drygate.

In an alley on the west side of the High Street, a little above the College, was the monastery or "place" and gardens of the friars

---

[1] 16th June, 1677.　　　　[2] Lib. Coll. N. D. p. 240.　　　　[3] Ibid. p. 166.

called the *Fratres Minores de Observatione,* or Minorites, founded *circa* 1476 by Bishop John Laing and Thomas Forsyth, rector of Glasgow.[1] No records of the foundation, nor of the extent of its property, are preserved, but in the Liber Protocollorum there is an instrument recording a grant to them by the chapter of Glasgow of a portion of the Ramshorn grounds adjoining the walls of their garden to the west for extending their buildings and garden.[2] An unfortunate member of this fraternity—one Jeremy Russell—was burned for heresy in 1599.[3]

On the other side of the High Street, near where the old College Church was afterwards erected, stood the more important convent of the Dominicans or Friars Preachers, popularly known as the Black Friars. Their church, which was surrounded by a cemetery, was begun to be built some time before 1246—probably in the preceding century. Although it did not probably come up to the description given of it by M'Ure, it must have been a fine old building. It was, M'Ure says, " the ancientest building of Gothic kind of work that could be seen " in the whole kingdom, as was observed by Mr. Miln, the Architect " to King Charles I., who when he surveyed it in 1638, declared that " it had not its parallel in all Scotland except Whittairn in Galloway."[4] Of its general appearance a representation has been fortunately preserved in the bird's-eye view of the college by Captain Slezer, which I have given in a subsequent page. This view must have been taken[5] shortly before the church was destroyed by lightning in 1670.

The Place or Convent was in the High Street to the west of the church, and it was richly endowed. There are notices of it in Glasgow deeds as early as 1270. In one charter of that date there is bequeathed to the vicars choral of the Cathedral a house which is described as " proximior Fratribus Predicatoribus in villa Glasguensi inter ipsos " fratres et domum Willelmi de Belledstane." There are many deeds in the Chartulary relating to the property of the order, some of them curious and interesting. In 1301, when Edward I. was in Glasgow, endeavouring to bring the western shires of Scotland under his dominion, he was lodged in the convent of the Friars Preachers. It was probably the only place in the town capable of receiving the royal retinue, and like other buildings of the Dominicans it was no doubt richly furnished. Edward at this time was constant in his offerings

---

[1] Spottiswoode.   [2] Lib. Protocollorum, No. 560.   [3] Appendix.
[4] M'Ure's History, 1st ed. p. 60.   [5] Page 125.

at the high altar, and at the shrine of Kentigern, in the Cathedral, and the sums which he paid on these occasions are preserved, and also, in some instances, the occasion of the gifts. On the 23d of August, 1301, he offered seven shillings in honour of St. Bartholomew. Two days afterwards he offers the same sum in consequence of "good news "which he had of the Lord Malcolm of Drumman, a Scottish knight, "having been captured by the lord John of Segrave." And on the 2d of September in the same year the occasion of his offering is "good "news which he had of the Castle of Turnberry."[1]

Among the endowments of the convent there is an old writ subscribed by two notaries, which mentions a chalder of meal as being paid "to the friers" furth of the lands of Balagan, with liberty of cutting timber, and also a right of fishing in Lochlemont (Loch Lomond).

For many years the convent shared, along with the chapter-house of the Cathedral, the merit of sheltering under its roof the more important assemblies of the university after its foundation in the middle of the fifteenth century. In the century following the prior and convent made an attempt to vindicate for their precincts the privileges of a sanctuary. The question came to be tried in a suit arising out of a sudden quarrel between two of the citizens, in which one of them wounded the other. The aggressor, according to the representation of the friars, "fled into the said place and sanctuary for girth, traist-"ing to haif bruikit the privilege of the samyn." But the friends of the injured man "be fource and way of deid tuke him furthe of the "porche kirk dure thereof, delivered him to the provost and baillies "of the said citie and chalmerlane of the castell thereof, qua hes and "wythaldis him, and will not restore him againe to the fredome and "privelege of the said sanctuary without thai be compelled: to the "grait hurt of the freedome and privelege of Halie kirk." Their suit was unsuccessful, and the court assoilzied the defenders, on the ground that the convent had failed to establish their alleged right.

The friars had a grant in 1304 from Robert, bishop of Glasgow, authorizing them to introduce into their convent the water of the Deanside or Meadow well—a spring which was then and for long afterwards in great repute—"Fontem quendam qui dicitur Meduwel in loco "qui dicitur Denside scaturientem in perpetuum conducendum in claus-"trum dictorum patrum ad usus necessarios eorundem."[2]

---

[1] Reg. Epis. Glasg. No. 548.   [2] Lib. Coll. N. D.

The whole property of this community was transferred to the university in the year 1568. Ten years later there still remained "a tene-"ment of howssis perteining sumtime to the saids Friers Predicatouris"[1] —possibly the one fronting the High Street, shown in Captain Slezer's view—but with this exception the only part of their buildings which appears to have survived the Reformation was their conventual church. It remained, though in a ruinous state, till the year 1670, when, as already stated, it was destroyed by lightning,[2] and what was afterwards known as the College Church—also now removed—was built upon its site.

The well-known pile on the same side of the High Street, farther up, till recently occupied by the college, is not of very ancient date. The building of it was begun only in 1632. Glasgow was the second of the universities of Scotland, and was founded in 1450. It had the papal privilege of a *Studium Generale*—the then technical term for a university—and a foundation by the Pope. It took for its model the famous schools of Paris and Bologna—adopting the same mode of teaching and examining, and prescribing the same text-books. The Pope in making the grant professed to be actuated by the fitness of the city "on account of the healthiness of its climate and the plenty "of victuals, and of every thing necessary for the use of man."

The first building, called the schools, in which the masters taught, was a house which had belonged to the parson of Luss, and which was afterwards called "the auld Pedagogy." It was situated in the Rottenrow, and is supposed by Professor Innes to have been in existence and used as a chapter-house before the papal foundation. It included a dwelling-place for students of arts, which was named *Collegium*, in which they had chambers and a common hall. This old building remained till the middle of the present century. The accompanying view of the ruins is taken from the north.

But the faculty did not long remain there. In 1459 they acquired from James, the first Lord Hamilton, a portion of the land in the High Street on which the present buildings were subsequently erected. The grant was in favour of Master Duncan Bunch, principal regent of the faculty of arts of the *Studium* of Glasgow, and it conveyed a tenement in the High Street, near the place of the Dominican Friars, together with four acres of land in the Dove Hill, contiguous to the Molendinar

---

[1] Munimenta Universitatis, vol. i. p. 120.   [2] Law's Memorials.

THE OLD PEDAGOGY IN THE ROTTENROW

Burn, on the condition that twice in every day, at the close of their
noontide and evening meals, the regents and students should rise
and pray for his own soul and that of Euphemia his wife, countess of
Douglas and lady of Bothwell; and that if a chapel or oratory should
be built in the college, the regents and students should also there
assemble, and on their bended knees sing an ave to the Virgin with

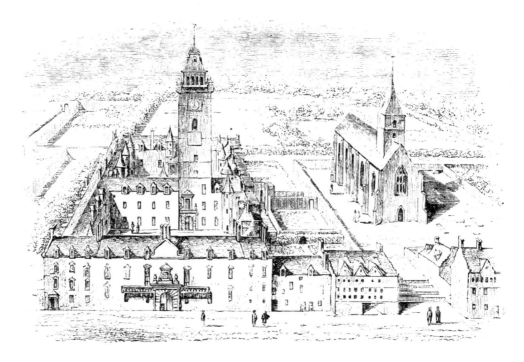

a collect and remembrance for himself and his wife.[1] To this ground
an addition was made in 1475 by "the annexation and union of Sir
"Thomas Arthurlees' place or manor to the pedagogy."

In 1563 the possessions of the University in the High Street were
still farther increased by a grant from Queen Mary of the manse and
"kirkroom" of the Friars Preachers, with thirteen acres of land in the
Dove Hill, with certain rents from tenements in the city and elsewhere.[2]
The occasion of the grant is stated to be the ruined state of the university and college—its schools and chambers standing half-built, and the
endowments of its teachers and the provision made for its poor scholars
having ceased.

[1] Munimenta Universitatis Glasguensis, vol. i. p. 9.   [2] Ibid. vol. i. p. 67.

The new buildings were begun, as I have mentioned, in 1632, and by 1656 the structure had been completed, with the exception of the court, in which the professors' houses were. The bird's-eye view of the college on p. 125 is from the curious work of Captain John Slezer, Theatrum Scotiæ, already referred to, and it may be accepted as a correct representation of what it was about the year 1660. Captain Slezer's work was not published till 1693, but the view must have been taken some time previous to 1670, as it represents the old church of the Black-friars, which was destroyed in that year.

Previous to the new erection the general chapters of the university met, as already stated, sometimes in the Cathedral and sometimes within the precincts of the Friars Preachers. The first general chapter, held in 1451 for the incorporation of members, met in the chapter-house of the Friars, and the last transactions recorded before the Reformation show us the university met in full convocation in the chapter-house of the Cathedral, while the faculty of arts held its congregation in the crypt at the altar of St. Nicholas.[1] On the 25th October, 1637, we find the faculty holding a meeting "at the castell of Glasgow"—the archbishop being at that time chancellor.[2]

In 1577 James V. issued a new erection or foundation, which more amply endowed the university, and in several respects changed its original constitution and character.

Within the precincts of the college in the High Street many of the students resided, as they had done in the old premises in the Rottenrow. They occupied apartments in the different courts, and dined at a common table. At first they appear to have paid no rent for their rooms, but after 1712 a charge was made for each room, varying from four shillings sterling to ten shillings for the session, according to the situation.[3] The students appear to have furnished their own rooms. Dr. Carlyle of Inveresk, who studied at the university in 1743, says: "I had my lodging "this session in a college room which I had furnished for the session at "a moderate rent. John Donaldson, a college servant, lighted my fire "and made my bed; and a maid from the landlady who furnished the "room came once a fortnight with clean linens."[4]

The accompanying view of the inner court of the college is interest-ing from its having been taken on the occasion of the rejoicings which

---

[1] Professor Innes.   [2] Munimenta, vol. iii. p. 379.   [3] Ibid. vol. iii. p. 513.
[4] Autobiography of the Rev. Dr. Alexander Carlyle, Edin. 1860, p. 99.

FINE ART EXHIBITION IN COURT OF GLASGOW COLLEGE

took place in Glasgow in 1761 on the coronation of George III. The smoke behind the steeple proceeds from a bonfire kindled in the High Street before the college gate. On this occasion the court was decorated with pictures supplied by the Foulises, who had at that time their studio within the college buildings. The illustration is copied from an engraving executed in their academy, and published at the time. It is farther interesting as showing the costume of the citizens of Glasgow in the

middle of the eighteenth century. The above view of the College is from a drawing made by Mr. Leitch in 1845.

Besides the garden behind the college, called "the great yard," there was constructed in 1704 a "Physic garden;" but to these gardens all of the students had not access—an unjust partiality having been shown by confining the privilege to "the sons of noblemen who are scholars." To each of this favoured class the faculty allowed "a key to the great garden " and Physic garden, providing the said privileged persons promise to " allow no other the use of the said key."[1] About this time the students appear to have been in the habit of acting plays, but eventually this was prohibited by the faculty under the pain of expulsion. In many other respects the faculty exercised a strict discipline over the students. On

[1] Munimenta, vol. ii. p. 421.

one occasion a student was fined for cutting the gown of another student on the Lord's day. On another the faculty deals with a student for challenging another to fight with swords. The wearing of swords by the students was strictly prohibited, and on one occasion a student is severely rebuked for having been "found by the Principal on Tuesday " last with a sword girt about him in the toun," and the sword is impounded. Another student is reprimanded for being "found drinking in " an ale-house with some touns people at eleven of the clock at night," and threatened with expulsion if it be repeated. Cases of riot and insubordination are frequent, and these are summarily dealt with by the college authorities. One singular piece of mischief practised by the students was to give in the name of some fellow-student, whom they wished to annoy, to be publicly prayed for in the church by name. This went so far that the professors had to interfere. A number of students were summoned before them and reprimanded, and one of them was expelled.[1]

But the faculty claimed a much larger power over the students than dealing with such cases of discipline. They asserted an absolute jurisdiction, extending even to criminal charges, to the exclusion of that of the magistrates of the city; and they put in practice what they claimed, for they had a prison of their own in the steeple to which delinquent students were consigned. On one occasion a student—John Satcher by name—was committed to this prison for sending a letter to the principal "conceived in very insolent terms." Thereupon some of the other students broke open the prison door and released John, who, as the faculty minute bears, forthwith "threw off his gown and withdrew him- " self from the college till this morning, when he was seized and put into " his former place of confinement." Subsequently the culprit "acknow- " ledged his great offence," and having "humbly begged pardon of the " principal and all the masters " he was reponed—the ringleader of those who had broken the prison door being subjected to a fine of eighteen shillings sterling.[2] The faculty also exercised the discipline of corporal punishment. One of their edicts in 1667 is that if any students occupying rooms within the college shall be "found guiltie of breaking the glass " windowes or doing anie other detriment to the hous, they shall be " furthwith publicklie whipped and extruded the colledge."[3]

But these were small matters. A case occurred when a student,

[1] Munimenta, vol. ii. pp. 373-379.   [2] Ibid. p. 415.   [3] Ibid. p. 340.

Robert Bartoune, was charged with murder, and the faculty did not hesitate, even in that case, to assert its jurisdiction and proceed to exercise it. The court was held in "the laigh hall of the universitie," on the 18th of August, 1670—Sir William Fleming of Farme, rector, presiding, with the dean of faculty and three regents as assessors. The indictment was given in by "John Cummyng wryter in Glasgow, elected "to be Procurator Fiscal of the said universitie, and by Andrew Wright "Cordoner in Glasgow neirest of kine to umquhill Jonnet Wright," whom Bartoune was charged with having murdered in her own house "by the shoot off ane gun." The punishment demanded at the hands of the faculty was that of death. The panel having pled not guilty, "an inqueist of honest men" (fifteen jurymen) was impanelled and the case proceeded to trial. A curious incident is recorded in the course of it, namely, that the jury, before giving in their verdict, demanded that the university should hold them skaithless in case they should afterwards be challenged for having taken part in the proceedings, "in "regaird they declaired the caice to be singular, never haveing occurred "in the aidge of befor to ther knowledge, and the rights and priviledges "of the universitie not being produced to them to cleir ther priviledge "for holding of criminall courts, and to sitt and cognose upon cryms "of the lyke natur." The rector and his assessors answered that the objection to the jurisdiction came too late, after they had agreed "to "pase upon the said inqueist in initio;" but notwithstanding "for ther "satisfactioune and *ex abundanti gratia*," the court agreed to hold them free "of all coast danger and expenses." The verdict was not guilty, and it is not unlikely that a sense of the responsibility which would have attended a different result did not fail to influence the jury."[1]

The magistrates, however, did not always recognize the jurisdiction thus claimed by the university. On one occasion (in 1711) when some students had been caught misconducting themselves in the city, the magistrates had them apprehended and brought before them, and compelled each of them to pay a fine before he was released. The university resented this, and demanded the restitution of the fines, under protest that if the magistrates refused they would be held liable "for all expenses "and damadges that the said Masters of the University may be putt to "in vindicating their right and jurisdiction over any of the scholars com- "mitted to their charge."[2] The result is not stated.

---

[1] Munimenta, vol. ii. p. 340. [2] Ibid. vol. ii. p. 400.

The burgh records also contain some curious notices as to the relations subsisting between the town and the university. The sons of burgesses appear to have enjoyed certain privileges and exemptions, and the magistrates were tenacious in asserting them. Among others, under date 16th November, 1626, notice is taken of an undue exaction made " by the Principal and Regents on the town's bursars quha are urgit to " gif ane silver spune at their entrie."

In the Muniments of the University are to be found many other interesting notices of student life, and of the customs of the college. One of the latter was that the students at one time prayed publicly by rotation in the classes. This practice was, probably, in many cases exercised injudiciously, and it ceased soon after the beginning of the eighteenth century, in consequence of a resolution by the faculty that it should be *gradually* discontinued. The minute bears that in order " that " it may be worn out by degrees, and with the less noise, the faculty " recommends it to the several masters that at these times when the " students used to pray they put it only on those of greatest gravity and " sobriety, and sometimes themselves to do it at these turns, and some- " times altogether to omit it."[1]

In 1634 Charles I. addressed an autograph letter to the Archbishop of Glasgow requiring him to see that the members of the college repair together to divine service in the Cathedral in their gowns, according to their degrees, forenoon and afternoon, and that they occupy seats to be specially appropriated to them.

When Beton at the Reformation carried with him to Paris the orna- ments and jewels belonging to the Cathedral, he took among them a silver staff, the history of which is interesting. It is thus described in an " Inventur of the Guddis and inspreth pertening to the College of " Glasgow," *circa* 1614: " Item in the Principal his studi ane silver staff " callit the rectors staff, of five pund sevin unce ane quarter unce veight, " quhilk Mr. James Balfure deane of Glasgow, Rector the yeir of God " 1560, gave to the bischop of Glasgow, quho carijt the same with all " the silver warke and hail juels of the Hie Kirk to Paris with him. " Notwithstanding the said staff, be the travels of Mr. Patrick Sharpe " Principal, was recoverit, mendit, and augmentit the yeir of God CIↃ. IↃ. " XC as the dait on the end of the staff bears."[2] The staff which the dean thus improperly gave to Beton, and which was recovered in 1590,

---

[1] Munimenta Universitatis Glas. vol. ii. p. 375.   [2] Ibid. vol. iii. p. 523.

was the present college mace. The "augmentation" of it must have been considerable, for while the original weight was five pounds seven ounces and a quarter, it now weighs eight pounds one ounce. It was originally constructed in 1465. It now bears the following inscription in modern letters: *Hæc virga empta fuit publius Academiæ Glasguensis sumtibus* A.D. 1465: *in Galliam ablata* A.D. 1560, *et Academiæ restituta* 1590.

A great part of the old buildings of the college has been destroyed, and the portions which remain have been converted to other uses, but it is to be hoped that the front to the High Street will be spared as one of the landmarks of Glasgow,[1] and that in its new premises the university will continue to deserve the character given to it by James Melville. "I daresay," wrote Melville in his diary, "there was no place in Europe "comparable to Glasgw for guid letters during these yeirs for a plentiful "and guid chepe mercat of all kynd of langages artes and sciences."

In one of the wynds running west from the High Street was the Grammar School. It was founded by Simon Dalgles (Dalgliesh), Official of Glasgow in the middle of the fifteenth century; and from a notarial instrument in 1508 we learn that, founding on the terms of the original grant, the chancellor of Glasgow claimed to be master of the school by virtue of his office, with the right to appoint and remove the teachers. But Sir John Stewart of Minto, the provost, on behalf of the burgesses, disputed his right and claimed the power of admitting all masters to "the mural schools and buildings assigned for the instruction of scho- "lars."[2] Of the result of the dispute there is no record. In 1578, as appears from an entry in the burgh minutes, the Grammar School was covered with thatch. The later building was erected in the beginning of the seventeenth century, and while it was being built the scholars met in the High Church.[3] Over the door of the school were the arms of Glasgow, with this inscription: "Scola grammaticor. a senatu civibusque "Glasguensis bonar. liter. patronis conditu."

At the foot of the High Street stood the old Tolbooth. We have no account of its appearance, or when it was erected. In the records of Our Lady College it is mentioned as the "Pretorium burgi de Glasgu "jacens in via S. Teneu ex parte boreali ejusdem." And in the ancient charters it is repeatedly mentioned as the place of meeting of the burgh

---

[1] The front of the College has since been removed, as noticed in the concluding chapter of this work. [2] Lib. Protocoll. No. 342. [3] Presbytery Records, 11th March, 1601.

courts—"the heid court of the burcht and citie of Glasgow halden in the "Tolbuithe thairof." From an entry in the council records in 1574 it appears that there were "buythis vnder the tolbuyth," the rents of which were appointed to be applied in "mendyng and reparyng of the tolbuyth

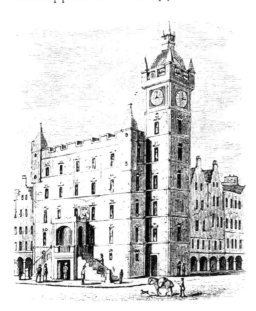

"and to na vther vse." This old building having become dilapidated was taken down, and a new tolbooth erected in 1626. This, as will be seen from the cut, was a fine picturesque structure. A traveller in the time of the Commonwealth describes it as "a very "sumptuous, regulated, uniform "fabric, large and lofty, most in- "dustriously and artificially carved "from the very foundation to the "superstructure, to the great ad- "miration of strangers, and is with- "out exception the paragon of "beauty in the west."[1] This build- ing served as a prison and as the place for the council meetings till early in the present century, when it was removed and the present building erected on its site.

When the old jail was taken down the magistrates had the good taste to preserve and repair the beautiful tower attached to it, now known as the Cross steeple. But it nearly experienced at the hands of their less worthy successors the fate which, somewhat later, befell the western tower of the Cathedral. The demolition of the steeple was actually under the consideration of the town council for several weeks, and it was only saved by the vote of a majority. This was in 1814!

They must have witnessed some curious incidents, those old tol- booths, and like all the other prisons in Scotland, till a comparatively recent period, they must have been the scene of much suffering. Pri- soners of all sorts were crowded together without classification; men and women often confined in the same apartment; and young offenders, imprisoned for trifling matters, locked up with hardened criminals,

[1] Franck's Northern Memoirs.

even murderers. Ill clothed most of them, cold and hungry, and in filth, imprisonment was then a real punishment. Those who could afford to bribe the jailer might fare better, for that functionary exercised a very despotic power, and had the means of subjecting his prisoners to painful suffering. Even so late as 1818, when Mr. Gurney visited the prisons in Scotland, his account of what he observed is almost incredible.

Our burgh records contain but few notices of the prison discipline in the old tolbooths of Glasgow; but one curious incident may be quoted which illustrates the relations subsisting between the jailers and their prisoners. In the year 1666 an individual called "Johne Rowat mer- "chand," held the office of jailer of the Tolbooth at the Cross, and one of his prisoners—committed for what cause is not stated—was "the Laird of Branshoyle." John had some dispute with his prisoner, which he ended by putting him in irons. Possibly the laird deserved it, but he had friends who brought the matter before the magistrates, and the jailer lost his place. He applied to be reponed, and his supplication and apology is recorded in the council minutes. After stating his appointment to the office of "keiper to their Lord- "ships tolbuith quhilk he hes attendit theis divers yeares bygane," it proceeds thus: "And laitlie ane of the prisoners therein, the Laird " of Branshoyle, haveing far excceded the bounds of ane prisoner " towards the supplicant, his keiper, trew it is that in ane passioune " the supplicant did exceid his power and commissioune, in laying " him in the irones, for the quhilk he is very sore grieved from the " bottom of his heart, albeit he was heighlie provocked therto: And " trewlie he dar say that he hes dearlie payit for it, for with the anger " he took at that tyme he hes never sensyne bein quyt of ane most " cruell collick and gravell, quhairby he was very lyklie to have lost " his lyfe and is not ʒit fullie quyt of it." He then acknowledges the justice of his dismissal, and craves the council "to pitie him at " this tyme seing their Lordships know he hes lived honestlie heirto- " foir, and come of honest and ancient parents within this burgh, besyde " that he is awand fyfe thowsand marks and hes the burdone of four " motherless childerin; and that your Lordships wald be pleased to " readmitt the supplicant againe to his charge, and be the grace of " God the lyk should never be sein in him againe."[1] He was reponed,

[1] Burgh Records, 2d October, 1666.

but he lost his place again soon afterwards for allowing a prisoner to escape.

The jailers in those days received no salary. They appear to have been remunerated by fees derived from the fines imposed upon prisoners of the class who could afford to pay, and in earlier times there were doubtless many such; but when only those of the baser sort, or those in absolute poverty came under their care, their emoluments must have been very small. A keeper of the Glasgow jail who had suffered from this cause applied to the town council in 1661, and there is a minute by which the treasurer is ordained "to pay to Charles M'Cleane " Jylor twentie punds for his extraordinarie paines in attending the " tolbuith this long tyme bygane *haveing got no profeit therby, having* " *only thiefes and lounes his prisoners.*" Witches being an exceptional class a special allowance was made for them. On one occasion the jailer gets "four score two pounds fourteen shillings four pennies Scots " money, depensed be him for the maintenance of the witches who " are prisoners here in the tolbuith be order of the Commissioners, from " the 22d of May last to this day."[1] And on a subsequent occasion " Alexander Cunningham servitor to the jayler" is allowed sixty-six pounds eight shillings Scots as "expenses in maintaining witches and " warlocks in the Tolbuith imprisoned by order of the Commissioners " of Justiciarie at Paisley."[2]

Our prisons now are in a very different state from what they were in the old times, and prisoners are treated after a different fashion; but it is questionable whether we have not gone too far in the opposite direction. A recent report presented to parliament on the subject of prisons tells us that now " the prisoner appears to feel that the prayer " for daily bread is rendered unnecessary by the solicitude of his cus- " todians; that nestling comfortably in his hammock he lives less rapidly " than before, and that he finds, in many instances, a peace and repose " to which as a law-abiding citizen he was perchance a stranger." We may quite accept the conclusion of the commissioners, that they have " abundant reason to think that, as a rule, imprisonment, as now " conducted, inflicts no injury, and that in a large proportion of cases " its punitive character is but little felt."[3]

---

[1] 4th September, 1697.　　　　　　　　[2] 12th March, 1698.

[3] Report by Mr. Briscoe, Inspector of Prisons, and other Commissioners, presented to Parliament, Session 1878.

Besides the old Tolbooth at the Cross there was a prison in the upper part of the town, which appears to have become necessary in consequence of the insecure condition into which the building at the foot of the High Street had fallen. This upper prison is mentioned in the burgh records in 1574 as "the heicht tolbuyth," and it was probably a very wretched and uncomfortable place. In the year 1605 there occurs an entry regarding a debtor imprisoned there, whose brother had procured ("purchest") his removal "out of ward of the heich hows "to the laiche tolbuithe," but the brother—probably in consequence of the insecurity of the lower prison—was obliged first to find caution that the debtor "sall remaine in waird in the laiche tolbuithe" until he has satisfied the debt for which he was incarcerated. After the Reformation the magistrates acquired the building on the south side of the Drygate, which had been occupied as a manse by the prebendary of Cambuslang, and fitted it up as a house of correction for vagrants and women of dissolute character. This building having also become unfit for the purpose, the magistrates, in 1792, obtained a lease from the College of a part of their property adjoining the old meal market in the High Street, and used it as a bridewell, but this was discontinued on the erection of the prison in Duke Street.[1]

At the foot of the High Street stood the city cross—the one erected after the ancient cross at the head of the street was superseded. Of what form it was there is no authentic record. At the beginning of the seventeenth century—perhaps earlier—the guard-house was built against or round it, and when the guard-house was in 1659 removed farther west—having been found an obstruction to the street—the cross was found to have been so defaced that it was thought necessary to remove it also. The minute of council which records this is interesting: "The same day [1st October, 1659] the Magistrats and Counsall "having receavit warrand and ordours for downe taking of the guard "house was buildit about and wpon the Croce, and in regard the "samyn Mercat croce throw the building of the said guard house thair- "upon, was altogether defaced, it is therefore now concludid to remove "the samyn with all convenient diligence and mak it equall with the "ground."

In each of the four streets that branched from the cross there were arcades or piazzas. Defoe, referring to these, says: "The lower

[1] Cleland's Statistical Tables, 3d edit. p. 97.

" stories for the most part stand on vast square doric columns with
" arches which open into the shops adding to the strength as well as
" the beauty of the building." But it was probably true of them
what Pennant said, that they were "too narrow to be of much service to
" walkers."[1]

The beautiful street which now stretches westward from the Cross
was in old times a country road leading to two chapels—one dedicated to St. Thomas of Canterbury and the other to St. Tanew or
Thenew, the mother of Kentigern, who, according to the Aberdeen Breviary, was buried there. In a deed in 1498 mention is made of " the
" chapel where the bones of the beloved Thenew mother of the blessed
" confessor Kentigern rest now in the city of Glasgow." It was surrounded by a burial-ground, now the site of St. Enoch's Square.
When M'Ure wrote his history in 1736 the remains of this old chapel
were still to be seen—a solitary spot in the country, surrounded by
cornfields. There appears to have been property in the High Street
held in connection with this chapel, as in a charter in 1419 a tenement in that street is described as lying between the tenement of
Stephanus de Pollok "et terram Sancte Tanew."[2] The name became subsequently corrupted to St. Enoch.

Not far from the present church, and near where the old chapel
had stood, there was a sacred well dedicated to St. Tanew, or Thenew,
which, before the Reformation, was much resorted to for cures. In 1586
James VI. addressed a letter to Mr. Andro Hay, commissioner for the
west country, in which, among other things, he condemned the practice
of people making pilgrimages to such chapels and wells; but I have little
doubt that for some time after that St. Tanew's well was resorted to. It
was shaded by an old tree which drooped over the well, and which remained till the end of the last century. On this tree the devotees who
frequented the well were accustomed to nail, as thank-offerings, small
bits of tin-iron—probably manufactured for that purpose by a craftsman
in the neighbourhood—representing the parts of the body supposed to
have been cured by the virtues of the sacred spring—such as eyes, hands,
feet, ears, and others—a practice still common in Roman Catholic
countries. The late Mr. Robert Hart told me that he had been informed
by an old man, a Mr. Thomson, who had resided in the neighbourhood,
that, at the end of the last century or the beginning of the present, he

---

[1] Tour in Scotland, 1771, p. 200.　　　　　　[2] Lib. Coll. N. D. p. 240.

recollected this well being cleaned out, and of seeing picked out from among the débris at the bottom several of these old votive offerings, which had dropped into it from the tree, the stump of which was at that time still standing.

The road or street leading to St. Tanew's chapel and well is in a charter of 1426 called the "magnus vicus extendens a cruce fore versus "Capellas Sancte Thomæ marteris et sancte Tanew."[1] In a later charter (1487) it is called "vicus Sancte Thanew,"[2] and in a still later deed (1548) it is called "the gait passing fra the west port to sanct Tenewis "chappil."[3] By the year 1520 this road or street had come to be spanned, at a point not quite half-way between the Cross and St. Thenew's Chapel, by the gate called the West Port.[4] The privilege of having "a free "Tron" in the city and barony of Glasgow had been granted to the bishops by James IV. in 1489, and the portion of the street lying within the port acquired the name of "the Troyngate," from the place of weighing being there. The outer portion, west of the port, obtained, about two centuries later, the name first of West Street and then of Argyll Street.

For a long time there must have been few houses in the Trongate, and most of these had gardens and fields behind them. In the charter of 1426 just referred to, the granter, Malcom Lytstare, burgess of Glasgow, sells to John Stewart, sub-dean of Glasgow, a tenement on the north side of this street or road, with the garden adjacent on the north. In 1505 there is a deed in which mention is made of "a garden with "pertinents" *in commune via sancti Tenew,*[5] and there are many other deeds of still later date in which mention is made of houses in the Trongate with gardens and orchards attached to them.

On the south side of the Trongate, on the site now occupied by the Tron Church, stood the collegiate "Church of the Blessed Virgin Mary "and St. Ann"—called in some of the old writs "our Lady College," and afterwards the Church of St. Mary. Mr. Robertson says that the erection and endowment were completed in 1549. The endowment may not have been completed till then, but the church must have been erected before 1528, as in a charter of that year of lands adjoining, mention is made, "nove ecclesiæ beatarum Marie virginis et Anne matris ejus."[6] There could have been no houses near it then, as it was surrounded by

---

[1] Lib. Coll. N. D. p. 244.   [2] Munimenta Universitatis Glasg. vol. i. p. 35.
[3] Munimenta, p. 248.   [4] Ibid. p. 73.   [5] Lib. Coll. N. D. p. 258.   [6] Ibid. p. 90.

a large burying-ground. After the Reformation the market for grass and straw was, by a minute of the town council in 1577, appointed to be held in this burying-ground—called in the minute "the New Kirk "yarde." It was required that one of the prebendaries of this church of St. Mary should be expert in playing the organ, and that he should perform on it daily according to the use and wont of the metropolitan church. He was also required to keep a school for the instruction of youth "in plain song and descant." This school stood in the Trongate, on the west side of the Collegiate Church, and is mentioned in the burgh records as "the scuile sumtyme callit the sang scuile." In 1575 there is an entry in the burgh accounts of a payment "to Thomas Craige of the "New Kirk scule for straye to the mending thairof and for onputyng of "the samyn xxij *s.*" (1*s.* 10*d.*), from which it appears that, like most of the other buildings in the city, it was thatched. Neither the "sang scule" nor the churchyard, nor any other portion of the collegiate property, ever belonged to the corporation. They held it in trust only for the benefit and endowment of the Tron Church, but they disposed of it nevertheless in 1588, along with some properties belonging to the corporation, at a time when they were greatly pressed for funds.[1]

Behind the Collegiate Church, within an open area, and on the site of what is now the presbytery house, stood the old manse of St. Mary's. It fronted the south, with its back to the church. It was a narrow two-story building, rough-cast, with a steep roof and crow steps on the gables. It had five windows in front, three in the upper flat, and one on each side of the door, which was above the level of the ground, and was approached by two or three steps. Around the house was a garden inclosed by a hedge. This old manse remained till the middle of the present century.

"Our Lady College" was founded by James Houston, sub-dean of Glasgow, in the early part of the sixteenth century. The provision made for the services embraced a provost, eight canons or prebendaries, and three chaunters. The number of the prebendaries was increased by subsequent benefactors. All the prebends were endowed, partly from lands and houses within or near Glasgow, and partly from the fruits of the parish churches of Dalry and Maybole. After the Reformation the revenues within the city were appropriated by the magistrates, but the prebendaries were allowed to draw their stipends until they died out.

---

[1] Burgh Records, 24th Dec. 1588.

Even subsequent to the Reformation, however, the church received (in 1650) an endowment of some value by a deed granted by the magistrates, with consent of the Stewarts of Minto, "for the use and profeit of their "two ministers serving the cure at the New Kirk [the Tron] as part of "their stepend." What has come of this endowment I do not know, but certainly it cannot be said of this church, whatever may be the case as to

the others in the city, that the support of its ministers has come exclu- sively from "the common good."

The Trongate has undergone many changes. The above view is from a drawing made in 1845.

Early in the fourteenth century the formation of the Gallowgate must have been commenced, as in the charter of 1325 already referred to mention is made of a tenement "in vico qui dicitur le Galogate." In other charters it is variously called *via furcarum; vicus furcarum juxta torrentem Malyndoner;* and *via furcarum tendens a cruce forali ad orientem portam.*

On the site now occupied by the old Saracen's-Head Inn, and just outside the City Port, stood the chapel called Little St. Mungo's, surrounded by a burying-ground. It was founded some time before 1500 by David Cunningham, archdeacon of Argyll. In a deed granted by him in that year, endowing the chapel, he describes it as "unam capel-"lianam cum capellano extra muros civitatis Glasguensis in communi "via furcarum extra torrentem de Malindoner et prope arbores vocatas "Sancti Kentigerni."[1] By *extra muros* the granter meant beyond the city gate. The churchyard was surrounded by trees. After the Reformation it became the property of Donald Cunningham of Aikenbar and Marion Lyon, his wife, from whom it was purchased by the magistrates in 1593 at the price of 200 merks—£13, 6s. 8d. according to the value of Scots money at that time—on the condition that the "chapell, hous, "and ʒaird" were to be maintained as an hospital for the poor. The magistrates did convert it into an hospital for lepers, and for some time maintained it as such; but, in breach of their trust, they conveyed it about the middle of last century to Robert Tennent, for the purpose of his building on it a hotel of the better class, which he did. This was the Saracen's Head.

Even so late as 1736, when M'Ure wrote his history, the Gallowgate extended no farther than the East Port. Beyond that was only a narrow country road, chiefly between hedges, leading to the old village of Camlachie. Between that port and the Cross, and not far from the old chapel, the street was crossed by the Molendinar Burn. Like St. Enoch's Burn, it crossed on the surface, and there was a considerable descent to it on each side, with stepping-stones in the stream for foot passengers. When it was swollen by rains people had to cross in carts or on horseback. The burn was a favourite place for watering horses and cattle, and Dr. Buchanan, writing in 1856, says he had conversed with old people who remembered it in that state.[2] Now a foul underground sewer, it was then a clear limpid stream. In the *Glasgow Courant* for 1755 there is an advertisement of a piece of ground at the Spoutmouth to be let, and one of the inducements held out to a tenant is its vicinity to the Molendinar as suitable for bleaching.

Beside the "trees of St. Kentigern" mentioned in the foundation charter of Little St. Mungo's Church, there was near the same place a well, called St. Mungo's Well—*Fons Kentigerni.* Like many of the old saints Kentigern is said to have had his bed, his bath, and his chair. The bed, Jocelin tells us, was hollowed out of the rock. He bathed

---

[1] Regist. Episc. Glasg. p. 501. [2] Desultory Sketches, p. 664.

in the Molendinar, and his seat, according to an ancient tradition, was *super lapidem in supercilio montis vocabulo Gwleth.* Gwleth, forming in combination Wleth, signifies *dew,* and hence, it has been said, the hill was called the Dew Hill, corrupted afterwards into the present name of Dow Hill. In a charter in 1581 it is called "Dowhill alias "Gersumland."[1]

The Gallowgate ended in a common called the Gallowmuir. The place of execution was there, and till near the end of last century the gallows—which gave their names to the street and the muir—was still standing. It was on the north-west end of the common, near the upper corner of what is now Barrack Street.

A continuation of the High Street, leading to the South Port or "Nether Barras yett," was inhabited chiefly by fullers and dyers, and from them it was called the "Walcargate"—in the old charters *via Fullonum*—a name which about the middle of the sixteenth century was superseded by that of Saltmarket.

In its earliest history—apart from its ecclesiastical position—Glasgow was only known as a salmon-fishing village, and the Clyde as a prolific salmon river. From the earliest times, accordingly, salmon-fishing was a valuable right; it formed a staple branch of trade, and the earliest of our records contain grants of rights of fishing conveyed along with houses in the burgh. In the charter by the master of the Temple already referred to (1180) there is conveyed along with the "toft" *unum rete in piscatione de Clud.* Down to a comparatively recent period, indeed, salmon-fishing continued to be one of Glasgow's most important industries. There are those still living who recollect the huts of the fishermen on the banks of the river. I recollect one of these within what is now the harbour of Glasgow, and I have seen the fishermen drawing their nets on green banks where there are now wharves and deep water. There was another hut close to the village of Govan, of which I am able to give a view on the following page, from an original drawing made about the year 1815. The quantities of salmon taken were sometimes very great, and the price of the fish was small. In 1748, when there had been a very plentiful supply, the *Glasgow Journal* of 18th July in that year announced that salmon was to be sold in the Glasgow Market at a penny the pound. In the early acts of parliament relating to the deepening of the river the rights of fishing were

[1] Reg. Epis. Glasg. p. 588.

carefully protected, but before long all protection had to be abandoned, and salmon-fishing in the Clyde above Dunbarton is now a thing of the past. The fishing rights of Renfrew were very extensive, and the Clyde

Trustees still pay upwards of £200 a year to that burgh as compensation for the loss caused by their operations.

Detached at first from the rest of Glasgow, and probably of a date as old as, or older than, most of the houses in the city, was a row composed of the huts or houses of the salmon-fishers. In a charter so early as 1285 it is called the *vicus pischatorum de prope pontem de Clud*[1]— a description which proves what I have already stated, that there was a bridge at this place anterior to the one erected by Bishop Rae. Afterwards this row is called "the Fyschergate," and Mr. Cosmo Innes suggests that it is to be identified with the present Bridgegate.[2] But it is not so. The Fishergate occupied what is now the lower end of Stockwell Street, that name having, in the early part of the sixteenth century,

[1] Reg. de Passelet. p. 400.   [2] Orig. Parochiales. vol. i. p. 14.

been adopted from a well, called the "Stok Well," which had for many years stood in the Fishergate. In a deed of sale in 1487 a tenement is described as lying *in vico Piscatorum juxta le Stok well;* and it is stated to be bounded by a certain tenement on the south, and by another tenement on the north—a description which could not be applicable to a building in the Bridgegate, which runs east and west. But the matter is put beyond doubt by two instruments in the recently published Book of Protocols, both of the same date—9th November, 1512—in one of which a tenement is described as situated in "le Fischaregait," and in the other the same tenement is described as lying "apud Stokwell"— showing that at that time the street was known by both names.[1]

For reasons to be afterwards stated it is not unlikely that the south end of the Fishergate was near to what was at that time the margin of the river.

By the end of the fifteenth century the fishermen had come to possess better houses, some of them with gardens attached. In a charter of 1487 mention is made of a tenement and garden belonging to John Leiche, fisherman, in the street leading to the bridge of Glasgow. They formed very much, no doubt, a community by themselves, and at an early period the magistrates established a court, which was held at the Broomielaw, called the Coble Court, which took cognizance of disputes among the fishermen, and of other matters relating to the river. Under date 21st April, 1589, is a minute of "the Coble court of Glasgw halden "at y Brumelaw thairof be honorabill men James Flemyng and Robert "Rowat baillees—Dempster Johnne Maxvell." On this occasion Niniane Hucheson, a fisherman, is decerned to pay to John Clarke, another fisherman, nineteen shillings as the price of "twa salmound fische," which he had taken from him "in a wrangous and maisterfull way." According to the value of money at that time this was equal to one shilling for each salmon.

The bridge which came in place of the one mentioned in the charter of 1285 was erected, as I have said, by Bishop Rae in the year 1350. It was only twelve feet wide, and, till altered in 1776, it had a very steep ascent to its centre. The late Mr. Reid (Senex) says he recollects having crossed it when it was still in that state. Before that time it had become very insecure, and carts and carriages, Mr. Reid says, generally crossed the river at a shallow ford immediately above the

---

[1] Liber Procollorum, Nos. 595, 596.

bridge.[1] So unsafe, indeed, was it, even a century before this, that the tacksman of the bridge was ordered by the magistrates "not to "suffer any cairtis with wheilleis goe alongst the brig vntill that the "wheilleis be taken off and the boddie of the cairt alone harled by "the hors."[2] In 1765 the magistrates endeavoured to close the bridge altogether against carts. This was resisted by some of the inhabitants of Rutherglen, and led to the bridge being widened and repaired.

For a long time the Fishergate, or Stock Well Street, was quite a rural locality. It was on the western extremity of the city, and the houses, many of which were quaint buildings with thatched roofs, were shaded by trees, and those on the west side had also gardens, with the open country behind them.

Till a comparatively recent period there were no streets in Glasgow besides those which I have named, and the population was very small. In the end of the sixteenth century (1581) the Confession of Faith was signed in Glasgow, at the same time as the rest of Scotland, and as the obligation to sign was stringent the probability is that among the Protestant part of the population, at least, the signature was very general, yet the Confession received only 2250 signatures. The subscription books were carried from house to house by the elders, and as it is recorded that all the names were got in High Street, Gallowgate, Trongate, Saltmarket, Bridgegate, and Stockwell, it may be inferred that these, with the Rottenrow and Drygate, comprised at that time the whole town. That no names were got in the two streets last named may be accounted for by the fact that it was there that the ecclesiastics and their dependants, the adherents of the old faith, resided. Among the earliest houses of importance in the city were the manses of the thirty-two canons of the Cathedral, already referred to, with their gardens and orchards, as arranged by Bishop Cameron about the middle of the fifteenth century. These, with the residences of the choral vicars and the officers of the Cathedral, were situated in the Rottenrow and Drygate and in the extreme upper end of the High Street, and down to the time of the Reformation they formed the centre of the city. It is not probable, therefore, that in this ecclesiastical region, under the shadow of the Cathedral, the elders would obtain any signature to the Confession of Faith that could possibly be evaded.

---

[1] Glasgow Past and Present, vol. iii. p. 540.   [2] Council Records, 18th Sept. 1658.

To say that the Confession received 2250 signatures does not by any means imply that so many of the adult population could write. A certain number would adhibit their own names, and those of the rest would be adhibited for them by some one—probably the session-clerk—having their authority to do so. This was done in all the parishes of Scotland when the Solemn League and Covenant was signed.

Even so late as 1708, after the Union, the population of Glasgow was under 13,000. In the first year of the present century, when a census was taken, it had increased to only 83,000.

Of the wonderful growth of the city after this time I must confine myself to a general notice. Much of the story has been well told in the attractive pages of Mr. Reid ("Senex") and of the late Dr. John Buchanan.

There continued to be gardens behind the houses in the Trongate till near the close of the last century. In the *Glasgow Journal* of 16th January, 1766, there is an advertisement of the sale "in whole or "in parcels of the garden at the head of William Anderson's tenement "and close of houses in Trongate;" and in 1789, in the *Glasgow Mercury*, the sale is announced of a garden "lying on the north side "of the Trongate Street, on the west side of the Candleriggs Street "and on the south side of Ingram Street, with an entry of 30 feet "wide from the Candleriggs into the said garden." Through this garden Brunswick Street was subsequently formed. In the same year (1789), Mr. Reid tells us "the whole of the Deanside brae was "vacant ground. The Deanside or Meadow well was situated on "a meadow at the west end of Greyfriars' or Buns Wynd, close to "a footpath leading up to the Rottenrow. It is now on the street "at 88 George Street, opposite the lane leading into Shuttle Street. "This well was then a rural spot—the whole lands on the west as "far as Partick being garden grounds and cornfields." In 1780 an advertisement in one of the local papers announces "summer quarters to "be let at the west end of Rottenrow, in the common gardens."

The Candleriggs was opened as a street in 1724, but for a long time there were few buildings in it. At first it was called the New Street, and it bears that name in M'Ure's History. At the corner of Candleriggs and Bell's Wynd was the Wester Sugar-house, among the first, if not the very first sugar manufactory erected in Scotland. It was established in 1667 by four merchants in Glasgow. Sugar was then a scarce luxury,

K

and it is only within a period comparatively recent that tea and coffee and potatoes came into use amongst us.[1]   M·Ure, referring to this Wester Sugar-house, says that "having got a little apartment for boiling "sugar, and a Dutchman as master boiler, the undertaking proved very "effectual, and their endeavours were wonderfully successful."   They

afterwards left this "little apartment" and erected a larger building. Other sugar-works were afterwards established, but for a long time they were all on a comparatively small scale.

So late as 1750 the head of the Stockwell, where the Trongate ended, was the western extremity of Glasgow—the old West Port marking the boundary.   Outside of this gate a market for the sale of cattle was held on the open road.   On the south side of the street adjoining what be-came Dunlop Street was a malt kiln and barn, and on the opposite side —near what was afterwards Virginia Street—was a small thatched

---

[1] Potatoes were first introduced into the Stewartry of Kirkcudbright in 1725.—Mr. Maxwell of Munches, quoted in Murray's Lit. Hist. of Galloway, p. 337.

hostelry for drovers. To the west of this was a farm-house, standing back from the highway, flanked by byres or outhouses, the gables of which projected to the road. In front of this house the cows were milked, and Dr. Buchanan, writing in 1851, says: "People are yet alive "who have witnessed this scene."[1] A few malt kilns or barns, with a one-storey thatched house here and there, occurred along the road, which was then called St. Tennoch's gate or the Dumbarton Road. The last to disappear of these old buildings was a thatched malt barn and kiln, which stood back from the roadway at the foot of Mitchell Street. It was taken down about the year 1830. The view of it on p. 146 is from a drawing made, I believe, about the year 1820. For a long time the only opening from the main road was the Cow Lone, afterwards Queen Street —a lane between old hedges, and an almost impassable quagmire.

The first mansion built in this rural locality was erected by Provost Murdoch on the south side of the road, and nearly opposite the farm-house just mentioned. This mansion afterwards became the Buck's Head Inn. Soon afterwards another house, similar in design, was built by Mr. Dunlop to the east of Provost Murdoch's. This fine old mansion still remains, but much disfigured by being adapted to business purposes. At the time of the erection of these houses the ground to the south was vacant all the way down to the Clyde, and on the other side of the street, towards the north, there were only gardens and cornfields. This was after the middle of last century.[2]

Virginia Street was opened in 1753. At the head of it, on the site now occupied by the Union Bank, stood the splendid mansion of Mr. Buchanan of Mount Vernon, "a Virginia merchant," erected in 1752. At that time, at the place which is now the bottom of the street, there was a small house, with a malt kiln and barn and a "kailyard" behind, and all around were cornfields and vegetable gardens. Miller Street was not opened till 1771. Before that date it formed the garden ground of Mr. Miller, a wealthy maltman. The garden extended back to what is now Ingram Street, and at the south end, facing the Trongate, were Mr. Miller's malt kiln and barns.[3] After the street was laid off no lots were sold for a considerable time—the locality being considered too far out of town! The first steading was sold in 1771, and the price was 4s. 6d. per square yard.[4]

[1] Glasgow Past and Present, vol. ii. p. 190.
[2] Ibid. vol. ii. p. 191.
[3] Ibid. vol. iii. p. 201.
[4] Desultory Sketches, p. 619.

Nelson Street, Brunswick Street, Hutcheson Street, and Glassford Street—at first called Great Glassford Street—were all opened subsequently to that date. Buchanan Street was opened in 1778. It may be interesting to give the advertisement announcing the opening of this street. It is dated April, 1777, and runs thus: "Andrew Buchanan, " merchant, has made improvement on his former plan, and now pro- " poses to take down his house in Argyle Street and to make the entry " to his intended street correspond exactly with opposite the entry lead- " ing into St. Enoch's Square. The lots are laid off 65 feet in front, " with sufficient room backwards for garden plots. The situation is very " pleasant and convenient, and affords a prospect rural and agreeable."

The Back Cow Lane was not converted into Ingram Street till after 1777. In June of that year the north-west portion of the Ramshorn grounds, then lying in grass fields, was offered for sale by the magistrates at the price of 2s. 6d. per square yard. These lands had originally belonged to the church. In a charter by the King, Alexander, in 1241, confirming to the bishop "terras suas circa Glasgu," the lands of "Ramnishoren" are included; and in a subsequent charter in 1494 they are described as "terras domini episcopi Glasguensis que appellantur " Rammyshorne."[1] The dingy old Ramshorn Church, which was erected there in 1720, is described by M'Ure—writing in 1736—as that "stately " and magnificent structure, the North-west Church, lying at the head of " the New Street in a pleasant valley." The church, indeed, when erected was quite out of the town, and surrounded by fields and gardens. When the ground was taken for the building, the tacksmen were paid the sum of £108, 16s. 4d. Scots, about £9, "in full satisfaction to them for loss " and damage by the rooting out of their cherry and apple trees, goose- " berry and curran bushes, kaill, leeks, and other ground herbs."[2]

In 1751 the Broomielaw Croft was chiefly in cornfields, and the portion of it facing the river was covered with the remains of an old wood. So late as the beginning of the present century broom brushes were growing on a rocky elevation at the foot of Robertson Street.[3] What is now Jamaica Street was then an enclosed field. It is described in an advertisement in the *Glasgow Courant* of 3d June, 1751, as "that field " belonging to the Merchants' House beautifully situated between the " Broomielaw on the south, and the West Street [Argyll Street] on the

---

[1] Lib. Coll. N.D. p. 258.   [2] Burgh Records, 13th January, 1719.
[3] Rambling Recollections of Glasgow, by "Nestor," 1879.

" north," and intimation is made that the field is "now planned out in a
" large open street of 45 feet wide, with convenient lots of ground for
" building upon." This was what became Jamaica Street, but with an
increased breadth. The first house built on it was the mansion erected
in 1761 by Mr. George Buchanan, which afterwards became the property
of Mr. Black of Clairmont. Mr. Black occupied it as his winter residence, and went out to Clairmont—now part of the city—to spend the
summer in the country.

The rise in the value of property in this locality has been very remarkable. In 1788, just after Buchanan Street was opened, a lot of
ground fronting the street was sold for *2s. 6d.* the square yard. In 1777
the magistrates resolved to dispose of "the towns building ground" in
Argyll Street and neighbourhood, and by their minute of 24th March in
that year they fixed the prices. They resolved that the ground in the
old green—the "Dowcat green," lying between Jamaica Street and
Stockwell—should be sold at *3s. 6d.* the square yard; that St. Enoch's
Square, the ground in Argyll Street "westward of Mr. Robertsons," and
the west side of Jamaica Street, should all be sold at *4s. 6d.* the square
yard; and that for the steading on the east side of Jamaica Street, "as
" it is a corner steading," the price should be five shillings the square
yard. Within the last few years ground in St. Enoch's Square has been
sold at prices ranging from £20 to £25 the square yard, and one lot was
sold as high as £50 the square yard; while in Argyll Street, near St.
Enoch's Square, the prices have ranged from £50 to £80, and one steading was sold at £100 the square yard. These were the prices paid for
the ground alone, over and above the value of the buildings at the time
of the sales.

By the rapid extension of buildings, what were till quite recently
rural villages have been absorbed into and now form portions of the city.
Anderston, Finnieston, Gorbals, Hutchesontown, Tradeston, Kingston,
and Calton—each till a recent period a detached village—are all now
parts of Glasgow. Anderston acquired its name from a Mr. Anderson,
then proprietor of the lands of Stobcross, who in 1725 formed the plan
of a village on part of these lands; but very few houses, and these of a
mean description, were then erected. At that time what is now Stobcross Street was the avenue to Stobcross House, the entrance to the
avenue being at what came to be known as the "Gushet-house" in
Anderston. The estate on which Anderston was built came into the

market in 1735, when it was bought by Mr. Orr of Barrowfield. At that time the projected village consisted of only a few thatched houses, one of them built of turf. About thirty years afterwards Mr. Orr projected another village farther west, on part of what was then an unproductive farm. This village he named Finnieston, in compliment to a Mr. Finnie, then a tutor in Mr. Orr's family. Such was the beginning of these important suburbs. In 1776 Mr. Orr sold the whole of the Stobcross lands west of Finnieston to Mr. David Watson, merchant in Glasgow. At this time there was nearly a mile of space between the westmost part of Glasgow and the first houses in Anderston. It was still a country road inclosed by hedges, with fields and gardens on both sides, and was then known as Anderston Walk. On the south side of this road, between Anderston and Glasgow, there was a piece of ground, part of the Broomielaw Croft, extending to something more than nine acres. So late as 1791 it consisted of open fields. It had been acquired in 1774 by Brown, Carrick & Co., manufacturers of lawn and cambric, in whose title it is described as a park or enclosure consisting of nine acres, one rood, and ten falls, bounded by the high road leading from Glasgow to Anderston on the north and by the river Clyde on the south; with "the "ground or grass on the water side opposite the said enclosure." The whole price paid for this property, now so valuable, was a ground annual of £46, 12s. 3d. for the field, and 15s. for the water side ground. Brown, Carrick & Co. used the ground as a bleachfield until it began to be built upon, when it became known as the village of Brownfield.[1] It is now in the heart of the city.

The extension of the city on the south side of the river has been equally recent. In the year 1650 Sir George Douglas and his lady sold the lands of Gorbals, with the office of bailiary and justiciary, to the magistrates of Glasgow, in trust for Hutcheson's Hospital to the extent of a half, and for behoof of the "Crafts Hospital," now the Trades' House, to the extent of a fourth, and for the City itself to the extent of the remaining fourth. In 1789 the property was divided among the parties interested, when the Trades' House acquired the portion on the west of the then small village of Gorbals. This portion was called Tradeston. The part which fell to the Hospital was called Hutchesontown. Part of this lot consisted of the portion of a field lying at the south end of Jamaica Street Bridge on which was a wind-mill. It

---

[1] Brown's History of Glasgow, vol. ii. p. 113.

is incidentally alluded to in the Presbytery records as early as 1599, in which year proceedings are mentioned against "Andro Nicolson miller "in yᵉ vindmylne on gorballis besyde Glasgow." The wind-mill was still standing in the beginning of the present century, and from it the field acquired the name of the Windmillcroft. In the paper from which I have taken some of these particulars—one of the pleadings in an action in the Court of Session between the magistrates and Mr. Galloway, a brewer, as to certain duties on ale and beer levied in Gorbals—it is added, " The Hospital having feued this ground for building there is now (1805) "erected upon it a village called Laurieston, including some elegant "buildings called Carlton Place. The other part of the Windmillcroft, "that upon the west side of Broad Street, now called Bridge Street, was "allocated to the Trades' House, and upon it has since been built the "populous village of Tradestown. The remaining part of Windmillcroft "was allocated to the town of Glasgow, and since the commencement of "this action a part of it has been feued out for the erection of another "village, under the name of Kingstown. The whole of these newly "erected villages, Hutchesontown, Lauriestown, Tradestown, and the "proposed new village of Kingstown, are situated without the bounds of "the parish of Gorbals."

Gorbals formed part of the barony of Blythswood, and was part of what was called "the six pound land of Gorbals and Bridgend." In the beginning of the seventeenth century the village of Gorbals was called Bridgend, and it consisted of only a few houses at the south end of the old bridge of Glasgow. In a charter by Charles II. in 1661 reference is made to "the lands of Gorbals and the town of Bridgend." It was afterwards erected into a separate barony. In 1607 the Archbishop of Glasgow granted to Sir George Elphinston a charter in feu farm of the barony of Blythswood, comprehending Gorbals and Bridgend, with the office of heritable bailie and justiciary, and power to hold courts. The charter declares that the inhabitants "shall have power of carrying on "merchandise and manufactures of all kinds, in the same way as any "other free burgh of barony." The inhabitants were thus formed into a community, and they held a tenement of land in the village, which was called "the community land." The barony was afterwards acquired by Sir George Douglas of Blackstone. All these villages now form part of Glasgow, and the site of the wind-mill is now deep water near the centre of the river, a little below the bridge.[1]

[1] *Glasgow and its Environs,* p. 47.

THE CITY PORTS AND MILITARY DEFENCES.

Although in some of the old charters properties are described as *intra muros civitatis Glasguensis*, it is certain that at no time was Glasgow a walled town. The expression "intra muros" meant simply within the ports or gates. Eneo Silvio describes the towns in Scotland in the fifteenth century as all unwalled; and John Major, who taught for some years in the University of Glasgow, writing in 1521, speaks of Perth as being the only properly walled town in the kingdom. Our burgh records afford sufficient evidence, that as regards Glasgow, at any rate, while there were several ports, there were no walls. At a time when pestilences prevailed in Paisley and elsewhere, there are repeated entries enjoining that the ports be kept secure. But behind the houses which formed the boundary of the city there appear to have been only back yards and gardens, separating them from the open country beyond, and we find repeated orders enjoining the inhabitants to keep their back premises sufficiently fenced, so as to prevent any one entering the city except by the gates or ports.

By an old ordinance "twa honest men of the town" were appointed to take charge in turn of each of the ports. This fell into desuetude, and the order was renewed in 1588, on the occasion of a pestilence breaking out in Paisley.

In 1574 there is an entry in the council records ordering "the four "ports to be kept daylie continewalie, and at ewin the portaris to deliver "the keyes to ane of the baillies." And again, "Ordains the Rattonraw, "Drygate, and Grayefriar portis to be made sure and lokit, and stand "lokit, and keyis thairof deliverit to the baillies, and nane to repair "thairthroucht without the special license of the provest and baillies."[1] An unlucky wight who disregarded this injunction is thus dealt with a few weeks after the date of the order: "Robert Thomsone is fund in the "wrang and amerciament of Court for the lifting of the myd tre of the "Port beside the Castelyett, it being lockit, and the porter at his denner, "at his awin hand, and entering thairat, it being lockit, and dwme gevin "thairupoune."[2] As regards other inclosures for the protection of the city, these are dealt with by ordinances such as this:—"31 October, 1588.

---

[1] 29th October, 1574.　　　　　　[2] 30th November, 1574.

" It is statut that everie persone repair and hauld clois thair yairds endis
" and bak sydis, swa that nane may repair thairthrow to the toun bot be
" the common ports, vnder the pane of fyve pundis to be taiken of ilk
" persone quha contravenis the same."

The Stable Green Port, as already mentioned, was near the wall
surrounding the Castle garden. On the opposite side of the Castle,
across the street called the Wyndhead leading to the Cathedral, was the
Castle Yett Port or Castle Port. A part of the wall connected with this
port remained till near the end of the last century, with an old tower
that formed its termination on the south. This tower was removed to
make way for that unsightly building the Barony Church. Besides a
port at the eastern termination of the Drygate there was another, which
is referred to in a deed in 1410 as "the Subdean port of Glasgow be-
" tween the Gyrtheburn and the street called the Dreggate." The Gallowgate or East Port stood, as already mentioned, immediately to the
west of the Old Saracen's Head Inn. The south end of the barrier or
traversing wall joined the face of an old two-storey thatched house.
The north end rested on an angle of the old churchyard wall of Little
St. Mungo. This port was taken down in 1749.[1] The West Port stood
originally a short distance westward from the cross, near the mouth of
the Old Wynd. Having become ruinous, it was in 1588 ordered to be
transported "to the Stockwalheid."[2] At the foot of the Saltmarket was
a port called in some of the charters the Porta Inferior, and in others
the South Port or Nether Barras Yett. The street leading from it to
the old bridge, now called the Bridgegate, is called in one old writ *via
extra portam Australem que ducit ad Cludam;* and in another, *via que
ducit a Porta Australi ad magnum pontem lapideum trans Cludam.*[3] The
original port was a considerable way back from the river, but in 1644 it
was by a minute of council ordered to be taken down and "buildit of
" new nearer the water." In this minute it is called "the Salt mercat
" port."[4]

Besides these ports others are referred to in the burgh records, and
regulations are also made as to keeping certain closes and vennels closed
by gates at the lower ends, some of them to be locked day and night,
and others to have a wicket by which the inhabitants are to have leave
to pass. The following entry occurs in October, 1588: "It is statut that

[1] Glasgow Past and Present, vol. iii. p. 674.   [2] 28th December, 1588.
[3] Lib. Coll. N. D. pp. 34, 35, 220.   [4] Minutes of Council, 14th Sept. 1644.

" Lindsayis port, the Stinking vennall, and the Grayfrier port to be all
" closit; the Scuile Wynd to be likwayis closit and keepit daylie, as vse
" was, be the maister of the scule; the wickit of the Grayfrier port to be
" patent to the nichtbouris besyd, and they to be ansuarable for the same;
" and the Rottin Raw port to be lockit nicht and day."

In June, 1639, " it is statut and ordanit that ane dyk be buildit at the
" Stockwallheid, and ane port put thairin; and to build ane dyk from
" the lithous [dye-house] to the custome hous, with ane port thairin,
" lykwayes ane betwixt the bridge and Johne Holmis hous, in ane
" cumlie and decent forme."

The dyke last mentioned in this minute was the Water Port. It
had two gates—one between the dye-house and the custom-house, and
the other between the custom-house and the house of John Holms at
the east end of the bridge, near the Bridgegate. The "custome hous"
was a small toll-house at the north-west end of the bridge, at which
were received the dues on goods brought into the city from the south
side of the river.

A view of the Water Port, but probably not a very correct one, is
given in Capt. Slezer's view of the bridge. Its exact position, however,
is shown in an old map or plan made in the year 1760, the accuracy of
which may be the more relied on that it formed a production in a law
suit between the magistrates of the city and Mr. William Fleming, afterwards of Sawmillfield, relative to a saw-mill belonging to the latter. It
shows the small "custome hous" at the north end of the west parapet of
the bridge, with the dykes on each side—one resting on the "lit house"
and the other on the house at the west end of the Bridgegate (see page
155). It shows also that there was then no water under the northmost
arch, and that the bank extended to about the centre of the second arch.
By that time, indeed, the bank was so high and the ground had become
so consolidated that a road passed under one of the arches. This fact
we learn from the deposition of one of the witnesses in Mr. Fleming's
case, who speaks of the slaughter-house as bounded by a road " leading
" from the foot of the Saltmarket Street *through one of the arches of the*
" *bridge* to the Broomielaw."

The Brig Port, which has been frequently confounded with the Water
Port, was of much older standing than the Water Port. It is mentioned
in the burgh records so early as the year 1588, but where it stood or at
what time it was removed I have not been able to ascertain. To

NORTH END OF THE OLD BRIDGE OF GLASGOW

Mr. William Brown, late of Kilmardinny, I am indebted for the annexed most interesting and hitherto unpublished view of the old bridge, taken by his father, Mr. James Brown. The date of the drawing is probably somewhere about the year 1776, by which time the two northmost

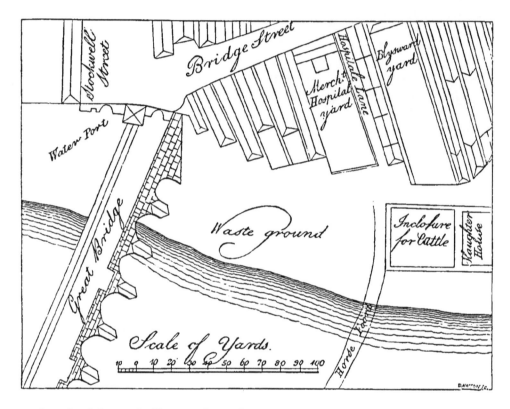

arches had been built up, but the bridge had not yet been repaired and widened.[1]

The illustration is specially interesting as being now printed from the original copperplate etched by Mr. James Brown himself. Whether the port or arch which forms so striking an object in this view is the original Brig Port I do not know. Mr. Brown was an accomplished draughtsman, and the etching may be accepted as a faithful representation of what the old bridge was twenty-five years before the end of the last century.

---

[1] The contract with Shaw, the mason, to widen the bridge was concluded in October, 1775, and as in May, 1778, there is a minute of council as to causewaying the bridge, the work was probably completed in that year.

I have mentioned that before 1776 the bridge had become so insecure that carts and heavy carriages passed the river by a ford. The order by the magistrates was that only "coaches and chaises" should pass by the bridge, and Mr. Brown's drawing is valuable as confirming this. It shows the coaches crossing the bridge and the carts crossing by the ford above. It shows also that there was a ford below the bridge as well as the one above it mentioned by Mr. Reid, and this is confirmed by a minute of the town council (24th November, 1767), which mentions "the foords above and below the bridge of Glasgow."

The only evidence I can find of any attempt to fortify the city was during the civil war, when the magistrates, for the protection of the town, ordered a trench or ditch to be made around it. The first notice of this which appears in the council records is under date 15th November, 1645, where "it is ordainit be the Committee of Estaites that fyve hundrethe
" bollis of meill be advancit for the vse of the people that cumis in to
" help to cast up the trinche about this citie, quhilk is to be payit out of
" som sowmes of monye the Provest is to receave for the vse of the
" publict; and becaus the meill can not be commodiouslie gottine, the
" said Provest Baillies and Counsell hes concludit to pay to everie man
" that cumis in to wirk at the said wark ten schilling scots for the haill
" time they wirk, in satisfaction of the peck of meill ilk man sould have,
" conform to the act and ordinance of the said Committee." In the following year there is an entry showing that the presbyteries in the neighbourhood were required to furnish men for this work: "24 March—
" ordains Jon. Johnston to go to the Presbiterie of Lanerk and get answer
" from them anent ther sending of men, or moneys to hyre men, to work
" at the trinch. As als ordains to wryte to the rest of the Presbiteries
" for ther deficiencie." And on the 9th of May in the same year the council "ordains the haill inhabitants of this burghe to come out ilk
" Mononday of the weik to the works." It is further declared that those who fail shall be "countit disaffectit to the caus in hand, and punishit
" *be the Sub Governour* according to the wull of the Magistrats." And again, on the 8th of August in the same year, "ordains that the Magis-
" trats tack up ane list of the haill horses in the toune, and caus ane
" competent numbir of thame serve weiklie at the trinche."

This trench does not appear to have been completed. The work was renewed at the time of the rebellion of 1715, the projected size of the ditch being twelve feet wide and six feet deep. Barricades were at the same time erected, and there are repeated entries on the subject in the burgh records of that year. Under date 29th October, 1715, there is a minute bearing " that in this tyme of common danger the toun is put to " vast charges and expences in fortyfieing the toun, and many other " wayes which they cannot evite, and that it is the advyce of his Grace " the Duke of Argyll, General and Commander in Chiefe of his Majestys " forces in North Brittan, the toun should be put in a better posture of " defence by drawing lynes of intrinchment about the toun in case of an " attack against it be the rebells and that the same be done with all " expedition;" therefore the treasurer is authorized to contract a loan to the extent of £500 sterling. Then follow numerous entries of payments for barricading the different ports, for barricades " at the Gallowgate and " St. Tennochs burn," for stopping the passage at Buns Wynd, and for wages and tools to the men working on the trenches.

The " lynes of intrinchment," however, if they were ever completed, which is doubtful, must have been of a very imperfect character, and for purposes of defence probably useless. There remains no trace of them now. In the formation of them, so far as they went, a good many gardens attached to the houses appear to have been invaded, for in the burgh accounts of 1715–16 there are repeated charges for the value of " Kaill " plants and Leiks quhilk were destroyed by the Trenches."

As a rule the Scottish people were all trained to arms. An act of James I. (1426), which was passed in a time of perfect peace, enacts that all merchants should import some armour and arms with their cargoes. In Glasgow—encouraged by the bishops and by the men of rank, many of them soldiers, who officiated as provosts—the people were early trained to military habits. Previous to the Union they had their "weapon " schaws." There were "buttis" in the Gallowmuir for "exerceiss when " schutting,"[1] and where for a long time regular drillings were held; and repeatedly the city raised troops and sent them to the field. A detachment of the citizens was led to Flodden by their provost, Mathew, Earl of Lennox, who was slain in that battle. In the reign of Queen Mary the citizens took part with the then Earl of Lennox against the Earl of Arran, afterwards Duke of Chastelherault, and an engagement took place at the Butts in the Gallowgate, near where the infantry barracks were afterwards erected. In this encounter—known as the Battle of the Butts —Lennox was defeated and about three hundred of the citizens were

---

[1] Burgh Records, 21st May, 1623.

slain; and the regent having entered the town gave it up to pillage. So unmercifully was this carried out that the very doors and windows of the houses were pulled down. The citizens had their revenge at the battle of Langside. A considerable body of them were in the army of Murray, and so much satisfied was the regent with their services that he conferred on several of the corporate trades substantial marks of his approval. Some of them had grants, with increased privileges and immunities; and the bakers had a charter for the erection of the well-known mills on the Kelvin, which came to be so valuable a property.

The burgh records contain many notices as to drillings and the raising of armed levies, and of "stents" imposed on the town to meet the expense. In 1589 the magistrates, on the requisition of James VI., raised a company of "fyftie hagbutteris to await on his Majesties service "in the north."[1] A stent was imposed for their support, and it was ordained that "the saidis hagbutteris be gratifeit with the soume of an " hundreth markis by and attour the soume of money sett doune for ane " daily wage to them, being ten shilling to everie ane of thame in the " day during their absence"—more than a shilling a day according to the then value of money—a liberal allowance for those times. The citizens generally had arms, and when occasion called for it the magistrates furnished them with ammunition—for example, in 1609, when a certain sum was "debursit of comand of the baillies for poulder to the " young men of the toun that tyme quhan the Dwik of Wertenbrig came " to this toun."

On a later date "it is ordainit that thair be electit thrie score of " young men apt to be tranit up in handlinge of thair armis and to begin " on Tuisday next; and the dreiller to have for his panes fourtie shillings " (3s. 4d.) ilk day for his cuming out of Edr. till he be dischargit, with his " hors hyre home and a field."[2] This was the year in which Episcopacy was abjured, and in which the famous Assembly was held in Glasgow. In the following year the "provest bailzies and counsell concludit that " thair be sent out ane hundreth men to the border to the common " defence;"[3] and by a subsequent order "all inhabitants within the " toun wha are myndit to carie musquattis are commanded to have " in redines ilk persone twa pund weght of powder, twa pund leid, " and five fadom of match." At the same time fifty additional men are ordered to the Border.

[1] Burgh Records, 12th and 19th April, 1589.   [2] 8th Sept. 1638.   [3] 10th April, 1639.

To meet these several expenses the magistrates, among other re-sources, "ordainit that publicatioune be made throw the toun be sound "of drum that the inhabitants of this burghe bring thair haill silver "plait to be bestowit in defence of the Commoun Cause in hand, con-"forme to the ordinance of the Committee at Edr."[1] And in the following year—which was the year of the meeting of the Long Parlia-ment—the provost "is appoyntit to go to Edinbrughe with the silver "and gold wark, the lint money and the contributions collectit for "the commoun cause."[2] In the same year "a perfyt catallog" was ordered to be made up "of the haill names of the persons within this burgh able for weir," and certain days were fixed for drilling. Three years later, as the troubles thickened, every one capable of bearing arms was called out. In that year—1643—Charles I. issued a proclamation for "putting of this haill kingdome on ane present "postoure of war," and the magistrates of Glasgow ordered that "in "everie ane of the four quarters of the toun everie man be in readi-"ness at all tymes with sufficient armes and that they use and exerce "the same;" and directions are given as to this, and officers appointed.[3] A subsequent order "ordains ane proclamatioune to be sent throw "the toune commanding all maner of persones betwixt sextie and "sextein to be in readiness with thair best armes, and to this effect "to cum out presentlie with their several capitaines, with match, "powder, and leid, and also to provyde themselfs with twentie dayes "provisioune to march according as they sall get ordours under the "paine of death."[4] A series of other warlike orders follow in rapid succession. All the ports are appointed to be guarded during the day as well as at night, and the officers of the burgh are appointed "to weir in tyme cuming everie man his sword and halbert." The "master of works is ordained to send to Holland for "sex scoir "sword blads;" and "eight tun of beir" is ordered to be supplied "for outreiking" a ship of war called "the Kings Eight Whelpe" conform to an order of the Committee of Estates. It was a stirring time, and the affairs of the unhappy king were getting sorely complicated.

It will be recollected that the Committee of Estates in Scotland concluded a secret "engagement" with Charles in the Isle of Wight, by which, in consideration of his undertaking to subscribe the Covenant,

---

[1] 15th June, 1639.
[2] 5th Sept. 1640.
[3] Minute of Council, 2nd October, 1643.
[4] 31st August, 1644.

the Committee agreed to commission an army to aid the king. In pursuance of this engagement the Committee proceeded to levy an army, and Glasgow was called upon to furnish a contingent. But Glasgow did not approve of this questionable alliance with the Cavaliers, and a majority of the magistrates, backed by the kirk-session, refused compliance, alleging as a reason that they were "not satisfied in their con- "sciences concerning the lawfulness and necessity of this present En- "gadgement."[1]   But they suffered severely in consequence. They were thrown into prison, and deprived of their offices. Four regiments of horse and foot were sent to Glasgow, with orders to quarter solely on the disaffected magistrates and council, and on the members of the kirk-session; and so strictly was the order executed that each individual had to find board and lodging for ten, twenty, and in some instances as many as thirty soldiers. The defeat of the Engagers by Cromwell, his visit with his troops to Glasgow, when he lodged in Silvercraig's house in the Saltmarket, his disputes with the clergy, and his interview with Zachary Boyd, the minister of the Barony parish— whose invectives against himself he punished by inviting him to dinner and inflicting on him a prayer of three hours' duration—are incidents well known.

The Restoration brought still more troublous times, and Glasgow again had its share of the suffering. Among other acts of oppression the citizens were disarmed by an order of the Privy Council requiring them to bring in their weapons, accompanied by a warning that " all who neglects to doe the samyn sall be looked upon as dissaffected " to the present government and punished accordinglie."[2]   But the people complained loudly of being deprived of their accustomed arms in times so unsettled, and so great did the outcry become that two years later the magistrates made an attempt to get the arms back. Their minute bears that "taking to their consideratioune the great " danger sundrie of our nighbours may fall in regard of the last pro- " clamatioune emittit anent the inbringing of armes, and that many " of our nighbors and com-burgesses may not now frielie trauell abrodd " as they wont to doe without carieing of some armes, it is therfor " concludit that the Provest sall ryd to Edinbrughe and petitioune " the Lords of his Majesties Privie Counsall for granting liberty to " our honest nighbors for carieing armes when they goe abroad."[3]   It

---

[1] Minute of Council, 23d May, 1648.   [2] Ibid. 22d April, 1665.   [3] 4th May, 1667.

does not appear what success the provost had in his mission. Probably none, for it was well known that the city was at that time far from being well affected to the Stewart dynasty, and the covenanting leanings of so many of the citizens gave great offence. The laws against such were rigidly enforced, and soldiers were quartered on those of the inhabitants who were suspected of having entertained the "outed" ministers, or of frequenting conventicles.[1] The magistrates and principal citizens were also compelled to subscribe a bond "that they their wyfes "bairnes servants and coaters sall not be present at any such conven- "tickles or disorderly meetings, but sall live orderly conforme to the "Acts of Parliament." This bond was subscribed by Provost Campbell, three of the bailies, and the whole council, and by several merchants and tradesmen. The total number who subscribed, however, was only 153. The Privy Council on this occasion sat for some time in Glasgow, and, to the scandal of the citizens, transacted business on Sunday in the forehall of the college during the hours of divine service, while those of the inhabitants who refused to sign were being plundered by the soldiers. Claverhouse chased into the city a number of persons whom he found attending a preaching near Strathaven, and massacred a considerable number of them near the Gallowgate Port. Of the Presbytery of Glasgow fourteen ministers were ejected from their livings. Several persons were hanged in the streets merely because they refused to conform to Episcopacy, and guards were placed at the city ports on the Sabbath mornings to prevent any of the citizens from attending services in the fields. Many of the townspeople were present at Bothwell Bridge, and the minister of the Barony parish, Mr. Donald Cargill, was executed at Edinburgh for complicity in that affair.[2]

On the occasion of the Duke of York coming to Glasgow, Provost Bell, a zealous royalist, announced the fact, and appointed "the haill "counsell to attend vpon the magistrates for waiting on him; that "the handsomest of the younge men of the toune be warined to beir "partizains in their hands to wait vpon him, and ordaines the inhabit- "ants to put out baill fyres at the heid of ilk close at such tymes as "they be warned by ringing of the bells."[3] The magistrates appear to have spared no trouble or expense on this occasion, for we find from a subsequent minute that their outlay amounted to 4001 pounds

[1] Minute of Council, 25th June, 1674. [2] 27th Feb. 1681. [3] 1st Oct. 1681.

L

12 shillings scots, a considerable sum in those days. On this occasion the duke lodged in Provost Bell's house in the Bridgegate.

On the abdication of James II. the city, as might be expected, was not slow to show its Protestant leanings. It raised a regiment of 500 men, and sent them to Edinburgh under the command of the Earl of Argyll. It got the name of the Scotch Cameronians, and became afterwards the 26th Regiment of Foot.

At the outbreak of the rebellion of 1715 the city again raised a regiment of 500 militia, and sent them to the camp at Stirling; and at the same time 300 stand of arms were sent to Glasgow from Edinburgh Castle for the use of the town. Soon afterwards we find the magistrates supplicating the Duke of Argyll "to give orders for removing of the 353 " rebel prisoners who are lying on the touns hands, and in custody in the " Castle prison, and easing the toun of the burden of them and of their " maintenance." The Castle Prison could not have been very secure at that time, as one of the reasons urged for the removal is that "these " prisoners require a guard of about ane hundred men always upon them, " without which they might have opportunity to escape."

In connection with the civil wars there is a curious entry in the burgh records regarding the son of one of the burgesses who had been engaged against the king's troops:—"13 January, 1694: the said day ordaines " the Mr. of Wark to pay to Adam Todd four dollars to help to pay *the* " *cure* of James Todd his son who was *deadlie woundit* at Killicrankie." The four dollars were well expended if the services rendered resulted in the cure of a person in such circumstances.

In 1745 the citizens of Glasgow and their neighbours were very forward in support of the government. About 3000 militia turned out, and from these was organized a regiment of 650 men, under the Earl of Home as their colonel, of which about 500 were Glasgow men, and the remainder chiefly from Paisley. They were marched to Stirling early in December, and were employed to guard the passes of the Forth.[1] In the *Glasgow Courant* of 12th February, 1746, they are mentioned as a regiment which made "a very fine appearance, notwithstanding it had " been raised and marched in nine days." On Friday the 27th of December, 1745, the Prince himself came to Glasgow, and took up his quarters in the fine residence of Mr. Glassford, afterwards removed to make way for Glassford Street. Writing to Mr. Maule the secretary of the Duke

---

[1] Cochrane Papers, Maitland Club, p. 117.

of Argyll, Provost Cochrane says, "On friday the clans with the Prince
" came to the town. They attempted to huzza two or three times as he
" went to his lodgings, but fell through it, our mob with great steadiness
" declining to join in it. Our people of fashion kept out of the way; few
" or none at the windows; no ringing of bells, and no acclamation of
" any kind. He appeared four times publickly in our streets, twice in
" all his mock majesty, going and coming from a review at our green,
" without the least respect or acknowledgment paid by the meanest
" inhabitant. Our ladies had not the curiosity to go near him, and
" declined going to a ball held by his chiefs."[1] One exception to this
was the notorious Miss Walkinshaw. Of a good family, which was
ruined by its adherence to the Stewarts, she became fascinated with the
Prince, and, regardless of her reputation, she accompanied him abroad
and lived with him there. She is said to have been handsome, but she
had no elegance of manners, and like himself she became a drunkard.
They often quarrelled, and sometimes fought.[2]

Dr. Thom, of Liverpool, writing in 1851, supplies an interesting
reminiscence of the unfortunate Prince in Glasgow. "Well do I recol-
" lect," he says, "Mr. William Walker, who died I think in 1820, taking
" me in 1815 to a spot in the Saltmarket two or three doors from my
" father's shop, and mentioning that under the then piazza, close to where
" we were, he had stood and seen the rebel army pass up from the review
" on the Green. The Pretender rode at their head. He was pale, and,
" in Mr. Walker's apprehension, looked dejected. He said he had a
" distinct recollection of 'Bonnie Prince Charlie' after the lapse of seventy
" years. He saw the rebel forces, when they had reached the Cross, turn
" to the left and march along the Trongate on their way to Shawfield
" House, at the bottom of the present Glassford Street, then the residence
" and head-quarters of the Chevalier."[3]

The want of all sympathy on the part of the citizens of Glasgow, and
the marked keeping aloof of the ladies, is said by Provost Cochrane to
have "fretted" the Prince—not the less so that, as Gib, who acted as
steward of his household, mentions, he dressed more elegantly when in
Glasgow "than he did in any other place whatsomever."[4] On the occasion of this visit of the rebel army, Glasgow was subjected in a contribution amounting in value to £10,000, which was subsequently repaid by
the government.

[1] Cochrane Papers, p. 66. [2] Ibid. p. 113. [3] Glasgow Past and Present, i. 198. [4] Coch. Papers, p. 110.

EARLY STATE OF THE LAND NEAR GLASGOW.

To pass to another interesting subject of inquiry regarding ancient Glasgow—the state of the country around the infant city. There can be no doubt that for a period long after the restoration of the see by David, the land around Glasgow, except that near the river, was waste muir, with probably a considerable amount of wood and bush land. A large district lying to the north and west was called the Bishop's Forest, but that name did not necessarily imply that it was all in wood. The term was frequently applied, as it still is, to ranges of land set apart and having privileges for the preservation of game; and there is evidence that in early times the southern division, at least, of Scotland was not by any means a well-wooded country.[1] The Bishop's Forest, whatever it consisted of, was of considerable extent, and certainly in some parts it was covered with wood. Probably also it abounded in wild animals. One of the legends told by the monk of Furness is that there being no men to plough the land, St. Kentigern commanded two deer which he saw on the edge of the wood to yoke themselves to the plough. They obeyed, and continued daily to perform their task. But on one occasion a wolf came out of the wood and attacked and devoured one of the deer, whereupon the saint commanded the wolf to take the stag's place in the plough. "This he did with great humility, and, yoked with the other stag, "ploughed up nine acres, whereupon the saint freely allowed him to "depart."[2] Whatever credence we give to the story, we may accept it as a memorial of the fact that in ancient times the Bishop's Forest was infested by wolves. Bishop Jocelin, indeed, to whom the monk's work was dedicated, might well accept the story of the wolf, for in his own time (1176) wolves abounded in the neighbourhood of his old monastery of Melrose; and in the following century (1225) there is an act of the Scottish Parliament empowering the monks of Melrose to set snares for wolves in Eskdale. Wolves, indeed, continued to infest the forests of Scotland till nearly the middle of the eighteenth century. The last was killed in Morayshire in 1743. Like the other old Caledonian forests, the Bishop's Forest at Glasgow contained also wild cattle, including the

---

[1] Sketches of Early Scottish History, p. 101.　　　　[2] Life by Jocelin, c. xix.

white species, of which remains are still preserved in the ducal domains at Hamilton; and by some accounts even bears were found in them.[1]

Even so late as the middle of the seventeenth century the lands around Glasgow—beyond the gardens and the few cultivated fields—must have been almost in a state of nature. From the inventory of the personal estate of James, Archbishop of Glasgow, it appears that the whole amount owing by "the fewaris, farmeris, tennants, occupiers and " possessiors of the lands and baronie of Bishops forist" for the crop and year 1632 was only £33, 6s. 8d. Scots, equivalent to £2, 15s. 6½d. of our money.[2] But this of course included only what was feued or under lease, and, as we have seen, the feu duties were very moderate. The Bishop's Forest embraced probably the whole of the Easter and Wester Commons, which, under the liberal administration of the bishops, the inhabitants were allowed to use as common pasturage and for casting peats, and for which no rent would be paid.

A portion of the ancient forest appears to have remained in its original state till so late as the year 1795. Brown, writing in that year, in describing the newly formed village of Anderston, says that the ground on which it is built "is bounded on the north by the wood of Blythswood, " the only remains of a forest, formerly belonging to Glasgow, in a " natural state."

Among the lands held in common by the citizens, besides the Easter and Wester Commons, were the Burgh Muir, and the district known as Garngad Hill. For some time after the flight of Beton, his faithful steward William Walker, continued to manage the temporalities, and to enter the "Rentallers;" but about the year 1568 the magistrates—following the example of the Duke of Chastelherault when he seized Lochwood —took possession of the common lands—as they did of many other properties and endowments belonging to the Church—and proceeded to dispose of them in lots to the inhabitants. Walker, whose heart was sorely grieved at this spoliation of his lord's benefice, wrote to the archbishop, then in France, that he had been "in great trublis, as is knawin " utuartlie be the changeing of the colouris of my hair q. was blak and " now is quhyte." In this curious letter, which is dated 6th April, 1569, Walker tells his master that he had been required and commanded by the provost and bailies of Glasgow to become a burgess, which he had refused, and in consequence of that refusal, he says, " I can in no wayis haif

---

[1] Caledonia Romana, p. 16.   [2] Hamilton's Lanarkshire, p. 149.

" justice ministrat unto me in quhatsumever actioun I haif ado befoir the
" provest and baillies." He goes on to tell that "al the borrow muir of
" Glasg on the Southe syde of the towne, and als Garngad hill on the
" north part of the toune, ar distribuit be provest baillies and communitie
" of the towne to the inhabitaris thairof, every ane his awin portioun
" conforme to his degrie, and hes revin it oute and manuris it this ʒeir
" instantlie, bot I wald have na parte thairof q [until] it plies God and
" ʒoure L. to make my parte, be ressoun I knew thai hade na power to
" deill ʒour L. lands w'oute sum consent of ʒoure L. or sum utheris in
" ʒoure L. name."[1] The archbishop, as already mentioned, was restored
by act of Parliament in 1600, but the feus which had been given off he
did not recover, and they were permanently lost to the Church.

It would appear, however, that the division had not been an impartial
one, and that the inhabitants did not get "every ane his awin portioun."
The people also had got alarmed lest the whole of the muir should be
thus alienated, and the land which the bishops had permitted them to use
as common pasture-ground for their cattle, taken away. We find accordingly, about this time, repeated protests made by the merchants and
deacons of crafts, in name of the community, against the alienation—
"geving furth or delying"—of any part of the "common muirs." Such
a remonstrance occurs under date 1st May, 1574, against a grant to one
James Boyd, and the parties making it protest that "the partis thereof
" ellis delt and geven furtht by [without] thair consent in tymis bigane
" suld nocht prejuge them but that thai may have tym and place for
" recalling and remeid thairof." Again, in 1576, a more formal protest
is made, and the magistrates are entreated "for the luf ye beir to God
" and the commoun weill of our toune" not to alienate any more of the
common lands, so necessary as pasture "for the sustening of our babies."
This touching protest was successful for the time, and under date 21st
June, 1576, there is a minute of council which bears that after mature
deliberation it was statute and ordained, "in respect that their com-
" moune muris, yet left wndelt and set furthe, will scarslie serue the
" tounschip for halding of thair guddis and furnesing fewall necessour,"
no part of the common muir shall in time coming be set or given in feu
to any person, "bot to ly still in communitie to the weill of the haill
" tounschip."

---

[1] Papers in possession of the Roman Catholic Church in Scotland. Contribution to Maitland
Club of the late Andrew Macgeorge, Esq. p. 24.

We cannot in our days so well understand the discontent of the people at the invasion and inclosure of commons. In Scotland, as well as in England, the land held in common was in the old time of vast extent. Only on the lower grounds, along the river banks and the sea, was the land appropriated and cultivated. The inland portion—upland, muir, and mountain—was, as a rule, not occupied for agricultural purposes, or specially appropriated at all, but served only to keep the poor and their cattle from starving. It was only as cultivation increased with greater wealth, and a higher civilization came to prevail, that the common land began to be inclosed, and the poor man's grazing ground appropriated by the neighbouring barons or burghal authorities.[1] But the ecclesiastics, who held the church lands, were the last to make these encroachments, and the appropriations by the magistrates of Glasgow of the "common muirs," which had been included in the patrimony of the Church, would probably not have been made by the bishops had they continued the feudal superiors.

In connection with the subject of commons, I may mention in passing that the proceedings of the Enclosure Commissioners in 1878 disclose the interesting fact that so late as that year there existed tracts of common land in England, forming part of a high and wild range of hills in Somersetshire, in which red deer still roamed at large.

Having referred to the common muir of Glasgow, which was on the north side of the city, I may mention that there stood upon it the small church or chapel of St. Roche the Confessor—called in a minute of council in 1647 "Sein Rokis Kirk." It was founded in the beginning of the sixteenth century by Thomas Muirhead, canon of Glasgow and prebendary of Stobo, and the cure was served by one of the order of the Blackfriars. It was surrounded by a burying-ground, which, when the town was visited by a pestilence in 1647, was used for the reception of the infected poor, for whose accommodation wooden huts were erected in it. From a corruption of the name of this chapel the district called St. Rollox took its name.

The portions of the land round Glasgow, which were saved from appropriation, continued till a comparatively recent period to be held in common by the inhabitants for pasturing their cattle. Certain parks in the locality now called Cowcaddens, and elsewhere, including the Green, were used for this purpose till near the end of the last century. The

[1] Scotch Legal Antiquities, p. 155.

cattle were collected every morning, and sent out to pasture on the common muirs, under the charge of herds appointed by the magistrates. In 1589 there is a minute of council appointing two individuals "to be " common Hirdis of the toun for this yeir to cum," one for the "nolt and " guidis aboue the croce" and the other "for the nolt and guidis beneth " the croce, and the rest of the nether pairtis of the toun." "Nolt and " guidis" mean black cattle and milch cows. The herds were required to give their oath of fidelity, and to find caution "for leill and trew " administratioun in their office."[1]   The cattle from the lower district were collected by the herd and driven through the west port, and up the common thoroughfare called the Cow Lone, now Queen Street, to the Cowcaddens parks, and he brought them home the same way in the evening.   At that time there was on the site of what is now the Royal Exchange a thatched farmhouse, with large dungsteads at either end.   Cow Lone, as I have previously mentioned, was then a rural, muddy lane, neither bottomed nor causewayed, and in wet weather the cattle often sunk in it so deeply as to get "laired"—causing the herd no small trouble in their extrication.   It continued in this state till so late as 1760, when it was causewayed.   Sometimes the cattle were taken westward by what was called the Back Cow Lone—now Ingram Street —a rural lane which led westward from the High Street by Buns Wynd, Shuttle Street, and Canon Street, till it joined the main Cow Lone. This practice of leading out the cattle to pasture continued till a comparatively recent period.   Dr. Buchanan, writing in 1855, says, "I have con- " versed with people who perfectly well remembered the last Town herd " collecting the cows and driving them along the streets and both of the " lones, in the manner now described.   His name was John Anderson, " and he lived in Picken's Land, Rottenrow.   I am in possession of his " horn, and a very primitive looking wind instrument it is."   It was made out of a cow's horn, with an indentation round the mouth- piece for the purpose of suspending the instrument from the worthy official's neck.

Originally there appears to have been a herd for the cows and a separate herd for the calves.   In 1579 there is an order of the town council by which "Matho Wilsone is maid and constitut calf hird, and " is ordanit to have vj^d (a halfpenny) for ilk calf, and his meit daily " about, or ellis xij^d (a penny) for ilk melteth [each meal] gif thai failzie

[1] 26th March, 1589.

" and to be poyndit thairfoir."[1] Perhaps the calves were pastured on the Green.   There was certainly a house for the herd there, situated near the site of Nelson's Monument.

No one was allowed to pasture his cattle apart from the common herd.   There is a minute which bears that " John Hogisyarde is fund in " the wrang and amercement of court for halding of ane kow by [apart " from] the herde, contrare to the statuts of the toune; quhilk kow was " fund and gottin in James Flemynges corne;" and the delinquent is ordained to make good "the skaitht to the said James."[2]

The prices at which the magistrates disposed of the common lands were very small.   The agricultural value of the ground was certainly not great, as may be judged from the fact that in 1712 the whole of the muir known as the Wester Common, extending to about 100 acres—now part of the city—was let to one James Bell at the rent of £11, 8s. 6d. That was probably all that could be then got for it; but the magistrates were not justified in permanently alienating lands which they held in trust—if not for the Church, to which they really belonged, at least for the citizens—at prices which were merely nominal.   On the 18th of June, 1730, they sold sixty acres of this Wester Common to James Rae, a merchant in Glasgow, at the price of £145, 16s. 8d. and an annual feu-duty of £5, 11s.   Taking the feu-duty at even twenty-five years' purchase, this is less than £285 for sixty acres of land.   And in 1747 they sold the remainder of the common, extending to between thirty and forty acres, to John Young, a tailor, at the price of £130 and a feu-duty of £1, 13s. 4d.   Again, on the other side of the city, the magistrates so late as 1764, sold to Hugh Tennent, a gardener, what is described in the conveyance as "the town's lands and muir of Easter " Common consisting of 42 acres," for payment of a feu-duty of only £10 sterling.   In the same way other valuable lots of ground were disposed of at prices equally inadequate.

THE PEOPLE, AND HOW THEY LIVED.

Of the personal habits of the people of Glasgow, and their mode of living in mediæval times, we have little information, but down to the

---

[1] 26th May, 1579.   [2] Council Records, 16th August, 1579.

fifteenth or sixteenth centuries these must have been of the roughest. And it was the same all over Scotland. Eneo Silvio describes the people as small in stature, but bold, the commonalty as poor and uneducated, eating flesh and fish, but bread a dainty.' In Froissart we get a picture of the Border Scots in one of their forays, in the year 1327, which is worth transcribing; and from the description which he gives of an army equipped for an invasion, we may form some estimate of the state of the people at large at that time. Their luxuries appear to have been few, but they were probably not without substantial means of living. "The Scots," writes Froissart, "are bold, hardy, and much in-"ured to war. When they make their incursions into England they "march from twenty to four and twenty leagues [miles] without halting, "as well by night as day; for they are all on horseback except the camp "followers, who are on foot. The knights and esquires are well mounted "on large bay horses: the common people on little galloways. They "bring no carriages with them, on account of the mountains they have "to pass in Northumberland; neither do they carry with them any pro-"visions of bread and wine, for their habits of sobriety are such in time "of war that they will live for a long time on flesh half sodden, without "bread, and drink of the river water without wine. They have therefore "no occasion for pots or pans, for they dress the flesh of their cattle in "the skins after they have taken them off, and being sure to find plenty "of them in the country which they invade, they carry none with them. "Under the flaps of his saddle each man carries a broad plate of metal, "and behind the saddle a little bag of oatmeal. When they have eaten "too much of the sodden flesh, they place this plate over the fire, mix "with water their oatmeal, and when the plate is heated they put a little "of the paste upon it and make a thin cake like a cracknel of buscuit, "which they eat to warm their stomachs. It is therefore no wonder "that they perform a longer day's march than other soldiers." When the English army on one occasion entered a camp which the Scots had just quitted, they found, among other things, says Froissart, "more than "three hundred cauldrons made of leather, with the hair outside, which "were hung on the fires full of water, and meat ready for boiling, and "more than ten thousand pairs of old worn out shoes made of undressed "leather, which the Scots had left there."[1]

In a curious document written in the early part of the sixteenth

---

[1] Chronicles—Johnes, vol. i. pp. 18–24.

century we have an account of how these shoes were made. It is a paper presented to Henry VIII., after the death of James V., by one John Elder, a clergyman, a native of Caithness, containing a project of union of the two kingdoms, and it contains some interesting notices as to the habits of the Highlanders. As a rule, he says, they go barelegged and barefooted, but in winter, when the frost is very severe, "we go " a-hunting, and after we have slain red deer we flay off the skin, and " setting our bare foot on the inside thereof, for want of cunning shoe- " makers, by your grace's pardon, we play the cobblers; compassing and " measuring so much thereof as shall reach up to our ankles; pricking " the upper part thereof with holes, that the water may repass when it " enters, and stretching it up with a strong thong of the same above our " said ankles. So we make our shoes—the rough side outward."[1] The custom of boiling the beef in the hide continued in some parts of Scotland till a very recent period. Burt says that in his time (1730), in some of the islands, the people still retained that custom.[2]

Men who fed on half-sodden flesh prepared in raw hides, and who made their shoes of undressed skins, would not be very particular as to how they were housed. Nor were they; for, as we have seen, they considered the occasional burning of their houses by the English a calamity more endurable than the expense of supporting their French allies.

In the Lowlands, including Glasgow and the other burghs, the dress of the men among the common people in the fifteenth century consisted chiefly of a doublet and cloak and a kind of short trews—the head being covered with a hat sometimes of basket-work and sometimes of felt, or with a woollen bonnet, while the legs and feet remained bare. Shirts were almost unknown, even among the better classes. Among women the kirtle or close gown was rarely accompanied either with the *wylicot* or under-petticoat, or with the mantle, and the feet were bare. From the poem "Peblis to the Play," by James I., we learn that in his time the women wore kerchiefs or hoods, and tippets about the neck. Some of the men wore hats of birch twigs interwoven, others flat bonnets. Their music was the bagpipe. A description is given of a tavern, with a fair linen cloth on the table, and a regular score on the wall, and the reckoning, which is twopence halfpenny each—about a penny farthing of our

---

[1] Holograph MS. quoted by Pinkerton, Hist. of Scotland, vol. ii. p. 397.
[2] Burt's Letters, vol. ii. p. 271.

money—is collected from the company in a wooden trencher.   Such would be a tavern in Glasgow about the year 1450.

In food there was hardly any luxury till James I., who had resided nineteen years in England, set the example of a better style of living. Under Robert II. the French knights could obtain no wine but at a great price.   The ale was no better than small beer, and the bread, when there was any, was of barley or oats.[1]   Among the common people milk and its various preparations formed a chief article of diet till a much later period.   Meat boiled with oatmeal, or fish, supplied the more substantial meals.   Bread and vegetables were luxuries, and were very little used—a circumstance to which, perhaps, may be imputed the prevalence of leprosy.[2]   The people generally, too, were much more gross in their tastes than they are now.   Even the higher classes indulged an appetite for coarse and strong-flavoured food which would astonish a gourmand of the present day.   At the royal table, in the thirteenth century, porpoise and grampus, fresh and cured, were regular items of provision.   In the following century the household books of James V. show repeated entries of payments for "pellok," the "phoca" or "selch," with the "cattus marinus," called sometimes "se cat," and the "polypus," as viands provided for the king and his court.   The flesh of the porpoise and seal, indeed, continued to be used till at least the end of the sixteenth century.   And this was not peculiar to Scotland.   In the accounts of the corporation of Rye, in 1448, we find twenty pence paid for a "porpais."   They were dearer at Lydd, for in the accounts of that corporation in 1449 there is a payment of six shillings for a porpoise, to be presented to no less a person than Jack Cade—called in the account "the Captain"—to propitiate his friendship in case of his ultimate success.[3]   Pike was in common use in Scotland, and there are notices of its having been sent to James IV. from Luss.   Cranes, swans, herons, bitterns, solan geese, and other birds of coarse flavour, were also esteemed as articles of food.[4]   Sturgeon was reckoned a great delicacy, and in the royal accounts in 1496 there is a payment of five shillings "to the man " that brocht the sture [sturgeon] fra Glasgo."[5]

After the Reformation the mode of living improved.   Vegetables and oatmeal were more used, and less flesh was eaten; but the habits of the

---

[1] Froissart.   [2] Pinkerton's History, vol. i. p. 154.
[3] Fifth Report on Historical MSS. pp. 492-520.
[4] Accounts of the Lord High Treasurer, preface, p. ccvii.   [5] Ibid. p. 277.

people were still coarse, and cookery was little cultivated. Fynes Moryson, a gentleman who travelled in Scotland towards the end of the sixteenth century, writing in 1599, says: "The Scotch eat much colwort
"and cabbage, and little fresh meat. Myself was at a knight's house
"who had many servants to attend him, that brought in his meat with
"their heads covered with blue caps, the table being more than half
"furnished with great platters of porridge, each having a little piece of
"sodden meat. And when the table was served the servants did sit
"down with us, but the upper mess [above the salt] instead of porridge
"had a pullet with some prunes in the broth. And I observed no art
"of cookery, or furniture of household stuff, but rather rude neglect of
"both, though myself and companion, sent from the Governor of Ber-
"wick about Border affairs, were entertained after their best manner.
"They vulgarly [commonly] eat hearth cakes of oats, but in cities have
"also wheaten bread. They drink pure wines, not with sugar as the
"English, yet at feasts they put comfits in the wine after the French
"manner." As to dress, he says, the common people wear coarse homemade cloth "and flat blue caps very broad. The gentlemen did wear
"English cloth, or silk or light stuffs. Gentlewomen did wear close
"upper bodies after the German manner, with large whalebone sleeves
"after the French manner, short cloaks like the Germans, French hoods,
"and large falling bands round their necks. The unmarried of all sorts
"go bareheaded, and wear short cloaks with close linen sleeves. The
"inferior sort of citizens wives, and the women of the country, wear
"cloaks made of coarse stuff, of two or three colours in chequer work,
"vulgarly called *plodan*." We may accept this description as in a great
measure applicable to Glasgow at that time.

Sir William Brereton, the traveller already quoted, writes thus of
the people in Edinburgh in 1634, and in all probability this description
also applied to Glasgow:—"The women wear and use upon festival
"days six or seven several habits and fashions: some for distinction
"of widows, wives, and maids, others apparelled according to their
"own humour and phantasy. Many, especially of the meaner sort,
"wear plaids, which is a garment of the same woollen stuff whereof
"saddle cloths in England are made, which is cast over their heads
"and covers their faces on both sides, and would reach almost to the
"ground but that they pluck them up and wear them cast under their
"arms. Some ancient women and citizens wear satin straight bodied

" gowns, short little cloaks with great capes, and a broad *boun-grace*
" coming over their brows and going out with a corner behind their
" heads, and this boun-grace is, as it were, lined with a white stracht
" [starched] cambric suitable unto it.   Young maids, not married, all
" are bareheaded—some with broad thin shag ruffs which lie flat to
" their shoulders, and others with half bands with wide necks, either
" much stiffened or set in wire which comes only behind; and these
" shag ruffs are more broad and thick than others."[1]

Ray the naturalist, who visited Scotland in 1661, describes the men
of the poorer class as wearing bonnets, and the women having a covering
of white linen on their heads, which hung down their backs.   "When
" they go abroad none of them wear hats, but a particoloured blanket,
" which they call a plaid, over their head and shoulders."   The magistrates of Edinburgh had, some thirty years previously (1631), endeavoured, but apparently without success, to put down this wearing
of the plaid over the head.   "It has now," the order prohibiting it
bears, "become the ordinar habit of all women within the city, to the
" general imputation of their sex—matrons not being able to be dis-
" tinguished from loose living women, to their own dishonour and
" scandal of the city."   When we come to notice the proceedings of
the Kirk Session of Glasgow we shall find that they also, perhaps
for the same reason, strictly prohibited the wearing of plaids over the
head by women in church.   There is a similar enactment about the
same time by the magistrates of Aberdeen, in which they condemn
" the uncivill forme of behaviour of a great many women of the burght
" of gude qualite quha resortes both to kirk and mercat with thair
" playddis about thair headis."[2]   In Aberdeen, curiously enough, men
were, in the sixteenth century, prohibited from wearing, not plaids only,
but blue bonnets.   The magistrates enacted that no burgess should
wear a plaid, under a penalty of forty shillings, and if he wore "a bleu
" bonatt" he was subjected in a penalty of five pounds.[3]   But the practice
of wearing plaids, in the case both of men and women, had become
inveterate, and it continued notwithstanding these enactments.

Another English traveller, Morer, writing in 1689, says he found
the Lowlanders in Scotland dressed much like his own countrymen,
excepting that the men generally wore bonnets instead of hats, and

---

[1] Brereton's Travels, p. 101.   [2] Burgh Records of Aberdeen, 6th June, 1621.
[3] Ibid. 5th October, 1576.

plaids instead of cloaks—the women wearing plaids when abroad or at church. "The children of people of the better sort," he says, "lay " and clergy, go generally without shoes or stockings. Oaten cakes, " baked on a plate of iron, are the principal bread, and they are fond " of tobacco." In Glasgow, till a recent period, it was quite common for the children of the well-to-do classes to go without shoes and stockings in summer, and it was the same in other towns. Captain Burt, speaking of the habits of the people in Inverness towards the middle of the eighteenth century, says, "Though the children of the upper " classes wear shoes and stockings in winter, nothing is more common " than to see them barefoot in the summer."[1]

Writing of his own recollection of the same period (1763), Mr. Maxwell of Munches says of the rural population of Galloway: "The " tenants in general lived very meanly on kail, groats, milk, gradden " —ground in querns turned with the hand, and the grain dried in a " pot, with an old ewe now and then about Martinmas. They were " clothed very plainly, and their habitations were most uncomfortable. " Their general wear was of cloth made of waulked plaiding, black " and white wool mixed, very coarse, and the cloth rarely dyed. Their " hose were made of white plaiding cloth sewed together, with single " soled shoes, and a black or blue bonnet—none having hats but the " lairds, who thought themselves very well dressed for going to church " on Sunday with a black Kelt coat of their wives' making."[2]

Linen was everywhere made at home, the spinning being done by the ladies, and also by the servants, during the long winter evenings. "Holland," which cost about six shillings the ell, was worn only by the wealthier classes.

In the burgh no doubt the people lived better than in the rural districts, and in Glasgow, whatever their food may have been, they appear to have consumed a considerable amount of wine. In early times it was only within burgh that the sale of wine was permitted at all, and when a cargo arrived it was first proved by the "tasters," and the price at which it was to be retailed in the taverns was then fixed. In the same way each brewing of ale was proved by the official taster before it was permitted to be sold, and the price was regulated according to the price of malt, and "efter the imposicioune of the worthi

[1] Letters, vol. i. p. 96.
[2] Murray's Literary History of Galloway, App. p. 337.

"men of the toune."[1]   Of wines, claret was most in favour in Glasgow, and indeed throughout Scotland.   It was imported from Bordeaux by French and Scottish traders.   The other wines used were chiefly those of Guienne and Gascony.   They were probably of a harsh and acid character compared with what are now imported, and the small quantity of sugar then consumed—most of which was imported from Italy, Sicily, and Cyprus—was chiefly used to mix with the wine.[2] The beer used in Scotland during the greater part of the fifteenth century was mostly imported from Germany.   When ale began to be manufactured in Glasgow, which it came to be to a large extent, it was made both from oats and barley or bere, and in the absence of hops it was flavoured with ginger and other spices and aromatic herbs, to fit it for keeping.   Women, called "browster wives," were then the only brewers, and for a long time the taverns were almost exclusively kept by them.[3]   In the old burgh accounts of Glasgow there are repeated entries of payments for "aqua vitæ" at the corporation dinners. This is not always to be confounded with brandy, to which, in earlier times as well as at a later period, the term was applied.   It was often applied to whisky made from malt.   In 1494 the exchequer rolls contain an entry of the delivery of eight bolls of malt to Friar John Cor to make aqua vitæ.   The quantity manufactured, however, was very limited. Till the sixteenth century the sale of distilled spirits was chiefly confined to the shop of the apothecary.   It was used only as a luxury or medicinally.   On two occasions there appear entries in the royal accounts of payments by James IV. "to the barbour that brocht aqua "vitæ to the king in Dunde."   At a later period French brandy was imported and used in considerable quantities, but the excessive use of whisky is quite a modern innovation.   From the burgh accounts it would appear that the amount of spirits consumed at our early city banquets was very small.

Down to the time of the Union claret was the wine principally drunk in Glasgow.   An English traveller who was there about 1660 says that the people "generally excel in good French wines as they "superabound with flesh and fowl."[4]   Another Englishman, who made an excursion in Scotland in 1704, writes that at the most common

---

[1] Acts of the Parliaments of Scotland, i. p. 683.
[2] Accounts of Lord High Treasurer, Preface ccviii.   [3] Ibid. p. ccxiii.
[4] Franck's Northern Memoirs calculated for the Meridian of Scotland.

taverns they had good French brandy and French wine—"so common "are the French liquors in this country." From a tavern bill in 1697 which has been preserved, we learn that claret was then charged 20*d*. (sterling) the quart. Morer, writing in 1702, says the Scots "have a "thin bodied claret at ten pence the mutchkin." After the Union the price was higher. In 1729 Burt states that claret was charged 1*s*. 4*d*. the bottle, and that it was soon raised to two shillings.[1] He says he found French claret—"a wholesome and agreeable drink—in "every public house of any note except in the heart of the High- "lands, and sometimes even there." The laird of Culloden kept a hogshead of claret on tap in his hall for all comers;[2] and at Arniston House, the country residence of President Dundas, there were sixteen hogsheads of clared used every year.[3]

ECCLESIASTICAL HISTORY.

The ecclesiastical history of Glasgow—not the history of the Church, but the proceedings of the ecclesiastics and the church courts, and the exercise of their jurisdictions, is in many respects curious, but my space does not permit more than a brief notice of it. The materials, indeed, are limited. With the exception of the Chartularies the only local record which we possess of the period before the Reformation is the Protocol Register, which Professor Innes believed to have been lost, but which was fortunately discovered by the Rev. Mr. Stevenson at Buckie, in Banffshire, among the collections of Bishop Kyle, and which has been since printed by the Grampian Club. It embraces only four- teen years—from 1499 to 1513—but it contains some curious and interesting entries, and casts considerable light on church life, and on the proceedings of the ecclesiastical authorities during that period. Besides collations and presentations to livings, questions of jurisdiction, and records of the conveyance of property, there are entries as to ecclesi- astical disputes, cases of libel for slander, the exercise of church disci- pline in cases of assault and slaughter, and other matters dealt with by the Archbishop of Glasgow and by the dean and chapter.

---

[1] Letters from the North of Scotland, vol. ii. p. 134.   [2] Burt.
[3] Domestic Annals of Scotland, vol. iii. p. 184.

The cases in which the discipline of the church was invoked to redress acts of violence are numerous, and in the worst of them the delinquents are priests. On one occasion Sir John Carnwath, a priest, is accused of having violently carried off *sub silentio noctis*, during the first week in Lent, the daughter of John Smyth, in the parish of Linton.[1] Another priest, Sir Bartholomew Blare—every priest had the prefix of "Sir"—is charged with "mutilating and dismembering" certain parishioners of Biggar in a conflict betwixt him and the said parishioners.[2] And Sir John Wanles, also a priest, is cited before the archbishop, "to "see and hear himself declared irregular and deprived of his rank, and "to be thrown into prison by the secular authorities and otherwise "punished, for the cruel slaughter of Adam Moscrop, scholar."[3] Many other cases of the same kind occur—acts of violence and licentiousness, and in one instance of theft—all committed by priests.[4] In one instance a priest, for using "loose and profane words" in presence of the chancellor, is ordained to confess his fault and ask pardon of the judge and the archbishop "*flexis genubus* on the floor of the court."[5]

There is another class of interesting entries in this old record relating to the forms observed on the induction of ecclesiastics. On the admission of Archbishop James Beton he is first received by the chapter, under letters apostolic addressed by the pope to that body. He is then received by the rector in name of the university and clergy of Glasgow; and lastly he is acknowledged by two of the bailies in name of the citizens to be archbishop of the see "and father and shepherd of their "souls."[6] On a subsequent occasion he takes the oath of office in the chapter-house of the Cathedral "by touching his breast and swearing on "the word of an archbishop and on the Holy Gospels." Induction is given to a chaplaincy, that of St. John the Baptist in the Cathedral, "by touch and real delivery of the chalice, book, altar, and ornaments "thereof."[7] And there is an interesting instrument recording the investiture, by the king in person, within the Abbey of Holyrood, of Sir John Symington to the chapel-royal of St. Ninian of Dundonald, in the diocese of Glasgow. The investiture on this occasion is recorded to have been made "by James IV. king of Scots, the true patron donator and "disposer thereof, by His Majesty personally taking the right hand of

---

[1] 20th April, 1504, Lib. Protocol. No. 80. [2] Ibid. No. 356.
[3] 14th April, 1511, Idem, No. 516. [4] Vide Ibid. Nos. 569, 570.
[5] Ibid. No. 442. [6] Ibid. No. 359. [7] Ibid. No. 399.

" the said Mr. John, and subscribing with his own Royal hand a writ
" containing the royal mandate."[1]   Another instrument records the investiture of Sir John Heriot, in the parish church of Drumman (Dry-
men), by leading the presentee "through the south gate of the church to
" the high altar, and delivering to him the keys of the church, the bap-
" tismal font, the bell rope, the high altar and ornaments thereof, Chalice
" and Book; all which were handled by the said Sir John in token of
" real possession obtained."   And two newly created canons of the
Cathedral are admitted by "making canonical obedience to the Dean
" and Chapter, by joining their hands, and falling on their knees, and
" taking the oath of the canons—placing the right hand on the breast
" after the manner of priests."[2]

Other instruments in the Protocol are interesting as relating to pilgrimages from Glasgow to Rome.   One of these records that Sir
Bartholomew Blare—the same individual, apparently, who had so mal-
treated the parishioners of Biggar—being, in expiation of his crime no
doubt, about to visit the shrines of the apostles Peter and Paul in Rome,
and "having taken a staff for support in his right hand, and in his left a
" pilgrim wallet, and setting out in name of the Father Son and Holy
" Spirit," committed to the protection of the pope and the see, himself
and his chaplaincy, and all his goods, "and all those adhering to him;"
and thereupon he asks instruments in the hands of the notary.   This he
does in the chapter-house, in presence of the chapter.   In another case
the notary records that the pilgrim priest, "taking his wallet, cloak, cap,
" and staff, and taking leave of the byestanders, advancing a little dis-
" tance, took his journey to his Holiness Pope Julius II."

In one case the chapter takes proceedings against George Lyle for
non-adherence to his spouse, and not treating her with matrimonial
affection;[3] and in another case the archbishop pronounces a sentence of
divorce.

In the beginning of the sixteenth century we have in the same
records examples of the attempts which had begun to be made by the
citizens to assert their independence, and of the collision into which
they came with the archbishop, in consequence.   In December, 1510,
there is a record of proceedings taken at the instance of the commissaries
against the bailies of the city and other citizens, who had "incurred the
" greater excommunication" for having done certain acts and made

---

[1] Lib. Protocol. No. 492, 6th Nov. 1510.   [2] Ibid. No. 572.   [3] Ibid. No. 362.

certain statutes against the jurisdiction of the Church, "namely, that
" none of the citizens of Glasgow ought to summon another citizen
" before a spiritual judge ordinary respecting a matter which could be
" competently decided before the bailies in the Court House of Glas-
" gow; and because they had fined one Alan Lethame a citizen, because
" he complained to the Official against another fellow-citizen." The provost, the Earl of Lennox, appeared before the chapter "as pleader for
" the said bailies, and procurator for the citizens to defend them," and
demanded to be furnished with a copy of the citation. This bears to
have been "done, Sabbath, 7th Dec. 1510."[1] But the time of independence had not yet come. In the following month the earl again
appeared and "publicly confessed and openly acknowledged" the act
complained of, and renounced, in name of himself and the citizens, "all
" statutes made against the liberty and jurisdiction of Holy Mother
" Church, promising never to put them in execution in time to come."[2]

All law business at that time was in the hands of ecclesiastics; and
notaries received their appointment from the archbishop, who had the
power of suspending them at his pleasure.[3] In one of the instruments
the notary styles himself "presbiter, notarius publicus, ac *scriba* "—writer
—the name adopted by his successors in the Faculty.[4]

Under the bishops and archbishops the religious life of the inhabitants was that of other cathedral towns. There were the usual services
in the High Church, in its choir and at its many altars. The Black Friars
had services in their church in the High Street, afterwards known as the
College Church; and in the collegiate church of St. Mary and St. Anne
in St. Thenew's Gate, now the Trongate, there were regular services.
At the Reformation these two last-mentioned churches became ruinous,
and thus there was then only one church for the city—the Cathedral—
with one minister, to whom a second was in 1588 joined as a colleague.
In 1592 the increasing population caused the church of St. Mary and St.
Anne to be repaired, and a third minister was then provided. A fourth
was appointed in 1595 to the Barony, which was separated from the city
in the following year. For this congregation, the crypt—for some time
called the Laigh Kirk—was fitted up. In 1622 the old Blackfriars
Church was added, having been repaired in that year. To accommodate
an additional congregation the western part of the nave of the Cathedral

---

[1] Protocolla, No. 498.   [2] Ibid. No. 504.
[3] Ibid. No. 428.   [4] Ibid. No. 501.

was fitted up in 1648. It was called the Outer High Church, and Patrick Gillespie was appointed its first minister. In that year Glasgow was divided ecclesiastically into four parishes, and in 1701 it was divided into six. In making this division the Magistrates and the General Session—for it was done at the sight of both—appear to have had regard solely to the number of "examinable persons" which would be in each division. The total number of such persons to be provided for was 9994, and how very equally the city was apportioned for their accommodation will be seen from the division made. There was first "the north quarter," comprehending the Drygate and Rottenrow "and "country places," and coming down to the Blackfriars' Church, "con-"taining of examinable persons" 1777. Second, the middle quarter, down the High Street to the Cross, containing 1685. Third, the east quarter, comprehending the Gallowgate and east side of Saltmarket, containing 1628. Fourth, the south quarter, comprehending the Bridge-gate and Goosedubs, containing 1648. Fifth, the south-west quarter, now the Tron parish, containing 1649; and lastly, the north-west quarter, beginning at the Tolbooth and "taking in all without the west port and "the west side of Stockwell, and comprehending the Candle Street and "Bells Wynd with the Grammar School Wynd and the Back Wynd," containing 1607.[1] This enumeration is interesting as showing how the population was located in the beginning of the eighteenth century. In each of the six divisions it will be seen there was an almost equal number of persons—the difference between the highest division and the lowest amounting to not more than seventy, and between the others much less. Other parishes were subsequently formed, and churches erected from time to time, till they amounted to ten—the present number. They are called the City Churches. The stipends of the ministers are paid by the city out of "the common good," but apart from what the church lands yielded, some of the churches—certainly the Tron and Blackfriars—had originally independent endowments and property, of which the corporation took possession. If the matter were investigated, and the magistrates were brought to account for all the property which they hold in trust for ecclesiastical purposes, it would probably be found that the city churches do not form such a burden on the proper resources of the community as is generally supposed.

In matters of discipline, after the Reformation, an entirely new order

---

[1] Burgh Records, 9th September, 1701.

of things succeeded to what had formerly prevailed in Glasgow, and the inhabitants found that under the presbytery and the kirk session, especially the latter, they were to be subjected to a rule very much stricter than they had experienced under the archbishops.

On the abolition of Episcopacy it might be supposed that all ecclesiastical matters would fall under the cognizance and control of the presbytery, but this was by no means the case. There were no parochial sessions till the middle of the seventeenth century, but in the General Kirk Session, instituted in 1572, a power arose which appears to have been at first above both presbytery and corporation. Its rule was despotic, and it claimed and exercised powers which would not be credited if we had not the records before us. They sat in secret conclave—the whole elders and deacons, being "sworn, with uplifted hands, to reveal "nothing that shall be voted in the session, nor the voters."[1] The original books of the session are unfortunately lost, but copious extracts from them had been made by Wodrow, and they are preserved in his unpublished "Life of Mr. David Weemes," the manuscript of which is in the library of the university. From these we obtain a curious picture of social life in Glasgow in those olden times.

To begin with, the kirk session exercised for a long time the right of patronage of the city churches. It was by them that the city was in 1648 divided into four parishes—the magistrates merely concurring. Even after the magistrates had obtained from the crown a gift of the patronage, the kirk session still insisted on appointing the ministers, and this continued down to 1717, when the magistrates, on the ground that all the churches except the Cathedral were maintained and endowed from funds dispensed by them, claimed to have a say in the appointments. This led to an arrangement in that year by which it was agreed that the session of the vacant church should be allowed to make the nomination, but that the minister should not be called until the approval was obtained, not of the magistrates only, but of the General Session. This continued for some time, but disputes arose which led to the proposal of other schemes, and as the parties could not agree it was at length settled in a judicial process that the magistrates had the exclusive patronage. This decision was the cause of a small "disruption," for it so displeased the General Session that a number of its members left the church, and

---

[1] Session Records, 24th October, 1588.

having erected a chapel in Canon Street, they termed it the meeting-house of the Free Presbyterian body.[1]

Under date 28th May, 1588, we find the kirk session intimating to the presbytery that the "exercise" of the latter cannot be permitted in the Blackfriars on Friday, because it "interfeirs with the preaching" on that day, and the presbytery is desired "to alter the day of their exer-"cise." The presbytery yielded, and there is an intimation afterwards "that preaching, *with consent of session* and presbytery, is to be in the "Blackfriars Wednesday and Friday."

Equally did the session dictate to the town council, and even interfere in the nomination of the magistrates. On the 26th of September, 1587, they sent to the council on the day of the election "to request that in "chusing the baillies men might be chosen that were fit for the office," but they added judiciously "*as near as possible.*" In 1644 we find them giving orders "that the magistrates shall attend the Tables at the Com-"munion in the Hie Kirk and keep order; and the Dean of Guild and "Convener and the old Magistrates in the New Kirk [the Tron]." This must have been no sinecure, if an order, which was enacted by the session in 1589, was enforced, that the "time of convening on Sundays of the "Communion" should be four o'clock in the morning—the "Collectors" being ordered to assemble in the High Church on these occasions at three in the morning.

But, indeed, early hours were generally observed in Glasgow at that time and for long afterwards. In a journal kept by an English student, one Josiah Chorley, who attended the university in 1670, the writer says—"The good orders of the College were very agreeable to mine inclination. "At five o'clock in the morning the bell rings, and every scholar is to "answer to his name which is then called over. The day is spent in "private studies and public exercises in the classes; at nine at night "every chamber is visited by the respective regents."[2]

Speaking of the religious life of the people, Mr. Chorley says—"The "Lord's days are strictly observed: all the scholars called to the several "classes, where after religious exercises, all attend the Primar and Regents "to church, forenoon and afternoon, and in the same order from church.

---

[1] Cleland's Annals, ii. p. 411.

[2] "Chorleyana, or a Register commemorating the most remarkable passages of God's providence "towards me from my nativity, by Josiah Chorley," MS., quoted by Professor Innes in Preface to Munimenta Universitatis, p. xxiv.

" Then in the evening they are called again to the classes, and then
" come under examination concerning the sermons heard, and give
" account of what was appointed the foregoing Sabbath in some theo-
" logical treatise, and then to supper and chambers." And he adds:
" There is also a comely face of religion appearing throughout the whole
" city, in the private exercises thereof in the families, as may appear to
" any that walks through the streets; none being allowed either in or
" out of church time to play or saunter about; but reading scriptures,
" singing psalms, &c., to be heard in most houses."[1] There is reason
to fear, however, that in many cases it was only "a face of religion."
Absence from church was in those days a grave offence, and persons
who were guilty of it, or of "playing or sauntering about," were severely
dealt with.   The duty of looking after such delinquents was imposed by
the kirk session on the magistrates and ministers, who, by a minute of
session of 14th April, 1642, were directed "to go through the streets on
" Sabbath nights to search for persons who absent themselves from
" church: the town officers to go through with the Searchers."   By
another minute the session directs the searchers, on the Sabbath, to
pass into the houses and "to apprehend absents from the kirk."   These
searchers, or "compurgators" as they were called, were also employed in
perambulating the streets on Saturday nights, and when at the approach
of twelve o'clock they heard any noisy conviviality going on, even in
a private dwelling-house, they entered and dispersed the company.
Another of their duties was to perambulate the streets and public walks
during the time of divine service on Sunday, and compel every one they
met abroad, not on necessary duty, to go to church.   At a later period
it was left optional to the delinquents to go home, and if they refused to
do so they were taken into custody.   This practice was continued till so
late as the middle of last century, when the searchers having taken into
custody Mr. Peter Blackburn, father of Mr. Blackburn of Killearn, for
walking on the Green one Sunday, he prosecuted the magistrates and
succeeded in his suit.   This caused the practice to be abandoned.[2]

On the restoration of Episcopacy the archbishops took a leaf out of
the book of the kirk session in the matter of compulsory church attendance, and this in a way that neither the session nor the town council liked.
It was one thing to compel the inhabitants to come to church to hear the

---

[1] Pref. to Munimenta Universitatis, p. xxv.
[2] Notes by Dugald Bannatyne, Esq., quoted in Statistical Account, vol. vi. p. 231.

" ministers," and a very different thing to have attendance enforced on the episcopal ordinances, and the orders of the prelates were to a great extent disregarded. In these circumstances Archbishop Fairfowl applied to the town council, and insisted on their enforcing the law; and this was followed, under date 3d April, 1666, by a curious entry in the records of the council. It bears that there was produced a letter " direct thereto " be the Archbishop of Glasgow in the quhilk his Grace declaires that " efter search he findes severall persones both men and weomen who " ordinarlie dishantes [dis-haunts—forsakes] publict ordinances and " flateres themselfes with hope of impunitie, but knew not from whence " thir confidence springes, and therefor thought it his Grace dewtie to " adverteis the Counsell that his Grace intendit, gif thair fynes be not " exactlie leived be them, to employ some of the officers of his Majesties " Melitia both to observe who withdrawes from ordinances, and also to " exact the penalties imposed by law which his Grace is verie vnwilling " to doe." This letter troubled the magistrates not a little. It was " severall tymes read," and, after much discussion, " it was concludit be " pluralitie of votes that it was better for the toune that thes fynes war col- " lectit and wpliftit be the Magistrates, to the effect they might be applyed " to pius vses, then that any sojers should have the collecting thairof."

But to return to the kirk session. Previous to the Restoration it would appear that certain pictures and crucifixes, saved from the general destruction, still remained in the High Church, and no doubt many such were to be found in the houses of those who adhered to the proscribed faith. By an act of an Assembly held at Aberdeen in 1640, it was ordered that all these should be removed, and the execution of this order naturally fell to the magistrates. But either they were slow to execute it, or the kirk session did not choose to wait for them, and accordingly we find the session issuing an order on the magistrates to take the necessary steps. " The session enacted that the Magistrates " will cause all monuments of idolatry to be taken down and destroyed " viz. all superstitious pictures crucifixes &c. both in private houses and " in the Hie Kirk;" and the magistrates appear to have acted on the mandate and made the search. But it had not been very successful, as " next day it was reported that they found only three that could be " called so viz. the five wounds of Christ, the Holy Lamb, and Quinti- " gerne ora pro nobis."[1]

[1] 8th January, 1641.

The kirk session was particularly severe on "swearers, blasphemers,
" and mockers of piety." By one of their minutes they appoint "some
" of their number to go through the toun on the market day, till the
" magistrates provide one for that office, to take order with banners and
" swearers." Swearers are ordained to pay twelve pence (a penny), and
for the second fault to be rebuked in church.

But the kirk session did not confine themselves to morals and church
matters. In the year 1598 we find the following curious entry: "The
" Session thinks good that the University, ministers, and Presbytery,
" take cognisance who are within the toun that pretend to have skill in
" medicine and hath not the same, that they who have skill may be re-
" tained and the others rejected." And a message is sent to the town
council "to see what course to take with such."[1]

The first regular assessment for the support of the poor was made,
as we have seen, in 1638, but at a much earlier period the kirk session
had been doing something in that way at their own hand. In 1595
they appointed a committee to prepare "a roll of the people who were
" able in the toun to be stented for helping the poor;" and this they
must have enforced, for there occur frequent entries afterwards of the
distribution by the session of the money raised for this purpose. They
also enacted that no beggars were to be allowed on the streets or at
doors, and they got constables appointed to see this enforced, but not
apparently to much purpose, as street begging continued for a long time
after that.

Immediately before the Reformation, and for some time after it, the
habits of the lower orders in Glasgow appear to have been far from ex-
emplary—the gentler sex being apparently worse than the men. In
1589 we find the town council specially convened "becauss of the mani-
" fauld blasphemies and evill wordis vsst be sindrie wemen;" and as a
preventive measure, "they haif concludit that ane pair joges be set upp
" vpon the goves, gangand up with thrie or four fut stepis."[2] The
magistrates also by another minute appoint two persons "to attend everie
" day about the Cross, but especially at the sitting of Justice Courtes, for
" executing ther decreits against blasphemers, raillers, cursers, and other
" vicious livers." Immorality prevailed to a large extent. The session,
as might be supposed, took such cases specially into its own hands, and
it was not slow to deal with them. Offences for which, in our day, there

---

[1] 14th Sept. 1598.   [2] Minute of Council, 3d June, 1589.

is no punishment, were visited with penalties which would startle offenders now if they were applied and enforced as they were in those times. A pillar was set apart in the churches, and there the delinquent was obliged to stand before the congregation, sometimes for six Sabbaths in succession, "bare foot and bare legged and in sackcloth," and in some instances "to be carted through the toun."[1] On a repetition, and if the offender had been excommunicated, reconciliation to the church was to be obtained after this fashion. He is "to pass from his dwelling house to the "Hie Kirk every Sunday at six in the morning, at the first bell, convoyed "by two of the elders or deacons or any other two honest men, and "stand at the kirk door, barefooted and bare legged, with a white wand "in his hand, bareheaded, till after the reading of the text, and then in "the same manner to repair to the pillar till the sermon be ended, and "then go out to the door again till all pass from the kirk; and after this "be received."

At such exhibitions the congregation looked on no doubt with becoming reverence, but not such was the case with a party of English soldiers who were quartered in the town in 1655, whose treatment of the ceremonial was the occasion of the following minute: "The Session "resolves that so long as the English continue in the toun they will put "no person on the pillar *because they mock at them.*"

It may be believed that immorality was not confined to the lower orders, but it is not to the credit of the session that even-handed justice was not meted out when the offender was of higher degree. It so happened that on one occasion there was found in this category no less a person than the Laird of Minto. But then he *was* the Laird of Minto. He had recently been provost, and he was a person of influence in the town. Accordingly, in the exercise of a prudent discretion, and on his paying the very moderate commutation of "20 lib" (£1, 13s. 4d.) "the "Session *pass the laird*, considering his age, and the station he held in "the town."

Even the ministers were not free from the charge of exercising occasionally an undue partiality in such matters, and it was the occasion of a minute in 1630, by which "the Presbytery censures the ministers "of Glasgow for dispensing with public repentance for money."

In matters such as marriages, games, and banquets, the session exercised a like despotic authority. In 1583 they decreed that there should

[1] Minute of Session, 1586.

be "no superfluous gatherings at banquets or marriages; that the price
" of the dinner should be eighteen pence [less than twopence], and that
" persons married shall find caution to that effect." In 1593 they "directed
" the drum to go through the town that there be no bickering nor plays
" on Sundays either by old or young, and that no person go to Ruglen
" to see vain plays on Sunday."

But apart from the restriction on the price of the banquets, it was
not so simple a matter to get married then as it is nowadays. There
was something more required than a promise to love, honour, and
obey. In 1591 the session enacted that "those who are to be married
" declare the ten commandments, Articles of faith and Lord's prayer,
" or else they shall be declared unworthy to be joined in marriage
" and further censured."[1] And following up this there is an entry
in the session records in the same month bearing that a marriage
had been actually stopped "till the man learn the Ten Commandments
"the Lord's Prayer and Belief."[2]

And the sentence of the kirk session was no mere *brutum fulmen.*
They enforced as well as pronounced it. They caused "a ward house"
to be constructed in the steeple of the Blackfriars' Church, and to
this prison they committed offenders. One person is sentenced to
confinement for eight days, and instructions are given "to the beddal
" to let *steeplers* get nothing but bread and water, or small drink, so
" long as they continue in the steeple."[3] An individual who had been
absent from "the examination" and the communion for several years
is committed to the steeple, and ordered to make public repentance
besides. In 1609 the session enacts that all offenders shall pay their
penalties personally before leaving the session house, "or be put in
" the steeple till it be paid."

In 1665 the manse of the Prebendary of Cambuslang on the south
side of the Drygate was acquired by the Earl of Glencairn, who in that
year sold it to the magistrates, who, as I have already mentioned,
converted it into a house of correction for persons of dissolute character.
Of this new prison the kirk session took advantage—the Blackfriars'
Church having become ruinous—and immediately afterwards there
occur entries in their records ordaining persons to be taken to the house
of correction, both men and women, and appointing them "to be whipped
"every day during the Sessions will."

[1] 20th Dec. 1591.   [2] 26th Dec. 1591.   [3] Session Records, 7th Sept. 1604.

But the session had still more alarming penalties in store for female delinquents—notably among these being ducking in the Clyde. The magistrates had themselves previously resorted to this mode of enforcing morality, as we find an entry in the burgh accounts of a payment in 1575 "to the officeris for dowking of Janet Fawside xld." (about five-pence).[1] But the kirk session improved upon this. By a minute in 1587 certain women are adjudged to be imprisoned and fed fifteen days on bread and water, and "to be put on a cart one day, and ducked "in Clyde, and to be put in the jugs at the Cross on a Monday," that being the market day. The ducking system seems to have proved a success, but as the duckers probably fared as bad as the ducked an ingenious device was resorted to in order to obviate that inconvenience. The session appointed a pulley to be made on the bridge, whereby the offenders "may be ducked in the Clyde." By the same minute the time of exposure at the pillar in the church is relaxed, and it is declared that for a single offence the punishment shall be "*only* eight days in the steeple, one day on the cockstool and one "day at the pillar."

I have mentioned the stringent measures which the session took to compel attendance at church. When the people were got there they were subjected to an equally rigorous censorship. In 1587 the session enacted "that all persons in time of prayer bow their knee to "the ground." In 1588 they ordered some ash-trees in the High Church yard to be cut down "to make forms for the folk to sit on in the kirk." But this was for the accommodation of the male sex only, for in the following year they ordain "that no woman sit upon or occupy the "forms men should sit on, but either sit laigh or else bring stools "with them."[2] By a later minute they ordained "that no woman "married or unmarried come within the kirk doors to preachings or "prayers with their plaids about their heads, neither lie down in the "kirk on their face in time of prayer, *sleeping that way;* with certi- "fication that their plaids shall be drawn down or they roused by "the beddel."[3] For the better preservation of order they got the town council to enact, on the occasion of the filling up of "the beddell- "ship of the Laigh Kirk in Trongait," that it should be the duty of that official not only to ring the bells, "but also to walk throw the "kirk in tyme of divyne service with ane whyt staff in his hand, as

---

[1] 6th Nov. 1575.   [2] 10th July, 1589.   [3] 3d May, 1604.

"wont to be of old, for the crubbing of bairnes and uthirs that maks
"disturbance in the kirk, and for impeiding of all abuses therin."[1]
I find a similar regulation in the minutes of the kirk session of Perth
in 1616, which ordains the session officer "to have his red staff in
"the kirk on the sabbath days therewith to wauken sleepers and to
"remove greeting bairns furth of the kirk."

Even in cases of separation between man and wife the kirk session
of Glasgow took it upon them to exercise jurisdiction. One occasion
is recorded when there came before them two married persons "who
"declare they are content to separate one from another till God
"send more love into their hearts;" and the man having undertaken
to give the wife a small yearly allowance, "the session consent to this."[2]

Nothing indeed appears to have escaped the cognizance of the
session. It might be supposed that at any rate the regulation of the
city ports would be under the exclusive control of the magistrates.
But no. "The Session enacted that the ports be shut on Sabbath
"at twelve o'clock," and that care be taken "that no traveller go out
"or come in the town, and watches to be set where there are no
"ports." By another minute "the Session enact that the ports be
"shut on Saturday night, and watches set to observe travellers."[3] By
a later order they enact "that the ports be well kept in time of sermon
"because of the highlandmen."

The influence of the session continued to be felt till far on in the
eighteenth century, and they appear to have had always considerable
funds at their disposal. When the first town's hospital was erected
in Clyde Street in 1735 it was arranged that, besides a tax on the
citizens, the sum of £570 towards the cost should be provided by
the joint contributions of the town council, the Merchants' House, the
Trades' House, and the general session, and of this sum the session
gave no less than £250—the town council giving only £140.

The records of the Presbytery also contain many curious entries
which throw light on the manners and customs of these early times.

I have referred to the general practice of carrying arms, and the
presbytery books afford evidence that in this the clergy formed no
exception. The following entry occurs not long after the Reformation:
"On Sunday 28th August 1587 William Cuningham when going up
"by the Wynd heid with his son Umphra and some other persons

---

[1] 25th March, 1665.   [2] 22d October, 1635.   [3] 18th August, 1637.

" abused Mr. Wemyss the minister of the Hie Kirk, and in coming
" down from the kirk the father and son attacked Mr. Wemyss with
" a quhingear and a pistolet, called him a liar, and struck him on
" the head and breast which made him retire.   Mr. Wemyss in fear
" of his life cast his goun over his arm and *drew his quhingear* in
" his defence.   The Cuninghams attempted to draw their pistolets
" but were prevented by the Parson of Renfrew, who coming doun
" the Rattonraw at the time, and seeing the scuffle *drew his quhingear*,
" and defeated the Cuninghams, who were sentenced to ask pardon
" of God, of the Kirk, of the Magistrates, and of Mr. Wemyss, first
" at the Wynd heid, and then before the Congregation of the Kirk."
The record goes on to say that " the Presbiterie hereon admonished their
" ministers to be diligent in their study, grave in their apparel and not
" vain with long rufils and vain gaudy toys in their clothing."

Repeated instances occur of the presbytery dealing with parties
who had used violence in churches.   On one occasion " Andro Granger
" grantis y^t he drew his quhinzeir vilfully in ye queer, ye preiching place
" of Glasgow, aganis Arthur Allan burges of Glasgw."   He expresses
his regret, and is appointed to make public repentance.[1]   On another
occasion the presbytery deals with John Stirling for forcibly entering
the kirk of Cadder, during the administration of the communion, " with
" ane drawin quhinzeir in his hand," whereby the people were put in
terror and the tables with the elements were " cassen to the grund."
For this act of sacrilege John was excommunicated.   He was subsequently released from this much-dreaded sentence, but only on his
finding surety to obey the injunctions of the presbytery.   What these
were is thus detailed: " Y^e first ye said J^{on} paye ye sowme of fourtie
" merkes, q^{r}of ten merkis to be gevin to the Kirk of Cader, and twentie
" lib to ye Collector in ye presbiterie to be bestowit to godlie wses;
" And y^t being done y^t ye said J^{on} mak his publict repentance in
" secklay^t bairfutit, bairleggit, and bairheidit, first in ye Kirk of Cader:
" 2 in ye Kirk of Glasgw: 3 in Leinzaie Kirk: 4 in campsie: 5 in
" monyaburt: and ye rest of ye said dayes in ye said Kirk of Cader,
" in maner of excommunicats—y^t is, standing at ye Kirk duir of everie
" ane of ye said Kirkis, yan entring to ye piller y^r in remaining q^{ll} ye
" sermont be endit; yan cuming fra ye piller and standing at ye Kirk
" duir q^l ye pepell be cum furt of ye Kirk, and swa to indure wnto

[1] 9th Dec. 1595.

" yᵉ next Synodall assemblie." It is to be presumed that John went through all this, as we hear no more of him.[1]

The fines levied in such cases were usually ordered to be applied to public works. The maintenance of bridges in those days was a matter of great importance, and we find many of the fines imposed by the presbytery of Glasgow were ordered to be applied "to repair yᵉ brig of "Inchbellie," to "big the brig of Kirkintillat," for "reparacioun of yᵉ brig "of Campsie," and other such purposes.

Among other offences dealt with and prohibited by the presbytery was "the playing of bagpipes on Sondaye from sun rising to its going "doun," and practising other pastimes after canonical hours under pain of censure.[2] This limitation of the time for indulging in amusements appears to have been only carrying out an extraordinary order which the presbytery had issued a few years before prescribing the limits of the Sabbath. Their minute bears that they "interpret the sabbath to "be from sun to sun—no work to be done between light and light in "winter and between sun and sun in summer."[3] It was not till fifty years afterwards that the presbytery declared that the Sabbath "shall be from "12 on Saturday night to 12 on Sunday night."[4]

Reverence to parents was strictly enforced in these times. On one occasion we find the presbytery dealing with a young man because of his being "gudget stubborne and a disobedient sone to his father"—a chief cause of his offence being that he had "cum by his father and his bonnet "on his heid, not salutand his father."[5]

Extravagance at bridal parties was strictly prohibited by the presbytery, as it was by the session. The latter, as we have seen, had in 1583 limited the expenditure to eighteenpence Scots. The presbytery ten years later relaxed the rule so as to allow forty pence—about fourpence of our money—for each person present. If anything was spent beyond that it was followed by a penalty.[6] Instances of the infliction of money fines by the presbytery are very numerous, and they appear, like those of the session, to have been enforced. Among the offences punished in this way, and also by the prescription of penance, are absence from church, non-attendance at the communion, "wirking on the Sondaye," and "leiding of cornes" on that day; and in one case punishment is awarded

[1] Presbytery Records, 14th May, 1595.   [2] 7th May, 1594.
[3] 17th January, 1590.   [4] 18th August, 1640.   [5] 6th February, 1598.
[6] 29th January, 1593; 22d April, 1594.

because the offender "ryidis on Sondayes to sek his dettis." And the presbytery, as a rule, were no respecters of persons. They ordered Lord Fleming to be summoned for being absent from the kirk of Lenzie on a particular Sunday when he was at Cumbernauld, because it was "the motive and greit occasion moving his tenantis to byd avay fra "yᵉ kirk."

We have seen how the kirk session exercised jurisdiction in cases of separation between man and wife, and an illustration of the extent to which a similar jurisdiction was exercised by the presbytery of Glasgow is found in a case of divorce, on the ground of desertion, which came before them early in the seventeenth century. A man and a woman—John Philpe and Helen Willsoun—appeared craving the authority of the presbytery for their marriage, notwithstanding an allegation that a former husband of the woman was still alive. The presbytery having "efter tryell founde that now it is mair than twentie yeiris since hir hus- "band left hir, quho since that time hes not been hard of, grantis libertie "to the saidis John and Helen to marie."[1]

Repeated cases also occur of the presbytery trying cases of breach of promise of marriage. In one case the offender, Helein Bull, confessed to "refusing to marie Johne Miller wᵗ quhome scho hes bein proclaimit "twyse, now being of mind to marie Patrik Bryce." She is adjudged "to mak hir repentance in hir paroche kirk of Leinzae for hir incon- "stancie, and forder to pay penaltie to the thesaurer of hir kirk the "nixt sondaye afore she entir to hir repentance."[2] In another case about the same time the lady was the complainer, and her swain having denied the promise, and there being no proof, she referred it to his oath. The minute of the presbytery is as follows: "Quhilk daye " Johnne gudden denyis he maid promise to marie Jonet Busset and "sweiris be his aithe yᵗ he maid na promise to marie hir—it being "referrit yᵗto be yᵉ said Jonet; Thairfore yᵉ Kirk absolvis yᵉ said Johnne "fra yᵉ said Jonetis psute and grantis to him libertie to marie in yᵉ Lord "quhat woman he sall pleis."[3] So frequent were such cases of breach of promise that we find the kirk session of Cambusnethan enacting "that "each pairtie to be proclaimit sould lay doun aucht merk, and the pairtie "rewer sould lose theirs, and the other sould get their aught merks vp "againe."[4]

But the presbytery did not confine themselves to pecuniary penalties.

[1] 1610. [2] 7th September, 1596. [3] 1st July, 1595. [4] 13th January, 1650.

N

Here is what an unfortunate wight had to undergo for "dinging" his stepmother. "Quhilk daye the Presbiterie ordaine Gavin Lekprevik, " for dinging of Marioun Maxwell his stepmother to be in the joggis " the nixt sondaye be the space of half ane hour afoir his minister sall " entir to the sermont, and to stand thairin the said space in linen " cleithes, bairfuttit bair leggit and bair heidit; and how sone his said " minister sall entir in the kirk to preiche Gods word, that he pas on " the piller within the said kirk, and thairon remane during the haill " tyme of the sermont, and at the command of his minister to ask God " his kirk and the said Marioun forgiveness on his kneis, for the sclandeir " he hes committit be the dinging of the said Marioun and that he find " souertie under the pane of xx lib money that he sall obey this ordi- " nance."[1]

One offence, with a rather startling designation, with which the presbytery appears to have had repeatedly to deal, was what is called in their records "smooring bairns"—that is, smothering children. For example: "three women parochinaris of Cadder accusit of smooring " thair bairnis in the nicht are referrit to the Session of Cadder to be " tryit thair;" and there are many other examples. The delinquents are chiefly women, but on some occasions the man appears and is " rebuked for being art and part in smooring the bairn." Some have supposed that these were cases of deliberate smothering—in plain words, child murder—but this was not so. They were merely cases where the child had lost its life through the carelessness or intemperate habits of the parent. The lightness of the punishment awarded, indeed, shows this. An early entry in the records bears that the presbytery " advises and resolves that smoorers of bairns mak thair repentance " two sondayes in sekcleith standing at the Kirk door."[2] And it is made still more clear by an entry in the following century, which bears that "a number of women in the town having overlaid their children " in their drunkenness the Presbiterie advise that the old Act touching " the repentance be revised and put in execution."[3]

Another crime with which the Presbytery of Glasgow, in common with all the other presbyteries in Scotland, dealt with exceptional severity was witchcraft; and some of their minutes on the subject are very curious. In the end of the sixteenth century there occurs this entry: "Qlk daye comperit Sibill Dowe and grantis y‡ scho said wordes

[1] 13th May, 1607. [2] 27th April, 1592. [3] 25th December, 1647.

" to hir fellow servant woman tuiching ye houlat hart [owl's heart] to
" be rubbit to ane manis shuldeir, to cause a man to luif ane woman;
" but scho usit not that thing in any sort."

Shortly afterwards we find the presbytery taking cognisance of a
case where an individual in the parish of Lenzie[1] had used the very old
practice of divination by "turning the riddle" to discover the guilty
party in cases of theft. The practice was to place the riddle or sieve on
a pair of tongs held and lifted up by only two fingers. The name of
the suspected party being mentioned, if the sieve trembled or was moved
round he was held to be guilty.[2] In the case referred to in the Presbytery of Glasgow the minute is as follows: "Quhilk daye compeirit Jo^n
" Robeson in Leinzie paroche and grantis y^t at ye command of margret
" prestik spous to Johnne braid, Christiane braid his dochteir past to
" Kate hopkin to desyr hir to cum doun and turne ye riddell upone
" yame y^t had tane away his cleithes: ye said Kate come, ye said Jo^n
" braid being afield, ye said Kate turnit ye riddell for his cleithes y^t he
" wantit." For this "greit and heynous sin" John Robeson is decerned
to make his repentance on the pillar and to ask pardon at God and his
kirk,—and Katherine Hopkin, for turning the riddle, is subjected to the
same penance.[3]

A similar superstition prevails at the present day in Shropshire. A
key is placed on a Bible, with the fingers of the party holding it placed
so as to form a cross. It is thus carried from house to house, and on
coming to the residence of the guilty party the key is supposed to turn
completely round.

Another case in which witchcraft was practised in the olden time was
for the purpose of getting mills to grind freely. With such a case we
find the Presbytery of Glasgow dealing on the 24th of March, 1602.
" Quhilk daye compeirit William grinla in ye parochin of Leinzae and
" grantis yat William baird in Balloche gart him gang w^t him to Annie
" forsyithe and thai bayth besocht ye said Annie for godis saik to cause
" ye mylne gang to grind ye said William bairds meill; and y^t ye said
" William baird opened his sek, and ye said Annie pat hir hand in ye sek,
" and efter y^t ye said mylne geid." At a subsequent diet the presbytery
find that the parties "have committed a capital crime replenischit with
" sorcerie," and understanding that the woman Annie is fugitive, they
remit the two men "to Lord Flemyng yair ordinar to underly punisch-

---

[1] Kirkintilloch. [2] Weirus de Magis Infamibus, c. 12, p. 134. [3] 9th December, 1601.

"ment for thair offence." Lord Fleming reserving to himself "yᵉ
"pecuniall sum" to be exacted from them, remitted them back to the
presbytery to prescribe the penance, and the presbytery for their "horrible
"sine" appointed them to make their repentance publicly in each of
three several kirks in sackcloth, "bairfuttit, bairleggit, and bairheidit, sex
"severall sondayes and to crave Gods mercie for declyning to praye to
"God and inclining to the said Annie."

On another occasion we find the presbytery ordaining the minister of
Rutherglen to summon the persons within his parish "quha in yᵉ tyme
"called ʒule days used Gysrie superstitiouslie and troublit yʳ nichtboars
"in yᵉ nicht tyme to yᵉ great offence of God and his kirk."[1] The
offenders are afterwards ordained to make public repentance. And on
a subsequent occasion the presbytery "ordaines James broun in Ruglen
"allegit gysor in womens cloathes to be summoned."[2] This relates to
the well-known and, as we now think, very innocent practice of young
men and boys going about at Christmas masked or disguised, and enacting in the halls or kitchens of the better classes a rude sort of play or
mystery. Sir Walter Scott, in "The Pirate," referring to this custom,
mentions a party "setting forth as maskers, or as they are called in
"Scotland, Guizards." The custom, I believe, dates from a very early
period. In Glasgow the party were sometimes called "Galatians"—no
doubt from the opening words invariably used by the first performer,
"Here comes I, Galatian."

On a later occasion the presbytery ordains Agnes Gourlay, "to mak
"publick repentance in sekclaith for charming kine."[3] The object in
this case was to produce good cream, and for the information of those
who may wish to repeat the experiment, I may state that the *modus
operandi* practised by Agnes was "casting some of the milk into the
"grup, and putting of salt and bread into the cow's lugs." The *grup* is
the trench for carrying off the sewage of the byre.

One peculiar case with which the presbytery dealt was that of Mr.
George Semple, minister of Killellan, who was accused by John Hutcheson, one of the bailies of Paisley, that "he had ane book of Mr. Michael
"Scotts of unlawful airtes; that he saw him buy Albertus Magnus; that
"he heard him speak of sundrie vnlawful conceits;" and, to crown all,
that "*he hard tell that he made ballads and sonnets.*"[4] There are among
ourselves some clerical gentlemen who collect curious books, and even

[1] 13th January, 1608. [2] 20th January, 1608. [3] 9th Dec. 1650. [4] 27th Oct. 1613.

some who write poetry, with whom it would have fared ill had they lived in those days. There were other charges against Mr. George, but the result of the trial is not stated.

Another case is interesting for a reason to be presently noticed. One Robert Stewart was accused "by a libelled summons," at the instance of the presbytery, of having refused to allow his child to be baptised, and for setting the authority of the presbytery at defiance; "as also for "invading [attacking] Mr. Jon Couper ane of ye ministers of Glasgw "doun y⁰ gait of Glasgw to ye blak frier kirk, touking him, dinging him "af y⁰ hicht of y⁰ cassie, minacing wᵗ wordes, minting to drawe ane sword "to him, and spewand out blasphemous filthie speeiches agains him." What is interesting in the case is that Stewart in his defence declined the jurisdiction of the presbytery, on a ground which has been frequently made the subject of observation in later times, viz. that the presbytery was both judge and prosecutor. "And being partie," he pleaded, "y⁰ "power of y⁰ Juge did failzie, for in y⁰ ane and y⁰ self same cause nane "can be bayt accuser and juge." So he appealed to the Synod and General Assembly. To this appeal the presbytery paid no regard, and having repeated their order to have the child baptized under pain of excommunication, Stewart "appellit fra ye said presbyterie to y⁰ kinges "maiestie and lordes of his secret consale." It seems to have been regarded as an exceptional case of high defiance of the church courts, and the presbytery appear to have themselves invoked the civil arm, for shortly after we find Stewart a prisoner in the castle of Glasgow, and two of the ministers appointed to confer with him there to ascertain "gif "he be penitent." What followed does not appear, there being no further mention of the case.

There occur in these old ecclesiastical records many other curious cases which my limits do not permit me to notice. But the chief business which occupied the presbytery was offences against morality—vice in all forms, profane swearing, blasphemy, personal violence, and homicide. At the period of the Reformation, as I have already said, the morals of the people of Glasgow and of the rural parishes adjoining must have been at a very low ebb, and during a long series of years there is hardly one page of the presbytery records in which there does not occur one or other of such cases. Among the offenders, too, were persons of all ranks, including both lords and ladies; and it is amusing to find the celebrated physician "Mr. Peter Lowe Doctor of chirurgerie" among those decerned to make repentance, and a complaint afterwards made of him for levity while under the penance; as the minute expresses it, for "not behaveing " him on the pillar as becomes."

Cases of homicide and other deeds of violence were frequent. Some of the latter I have already mentioned. Of the former, one is curious for the reference it contains to the practice of offenders in such cases compounding with the relatives of the slaughtered man. The minute of the presbytery is as follows: "Ordenis Jo^n Levingstoun in Inchevod to " produce yis day viii dayes before yame Lettres of Relaxation fra ye " horne, and respet he hes fra ye slauchter of wmq^{ll} Jo^n Adame: As also " ane *Lettir of Slayance* for y^e said slauchtir fra y^e said wmq^{ll} Jo^{ns} wyfe, " bairnis, kin, freindes and alyance for ye said slauchtir. And ordanis " y^t minister of Campsie to summond y^e said wmq^{ll} Jo^n wyfe and bairnis " before yame yis daye viii dayes, that yai may declair gif yai be ag$_3$reed " w^t ye said Jo^n Levingston and satisfeit for ye said wmq^{ll} Jo^n Adames " slauchtir."[1]

On another occasion Arthur Colquhoun is arraigned before the presbytery "for the cruelle murther of wmq^{ll} James Pincartoun his " brothers son quha had not affendit him." He is ordained "to under- " lye ye censure of ye kirk for ye saming," and subsequently he is excommunicated.[2]

A few pages on we find an individual dealt with "for swearing and " blasphemy;" another for coming into the church of Cathcart armed with hagbut and steel bonnet, and making a disturbance. A little farther on, Matthew Fleming, merchant burgess of Glasgow, is delated for having " in ane rage and anger" struck off the hat of Mr. John Young, minister of Beith, "on the high street of Glasgow," for which "hevie sclander to " Godis kirk" he is ordained to make his public repentance.[3] John Hamilton, younger of Preston, and another, are charged for a "sclandeir " offerit to ye kirk and presbiterie of Glasgow be ye hurting done be " yame of Robert Hamilton of Silveston and Andro Hamilton of Let- " thame in ye effusion of yair bluid wpone ane Sondaye eftir nwn amangis " ye middis of ye pepill cuming fra ye hie kirk at ye wynd heid of Glasgw " immediatelie eftir ye preeching."[4] A parishioner of Campsie is en- joined penance for having "interrupted his minister in the pulpit by " mony proud wordes before the lettir prayer."[5] And a woman is

---

[1] Presbytery Records, 7th Feb. 1595.   [2] 8th April, 1600.
[3] 31st October, 1603.   [4] 25th April, 1598.   [5] 7th May, 1606.

charged with "laying doun twa twynes [twins] at y: door of ane poor "honest man." Cases of ordinary discipline for immorality occur, with wearisome regularity, at almost every diet of the presbytery, as do likewise cases of Sabbath-breaking. On one occasion an individual is charged with "y͏ᵉ sclandeir done be slaying on y͏ᵉ Lordes daye of salmont "and red fische;" and accusations for attending stage plays on Sunday are frequent—these, curiously enough, being almost invariably enacted at Rutherglen.

Of charges against ministers there are few, but they do occur occasionally. One of the presbytery, Mr. David Weems, is accused that he is "fund to be declynand in doctrine, negligent in preparacioun, and "in his teaching hes gevin occasioun of lauchtir; and aftymes to be "overtaine w: drink."[1] Another minister is charged with the crime of usury—receiving interest on certain sums he had lent. In this case the proceedings are voluminous and protracted, for usury in those days was a serious offence.

The records of the presbytery contain also some curious notices regarding their forms of procedure. For example, we are accustomed to suppose that only a minister can be moderator at meetings of a presbytery, but it was not always so. On one occasion there were in the Glasgow presbytery two candidates for the office—one a minister and the other a schoolmaster—and the schoolmaster was elected.[2]

The ministers, as a rule, were educated gentlemen, many of them belonging to the best families; and they were undoubtedly the true patriots of the time. Repeated evidences of this occur in their records. In the time of the Commonwealth there was read in the Presbytery of Glasgow a letter from the Presbytery of Edinburgh, subscribed by Mr. Hugh M'Kail, pointing out the expediency of ministers of their own accord contributing to the defence of the country, and suggesting the levying of a regiment of horse in the interests of Cromwell. This was agreed to—the whole members contributing in proportion to their stipends.[3] The regiment thus raised by the Presbytery of Glasgow was called "the ministers' regiment," and was commanded by General Strachan.

For a long time there were no pews in the churches in Glasgow, and when seats came to be provided they were free. They were first let in 1667, and one of the bailies and the master of work was

[1] Presbytery Records, 29th October, 1600. [2] 11th March, 1600. [3] 16th July, 1650.

appointed "to visit the haill seats and lay on the quantitie of mailles "thairon."[1]

The ministers had, indeed, much need of seat-rents. Out of the ample possessions which belonged to the church at the Reformation the rapacity of the nobles left but a scanty remnant for the support of the ministers, and their stipends in the end of the sixteenth century were miserably inadequate. There is an incidental notice of this in a minute of presbytery in 1595. It bears that the Presbytery of Glasgow consists of six churches, viz., Glasgow, Govan, Rutherglen, Cadder, Lenzie, and Campsie, "and of the said sex Kirkis thair is the minister "of Campsie ane auld man having onlie in yeirlie stipend fourscoir and "sex lib [about £9] and the minister of Leinzae onlie in stipend fourtie "aucht lib with the vicarage worth twentie merkis in the ȝeir [alto- "gether under £7] and the saidis ministers of Campsie and Leinzae "throch povertie keipis nocht the dayes of presbiterie."[2] No wonder. The object which the presbytery had in view, however, was not the increase of the emoluments of these poor gentlemen—which was probably at that time hopeless—but to get the General Assembly to cause the church of Monkland and some other churches to be joined to the Presbytery of Glasgow so as to increase the number of members necessary for the despatch of business. At a period long after this the stipend of the first charge in Glasgow was only 500 merks—equal at that time to £27, 15s. 6d.; that of the second charge was 300 merks—£16, 13s. 4d.; that of Cadder was only 68 lib. vis. viiid. and three chalders—in all £14, 17s. 6d. In many cases residence was impossible for want of a house, and the minister of Cadder had to reside and study in the steeple. It was true what Knox wrote, that "thair was none within the realme more "unmercyfull to the poor ministers than war thei whiche had the greatest "rentis of the churches."[3]

---

[1] Minute of Council, 16th Dec. 1667.   [2] Presbytery Records, 16th March, 1595.
[3] Knox's Hist. vol. ii. p. 128.

MUNICIPAL AND SOCIAL HISTORY.

To return to the corporation. The manner in which the magistrates conducted the affairs of the city in early times was in all probability much the same as prevailed in other burghs. So far as can be judged from the records they appear to have acted, on the whole, with intelligence and discretion, and with a considerable amount of public spirit. Some notices of their proceedings, and of the manner in which they conducted municipal affairs, cannot fail to be interesting.

When left with perfect freedom of action we find them, as a rule, acting equitably and with prudence; but they lived in unsettled times, and had sometimes to bend to circumstances. On one occasion they were obliged, against their own judgment, to issue an order to eject from his holding a valued servant, "John Hamiltoune their tenant "in Provand," on account of his "keeping of conventickles"—the reason recorded being "that the secreit counsell is insensed against "the toune for suffering him to doe the samyne," and that his removal had become necessary "for preventing, therfor, the danger the toune "may sustein."[1] In the same way they had to submit to the disgraceful order of the privy council which required "the wyfes and families "of all vtted ministers" to be expelled from the city.[2] In 1645 they showed a want of discretion when, on the victory of Montrose at Kilsyth, the magistrates then in office gave expression to their sympathies with what they thought to be the winning side by inviting the marquis to Glasgow and entertaining him sumptuously. But they speedily paid the penalty of their indiscretion, for in the following month, Leslie having gained the battle of Philiphaugh, his first act was to lay Glasgow under a heavy contribution, which he jeeringly told the magistrates was to pay the interest of the money they had expended in entertaining Montrose. And this was not the only penalty they had to suffer, for when the magistrates came to be elected immediately afterwards the Committee of the Estates of parliament interfered and insisted on the exclusion from office of all those who had been "actours in the capitu- "latioune with James Grahame."[3] They had no doubt a difficult part

---

[1] Burgh Records, 5th Oct. 1678.   [2] 22d March, 1679.   [3] Minute of Council, 30th Sept. 1645.

to play, but at the Revolution the favours conferred on the city showed how much the government of William and Mary was satisfied that the bulk of the inhabitants had been true to the Protestant cause, and that the authorities, on the whole, had been careful of the maintenance of order in very trying times.

In the administration of justice the magistrates appear to have shown considerable vigour, and if the constitutional liberty of the subject was sometimes invaded—as undoubtedly it occasionally was—the error was generally on the side of equity, and the act one of poetical justice. Some of the punishments awarded were certainly of the latter character. On one occasion " Richeart Herbertsoun fleschour" was brought before them "for the maist barbarus bangsterrie done be him against James " Watsoun flescheour, and for stiking of the said James Watsouns grit " dog." The slain dog was represented as worth £2 sterling, and " maist necessar and profitable to him;" and James craved "to be fred " of the said Richearts oppressioun, bost, and bangsterrie, in tyme cum- " ing and to mak the said James satisfactioune and recompens for his " said dog." Richard having appeared and confessed, the punishment awarded was that he be "wardit qll monanday next and that day stockit " at the croce, and *the dog to be laid befoir him*," and thereafter to be put in sure ward till he find security to keep the peace.[1] On another occa- sion a person described as "ane idill vagabound" is apprehended "upon " suspitione" of having committed an assault on a young child. There is no trial, and no evidence whatever is taken, but on the strength of the *suspicion* only, and of the assumed fact that he *is* an idle vagabond, he is ordained off-hand "to be laid in the stokis qll the evening, and " thairefter put out of the toun at the west port, *and banist the same for-* " *evir;* and gif evir he be fund within this toun heireftir, of his awin " consent, *to be hangit* but [without] ane assyze."

But although the magistrates, as a rule, dispensed even-handed justice, they undoubtedly did so in many instances in a very arbitrary way, and with little regard to constitutional forms. To such an extent had this come to be carried by the magistrates who came into power after the Restoration, that it became a public scandal, and in 1684 we find the following minute by their successors: "The same day the " Magistrats and counsell considering the great clamour made be the " tounes people by the abuses committed be the lait Magistrats these

---

[1] 25th January, 1612.

" few yeirs past by decerning severall persones to pay debts and soumes
" of money to others, and extorting and exacting fynes from several
" of them, without vsing ane probatioune or decerning any formall
" sentence against them in public court, far contrair to the law and
" pratique of the burgh: for remeid therof it is enacted and con-
" cluded that in tyme cuming none of the Magistrats within the burgh,
" Baillie of Gorballs, nor Watter baillie, shall have power to fyne any
" persone except by conveining the transgressors in a public court."[1]

The arbitrary committing of suspected persons to prison—often
on the mere verbal orders of a magistrate, and without ever bringing
them to trial, was a practice not confined to Glasgow. Mr. Hector
gives many instances of the same kind occurring in Paisley even
so late as the end of the last century. Here is one taken out of
many from the judicial records: " May 6, 1791, Archibald Bogle incar-
" cerated by order of Bailie Brown on suspicion of desertion. May 17
" liberated by order of Bailie Brown." Thus, adds Mr. Hector, Bogle
was imprisoned eleven days without a warrant, and liberated probably
after the bailie had discovered that there was no foundation even for
suspicion.[2] And there are many other similar cases.

From an incidental notice in one of the council minutes we learn
the interesting fact that the magistrates of Glasgow, like some of the
rulers in Eastern cities in Scripture times, were in the custom of standing
in the public street, near the cross, to hear the suits of the citizens
and to dispense summary justice. On one of these occasions a person, described as a merchant burgess, addressed the provost in dis-
respectful and abusive terms—the crime being aggravated by the fact
that some distinguished strangers were standing by. The whole scene
is so curious, and it is so graphically described in the record, that I need
make no apology for transcribing it: " 2 April 1678 The quhilk day
" the Baillies and Counsell being conveined anent the complent given
" in befor them by John Grahame Procurator Fiscall of this burgh
" against Thomas Crawforde, merchand burges thereof, makand mention
" that upon yesterday the 1st of April instant James Campbell present
" Proveist of the said burgh with sundrie utheris, the Magistratis and
" uthir burgessis, being standing on the plaine stones beneth the tol-
" buith, *the place ordinarie for the Magistratis ther waiting and attending*
" *to heir the Complents and grievances of the burgesses and uthirs, and to*

---

[1] 27th October, 1684.   [2] Judicial Records of Renfrewshire (second series), p. 221.

"*give them justice incumbent to their office accordingly;* And at that tyme
" being about thrie houris in the afternoone, several persones of qualitie
" and strangers war standing besyd, the said Thomas Crawforde in
" ane arrogant and prowd maner, without consideratioune or respect
" that he, as a burges of this burgh, oweth to his Magistratis to whom
" he is sworne be his burges oath to give them all dew obedience,
" most contrair therto, in a furious way come to the said James Campbell
" Proveist, and there fell in questioning him about sundrie things, and
" did challing him therupone; and the Proveist having desyred him
" severall tymes to desist *becaus of the straingers, onlookers* and mar-
" velling at the Proveists patience, and the miscarriadge of the said
" Thomas, Trew it is the said Thomas wold nowayes decist but said
" in a disdainful way to the Proveist that he knew his malice and
" wold byd the butt of it &c." The fiscal accordingly craved the
council " to wnlaw and fyne him, and to rive and destroy his burges
" and gild brother ticket, and to cry down his fredome;" and this
is ordered to be done.

On various other occasions the magistrates showed that they were
tenacious of their dignity, and repeated notices occur in the burgh
records of parties being punished for behaving disrespectfully toward
them.   On one occasion " William Watson alias Blackhous William,"
is accused of " contempt and misbehaviour done be him to the magis-
" tratis in uttring disdaynful speiches to thame, *with his bonet on his*
" *head,* and being desyrit be ane of his nychtbors to tak af his bonet
" and reverence the magistratis, answerit and said, with bannyng, that
" he would not take af his bonet to the baillie." The culprit having
" confessit his misbehaviour," and the magistrates having " fund the
" same ane hie and proud contempt and evill example to utheris to
" do the lyke," inflicted a fine of ten pounds (16s. 8d.).   But in this
case, as in too many others, punishment did not bring reformation.
Blackhouse William had been unable to pay his fine, and having
been consigned to durance he threatened to set fire to the prison,
and actually attempted to do so, protesting at the same time that
" he wad naither acknowledge provest nor bailie, king nor casart,"
and for this he was again arraigned.   The opprobrious words he denied,
but he " confessit that being wardit in ane hie chalmer of the Tolbuth
" he pat fyre in ane pekle straw in his anger." This time justice was
vindicated by the offender being " ordanit to be wardit *in ane unfree-*

" *mans ward* quhill the morn, being mercat day, and then to walk
" bare heidit to the croce, and after being put in the irnes thair be
" the space of 4 hórs, he is humblie on his kneis to ask God mercie,
" and the baillies pardon, for his hie and proud contempt."[1]

Some of the punishments for theft are curious: " George Mitchell
" being apprehendit for thift is decernit of his confessioune that gif
" ever he be apprehendit within this citie in tyme cumyng to be brunt
" on the schoulders and cheik and to want ane lug out of his heid."[2]
The punishment of mutilation by cutting off an ear was common also
in the old English burghs, and in some of them it was practised
after a somewhat singular fashion. In the ancient town of Lydd
there was an ordinance in the year 1460 that in cases of petty theft
the offender was to be nailed to a post by the ear and left there " with
" a knyffe in hand." He might choose the time of his liberation, but
he. could only effect it by cutting off his own ear.[3]

At an early period we find special provision made for conducting
the deliberations of the council with becoming dignity and order. By
a minute in 1589 " it is statut, for keeping of a dew gravitie and
" amitie in counsall, and reverence to be borne to the provost baillies
" and honourable counsall of the toun, that quatsumever he be that
" injureis ane vther in counsalhous, be word or deid, salbe depryvit
" immediatelie of the counsall, and will nocht be admitted for the
" space of thrie yeiris thairefter, besyd vther punischment that the
" counsall sall think meet to enjoyne to thame for the tyme."[4]

There were no reporters in those days, and not only were all the
deliberations of the council in secret, but the members were strictly
forbidden to reveal anything which occurred or was said there. At
an election of magistrates in 1584, the minute, after narrating the nomi-
nations, proceeds thus:—" Attour everie ane of the persounes foirsaidis,
" suorne vpoun this present counsell, is content and consentis that
" thay and everie ane of thame quha happinnes to oppin and reueill
" ony mater, purpois, or caus votit, proponit, and concludit, within
" the Counselhows, or yit the votis of the Counsell, to ony persounes
" nocht being counsallouris, that thay and everie ane of thame, immediatly
" efter tryall and knawledge had thairof, salbe depryuit in likemaner,
" and neuir to bee vpoun counsell thaireftir as vnwordie thairof."[5]

---

[1] 22d Feb. 1612.   [2] 24th Aug. 1599.   [3] Fifth Report on Hist. MSS. p. 530.
[4] 4th Oct. 1589.   [5] 10th Oct. 1584.

From the same minute we learn the curious fact that one of the council at that time acted as doorkeeper, and that this duty was imposed for each diet, on the latest comer: "Attour it is statuit and ordaint "that sik of the counsell quha cummis hindmest to the Counsell at "tymes requirit, thay being warnit, sall keip the dure quhill [until] "the nixt that cummis relief him, and the hindmest of all to keip "the dure quhill the counsell ryse for that tyme."

Nor did the council encourage large deputations in those days. A minute of the middle of the seventeenth century informs us that "Johne Hall being knocking at the Counsall hous doore desyring to "have entrie, and it being granted that he sould com in his alon "and speak quhat he pleased: because he was not permittit to com in "with ane multitud at his back he refused to com in but protestit at the "door."[1]

In connection with the subject of the maintenance of dignity I may mention here a curious question of precedence which occurred at the beginning of the present century. The point was raised in 1803 in the convention of royal burghs, and had respect to the precedence of the Provost of Glasgow and the Provost of Perth at the meetings of the convention. At these meetings the seats which had, for a considerable time, been occupied by the members were as follows: The Lord Provost of Edinburgh occupied the chair; the commissioner from Glasgow sat on his right hand, and the commissioner from Perth on his left. The two commissioners from Edinburgh sat opposite the chairman, and the other members sat without any prescribed order. But the commissioner from Perth insisted that thereafter he should sit on the right hand of the chairman, and that the commissioner from Glasgow should take the less honourable place on the left. One of the grounds on which this demand was based was a letter from James VI. in 1594, directed to the earl marischall, commanding him to place the commissioners of the burgh of Perth in parliament in the second place, and next to the commissioners for Edinburgh. But this was no precedent, as at that time Glasgow was not represented in parliament at all. Another and a better ground was that Perth was made a royal burgh at an earlier period than Glasgow. The case was discussed at great length, and long printed pleadings were lodged by the parties. The result was that the convention, at a meeting in

---

[1] 23d April, 1659.

July, 1804, decided "that the Provost of Perth had no title to the
" seat claimed by him as his right; neither has the Provost of Glas-
" gow, or any member of Convention, a right preferable to another
" to occupy the seat on the right hand of the President thereof, and
" therefore they dismissed the claims of the parties." Against this
judgment the Provost of Perth protested, with a view, as was supposed,
of bringing the question before the Court of Session, but he allowed
the matter to drop.[1]

In the earlier times when the interests of the bishops depended so
much on the prosperity and influence of their burgh, the provosts were
selected not from among the citizens, but from among noblemen and
gentlemen of rank whose position and power would prove useful to the
bishop and the town in cases of emergency. Thus we find such persons
as the Earl of Lennox, Lord Boyd, Sir George Elphinston, Crawford of
Jordanhill, the Stewarts of Minto, Houston of that Ilk, Hamilton of
Cochno, and others occupying the position of chief magistrate. Latterly
it came to be the practice with the archbishops to give grants of the
office during their own life. An example of this occurred when Archbishop Boyd appointed his kinsman Lord Boyd to be provost during
his (the archbishop's) lifetime.[2]

These old provosts were frequently the leaders of parties in the
council, and among the citizens each had his own partisans and his own
peculiar policy. In the beginning of the seventeenth century we have
a glimpse of a small local commotion arising out of one of their party
disputes. When Sir George Elphinston was provost a change was made
in the system of municipal election, which Sir Matthew Stewart of Minto
thought would be injurious to his local influence. Sir Matthew succeeded
in enlisting the sympathies of the crafts, who took to arms, and "climbing
" up to the platform of the market cross proclaimed their remonstrance
" against the new arrangements in the sight of the magistrates who sat
" in their Council house close by." Nothing seems to have come of the
rising, but some collisions followed, and the two knights and their
principal supporters were imprisoned for some time in Linlithgow on
account of "the general insolency" of which they had been guilty.[3]

The fate of these two great families, who gave so many provosts to

---

[1] The pleadings and the decision will be found in a volume of Law Papers in the office of the
Town-clerk of Glasgow.

[2] 1st October, 1577.   [3] Privy Council Records.

Glasgow, was a sad one. A mural tablet in the Cathedral commemorates the names of eight Stewarts of Minto in succession, "knights "created under the banner." When M'Ure wrote his history, in 1736, the family, he tells us, was "mouldered so quite away that the heir in "our time was reduced to a state of penury little short of beggary." Of the other family, Sir George Elphinston, the favourite friend and servant of King James, who acquired a great estate in Glasgow, and rose to be lord justice-clerk, "died so poor that his corpse was arrested by "his creditors and his friends buried him privately in the chapel adjoining "his house."

As a rule the provosts did not reside within the burgh, but on their own domains—coming only to the city on occasions of emergency or special business, and on these occasions, especially when they rendered any special service, they were usually rewarded by some present, generally wine. For example, under date 18th June, 1583, we find "given "to Agnes Broune for wyne presentit to the proveist in time of trublis, "being caused to abyde in this toune for pacifeing thairof xiij li vis. viij*d*." On another occasion the council minutes bear that the provost had remained in the town "for pacifeing the trubles betwix the merchandis "and craftsmen;" and no doubt on that occasion also he would be suitably entertained. At the time when Lord Boyd was provost there are repeated entries of presents of wine to him. One is of "twa hogheidis "wyn gevin and presentit to my Lord Boyd at the haill townes com- "mand xxxiij lib. vis. viij*d*." It must have been very light claret, as the price of the two hogsheads was, in our money, little over £4. Again, in 1575, there is a present of a half tun of wine to the provost; and again a tun in 1577—the last bearing to be an expression of the gratitude of the town "in keiping of thame fra syndry particular raiddis to the court, thaj "being charget thairto, and salfing thame fra wther intenementis."

But besides such gratuities there appear to have been both "fees" and perquisites paid to the provosts and bailies. Thus in 1573-4 there occurs an entry of a payment "to my lord provost for his fie xiij lib. "vjs. viij*d*. (£2, 4s. 6*d*.) and to thrie of the bailies for their fies xx lib." (about £1, 18s. each). And from a subsequent minute of council it appears that each year the fees paid by two of the burgesses entering in that year were given to the provost, "quhilk hes bein in vse thairof of "befoir."[1] In subsequent years the fees vary in amount. They appear

---

[1] 28th June, 1595.

to have been discontinued before the end of the seventeenth century, and in 1720 a small fixed allowance was made to the provost. On the 31st of March of that year a minute of council bears that "in respect the " provest as Chiefe Magistrat whiles in that station is obliged to keep up " a post suitable thereto, and cannot but be at considerable charge in " furnishing his house with wines for the entertainment of gentlemen " who may have occasion to wait on him at his house, it is their judgment " there should be forty pound sterling settled upon the provest yearly for " defraying the said charge and he may therewith furnish himself with " what wines he thinks most fitted." This payment continued to be made down to the passing of the first reform act, when it was abolished. The last payment to the provost was made on the 30th of September, 1833.

With the exception of cocked hats and chains I am not aware that, except perhaps the provost, the magistrates of Glasgow had until quite recently any distinctive costume. But they may at one time have had such. One of the sumptuary laws of James VI. was "that the Provest " bailzeis and some of the principallis of thair counsall of the burrowis of " Edinburgh, St Johnstoun, Dundie, St Andrews, Glasgow, Striveling and " Aberdeyne sall weare gownes of reid scarlatt cloathe with furringis " aggreable to the same vpoun Sondayis and all vtheris solemne dayis."[1] If this was ever acted on may it not have been the origin of the scarlet cloaks which in later times were worn by the "tobacco lords" and other merchant princes of Glasgow? It was certainly not till a later period that the magistrates came to wear gold chains and medals, but there is evidence that as early at least as 1627 the provost had a distinctive hat, as there is an entry in the burgh accounts for that year of a payment "for ane hatt and string to the provest." In 1720 the town council enacted that the provost should wear a velvet court dress. The gold chains were for the first time introduced in 1767, and were then, as the minute bears, "delivered to the magistrates to be worn by them as badges " of honour."[2] The cocked hats continued to be used till 1833, when they were abolished at one of the first meetings of council after the passing of the reform act. At the same time a motion was made to abolish the gold chains and medals also, and to melt them down "for the " common good;" but this proposal of ill-judged parsimony was happily

---

[1] Proclamatioun anent the Habits, 1609.   [2] Minute of Council, 15th January, 1767.

defeated. It was not till 1875 that official robes were adopted for the provost and bailies and the town-clerk.[1]

It was perhaps to keep up a martial spirit among the citizens, as well as for their own dignity, that, besides two drummers, the magistrates in old times maintained a trumpeter and a piper—the last-named functionary being sometimes described in the burgh records by the euphonious title of "the touns minstrel." By a minute in 1675, appointing one John M'Caine to the office, he is designed as "commoun pypper or minstrel," and he is directed "to goe throw the toune every day morning and "evining or at such tymes the magistrats sall appoynt—vsing his office." His salary is fixed at a hundred merks—£5, 11s. The trumpeter had the same salary, "by and attour some little thing at the magistrates pleasour "to be payit to him that day he sall have occasioune to ryd in the militia." He was also to be "obleist to wait and attend wpon the magistrats for " goeing of errands or quhan they sall be pleased to send him."[2]

By an earlier minute all the town's officers, as well as the drummers and piper, are appointed to be dressed in "coit, brekis, and hoiss of red "kairsey claithe." On one occasion, where an order is made for new uniforms, the quantity of cloth allowed to each is fixed at "fyfe eln;" but "becaus Andro Stark, Wm. Letham, Rob. Wilsoun, elder, and " Robt. Glasgw ar biggar nor the rest of bodie, to ilk ane of thame "half ane eln mair." The clothes are all "to be maid be thair selfs *in* "*jupe fassoun.*"[3] When, in the following year, a drummer fell to be appointed, the magistrates, having in view the making of the clothes, preferred a tailor to the office, and it was made a condition of his appointment that he should undertake "to learne Jon. Jeimesoune, his " collig, the tailzeour craft swa long as y[e] counsall sall appoint, becaus " they are onlie thame twa to be drummers."[4] The drummers appear to have quarrelled on a question of precedence, and the magistrates were obliged to interfere. This they did by a minute which "ordainis " the drummers to touk throughe the towne weik about, and he who " toukis for the weik sal onlie have power to touk to the haill Lords and " strangers sall cum to the town for that weik." The minute concludes with an admonition to them "to leave [live] together peacablie as bre- " ther and not wrang or injure utheris."[5] The wages of the drummers were paid by a special tax on the inhabitants.[6]

---

[1] Minute of Council, 19th January, 1875.　　[2] Burgh Minutes, 3d April and 4th August, 1675.
[3] 11th June, 1625.　　　　[4] 16th June, 1627.　　　　[5] 12th Feb. 1642.　　　　[6] 5th July, 1676.

In other matters, besides piper and drummers, and officers in scarlet uniforms, the magistrates, after the Reformation, made provision for their personal dignity. In 1610 a charge appears in the burgh accounts "for grein silk, fustean, and other furnesing to the twa grein claiths to "the Counsall satis in the kirkis heich and laich."[1] Some thirty years afterwards there is a minute of the council which "ordains ane velvot "cuschein and ane velvot black cloth to be laid in the kirks before the "provost in tyme cuming."[2]

It is pleasant also to notice that in early times the Glasgow magistrates, with all their troubles, had a regard to the amenities of social life. They had flowers on the council table, and, what is curious, they had flowers also placed on their seat in church. In their accounts towards the end of the seventeenth century there occurs a payment for "roses and flowers furnished to the Counselhous and kirks, and to the "Magistrats and Counsell;"[3] and there are subsequent payments for "flowers yearly to the Counsell hous and seats in the Churches."

They were kind to the poorer class of citizens, and liberal in their charities. Their records abound with examples of this. The payments to people in destitute circumstances are frequent, and there are also repeated instances of a kind consideration for those not actually in poverty, but requiring temporary encouragement and assistance. For example, a working man had his horse stolen, and the magistrates "ordain the Master of wark to pay to him four rex dollars for helping "to mak vp the loss." A poor "student of philosophie presently lawried "or to be lawried"—that is, laureated, about to take his degree—is allowed twenty-four pounds scots "for supplying his present wants and "helping him to buy cloathes and books." Another poor scholar has a gift of six pounds scots "to help to buy him a coat." On another occasion the master of work is ordained "to buy and provyde for ane "poor boy going to the College, being a burges sone, ane cloak goune, "and ane hatt, of the qualitie as the magistrats sall appoynt him." Again, one John Gemmell, merchant, "in respect he is knowne to be ane "verie honest man and hes lost his stock by sea venter," is granted a loan of 200 pounds scots. Early in the seventeenth century (1626) there is a payment of "fourtie merk to ane Grecian bishop." A sum of "twenty pundis" is paid to "ane distressed gentleman." There is an order "to pay to Antoine Nauder a Frenchman thrie rex dollars to help

[1] 17th August, 1610. [2] 2d Sept. 1643. [3] 29th Sept. 1683.

" to carry him and his wyfe off the town, he having left his countrie for
" his religion." The magistrates on another occasion send certain persons "throw the toune for collecting a contributioune for releiving of
" Walter Gibsone skipper at Innerkeithing and Jon Reid his mate, from
" their slaverie, being prisoners with the Turks;"[1] and there are many
similar cases.

For a long time the magistrates paid an allowance or annual pension
to a "chirurgian" for the benefit of the poorer class of citizens, and
among the practitioners thus subsidized was "Mr. Petir Lou," a name
well known in the medical history of the city, of whom mention has
already been made. The amount paid to this gentleman appears in a
minute of the town council in 1608: "Gifen to Mr. Petir Lou chyrurgin
" for his pensioun addettit be the toun to him liij£ vi*s.* viij*d.*" (£4, 8*s.* 10*d.*)
Subsequently the city paid also for the services of a physician, but this
practice was discontinued in 1684, at a time when the finances of the
burgh were at a very low ebb. The minute on the subject is curious:
" 27 October. The said day the Magistrats and counsell considering the
" sad condition the toun is in throw the great debt they are resting, it
" is theirfoir concludit that the toun shall make use of no persone as
" the touns physitian or chirurgian in time coming, and if any person
" who is unwell, *and deserves to be cured*, wpon their applicatioun to any
" of the Magistrats they are empowered to recommend them to any
" physitian they shall think fitt." Apparently they had not been particular as to who they employed in cases which they thought deserving
of cure, as in the same year in which they discontinued the employment
of a "chirurgian" there is an entry in the records of a payment "to the
" mountebank for cutting off umqll Archibald Bogles leg." The mountebank was paid for this service "60 lib" (£5), a sufficiently liberal fee
considering that his patient, being described as deceased, had probably
died under his hands.

But although the magistrates ceased to pension a physician, they
continued to retain the services of a person skilled in lithotomy, and
there is a minute bearing that a certificate having been produced in
favour of Duncan Campbell "subscryvit be the haill doctors and most
" part of the chirurgians in toune of his dexteritie and success," they
appoint Duncan to the office to operate on the poor "in place of Evir
" McNeil who is become unfit to doe the same through his infirmitie."

---

[1] 30th October, 1676.

The reason for the appointment appears to have been that the regular surgeons did not operate for that disease. It is curious to note from the council records that the disease appears to have prevailed chiefly among children. To what cause its prevalence at that time is to be ascribed I do not know. When, long afterwards, it was proposed to shut up the public wells in the city a committee of the town council issued a pamphlet containing reports by medical men, in which, among other things, it was stated that the well water contained lime, especially sulphate of lime, and the opinion was expressed that "lime is generally "the cause of gravel and stone." But exception has been taken to the statement that there was so much lime in the Glasgow water as to cause the disease. In our own time certainly calculus has been comparatively rare in Glasgow.

An amusing example of the control exercised in old times over medical men practising within the burgh is to be found in the "Seal of "Cause" which the magistrates granted on 16th August 1656 in favour of the "Chirurgeounis and Barbouris"—these two professions being at that time united in one corporation. A seal of cause was a local charter of incorporation granted by the magistrates, in which was defined the conditions on which it was granted. In the one in favour of the surgeons and barbers—by which that corporation is authorized to exercise within burgh "the art of chirurgeourie and barbourie"—there occurs the following clause, which is too good to remain buried in the charter chest of the corporation. It provides "That no free mane presume to "taik ane uzr freamans cuir af his hand untill he be honestlie payit for "his bygaine paines, and that at the sight of the baillies, with the "udvyce of thair visitour, in caice the patient find himself grived by "the chirurgiane, under the payne of ane new upsett; excepting always "libertie to the visitour and qrter maisters to tak patients from ane "free man not fund qualified for the cuiring of them, and to put them "to ane more qualified persoune as shall be thoght expedient after exact "tryall."

Bloodletting in Glasgow, as elsewhere, was universal among all classes; the usual season being spring. As a rule it was done by the barbers, and it was this, no doubt, that led to their being united in the same corporation with the surgeons. This branch of their profession was symbolized in the sign over the barbers' shops, which remains over many small shops to the present day. The bare pole—

a pun on poll—referred to the shaving of heads. The red strip painted round the pole indicated the bloodletting, and the basin suspended at the end represented the vessel which received the blood. In the Accounts of the Lord High Treasurer, under date May, 1491, there is a payment to "a leyche that leyt the king blud;" and in another entry we have the payment of 12*s*. to M'Mulane the barber "for the "leichcraft done be him to the litil boyis of the chalmire." But James IV. not only had blood let but he practised the art himself as an amateur, and he bribed his attendants to allow him to operate on them. In the royal accounts there occurs a payment "to Domynico "to gif the king leve to lat him blud."[1] Even the lower animals were subjected to spring bleeding. In a book of accounts of the nunnery of Radegunda, in the year 1449, there is an entry of the payment of twopence "for bleeding the cart horses on St. Stephen's day."[2]

A few instances occur of the encouragement of literature by the magistrates in a small way. In 1661 the sum of ten dollars is ordered to be paid "to James Cerss, Philomath, for dedicating his Almanack "to the toune."[3] I have not seen any copy of this Almanack, but it was no doubt a continuation of it that was printed by Robert Sanders in 1667 and subsequent years. The first of these which I have seen is entitled "A new Prognostication for the year of Christ 1668 being "Bissextile or Leap-year, with many fairs not heretofore insert, by "J. H. Philomathes. Printed at Aberdene and imprinted at Glasgow "by Robert Sanders Printer to the Town and are to be sold at his "shop. M.DC.LXVII." The others bear only to be printed by Sanders, but they had been all compiled in Aberdeen, and they all contain the usual prognostications of weather; "dismal and perillous days;" directions for letting blood, &c. Copies of these old Glasgow Almanacks must be now extremely rare.[4]

In the year 1662 the burgh accounts show a payment of twenty dollars "to Mr. Johne Andersoun ane of the doctors of the Grammer "school for divers respects and for dedicating a book to the magis- "trates." On another occasion the treasurer has "ane warrand for "the soume of eight rex dollars payed to Mr. Wm. Geddes minister "for his incuradgment to print the twa books called a Memoriall

---

[1] Accounts of Lord High Treasurer, cclxxx.

[2] MSS. of Jesus College, Cambridge. Second Report on Historical MSS., p. 120.

[3] 1st October, 1661.

[4] The only series of them which I have seen was in the possession of J. Wyllie Guild, Esq.

" Historicum and another book sett out be him."[1] On a later date
the treasurer is ordained " to pay to James Robison Schoolmaster
" three guinzeas for his encouradgment in compiling and printing a
" litle book entituled a dialogue betwixt a young Lady and her School-
" master shewing the right way of sillabing."[2] And in 1736—the year
in which M'Ure published his well-known history—there occurs this
entry in the burgh records: " Remit to the Annual Committee the
" petition given in by John M'Ure, Writer, craving some consideratioun
" for defraying his charges in putting forth a book which he calls the
" Hystory of the present state of the City;"[3] and no doubt the petition
received a favourable answer.

The magistrates did something also in the fine arts. But not much.
In 1641 they ordain the treasurer " to have ane warrand to pay to James
" Colquhoun fyfe dollars for drawing of the portraict of the toun to
" be sent to Holland."[4] It would be interesting if this old view of
the city could be recovered. We are indebted also to the public spirit
of the magistrates of that time for the portraits of royal personages
which we have in the Corporation Galleries. In 1670 there is a minute
by which " it is appoynted that the provest wrytt to London to the
" Deane of Gild to buy for the tounes use the portrators of King Charles
" the First and Secund *as also ane carpett.*"[5] But the dean succeeded
in getting only one portrait—that of Charles I., and two months afterwards there is a warrant for the price of it: " twenty fyve punds starling
" for the kings portratour." Seven years afterwards the order is repeated to procure the other, " that it may be hung in the Counsell-
" house with the rest now there." In 1708 the provost reported that
he had bought from Mr. Scougall, limner in Edinburgh, the portraits
of William and Mary, " both of full length for twentie seven pounds
" sterling." Queen Anne's portrait, by the same artist, was added to
the collection in 1712 at the price of £15, and that of George I. in
1715 at the same price. We are all familiar with the stone statues
of the Hutchesons, the founders of the hospital bearing their name.
One of these, that of Thomas Hutcheson, was executed on the order
of the magistrates. The artist was one James Colquhoun, and the
price paid was 500 merks, about £28 of our money—a good price
considering the time and the character of the work.

---

[1] 17th May, 1684.   [2] 21st Sept. 1723.   [3] 4th October, 1736.
[4] 12th June, 1641.   [5] 4th June, 1670.

In early times the magistrates in their corporate capacity appear to have exercised a generous hospitality. "Corporation dinners" were of frequent occurrence, and there are some curious notices of these banquets three hundred years ago. They appear to have been held in different taverns by rotation, so as to distribute the favour equally. And our old rulers were not above running up a score, though no doubt they honestly cleared them off periodically. On one occasion we find an order by the council "to take ane account of what reckon- "ings is restand in any taverns in the toune that hes been spent wpon " the tounes accumpt this last yeir, that warrand may be granted for " paying the same."[1] Of special corporation banquets there are re- peated notices. Under date 4th July, 1573, there is an entry of a payment "to Bessie Douglas for the provost baillies and counsales " dennaris on Witsonyisday xiij lib. vi*s*. viii*d*.,"—about £2, 5*s*. according to the value of money at that time—not a very extravagant amount certainly. In the following year another "bancatt" took place in the house of Catherine Steward, on the occasion of "the seeling of the " provosts commissioun." The expenditure on this occasion was xviij lib., a trifle over £3, but this is increased to a small extent by two subsequent payments—the first "to Robert Lettrik, officer, for aquavitie " furnisit to the bancatt vi*s*.," a little more than a shilling; and the second x*s*.—about two shillings of our money—"for cairage of wyne and flour " fra Edinbrugh to the bancatt at Catho Stewardis." In 1575 there is a payment to Euphame Campbell "for ane bankat maid to the " provest baillies and counsale and wtheris, dekynnis and honest men, " at command of the baillies;" and on 24th May, 1656, the council "appoyntes the tounes dennar on the first Tysday of June next to " be made reddie in Thomas Glenis hous, and the Dein of Gild to " have ane cair thereof and of thais quha sould be invited thairto."

The hospitalities of the corporation cost more in our days, but considering the importance and wealth of the city the annual expendi- ture under that head has been moderate enough—not exceeding, on an average of the last ten years, about £400. There have been ex- ceptional occasions, such as in the year of the Duke of Edinburgh's marriage, when the city spent in hospitalities nearly £1600.

The magistrates also in the old times, as now, kept the king's birthday. On one of these occasions we find this entry in their minutes: "Ordeines

---

[1] 29th September, 1682.

" ane warrand to be grantit for 41 lib 10s. (£3, 9s. 2d.) as for expensis of
" vyne and confeitis spent at the croce upone the fyfte of July the kingis
" daye—my Lord of Glasgw being present with sundrie uthir honorabill
" men."[1]   And a similar charge appears in the following year.

   In presents to their provosts, as well as to the bishops and to
strangers, the corporation accounts show various payments.   In the
burgh accounts in 1609 we find a charge of fifty pounds Scots (£4,
3s. 4d.) " propynit be the toun to the baptisme of the provests barne,"
and for " sugir and sweit meitis " on the same occasion.   In 1684
there is an order to pay to John Finlay, maltman, the sum of 89 lib.
9s. (£7 odds) " quhilk was spent in his hous at severall tymes be the
" magistrats on the touns account."   Another charge is for " vyne,
" confeits, and breid, and sum aill, furnist and send to the Counsal
" hous that day the lard Auchinbrek was made burges."   One of the
gifts of wine by the magistrates may be noticed as illustrating the
change in the position of the archbishops after the Reformation.   We
can imagine what must have been the grandeur of the ceremony, and the
lavishness of the expenditure, at the installation of a bishop such as
Cameron.   When Boyd of Trochrig was " admitted bischop " in 1573
the town council appear to have thought it sufficient to present, and
the bishop perhaps thankfully received " ane gallon of wyne," for the
price of which a charge appears in the burgh accounts.[2]   But as a rule
the magistrates, after the Reformation, were kind to the archbishops
and repeatedly made them presents.   On one occasion there is a charge
for " silver work given to the ladie Elphinstoun the bischops daughter
" at her marriage."[3]   On another there is an entry of " the sowme of twelfe
" hundreth threttie sex pounds (£103) payit for French wynes given
" be the toun to the archbishop of Glasgw and utheris this last yeir."[4]
And there are many similar entries.

   There occurs also in the burgh records a curious series of charges
for wines and confectionery purchased by the magistrates and disposed
of as gifts to parties to whom they were indebted for services rendered
to the town, or whom they desired to propitiate.   Between Dunbarton
and Glasgow there never was any great cordiality, yet in 1607 a sum is
paid " to Symon Stewards wyfe for vyne presented to the baillies of
" Dunbarton."   In 1668 there is a payment of nearly £80 sterling " for
" some wynes was disposed of to some noblemen for their courtesie and

---

[1] 19th August, 1609.   [2] 12th October, 1573.   [3] 5th Oct. 1667.   [4] 25th June, 1681.

"favour showne to the towne." In 1670 there is again a considerable sum "for twa hogheids French wyne, twa rubors, and ane butt of sek, "sent to Edinburgh *to some persones.*" A few years afterwards, 1674, Donald M'Gilchrist has a warrant for 240 pounds Scots "debursit be "him for French wyne given be the toun to Sir John Harper at severall "tymes for service done be him to the said burgh." In 1686 the council "appoints the provest baillies and Dean of Gild to gratifie such of "the tounes friends as they shall think fitt by sending them what wynes "they think convenient on the touns accompt." In 1688 the treasurer is ordained to pay to Bailie Bell the sum of £12 sterling "for ane "hodgeshead of sack, and £14 sterling for half ane tun of French wyne, "and £7, 16s. 8d. more for two cask of rasenis and two cask of figs, all "furnished by him on the touns account whilk were given to severall of "their friends the last year." On one occasion a warrant is granted to the treasurer for the sum of £10 sterling, which had been paid by him in Edinburgh "to ane friend *for doeing the towne ane guid turne.*"[1] And on 20th April, 1695, the council "appoints the thesaurer to have "allowance in his own hands of 200 merks payed out be him as the "price of ane hogsheid of wine *given to a friend of this toun whom it is* "*not fitt to name.*"

There can be little doubt that one reason of the city spending so much in wine was that the taverns, which originally were almost entirely in the hands of women, were, many of them, now kept by officials of the burgh—bailies, deacon-conveners, and others. This had given rise to some scandal; so much so that in the end of the seventeenth century the town council was obliged to take up the matter. Their minute bears that they had taken to their consideration "the severall abuses hes been "committed these severall years past by electing and choiseing of magis- "trats and deacon-conveners in this burgh who keped change and publict "taverns, which occasioned much debaushire and drunkenness, and poor "people to spend their money needlesslie in said taverns; It is therefore "hereby enacted statute and ordained in all tyme comeing that nae "person or persones be elected and choisin to bear office as Proveist, "baillies, Dean of Gild, Deacon Convener, Baillie of Gorballs or as "Water baillie, wha keipis ane publict tavern or change house."[2]

Another commodity more harmless, and more characteristic of the city, was largely used by the magistrates as the medium of expressing

---

[1] 22d March, 1656.   [2] 4th Oct. 1690.

their good-will—namely, herrings. At a very early period the curing of salmon and herrings, both for home consumption and for the French market, was an important branch of trade in Glasgow, and Principal Baillie states that by the middle of the seventeenth century it had greatly increased. In the sixteenth and seventeenth centuries the consumption of herrings was much greater among both the middle and lower classes than it is now. At that time they formed the principal food of the reapers in harvest, and they formed, with oaten cakes, the entire sustenance of the numerous class of seamen employed in the fishery. Seven herrings to each man for a meal was the common allowance. The shoals came much farther up the firth then than they do now; and in some seasons, in the beginning of the seventeenth century, it is said that not less than nine hundred boats have been employed in the herring fishery within the Cloch. When the fish did not come into the lochs in large quantities, the fishermen were in the practice of making three voyages during the season to more distant grounds. Each boat paid to the crown one thousand herrings for each "drave" or voyage.[1] These were called the "Assise herrings," and for a long time the Argyll family held a grant of the crown's right to this tax on the Firth of Clyde, for which they paid a reddendo of 1000 pounds Scots—£50—per annum. Their profit must have been considerable, for in the old rentals of the Argyll estates the annual value of the assize herrings is larger than the whole rental of the estate of Roseneath.[2] Some of the Canon lands of Glasgow were held for the payment of so many cured herrings. In a retour of the seventeenth century it is stated that Lord Boyd held certain of these lands in the parishes of Largs and Dalry for the yearly payment, inter alia, of "6000 halecum rubrarum"—red herrings.[3]

The greater part of the herrings caught in the Clyde were taken to Greenock—which, indeed, owed its foundation and first rise to the herring fishery—where they were bought by the Glasgow merchants, and, after being cured there, were exported to foreign markets. In 1564 no less than seventeen hundred lasts of herrings—that is, twenty thousand barrels—were exported from Greenock to Rochelle alone, besides what went as usual to the other ports of France and the ports of the Baltic.[4]

---

[1] Brown's History, vol. ii. p. 312. [2] Fourth Report on Historical MSS. p. 481.
[3] Ponts Cuninghame Topographised. Edit. by Mr. Dobie, p. 375.
[4] Brown's History, vol. ii. p. 315.

But the quantity consumed in Glasgow must have been also very great. The magistrates, as I have said, used them to a large extent in making presents, and it is curious to note that the fees which they paid yearly to the counsel permanently retained for the city consisted in part of barrels or half barrels of these fish. In 1612 there is a minute of council, entitled "Act anent herrings to the Touns advocates," which bears that the magistrates, "for the great and thankful service dune be "John Nicoll wryter in Edr. to the toun," in a case specified, "*and for* "*the expectatioun quhlk they haif of his service to the toun,* hes ordainit "the thesaurer and Mr. of werk to send ane half barrel of herring to "him, for this yeir only; with twa half barrels to Mr. Alexr. King; twa "to Mr. Thomas Hendersoun; ane to Mr. Wm. Hay, and ane to James "Winrame with 10 lb to ilk ane of their clerkis."[1] In the following year there is a payment to Jonet Lugie "for ane hoghead of herring to "be sent in barrelis to the tounes men of law." Under date 13th December, 1628, there is a minute bearing that "the provest bailyeis and "counsell hes aggreit and condescendit to give yearlie to maister John "Robertsoune advocatt, last chosen for them agent for the toun, ten "pund of yeirlie fiall, and twa half barrellis hering, as the rest of the "tounes principall advocatts gettis, during the tounes will and plesour "allenarlie." And after this there are repeated entries of payments for barrels and half barrels of herrings to the town's advocates and others. By an entry in the burgh accounts of a later date we learn that the sum paid for "the Advocatts herring" for the year 1666 was 187 lib. 16s. 8d. (£14, 18s.)

But Glasgow was not alone in the practice of propitiating her friends, and in showing her "gratitude for favours to come," by occasional gifts. In the English corporations in very early times it was the custom to give presents to men in office or persons of influence to whom they looked for favours. Examples of this are found in the records of Bridport and Faversham and other places, and curiously enough, in the case of the last-named corporation, the gifts, as in Glasgow, consisted in a great measure of herrings. So early as the year 1305 we find the magistrates of Faversham sending a gift of 4000 herrings to the sheriff of Kent. The price of the 4000 was 20s. Again 1000 herrings are sent to "Elyas the clerk;" 2000 are sent to the constable of Dovorre, and other quantities are sent in gifts to various other persons.[2] The articles

---

[1] Burgh Records, 19th December, 1612.   [2] Sixth Report on Historical MSS. p. 504.

which form the subjects of presents by the town of Bridport and other corporations are bread and wine, chickens, fish, beef, oats, and articles of horses' trappings.[1]

In Glasgow, when we come down to the times after the introduction of tobacco, we find the town's presents made sometimes in that commodity. For example, on 3d May, 1701, the treasurer is authorized to pay to the deacon convener fifty-one shillings scots (4*s.* 3*d.*) "as the "pryce of four pound of tobacco presented be him to the Provest and "given be him to one of the touns friends at Edinburgh, and of a bag "about the same." In England a century earlier tobacco was a much more expensive luxury. When the Earl of Northumberland was confined in the Tower for his supposed complicity in the Gunpowder Plot one of the items of his expenses was £3, 10*s.* for 2 lbs. of tobacco.[2] But in Glasgow also, at a later period, tobacco became a luxury too expensive for presents to any friends of the town. At the outbreak of the first American war it rose in price two thousand per cent., and Mr. Glassford and other large holders among the "tobacco lords" made large fortunes.

DISTINCTION OF CLASSES.

The mention of these magnates leads me to notice the extraordinary distinctions of class which prevailed in these times. During the reign of the Tobacco lords—the then merchant princes of Glasgow—they had a privileged walk at the Cross, which they trod arrayed in long scarlet cloaks and bushy wigs; and such was the state of society then, that when any even of the most respectable master tradesmen of the city had occasion to speak to a Tobacco lord, he required to walk on the other side of the street till he was fortunate enough to catch his eye, as it would have been presumption to have made up to him.[3] It was dangerous, indeed, for a plebeian to quarrel with any of these magnates. It exposed him to the risk of ruin. We have a similar description of them by Mr. Reid (Senex). "I am old enough," he says, "to remember our "Tobacco lords with their bushy wigs and scarlet cloaks perambulating

[1] Sixth Report on Historical MSS. p. 490.
[2] Papers of R. Cholmondeley, Esq. Fifth Report on Historical MSS. p. 354.
[3] Principal Macfarlan and Dr. Cleland, art. in Statistical Account, vol. vi. p. 232.

" the plane stanes at the Cross, and keeping the other classes at a
" respectful distance. No lady would venture to walk upon this aris-
" tocratic promenade, but as soon as she came near King William she
" directly crossed to the south side of the Trongate, and continued her
" course under the pillars, which then, with the exception of the plane
" stanes, formed the only flagged footpath of that bustling thoroughfare.
" It was with no little admiration and wonder that I beheld the powdered
" flunkies of these lords frisking across their barricaded courts, dressed
" in plush breeches, with thread stockings, dashing shoe buckles (which
" nearly covered the whole front of their feet), with massy brass buttons
" on their coats, and gold bands on their hats."[1]

As trade increased and wealth became more diffused the middle
classes became more independent, and after the opening of the public
coffee-room in 1781 the more marked separation of classes gradually
disappeared.

But previous to the beginning of the seventeenth century the distinctions of class were still more marked than they were when the tobacco
lords strutted in front of the Tontine. This was more especially shown
in the marked separation between the craftsmen and those who called
themselves merchants. Socially the latter asserted a precedence which
was carried so far that in musters of the citizens, and at weapon schaws
and other public occasions, the merchant kept aloof from the craftsman,
and would not even serve in the same Company with him. But the
separation was still more marked in the matter of trade, for the merchant
denied to the craftsman the right to engage in any mercantile specula-
tion, affirming, to use the words of old John M'Ure, "that they were
" to hold every one to his trade and not meddle with theirs." It is a
true description which M'Ure gives when he says that to such an extent
was this carried that "there arose terrible heats strifes and animosities
" betwixt them which was like to end with shedding of blood, for the
" trades rose up in arms against the merchants."[2] Mr. Crawford, in his
History of the Trades House, ascribes this feeling in a great measure to
religious causes, namely, to the adoption by the craftsmen generally of
the doctrines of the reformed religion, while those of the merchant rank
adhered to the tenets of the Church of Rome.[3] But the cause lay much
deeper than this, and it had begun to operate previous to the Reforma-

---

[1] Glasgow Past and Present. [2] M'Ure's History, p. 157.
[3] History of the Trades House, p. 45.

tion. The more opulent class of burgesses, constituting the merchant rank, had, in Glasgow and other considerable burghs, enjoyed for a long time a monopoly of influence and power, and they viewed with distrust the growing importance of the artisan burgesses or craftsmen. These, on the other hand, rising as they now rapidly were to wealth and importance, viewed with jealousy the position of the merchants, and their attempts to exclude them not merely from a participation in municipal government, but even from those mercantile adventures which were becoming such sources of wealth to the enterprising trader. The parties were ultimately brought together by friendly mediation, and an arbitration was entered into which, in 1605, resulted in the well-known decree called the Letter of Guildry, which was ratified by the magistrates and subsequently confirmed by the king and parliament. By this important deed the Dean of Guild Court was established, and its jurisdiction defined; the relative rights of the merchants and craftsmen were finally adjusted; and, as expressed in a minute of the town council in 1605, it was settled that there was to be no more at any "muster, weapon-shaw- " ing or other lawful assembly, any question strife or debate betwixt " merchant and craftsman for prerogative or priority, but they and every " one of them, as one body of the commonweill shall rank and place " themselves together but [without] distinction as they shall happen to " fall in rank."[1]

TRADE AND COMMERCE.

The trade of Glasgow is a large subject, and I can only glance at its early history. Before the seventeenth century there was little trade of any kind in Scotland, and few or no manufactures. Even the commonest articles of daily use, such as horse-shoes, harness, bridles, and saddles, were imported ready-made from Flanders. Yet there was, in the middle ages, trade to some extent, and probably a good deal of it was in the hands of the religious bodies. There is a charter by William the Lion granting to the monks of Scone exemption from customs duties for one ship and its merchandise, showing that these monks were at that early period carrying on a foreign trade. But by the middle of the

[1] 16th Feb. 1605.

seventeenth century there was a great change, and the trade of Glasgow in particular had by that time, for so small a place as it then was, become considerable. In the reigns of James VI. and Charles I. a considerable traffic was carried on by traders carrying goods of home manufacture from Glasgow into England, and bringing home "merchand waires."[1] Under the liberal administration of Cromwell, too, Scotland generally— hating him though she did—could not but acknowledge the advantages she possessed in perfect freedom of commerce. A Scotch vessel was then at liberty to carry a Scotch cargo to Barbadoes and to bring the sugar of Barbadoes into the port of London.[2] Speaking of the merchants of Glasgow, Franck says that in 1650 their commerce was extensive. " Moreover," he adds, " they dwell in the face of France with a free trade. " The staple of the country consists of linens, friezes, furs, tartans, pelts, " hides, tallow, skins, and various other small manufactures and com- " modities."[3] In the report "on the Settlement of the Revenues of " Excise and Customs in Scotland" made to Cromwell by Thomas Tucker in 1656[4] he speaks of Glasgow as "one of the most considerable " burghs, as well for the structure as the trade of it. The inhabitants, " all but the students of the College which is here, are traders and dealers " —some for Ireland with small smiddy coals in open boats from four to " ten tons, from whence they bring hoops, rungs, barrel staves, meal, " oats, and butter; some for France with pladding, coals, and herring, of " which there is a great fishing yearly in the western sea, for which they " return salt, pepper, rosin, and prunes; some to Norway for timber; " and every one with their neighbours the highlanders, who come hither " from the Isles and Western parts."

The Restoration came, and with it the Scotch regained their inde- pendence, but they soon found, to use the words of Lord Macaulay, that "independence had its discomforts as well as its dignity."[5] The English Parliament treated them as aliens. A new Navigation Act put them on almost the same footing with the Dutch, and high, and in some cases prohibitory duties were imposed on the products of Scottish in- dustry. But there was no redress—nothing for it, in short, but a union of the kingdoms, for which matters were now fast ripening.

Yet previous to that event the trade of Glasgow had, as I have said, become considerable. We may form some idea of it from an account

---

[1] See Minutes of Council, 1625.　　　　[2] Ordinance in Council, 12th April, 1654.
[3] Northern Memoirs.　　[4] Printed by the Bannatyne Club.　　[5] History, vol. iii. p. 253.

preserved in one of the acts of the Scottish Parliament of the year 1698, relating to the affairs of a once opulent but then reduced Glasgow merchant, a Mr. James Gilhagie. He had applied to Parliament for relief, and a state of his mercantile transactions and his losses is embodied in the act. It bears that besides the lands of Easter Craigs and Kennyhill, of which he was proprietor, Mr. Gilhagie had possessed houses in Saltmarket and in the neighbouring streets, besides his plenishing in them, and "his two well furnist buiths and merchant ware." All these had been destroyed by the great fire in 1677, causing a loss of 20,000 merks—more than £1000 sterling. He possessed a ship, which was lost with all her cargo, consisting of French wines, causing a farther loss of £500 sterling. He had been largely engaged in coal works near Glasgow, by which he had lost 20,000 merks more; and he had been engaged in adventures from Glasgow to Archangel, Madeira, and the Canary Islands. This was in the time of William III.;[1] and there were many other merchants in the city at that time whose transactions were very considerable.

But when the Union came the trade of Glasgow received a great impetus. There was a general outcry against it at the time, and at first it certainly was productive of some changes which were unpopular. Among other things the days of cheap claret came to an end, as Scotland, after the Union, had to cease importing French products. But notwithstanding the opposition, it soon became apparent that this important political measure was to be the cause of increased prosperity to all Scotland. In conformity with England she had to cease exporting her wool, but on the other hand she found in England a market for wool and linen, and a greatly enlarged demand for grain and Highland cattle. In the first year after the Union the total revenue from the excise in Scotland was, in round numbers, £35,000. In 1808, after the lapse of a hundred years, it had increased to £180,000—more than five times the produce of the first year.

Until the beginning of the eighteenth century the trade of Glasgow, besides herrings, consisted chiefly of coarse woollen goods and sugar. The rise of the last-mentioned industry, in 1667, I have already noticed. The first "manufactory" which the city possessed was established in 1638. It was a weaving factory, and the magistrates hastened to encourage the novel proposal, and to offer liberal terms to the projectors.

[1] History of the Merchants' House, printed for Private Circulation, 1866, p. 526.

P

Marking as it does the commencement, though in a very small way, of a new order of things which was destined to contribute so largely to the prosperity of the city, it may be interesting to quote the minute of the town council on the subject. It is entitled in the burgh records, "Anent the Manufactorie," and is as follows:—"31 January 1638. "The said day foirasmeikle as Robert Fleyming merchand, and his "pairtineris, ar of mynd and intentioun to erect and tak up ane hous "of manufactorie within this burgh, quhairby ane number of the poorer "sort of people within the samin may be imployt and putt to wark; "And the said provost bailies and Counsall considering the grait good, "utilitie, and proffeit will redound to this brught and haill incorporation "thairof thairby, they have concludit, all in ane voyce, for the said "Robert his better encuragement to the said good wark to sett to him "ane lare and tak of thair grait ludging and yairds att the back thairof "lyand within this burght in the drygaitt, except the twa laich foir voultis "and back galreis at the back of the samin lyand be eist the entrie of "the said grait tenement, and of the buithe under the tolbuithe pre- "sentlie occupayt be James Wood, all maill frie or ony othir kynd of "deutie, during the space of fifteen yeirs eftir his entry." But the days of free trade had not yet come. The incorporation of Weavers got alarmed, and it was reported to the town council, on the 5th of May following, "that the weivors friemen feirit that the erecting of the manu- "factorie suld prove hurtfull and prejudiciall to thame," and they insisted that provision should be made that anything required to be woven *by the citizens* should be done by the incorporation of weavers only. The projectors yielded, and "thairfoir," as the minute of council bears, "Patrick "Bell, ane of the undertakeris, for himself and in name of his partineris, "was content that it suld be enactit that there sould be no woovis wovin "of tounis folkis thairin be thair servandis in hurt and prejudice of the "said friemen, bot be thais onlie quha ar frie with this calling." Such was the first manufactory in Glasgow, and such the ideas then prevailing as to freedom of trade.

But the real commencement of commercial enterprise was subsequent to the Union, and it began in Glasgow, as already mentioned, with her trade with the American colonies. The tobacco trade commenced in 1707. The Glasgow traders had at first no ships of their own, and their first ventures to Maryland and Virginia were in vessels chartered from Whitehaven. It was no doubt to trade carried on in such vessels, at an early period, that Tucker in his report to Cromwell refers when he says, writing in 1656, "Here hath been some [merchants] who have " adventured as far as Barbadoes, but the losses they have sustained by " reason of their going out, and coming home late every year, made " them discontinue going thither any more." It was not till eleven years after the Union that a vessel belonging to Glasgow crossed the Atlantic.

How very limited the trade of the city was, however, till far on in the eighteenth century we may judge from the state of banking in the city at that time. Banks, indeed, were unknown in Glasgow till a comparatively recent period. The Bank of Scotland, soon after its institution in Edinburgh, made an attempt to establish a branch in Glasgow, but it proved unsuccessful. The trial was renewed in 1731, but again it failed. At that time the small amount of bank accommodation that was required was provided by private traders. An example of this is found in an advertisement which appeared in the Edinburgh *Evening Courant* in July, 1730. It was inserted by "James Blair merchant at " the head of the Saltmarket in Glasgow"—*merchant* being the designation then adopted by the shopkeepers—and he intimates that at his shop there "all persons who have occasion to buy or sell bills of " exchange, or want money to borrow, or have money to lend on in- " terest, &c., may deliver their commands." The Royal Bank was established in Edinburgh in 1727, and the effect of its rivalry was to cause the temporary stoppage of the Bank of Scotland in the following year!

At first the foreign trade of Glasgow was confined to few hands, but it rapidly developed, and, along with it, other branches of industry. Sir John Dalrymple, writing shortly before 1788, says: "I once asked the " late provost Cochran of Glasgow, who was eminently wise, and who " has been a merchant there for seventy years, to what cause he attri- " buted the sudden rise of Glasgow. He said it was all owing to four " young men of talent and spirit who started at one time in business, and " whose success gave example to the rest. The four had not ten thou- " sand pounds amongst them when they began." These four gentlemen were Mr. Cuningham of Lainshaw, Mr. Spiers of Elderslie, Mr. Glassford of Dugaldston, and Mr. Ritchie of Busby—the estates here named being all purchased out of their acquired wealth.[1]

[1] Dr. Strang, Glasgow and its Clubs.

It would be interesting to trace the history of the trade in coal, which in later times became so important, and to which Glasgow owes so much of its prosperity, and to know the prices at which that article was sold, but the notices on the subject are scant. The earliest mention of a coal-work in Scotland occurs in one of the Dunfermline charters in 1291.[1] The workings in all coal-mines must have been for a long time on a very small scale, and the pits or shafts of very limited depth. A certain quantity was used for firing, but peat formed the common fuel of the country. Furze was also used and wood where there were forests. In the high grounds of Ayrshire there appears to have existed an extensive forest, and even at Preston, now so surrounded by coal-mines, wood was used as fuel for the salt pans. But generally wood had become a scarce and valuable commodity.[2] Coal must have been imported as fuel previous to 1283, as in that year the municipal statutes of Berwick contain regulations for selling it alongside the vessels importing it. By the beginning of the fifteenth century it had become a common article of merchandise.[3] In the following century, when it was more wrought in Scotland, it was occasionally exported, but the general supply was so small that in 1563 an act was passed prohibiting the exportation—the statute bearing that coal was often used as ballast for ships, and that the export caused "a most " exorbitant dearth and scantiness of fuel." Writing in the reign of James I. Eneo Silvio describes Scotland as a cold country, generally void of trees, but, he adds, "there is a sulphurous stone dug up which is "used for firing," and these, he says, were distributed to the poor at the church doors where the country was denuded of wood.[4]

There is an entry in our burgh records under date 19th August, 1578, from which we learn that the Archbishop of Glasgow had let " the coil- " heuchtis and colis withtin the baronie of glasgw for the space of three " yeris, for the yeirlie payment to the said reverend father of forty pundis " money, togeddir witht threttene scoir and ten laidis of colis." At this time the pound Scots had come to be worth only about two shillings and sixpence sterling, so that the rent of all the coal within the barony, with the use of the existing shafts or openings, was only £5 per annum and 270 "laids" of coal. The term laid or load, as applied to coals, is

---

[1] Scotland in the Middle Ages.   [2] Professor Innes, Preface to Chartulary of Melrose, p. 16.
[3] Early Records of Mining, by R. W. Cochrane Patrick, Esq., p. xliv.
[4] Descriptio Asie et Europe, Paris, 1534.

not now used in Lanarkshire, but in some other districts it is. In Haddingtonshire, where the term is still employed, there are seven laids in a ton of coal. That gives 320 pounds to a laid, or very nearly what is practically the burden of a pack-horse. This, it is highly probable, was the quantity represented by the "laid" in the archbishop's lease. From another entry in the council minutes four years before this time[1] we find that the price of "a laid of colis to the tolbuytht" was twenty-two pence Scots, or less than 2½*d.*, and as that was for only a single laid we may safely assume that the value of what the tacksman had to deliver would be at most not more than twopence the laid. At this rate the entire rent drawn by the archbishop for all the coal within the barony was only £7, 5*s.* per annum.

In 1621 the lords of the privy council fixed the price of coal at seven shillings and eightpence (7⅔*d.*) the load.[2] But from the accounts of the household expenses of Archbishop Sharp in 1665 we find him paying 10*d.* a load for coal.[3] From another notice in the privy council records it appears that in the year 1621 the average weekly gains of a collier's family was about five merks (5*s.* 6*d.*).

In 1655 the magistrates let the coal in what is termed in their minute "the muir heughe," to two of the burgesses, Patrick Bryce and James Anderson. The terms of the agreement were that the town should "deburse for advancement of the said work twa thousand merkis Scotis" (£111, 2*s.* 2*d.*). The tenants were to have the first year free, and thereafter to pay to the town yearly 600 merks (£33, 4*s.*), and at no time to charge more than four shilling (fourpence sterling) for the hutch of coals —the hutch to contain nine gallons. They were to be bound "to keep "the work on futt threttein yeirs," and to employ eight hewers and no more. This arrangement does not appear to have been successful, or else the coal accessible by the shallow workings then in use had become exhausted. There is a minute accordingly by the town council some ten years afterwards, which bears that coals have "become verie scant "and dear, so that the hutch bought of befoir on the hill for four shilling "is now bought for no less than six shilling (sixpence), and that in re- "gard of the decay of the coall hewes about the towne quhilk maks "ane great outcry among the inhabitants and mainlie the poor, and the "magistrats and counsell knowing the same to be most trew, and being

<hr>

[1] 5th May, 1574.   [2] Privy Council Records.
[3] Maitland Miscellany, vol. ii. p. 524.

" informed that coalles may be win and gottin in their awin land in Gor-
" balles, they have therefoir concludit to give to Patrick Bryce Weaver
" ane thousand marks moneye (£55, 11s.) to sett down there twa shanks
" presentlie." The pits could not have been very deep which were put
down for that sum.

The late Mr. James Baird of Cambusdoon repeated to me in 1875 a
statement made to him some fifty years before by an old man, William
Wotherspoon—then seventy-eight years of age—to the effect that when
he was a boy of fourteen he was in the habit of carting coals from the
Greenend pit of the Calder Ironworks to Glasgow (a distance of nearly
twelve miles), where he sold them in the Gallowgate for fifteenpence the
cart—this sum being all he got to meet the price which had been paid
for the coals at the pit mouth and for the carting. This would be about
the year 1760. Wotherspoon occasionally got employment for his cart
in returning, and he saved money. He became, Mr. Baird told me, a
very strong man, and was able to lift two and a half hundredweight in
each hand. I do not know what quantity of coals was in the cart, but it
would probably be about nine or at most ten hundredweight.

That fifteenpence was the usual market price of a cart of coals delivered in Glasgow in the middle of the eighteenth century is confirmed
by the early accounts of the Town's Hospital. M'Ure says[1] that the
directors had it in design " to publish Regulations together with an
" abstract of the first year's management," and these particulars did
appear in a little volume, now very scarce, printed in Glasgow in 1742.[2]
Among the items of expenditure for the year 1737 given in this report
I find: " Coals, 560 carts, £29, 13s. 2d."—that is, less than 1s. 3d. the
cart. When Gibson wrote his History of Glasgow in 1778 "a cart of
" coals," he tells us, contained nine cwt., and we may assume that it was
the same in the earlier part of the century.

By the beginning of the eighteenth century Glasgow had become
known for its manufacture of plaids—that indispensable article of apparel
in early times; and when the magistrates resolved to make a present to
the Princess of Wales the minute of council bears that "it was judged
" not improper to send to her Highness a swatch of plaids as the manu-
" facture peculiar to this place, for keeping the place in her highness'
" remembrance."[3] A number of plaids were forwarded accordingly, and

---

[1] P. 315.   [2] A Short Account of the Town's Hospital in Glasgow, 1742.
[3] Burgh Records, 26th August, 1715.

were graciously accepted. The letter by the magistrates to the princess describes the plaids as "what are generally used in Scotland by our "women for covers when they goe abroad and by some men for the "morning guns [gowns?] or for hangings in bed chambers." This was at the time of the outbreak of the rebellion of 1715, and the city trans-mitted at the same time to the king what he, no doubt, valued more than the "swatch of plaids"—namely, an offer to raise and officer a regiment of five hundred men. The offer was received with thanks, but the magistrates were informed that the government had already taken such precautions as would render it unnecessary to put the city to that expense.

At a subsequent date we find the magistrates making regulations as to "linnen and cotton handkerchiefs," the manufacture of which had also been introduced in Glasgow, and there is a statute directed against the use of false or loose colours, and against handkerchiefs "being made "shorter in length than they are in breadth."[1] The foreign trade of the city increased rapidly. In the year 1775, in the single article of tobacco, Glasgow imported from America no less than 57,143 hogsheads, being more than a half of all the tobacco imported into Great Britain in that year.[2]

The subsequent history of the trade and commerce of Glasgow does not fall within the scope of these notices. The increase in the commer-cial prosperity of the city after the middle of the eighteenth century was very rapid. Many causes combined to produce this result, and not the least among them was the deepening of the river.

THE RIVER AND HARBOUR.

I have as yet said very little of the river, but the subject is well deserving of attention, apart from its connection with the trade and commerce of the city. The physical history of the Clyde, and the wonderful changes which in the course of ages it has undergone, are matters of the deepest interest.

It is certain that at a time not remote, geologically speaking, but not so late certainly as the beginning of the Christian era, the district

---

[1] 11th March, 1726.   [2] Denholm's History, p. 213.

through which the Clyde flows was the bottom of an inland sea, of which Loch Lomond, with its tributary valleys, formed a branch.[1] Dr. Bryce conjectures that it was an estuary connected with the sea by a narrow strait near Erskine, where the hills on either side press close upon the stream.   This estuary, whose limits reached as far as Johnstone and Paisley, was narrowed upwards by the projecting Ibrox and Pollokshields ridges, but again widening out to wash the base of the Cathkin and Cathcart hills, swept round north-east in a wide bay so as to cover what is now the Glasgow Green and the suburb of Bridgeton. The water would then enter probably about Bothwell or Rutherglen.[2] That the sediment formed over this tract of the Clyde valley during this early period was deposited under marine conditions is conclusively shown by the discovery of marine shells and other organisms in various localities near the river.

At what period this state of matters existed it is impossible to say, but we have unquestionable evidence that what is now the Trongate, with other lower streets of Glasgow and many parts adjacent, were covered with water at a time when the district was occupied by man. The discovery in 1830 of a canoe on elevated ground at Castlemilk, at a place a long way back from the river, and of the bones of a whale, which must have been forty feet in length, near Erskine in 1855, together with canoes in the Trongate and other localities far above the present level of the river—all of them covered by strata of transported sand and gravel—show clearly enough that there has been an elevation of the land, and that it took place within the human period.   The discovery in the Green, in 1876, of a beautiful Roman bowl of Samian ware, four and a half feet below the surface—covered as it was by stratified sand—has been pointed to as evidence that another elevation had taken place since the Roman occupation, but the weight of evidence is entirely against that hypothesis.   The whole subject is interesting: it has given rise to much controversy, and relating as it does to the ancient condition of what is now a part of the city, it will not be out of place to notice shortly the facts which have been ascertained.

To begin with the canoes.   One of these was discovered in 1780 when digging the foundation for St. Enoch's Church; and what made this discovery the more important was that within the canoe was

---

[1] Geological Researches, by Mr. Smith of Jordanhill, p. 67.
[2] Geological Notes of the Environs of Glasgow.

found a beautiful polished stone hatchet or celt, one of the instruments, no doubt, by which it had been fashioned. Another canoe was found at the Cross, while excavating the foundation for the Tontine buildings. In 1824 one was found in Stockwell Street, near the mouth of Jackson Street; and another was discovered as high up as Drygate, on the slope behind the new prison. One of these ancient vessels was in a vertical position with the prow uppermost, as if it had sunk in a storm, and there were found within it a number of marine shells.[1] At a later period a considerable number of canoes of the same description were found on the lands of Springfield, on the south side of the Clyde, and others were found at Clydehaugh. The average depth at which these last were lying was about 19 feet from the surface of the ground, and they were all at a distance of more than 300 feet from the modern margin of the river. They were all imbedded in and covered by stratified sand, which bore the clearest marks of having been deposited by the action of water. Whether this was so in the case of the canoes found at such high elevations as the Drygate, has unfortunately not been ascertained. That canoes were found in these localities is undoubted, but we have no account of the state of the soil around or over them at the time of the discovery.

All the canoes were of the most primitive kind. They were formed of single oak-trees roughly scooped out—some more carefully made, and others so rudely constructed that the roots had not been entirely cut off, but merely rounded in a rough way, and fire employed to burn out the interior.[2] I subjoin a representation of two of the canoes which were found at Clydehaugh in 1852,

No. 1.

from drawings made at the time by Mr. Robert Hart, which he kindly permitted me to copy. No. 1 is the largest and finest of the group, measuring 14 feet in length, 4 feet 1 inch in breadth, and 1 foot 11 inches deep. It has been hollowed out of a magnificent oak, cleanly sawn

[1] Sir Charles Lyell, Antiquity of Man, 1st edit. p. 48.
[2] Account of Ancient Canoes found at Glasgow, by John Buchanan, Esq., LL.D.

through at the thickest part. There has been a seat across the middle, and on the bottom there are rests for the feet of the rower. The end is closed by two boards joined, and at the centre where they meet a vertical incision has been made in each edge all the way down so as to form a sheath into which a thin slip of oak had been neatly

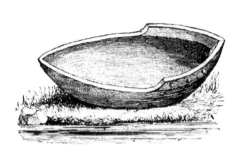

No. 2.

introduced, and made to draw out when necessary. In this way the seam caused by the meeting of the two boards has been made completely water-tight. No. 2 is a very curious little vessel. It was 10 feet long, 3 feet 2 inches broad, and 1 foot deep. The sides were perforated by a number of holes. These were for fixing the two quarter boards, as shown in the sketch. The boards had been separated from the canoe in raising it, but they were found by Mr. Hart and fitted into their places. The wooden pegs were as well made as if they had been turned. The quarter boards were half checked in the gunwale.

Referring to these Clydehaugh and Springfield canoes, the late Dr. Scouler, than whom, on such a subject, there can be no higher authority, says, " The depth at which they are found is that of the present channel " of the river, and cresting waves were quite competent to have carried " down all the beds of sand and gravel by which they were covered. " Here then we may infer that no geological change of any importance " has taken place in this part of the valley of the Clyde. But besides " these canoes there were others found which do indicate geological " changes—that is, changes in the relative position of the sea and " land from elevation. Thus, in the case of the canoes found in Lon- " don Street and at the Tontine, although they were buried at the same " depth from the surface, they are more than twenty feet above tide " mark ; in other words, what was once the channel of the river has " been elevated by that amount, and consequently these last canoes " must be of greater antiquity than those found at the lower levels " of Springfield and Clydehaugh. The history of canoes found at " such elevations as Drygate would carry us back to a much higher " antiquity, but, unfortunately, beyond the undoubted fact of canoes

" having been found in these places, we have scarcely any information.
" If they were found imbedded under transported sand and clay they
" would point to a very great antiquity, but it is possible the aborigines
" may have left them in such places for concealment or security. The
" result, however, of what we have on undoubted evidence, is that
" no elevation of the land amounting to more than twenty feet has taken
" place since the estuary of the Clyde was navigated by these ancient
" canoes."[1]

The organisms existing in the superficial deposits that now fill the
Clyde valley tell clearly their own tale. The boulder clay, the oldest of
these deposits, is the product of a sheet of land ice that descended from
the higher levels of the country to the sea-level during the glacial period,
and deposited there its burden of stones and other rubbish—the land
being then much lower under the sea than at present. The next series
of beds in the Clyde valley—namely the older sand beds and brick clays
—still testify to the presence of the sea by the arctic marine fauna contained in them. These deposits were succeeded by an upheaval of the
land of probably twenty feet, when we have evidence of a sea of less depth.
It was after that upheaval that the sands and gravels were laid down
which form our raised beach beds, and which contain a marine fauna still
living in the Clyde waters; and the probability is that the earlier canoe-
men lived during this period. And next we have evidence of a farther
rise of perhaps twenty feet more—which is Dr. Scouler's conjecture—and
this, the latest rise, shut out the sea from the Clyde valley above Bowling,
as well as out of Loch Lomond, where similar marine deposits are found.
After this last rise the Clyde would for a long time run through a tract
of country with no proper river channel, and the deposits then laid down
would be of fresh-water origin. The matter thus deposited will fully account for the rise in the bed of the river and of the bordering land, as well
as for the river shifting its channel from time to time, without resorting
to the hypothesis of any further upheaval. There is, as is well known,
a tendency in all tidal rivers that flow through a flat tract of country not
only to gradually elevate their beds, but likewise the land on either side,
so long as the river is allowed to remain in a state of nature. This silting up of the river valley goes on, of course, most rapidly when the river
is in flood, and it is hastened when the downward current is checked by
an advancing tidal wave. The deposit, too, will be greatest in the river

[1] Paper read at meeting of Archæological Society of Glasgow, 2d May, 1844.

itself, as there will be always more sediment there than elsewhere. The river will thus come to flow on higher and higher levels, till at last it bursts its bounds and takes a new course over lower ground. That this was the case with the Clyde in its later history is certain, for we have evidence of its having changed its course more than once within a limited tract of country both above and below Glasgow.

That the canoes found at Clydehaugh were at least as old as the time of the Roman occupation there can be no doubt. The probability is they were much older. If, then, their presence in the places where they were found precludes the hypothesis that any elevation of the land has occurred since they were left there, and if the deep covering of stratified sand over them can be accounted for by periodical floods, still less do we require to resort to the theory of elevation to account for the position of the Roman bowl found in the Green. There is abundant evidence that in times long after the departure of the Romans our Green was a low-lying swamp, repeatedly covered—perhaps covered every year—by floods or "spates," every one of which would leave a deposit of sand or clay. The place where the bowl was found was on the slope of the Flesher's Haugh, four and a half feet under the present surface, and about twelve feet above the then level of the river. But this by no means implies that the spot was so much above the level of the river when the bowl was left there. I have referred to the process of elevation caused by the deposit of matter brought down by the river, but we are in possession of actual data which show that by the improvements carried on in the Clyde, by deepening and otherwise, the bed of the river has been greatly lowered since 1758, when these operations commenced. So much has this been the case that between that year and 1876—the year in which the bowl was found—the level of low water in the harbour of Glasgow had been lowered to the remarkable extent of eight feet. We have no information how much it had been lowered above the harbour. The extent was no doubt less there than eight feet, for a weir was formed towards the end of the last century above the harbour to protect the foundations of the then recently erected bridge at the foot of Jamaica Street. This weir remained till 1842, when it was removed, and another erected on the under side of Stockwell Bridge, and this again was removed in 1852 to allow of the erection of Victoria Bridge. The formation of these weirs would, of course, from the time of their erection, prevent so great a lowering of the bed of the river as that which was taking place below; but that a process of lowering above the bridges had been going on for a very long time is certain, and it must have been hastened to some extent by the large quantities of sand which we know the inhabitants were in the custom of taking from the bed of the river below the old bridge of Glasgow. The foundations of this old bridge had been laid in what was then the bed of the river by Bishop Rae in the year 1350, and when the bridge was taken down in 1850 the remarkable fact became apparent that the original foundations had stood no less than five feet above the modern bed. It was also found that means had been taken from time to time to compensate the lowering process by artificially raising the portion of the channel immediately adjoining the piers, partly by compact masses of stone and partly by strong ranges of piles. The old foundations had been laid on beams of oak, and it is interesting to know that when these were taken out, after the lapse of 500 years, they were found to be as fresh as when first put in. This, however, is not so surprising when we know that the older canoes found under the Trongate were comparatively fresh when found, although they had been made from oaks which must have been growing where Glasgow now is at least four thousand years ago.

As showing also that the river was formerly broader, as well as its bed higher, than it was in our day, it is important to note that the bridge as built by Bishop Rae consisted of eight arches. Of these the two nearest the northern bank were built up, and the pier on that side removed in or before 1776, having by that time become of no farther use owing to the lower level and consequent contracted breadth of the river —the space being filled up with earth. From this it may be inferred that the brink of the river was, in Bishop Rae's time, considerably nearer the row of fishermen's houses than the present Stockwell Street, which probably occupies their site.

On the moderate assumption, then, that the depression of the bed of the river above the bridges amounted since the time of the Roman occupation to six feet, it will follow that the place where the Samian bowl was found was, in the Roman time, not more than six feet above the then level of the river; and deducting a foot of soil—which the contractor who found the bowl reported was over the stratified sand and clay—there remains a depth of only five feet of transported sand, which may easily be accounted for by deposits left by floods during the fifteen centuries or more since the bowl was lost in this swampy spot.

How frequent were these floods or "spates," and to what a depth the water attained, the present generation can have little idea. From the diary of Mr. George Brown, already quoted, we learn that a great flood occurred in 1712; and we have some interesting particulars of this flood from another eye-witness, Mr. James Duncan, Bookseller—the first, by the way, who introduced the art of type-making in Glasgow. Mr. Duncan, speaking in 1735, as a witness in the lawsuit between Mr. Fleming and the corporation already referred to, and himself at that time a man of eighty, says: "In the year 1712 there was an excessive "high speat in the river. At that time the deponent saw a boat swim "over the bridge at the foot of the Saltmarket and swim up the said "street opposite to the north gavel of the tenement lately built by "Thomas Blackstock, the south end of which house fronts the Bridge- "gate street, and there the deponent saw the said boat take in some "people who came off an old house which then stood there; then the "said boat swimed down to the foot of the Saltmarket street and up to "the foot of the Closes in the Old Yards, and there the said boat also "took in some people who were in houses at the foot of the said closes, "and carried them up the Saltmarket street."

Another flood fell under the personal observation of Mr. George Brown on the 11th of September, 1746. On this occasion, he tells us, "the river rose to such a height as to cover all the Laigh Green, to over- "flow the Bridgegate till near Allan Stevenson's house, the Stockwell "till near James Corbet's house, and the Saltmarket till it stopped the "entry into the Bridgegate."[1] Another Glasgow citizen, Mr. Reid ("Senex"), gives us his own recollections of two other great floods. Referring to one which occurred in 1782 he says: "In King street the "river reached the second shop above the Mutton Market. I stood on "the upper step of that shop on the 12th of March of that year, and "while I was there a boat arrived close to me, having been through the "Bridgegate with provisions for the inmates of houses in that quarter. "Both the markets were inundated, and I remember how the flood cleared "them of rats." This flood covered all the lower parts of the Green, "and the then village of Gorbals was so completely surrounded that it "seemed like an island rising up in the midst of an estuary." The river on this occasion rose twenty feet above its ordinary level. Speaking of another flood in 1808 Mr. Reid says: "I was living at that time in a

[1] Diary of George Brown. Privately printed 1856.

" self-contained house on the south side of the city, quite detached from
" any other, but the ground on which it was built was a little higher than
" the surrounding grounds. At night the river had put out all the fires
" of our lower apartments, and when I went to bed it stood three feet in
" our dining room. Outside of the house the water all around was
" deeper than the height of a man, and it was running past us with the
" rapidity of a mill race. I think that we were not less than 400 feet
" from dry land." Mr. Reid adds that on the evening of the next day,
the river having fallen considerably, he ventured to attempt his escape
from the house—tying his clothes in a bundle and carrying them on his
head; but even then the water was as high as his shoulders. The rest of
the family did not get away till the day following. In this flood the
Green was again covered, and a young man sailing over it in a boat lost
his life.[1] It is quite possible that the Roman bowl may have been dropt
from a boat in similar circumstances, and covered by the deposits of
subsequent floods. In 1816 there was another great flood. On this
occasion the Clyde rose seventeen feet, again submerging the Green; and
there were many floods after that till the continued deepening of the
river put an end to them.

Almost every flood covered the Green. Mr. Reid tells us that even
in his recollection the "Laigh Green" lay so low, and its surface was so
irregular, that a very slight rise in the river, and sometimes even a heavy
fall of rain, left it under water.[2] And Mr. Hart, to whom I have
already referred, and whose testimony as a man of science is peculiarly
valuable, told me he quite recollected that after each flood a stratum of
sand or mud was left on the Green often an inch thick.

The extent and effect of these floods is further illustrated by a curious
advertisement which appears in the *Glasgow Mercury* of 28th November,
1781. It announces "that there is a Ferry boat or lighter Lying in a
" park adjacent to the Green of Glasgow possessed at present by John
" King, late Deacon of the Fleshers, supposed to have been cast in by a
" flood more than twelve months byegone;" and it intimates that the
owner may have it on defraying charges. So that we have it here stated,
as an ordinary occurrence, that a boat, so large as to be described as a
ferry-boat or lighter, was left by the flood, not on the Low Green, but in
the "park adjacent"—namely, the Fleshers' Haugh. From all these

---

[1] Glasgow Past and Present, vol. i. pp. 81, 82.
[2] Old Glasgow and its Environs, p. 60.

facts it is easy to understand how the Samian bowl could in a long course of centuries have come to be covered by strata of transported sand. The whole Green, indeed, may have been under water during the Roman occupation, without resorting to the hypotheses of a subsequent elevation of the land. And it was the same with the low-lying lands farther down the river. Even at Dumbarton the land between the castle and the town was, so late as the beginning of the eighteenth century, "an impassable morass."[1]

But the proof that there has been no elevation since the Roman period, or even since the probably earlier time of the canoes which were found at Clyde Haugh, is much stronger than Dr. Scouler had supposed. His inference that no geological change of any importance had taken place in this part of the valley of the Clyde was founded on the assumption that the site of the canoes was that of the channel of the river; but he was not aware of the important fact, since supplied in the valuable work of Mr. Deas, that there exist plans and sections which show that at this place the bed of the river was, in 1853, fully seven feet lower than what it was a hundred years before—namely, in 1758. In other words, the site in which the canoes lay was all that depth below the level of what had been the bed of the river even so late as the middle of the last century.

How then did they get there? That they were not purposely buried at that depth is clear, for they were covered with strata of transported sand which had been quietly deposited around and over them. The only inference is that all the low-lying land adjacent was under water at the time when the canoes were left there, and that it has been since filled up by debris and detritus brought down by the river subsequent to the last elevation of the land. This hypothesis receives confirmation from the fact that in digging the trench for the quay wall of the Victoria Dock in 1875 there was found another canoe, about twenty feet from the then bank of the river, and at a depth of upwards of fifteen feet from the surface. It was covered by stratified sand and gravel, and lay at a point nearly eight feet below the level of what had been the bed of the river in 1758.

But other discoveries made in the course of the operations by the river trustees in the same locality gave still more interesting results— results which not only afford evidence of changes in the bed of the

[1] Defoe's Tour, 1727.

river, but which tend to show that the land at this place was under water at a period not by any means so remote as might be supposed. In the course of excavations at a point about 200 feet from the present bed of the river the workmen uncovered the remains of an ancient pavement or causeway—the centre of it lying at a depth of more than twenty feet from the present surface, and the extremities at depths varying from nine to ten feet. The stones highest situated were covered with a muddy soil, and were about the present high-water level. From this point the causeway appears to have sloped downwards and then risen again; and the stones at the lower levels were covered with beds of stratified clay, and gray and brown sand, alternating with beds of leaves in which hazel nuts were found. The greater part of the clay was arenaceous. The lowest point at which the stones were found was fully ten feet below what had been the level of low water in 1758. The pavement was thirty feet broad, and was traced to a length of 200 feet. From the positions and levels of the stones the probability is that they formed a causeway across—not the present bed of the river, but across an older channel more to the north, and that since that time the river has formed a new bed for itself. If the lowest of the stones were, when found, in the position in which they were originally laid, the river must have been then flowing on a lower level. It is possible that a flood, bursting through when the new channel was opened, may have undermined the centre of the causeway and caused the stones to fall down; and this is the opinion of a gentleman connected with the operations of the river trustees who saw the stones when they were discovered; but it is more probable that the old level of the river where the stones were laid was lower than the present. I have already referred to the habit of rivers to silt up their old channels, and this I apprehend was the case here. The river would silt up the channel over the causeway, and afterwards seek a new course for itself farther to the south, and there again it would proceed to raise its bed until its low-water level was in 1758 ten feet above the level of the causeway. However that may be, the important fact with which we have to do is that the stones were covered with beds of stratified sand and clay and beds of leaves, the aggregate depth of which was nearly ten feet.

The first inquiry which suggests itself in regard to these stones is, to what age are they to be ascribed; and here we are assisted by a material fact. The stones are all tool-marked, and the marks are

Q

those of several kinds of iron tools. Therefore, whoever placed them there were acquainted with the use of iron, and there is every reason for supposing that they belong to the Roman period. But if so there has been no elevation of the land here since the time of the Romans. The evidence, in short, is equally conclusive with that afforded by the Roman ford at Drip on the Forth, above Stirling, at which place a depression of twenty or twenty-five feet would now lay the whole of that country under the sea.

But there are still farther grounds for concluding that this old causeway is not pre-historic. The beds of leaves and nuts with which it was covered contained fragments of wrought coal. More than this. In close proximity to the stones, and covered by the same stratified deposits, were found logs of oak bearing distinct marks of the ends having been cut with axe and saw. For these interesting facts I am indebted to Mr. Deas, who also furnished me with sections of the excavations, showing where the canoe was found and the position of the logs and stones. One of these stones I had an opportunity of examining, and I found the tool-marks on it very distinct.

Here, then, we have unmistakable evidence that at a time within the historic period the river, at this part of the valley, was on a lower level than it was in the last century, and that it and the adjoining land have been raised, not by upheaval, but by the gradual deposit of sand, clay, and gravel.

That the river, at and below Glasgow, was deeper in the twelfth century than it was in later times there are, I think, pretty clear indications from history. In the reign of Malcolm Ceanmor the kingdom was, in 1164, invaded by Somerled, who, it is recorded, having assembled a large force, and collected a fleet of 160 ships, "landed at Renfriu" with the intention of subduing all Scotland; but he was attacked and defeated by the people of the district, and with his son Gillecolm slain—the defeat, by the way, being ascribed in a contemporary poem to the merits of St. Kentigern.[1] It is very certain that in the last century Somerled could not have carried to Renfrew a fleet containing an army, with all the accompaniments necessary for so formidable an invasion, if the depth was no more than one foot at low water, which was all that it was on some of the shoals there in 1758. In early times the river came close to Renfrew, and it continued to do so till at least as late as the middle of the

---

[1] Chron. Manniæ, quoted by Mr. Skene, Celtic Scotland, vol. i. p. 473.

seventeenth century. This will be seen from Blaeu's map,[1] which shows a branch of the river coming close to the town and forming the island called the Sand Inch, which has since become joined to the mainland. On this island stood the ancient castle of Renfrew.

We have another proof from history of a greater depth in the river in the middle ages. Fordun tells us that King Alexander raised an army and with his fleet sailed for Argyll to subdue that wild district, but a storm having arisen he was obliged to put back, "and he brought up at "Glasgow in safety." The king's ships were not, of course, like those of modern navies, but in order to be fit for a sea voyage, and to be capable of carrying the troops and stores necessary for the subjugation of a province, they must have been of dimensions far beyond those of the insignificant craft which alone could come to Glasgow in the middle of the eighteenth century, when the depth of water in the harbour was only fourteen inches at low water, and at high water did not exceed 3½ feet.

One reason, besides, for predicating that the Clyde in its present channel would be deeper in the middle ages than during more recent years is to be found in the fact that recently the river must have been silting up its bed more rapidly owing to the increasing cultivation of the land throughout its area of drainage—the land when cultivated being, of course, more rapidly denuded of its soil than when it lay uncultivated and covered with dense vegetation. The same fact has been observed in all the large river valleys of the country.

A farther evidence still that the depth of water in the river was greater in the middle ages than it was in later years is afforded by the fact that in former times herrings came up as far as Renfrew, and were fished for there. This interesting fact we learn from the great charter granted by David to the monastery of Holyrood (circa 1143), by which the king conveys to the monks "unum toftum in reinfry," with a right not only of nets "ad salmones," but "et *ibi* piscari ad allechtia libere"—a free right of fishing herring there, that is, at Renfrew.[2]

Before leaving this subject I may mention a fact pointed out by the late Mr. Smith of Jordanhill, which goes to prove that no elevation of the land near Glasgow (otherwise than by deposits from the river) has taken place since the Roman occupation. It is this, that the Romans had evidently constructed their great wall at both ends with reference to what is the present water level; and in this Mr. Smith is corroborated

---

[1] Ante, p. 115.　　　　[2] Liber Cartarum Sancte Crucis, p. 5.

by Mr. Dobie Wilson, a sound antiquary, who resided near the Clyde terminus of the wall.

I may also mention, in passing, an interesting fact pointed out by Dr. Scouler, which had not been previously noticed, namely, that the constructors of the earlier canoes were contemporary with two animals of whose existence near Glasgow we have no historic record, viz. the reindeer and the *Bos primigenius*, remains of which were found in the Clyde and brought up by the dredge near Whiteinch. These animals, Dr. Scouler surmises, the ancient inhabitants of what is now Glasgow must have hunted with no other implements than those of stone and bone, and in a state of barbarism similar to that of the Fins, so graphically described by Tacitus. The *Bos primigenius* survived till a comparatively late period, but the reindeer, and the stone implements found in one of the canoes, take us back to a very remote age.

Dr. Scouler suggests that these early settlers were of the primordial Aryan race, the descendants of Japhet, who dwelt somewhere about the rivers Oxus and Jaxartes, and on the north of the mountainous range called the Hindoo Koosh, and to whose language, the Sanscrit, so many of our words may be traced. There can be no doubt that the Celts who came to inhabit our Western Highlands, and all the district around Glasgow, were of this great family, but it is doubtful if the first canoe-men were of that race. They were more probably the men of the second stone age—the aborigines whom the Celts found there, and whom they either mingled with or exterminated.

The inscription on one of the most ancient of the sculptured stones of Scotland, that at Golspie, may have some connection with the early Aryan settlers. Dr. Moore of Hastings, in his work on the Ancient Pillar Stones of Scotland, reads the inscription as being in the ancient Sanscrit character, and supposes the stone to have been erected to a Buddhist missionary by his followers, who introduced much of their system into the west at a period long before the Christian era.[1]

In the history of the Clyde nothing is more interesting than the wonderful progress made between the comparatively recent time when it was a shallow stream at Glasgow, capable of floating only small craft drawing two or three feet of water, and the present time when the largest ships can come up to the harbour.

---

[1] Paper read by Dr. Stuart, author of the Sculptured Stones of Scotland, at meeting of the Glasgow Archæological Society in 1865.

From 1752 to July, 1770, a period of eighteen years, the total revenue derived from the river was only £147, 0s. 10d. For the year 1878 it amounted to upwards of £217,000.

The first attempt towards deepening the river was made in 1740. In that year, under date 8th May, the following entry occurs in the minutes of council:—" Which day the Councill agree that a tryal be made this " season of deepening the River below the Broomielaw, and remit to the " magistrates to cause do the same, and go the length of £100 sterling of " charges thereupon, and to cause build a flatt bottomed boat to carry off " the sand and chingle from the banks." For 1878-9 the expenditure, including new works, was for that one year upwards of £450,000. The total amount expended by the Trust from 1770 to 1879 amounted to nearly eight and a half millions sterling.

When James Watt made his report in 1769 the depth of water within the harbour at low water was only fourteen inches, and at high water three feet three inches. The depth at low water at the same point is now four-teen feet, and at high water twenty-four feet. Even till within the last few years vessels of 15 feet draught were two, and often three tides in the river in their passage up or down, being, from the shallow state of the channel, afloat for only one hour or so before and after high water. Now vessels drawing 22 feet leave Glasgow two or three hours before high water and get to sea in one tide.[1] In 1812 our first steamer, the tiny *Comet*, with a draught of only four feet, grounded at Renfrew, although Henry Bell was careful to regulate her time of sailing so as to avoid low water. This was told to me by Mrs. Bell, who said she was on board at the time. "And what was done then?" I asked. "Oh," was the reply, " the men just stepped over the side and pushed her across the shoal." Over this same spot, not many years afterwards, the great iron-plated line-of-battle ships, the *Warrior* and *Black Prince*, with all their machinery on board, passed with water to spare.

Previous to 1662 there was no quay at all at the Broomielaw. Under date 24th July of that year the following minute appears in the council records:—"The said day it is concludit for many guid reasons and con-" siderations for the moir commodious laidining and landing of boats " that there be ane little key builded at the Broomielaw, and that the " samyn be done and perfectit with the best convenience be sight and " advys of the magistratis Deane of Gild and Deacon Conveiner." This

---

[1] The River Clyde, by James Deas, 1876, p. 13.

first structure, which extended above what is now the site of Jamaica Street Bridge, appears to have been of stone, but it must have been of very small dimensions. In the following year the council "appoynts " the key at the Broomelaw to be heightit twa stones heigher nor it was " ordained to be of befor, and ordains the Deane of Gild to try for moir " oakin timber *aither in the Hie Kirk*, or back galrie, for facing the " samyn." The zeal for the preservation of the Cathedral, which the magistrates had evinced in the earlier part of that century, appears not to have been shared by their degenerate successors. They seem to have forgotten, or they did not choose to remember, that one of the reasons stated in the act of Parliament, passed only thirty years before (1633), by which so many grants and privileges were confirmed to them, was "the great charges susteinit be thame in upholding the " great kirk of Glasgow."

Even with the aid of oak from the Cathedral, however, the first wretched structure appears to have been found of little use, and the first quay, properly so called, was built in 1688. But this also was of very small dimensions, and the total cost of it did not exceed £1600. At the present time there are four miles of quayage; and, besides the large dock on the south side of the river, there is on the north side at Stobcross a magnificent dock, having a water area of thirty acres, capable of accommodating one million tons of shipping per annum.

Below the Jamaica Street bridge, what was within my own recollection a pleasant green on which clothes were bleached, is now deep water crowded with shipping. So late as 1839 the river above what is known as Napier's dock was only 168 feet wide. The width there is now upwards of 400 feet, and vessels of 3000 tons burthen float where at that time stood one of the largest cotton mills in the city.[1]

So few vessels came to Glasgow that not till 1667 was any shipping register kept. In that year it was ordained that "ane book be " maid, and to ly in the Clerks chamber, to the effect that the entrie " of each ship that come in this river of Clyde may be booked thairintill."[2]

Previous to 1780 Glasgow was a mere pendicle to the ports of Port-Glasgow and Greenock. It was not till that year that it was made an independent port.

In the report of Mr. Tucker to Oliver Cromwell, already referred to, he says that in 1656 no vessels of any burden could come nearer to

---

[1] The River Clyde, by Mr. Deas, p. 12.   [2] Burgh Records, 5th Oct. 1667.

Glasgow than fourteen miles, where they unladed and sent up all commodities by three or four tons of goods at a time, in small cobles of three, four, or five, and none above six tons burthen.   The first vessel of any size that arrived at the Broomielaw was a small schooner called the *Triton*, belonging to Mr. Cunningham, which landed some French brandy on the 17th of May, 1780.[1]   This was twenty-two years after the commencement of the operations for deepening the river.   The contrast now afforded by the forests of masts of ocean-going ships and steamers is very striking.

Previous to the year 1767, when the Jamaica Street Bridge was commenced to be erected,[2] and before the weir had been formed to protect its foundations, the river was navigable for small craft up to Rutherglen, where there was a small landing quay.   Mr. Reid says he was informed by the late Mr. Alexander Norris, of Greenhead, "that in his younger " days he had frequently seen vessels sailing up the river to Rutherglen, " and passing under the arches of the old bridge.   These vessels were " mostly Highland boats loaded with herrings, ling fish, eggs, and farm " produce; and sometimes there were at that period more vessels lying " at the harbour of Rutherglen than at the Broomielaw; which by-the- " bye," Mr. Reid adds, "was not wonderful, as I once saw the Broomielaw " harbour with only a single gabbart lying in it."[3]

Ure, in his interesting history, suggests that in very early times Rutherglen was the only place "of mercantile importance in the strath "of Clyde," and that it probably had almost all the shipping trade. That it was a port is certain, and the ship on the ancient seal of the burgh is confirmatory of this.   But there is little doubt that as early as the reign of David I. Renfrew, which then adjoined the river, was also a shipping port.   Among the gifts of that king to the Abbey of Kelso were a toft in Renfrew, *and a ship*, and a net's fishing in the river.[4]   It is true, however, what Ure says—writing in 1793—"that till of late " gaberts sailed almost every day from the quay of Rutherglen to " Greenock—the freight being chiefly coals."[5]

---

[1] *Glasgow Mercury*, 18th May, 1780.

[2] The foundation stone was laid on 29th Sept. 1767, and it was opened for traffic in 1772.

[3] Glasgow Past and Present, vol. iii. p. 820.   [4] Liber de Kelso, p. 5.

[5] History of Rutherglen and East Kilbride, by David Ure, A.M.

SANITARY CONDITION OF CITY—HABITS OF THE PEOPLE.

With the extension of trade and the increase of wealth the habits of the people became more gradually refined, but until after the middle of the last century their social condition and sanitary arrangements—although in advance of the other towns in Scotland—present a striking contrast to the present state of matters.

For a long time it was the custom of the inhabitants in the High Street and Trongate to throw out their ashes and other refuse—to have, in short, what the council records call their "middings"—in front of their houses. In the buildings there was no uniformity. All along the Trongate, and also in Argyll Street, there was in early times an irregular succession of thatched houses, with kilns and other erections, some nearer the centre of the street and some farther back, and the space between the houses and the roadway was used not for ashpits only, but for the deposit of every kind of refuse. In 1589 there is an order by the magistrates "that na midding be laid vpoun the hiegat;" but no attention seems to have been paid to it, as we find the practice continuing till near the end of the next century. It was a time-honoured institution with which the magistrates appear to have been for a time powerless to grapple. So great had become the nuisance caused by throwing all sorts of refuse on the side of the street, and so great the accumulation of water in consequence, that, as we learn from a minute of council (5th May, 1655), many of the inhabitants on the north side of the Trongate were obliged "to mak brige stones"—stepping stones—through the water lying between them and the street "for entrie to thair houssis." This obliged the magistrates to interfere again—not this time, however, to prohibit the ashpits, but to secure a free passage for the sewage water along the street. To effect this there is a minute of the town council, under date 20th September, 1666, which bears "that the syre in Trongait, on the "north syde therof from Hutchesounes Hospitall to St. Tenowes burn, "was levelled and maid once straight for convoyeing away the water "that way, but now of lait divers persones, yea almost all who hes "houses and killes narrest the said syre, casts in stra ilk ane foiragainst

" their awin land to mak fuilzie of, quhilk stops the passage of the water
" should goe that way, and jorgs wp so that filth and myre is made to be
" sein in the gutters quhilk is verie lothsome to the beholders; and the
" said Magistrats taking this to their wyse consideratioune, and being
" desyrous that that abuse should be remeided, they therfoir do heirby
" statut and ordaine that no maner of persones presume to do the lyk
" hereafter, but that everie heritor or tennant of the said lands narrest
" the syre keep the same frie ilk ane foir against themselfes for thair
" parts therof to the effect the passage of the watter be not gorged or
" impeided thereby."

But the "hiegate" was used for other purposes than dungsteads.
Swine were allowed to go at large through the street;[1] "stanes and
"tymmer" were deposited on its sides; "skynnis" in heaps were laid
upon it; it was used as a place for "drying lint," and women washed
and "stramped" clothes and yarn and other articles there.[2] So much
was it a matter of course to lay bulky articles on the street, that in 1589
the magistrates thought it only necessary to order that such articles as
stones and timber should not lie on the street "langer nor zeir and day."
But they drew the line at peat stacks. It had actually been the custom
to erect not only these, but hay stacks on the sides of the Trongate; and
in the year last mentioned we find it enacted "that na truff stakis be
"maid vpon the foirgait under the pane of xvjs. ilk falt." It takes a long
time, however, to eradicate old habits. In the following century the
skins, the timber, and the peat stacks are found still encumbering the
highway, and under date 6th October, 1610, there is a statute directed
against each of these nuisances; while so late as the middle of the
eighteenth century the inveterate middings are still the subject of prohibitory minutes of the council. Probably some of them lingered to a
still later period. So late as 1795 a petition was presented to the
magistrates praying for the removal of all hay stacks in the Trongate,
but it was unsuccessful.[3] It has been said, however, and it is in all
likelihood true, that to the space which these dunghills and stacks and
rubbish occupied in front of the houses we owe in part the exceptional
breadth of the Trongate. The booths or "crames" for merchandise
which projected from the houses, contributed also to secure the present
breadth of this fine street.

[1] Advertisement by Magistrates, 1758.   [2] Minute of Council, 11th Oct. 1623.
[3] Burgh Records, 4th Nov. 1795.

But the nuisances mentioned were nothing to another of which we find the magistrates taking cognisance. What would be thought nowadays of the butchers using the sides of the most public streets in the city as the places for slaughtering cattle! The minute of the town council on this subject, 20th September 1666, speaks for itself:—"The " same day forsuameikle as the Provest baillies and Counsell taking to " their consideratioune that it has been the vse and custome of the " fleshers of this burgh heirtofoir to slay and bluid the wholl bestiall " they kill on the Hie street in Trongait on both sydes of the gait, " quhilk is very lothsome to the beholders, and also raises ane filthie and " noysome stink and flew to all maner of persones that passeth that way " throw the king's hie street, and is most unseimlie to be sein that the " lyk should be done thereon; And the said Magistrats and Counsell " vnderstanding that the lyk is not done in no place within this king- " dome or outwith the same in any weill governed citie," therefore the fleshers are commanded "ilk ane of them to provyd houses in " baksyds for the doeing thereof, as is done in Edinburgh and uthir " weill governed cities, and that betwixt and the term of Witsunday " next to come."

This statute, however, like those against other nuisances, appears to have been only partially obeyed, as three years after[1] there is an order by the magistrates forbidding "the fleschers in the Land Mercat to kill " any muttone or heidron [heifers] on the hie street and that they keip " their filth and pynches [offal] aff the foir gate." The butchers appear to have been in the habit also of leaving live cattle on the public street all night, and there is an order of the council in 1664 prohibiting this.[2] About the year 1755 the magistrates erected a new market in King Street, and it was not till then that a public slaughter-house was provided. It was situated at the foot of Saltmarket, on what was then called the Skinners' Green.

Towards the end of the seventeenth century, however, the work of sanitary reform was progressing, and not only were the "syvers" ordered to be kept clear, but the streets and closes were appointed to be swept clean, and all accumulations of refuse to be removed off the streets. By a minute of council[3] the magistrates order that each inhabitant shall clean the street in front of his house, and that no one within the ports shall lay any filth "upon the hie streets without the drop of the houss

---

[1] 14th August, 1669. [2] 15th October, 1664. [3] 29th October, 1670.

"excepting that quhilk they sall caus tak or carie awaye *within eight* "*and fourtie hours* after the laying out therof." By a later minute[1] it is ordered, under stringent penalties, "that the streets be clated and "made clean once every week."

These enactments were followed up, some ten years later (1696), by a long statute, entitled "against nestines," which contains a prohibition against *casting out at windows*, by day or night, any dirt or filth of any kind—the practice of the "gardyloo," in short, which thus appears to have prevailed in Glasgow as well as in Edinburgh. Great care appears also to have been taken to prevent any one going to or coming from places where "the pest" happened to be prevailing. For example, on 23d October, 1588, there is an order of the council "that in consider- "atioune of the apparent danger of the pest now in Paisley na persone "indwellar within this toun, because of the mercates of Paisley and "Kilmacolm approcheing, pas or repair furth of this toun thairto vnder "the pane of fyve pundis to be tane of ilk persone repairing thairto, and "banisched furth of the said toun for ʒeir and day, without lief asked "and geven be the baillies." At a later period (1625) the magistrates, "being certainlie informit of the contageon of the plage of pestilence "within the Kingdom of Ingland, at God's will and pleasour, quhilk "daylie increises and that ane great number of merchands burgess are "daylie passand therto with merchand wairis, and cuming back with "wairis to this countrie, and speciallie to this burghe, quhilk is very "dangerous not only to this burghe bot to the haill countrie about," it is ordered that no one shall go to England until his name is first entered in a roll stating where he is going, and that he bring back testimonials with him. In reference to another pestilence in 1644 the inhabitants are commanded to "fence and build up their close foots and yards that "no passage be had throw ther closes, and lykwayes that no inhabitants "within this burgh suffer any strangers to enter the samen, or recept "them into their houses, without testimonialls to be shawne to the "magistrats, and that nane of the inhabitants that ar now furthe of this "burghe in these bounds be receavit within the samen to ther ounc "houssis till they shaw the magistrats ther testimonialls." There occur at different times various other minutes of council to the same effect. With all these precautions, however, the town was more than once visited by the plague, and on one of these occasions, in 1647, the Faculty of the

---

[1] 17th January, 1685.

university retired to Irvine "tempore pestis," and held their meetings and conferred degrees there.[1]

Yet notwithstanding these visitations, and the necessity of the enactments against nuisances, Glasgow was in early times a bright and cheerful city; and before the end of the seventeenth century, by which time much of the "nestiness" had disappeared, it was, as regards general cleanliness, in advance of every other town in Scotland—Edinburgh not excepted. This is the testimony borne by all early travellers who visited the city, and, what is curious, they nearly all concur in describing the town itself as more beautiful than the capital. One writer, who was with the army of Cromwell when it occupied Glasgow, says: "The toun " of Glascow, though not so big nor so rich, yet to all seems a much " sweeter and more delyghtful place than Edinburgh."[2] Another Englishman, already referred to, Richard Franck, who visited Scotland during the Protectorate, speaks of "the splendour and dignity of this " city of Glasgow, which surpasseth most if not all the corporations in " Scotland. The people were decently dressed, and such an exact de- " corum in every society represents it to my apprehension an emblem of " England."[3] Sir Walter Scott, referring to this account by Franck, says, "The panegyric which the author pronounces on Glasgow gives us " a higher idea of the prosperity of Scotland's western capital during the " middle of the seventeenth century than the reader may have perhaps " anticipated. A satirist with regard to every other place Franck de- " scribes Glasgow as 'the nonsuch of Scotland,' where 'an English florist " 'may pick up a posie.' Commerce had already brought wealth to " Glasgow, and with wealth seems to have arisen an attention to the " decencies and conveniences of life unknown as yet to any other part " of Scotland." Morer also, who wrote in 1689, says that "Glasgow has " the reputation of the finest toun in Scotland, not excepting Edinburgh, " though the Royal city." Defoe, writing at a later date, says of Glasgow, "It is one of the cleanliest, most beautiful, and best built cities in " Great Britain."[4] And Mr. Campbell of London, the architect of the celebrated Shawfield mansion, writing in 1712, describes Glasgow as " the " best situated and most regular city in Scotland."[5] Of Edinburgh Sir William Brereton gives a less flattering account. Writing in 1634, he

---

[1] Munimenta, vol. ii. p. 312.   [2] 22nd October, 1650. Several Proceedings in Parliament.
[3] Franck's Northern Memoirs.   [4] Tour through the Island of Great Britain, 8th edit. vol. iv. p.117.
[5] Vitruvius Britannicus, London, 1717.

speaks of the High Street as being certainly a stately and graceful street; but of the houses and habits of the people, he says, " I could never pass " through the hall but I was constrained to hold my nose—their cham- " bers, vessels, linen, and meat but very slovenly."[1]

As regards house accommodation and mode of living the habits of the Glasgow people were of a very simple kind. It was a long time before the houses even of the wealthier merchants extended beyond what in our day would be considered modest dimensions for tradesmen. Till some time after the beginning of the present century the better classes lived in flats, and every room in the house, except the dining-room, contained a bed, and sometimes the dining-room also, either openly or behind a screen, and the mistress of the house received her visitors at tea in her own bed-room. Tea was till a comparatively recent period a luxury confined to the upper classes, and even with them the consumption was very limited compared with what it is now. I have before me an advertisement cut out of a newspaper of 1787, in which a lady advertises for a nurse to take charge of a child recently weaned. She is to be " not under twenty-eight years of age; a widow, and one " above the rank of a common servant, would be preferred; the wages " £6 per annum, *but not permitted to drink tea.*"

In the beginning of the century the rents of the houses in Glasgow were moderate enough. Dwelling-houses of a respectable class, in flats, were let from £8 to £12 a year; and shops or market booths for about £10, few being so high as £20.[2]

It was owing in part to the restricted house accommodation that taverns were so much frequented by the better classes. Most of the physicians and lawyers in large practice were consulted each at his tavern, and gentlemen met there in the evenings at their clubs. On these occasions, as a rule, the score was moderate—seldom exceeding fourpence or at most sixpence for each person. In some few cases lawyers saw their clients in their own houses. One of these was Mr. Huchison, who carried on his business in his own house on the north side of the Trongate, next the old Tolbooth—probably on the site of what was afterwards the Tontine Exchange and Coffee-room. The house is described in one of the family deeds as " that large heich tene- " ment back and foir at the corse." Into the interior of this old house, before the middle of the seventeenth century, we have an interesting

---

[1] Brereton's Travels, p. 103. [2] Glasgow and its Clubs, p. 109.

peep supplied by Mr. Hill. "There is a tradition," he says, "which I "had from an old friend and connection of the family, that in Mr. "Huchison's business-room, situated most likely on the ground floor, "on the opposite side of the close from the dining-room or entrance-hall, "there stood a long fixed oak table with his papers at one end and at "the other a large silver drinking tankard always replenished with wine "or ale for the refreshment of clients, without ceremony or show of "particular invitation."[1] His valuable papers were kept in a bed-room above, in a Dutch-built spring-locked "kist." This old chest is still extant.[2]

At that time the usual dinner hour was not later than twelve o'clock. Afterwards the better classes dined at one. The next meal was at four, and was called the "four hours," a term which continued for a long time, and which I have myself heard an old lady use so late as 1820 when calling the children to tea. When there was a dinner party the hour came to be three, and this continued till about 1780. With these early dinner hours supper parties were frequent. After tea, when the family was alone, the lady of the house usually washed the china cups with her own hands at table. Almost every lady made her own markets—not in shops, but in the public markets, for there alone could the chief domestic supplies be obtained. The market for butter, eggs, and poultry was at the Cross. Butcher-meat was to be had only in the markets in King Street and Bell Street, and vegetables in Candleriggs. The meal and cheese market was opposite the college, and fish was only sold in King Street.[3] At a later period there was a market for butcher-meat in Anderston. Butter-milk was an article much in demand. It was sold at the Cross till after the middle of the seventeenth century, when an order of the magistrates "ordaines the sour milk mercatt quhilk is now "keiped at the croce to be transported thence and keiped at the Gallow- "gait brige heireftir."[4]

In the autobiography of Dr. Carlyle we have some notices—interest-ing because written by a contemporary—of the state of Glasgow when he went there to study in 1743. He was then a young man of twenty-one, well connected, and had introductions to the best families in the place. He had previously studied in Edinburgh, and he contrasts Glasgow unfavourably with the capital—"not in point of knowledge," he says,

[1] Huchesoniana, p. 29.　　[2] Ibid. p. 26.　　[3] Glasgow and its Clubs, p. 159.
[4] 24th June, 1661.

" or acquirements in the language or sciences—for in Glasgow learning
" seemed to be an object of more importance and the habit of application
" much more general—but in their manner of living, and in those accom-
" plishments, and that taste that belong to people of opulence and persons
" of education.   There were only a few families of ancient citizens who
" pretended to be gentlemen, and a few others who were recent settlers
" who had obtained wealth and consideration in trade.   The manner of
" living, too, at that time was but coarse and vulgar.   Very few of the
" wealthiest gave dinners to any body but English riders, or their own
" relations at Christmas holidays.   There were not half a dozen families
" in town who had men servants: some of these were kept by the pro-
" fessors who had boarders.   The principal merchants took an early
" dinner with their families at home, and then resorted to the coffee-
" house or tavern to read the newspapers, which they generally did in
" companies of four or five, in separate rooms, over a bottle of claret or
" a bowl of punch."[1]

Tavern bills were moderate at that time even in the capital.   Dr.
Carlyle, still speaking of the year 1743, says: " There were ordinaries for
" young gentlemen in Edinburgh at fourpence a head, for a very good
" dinner of broth and beef and a roast and potatoes, every day, with fish
" three or four times a week, and all the small beer that was called for
" till the cloth was removed."[2]   And prices would be at least as cheap in
Glasgow.   More than thirty years after Dr. Carlyle's time one William
Chalmers advertises " that he keeps an ordinary at his Poultry and Beef
" Steak Office opposite the Post Office Princes Street, where gentle-
" men will be served with a good substantial dinner of fine Broth
" or Marrow-bone soupe, and Meat both roast and boiled, at the cheap
" rate of 6*d.* each."   In the country the charges at most inns were still
more moderate.   Dr. Carlyle, travelling in 1744, came to Whitburn,
where he was detained by stress of weather for several days, and when he
came to pay his reckoning he was surprised to find that the charge for
lodging and board for four days was only 3*s.* 6*d.*

Here is another picture of Glasgow life, drawn by one of the citizens
well known in the beginning of the present century—Mr. Dugald Bannatyne—who was for many years secretary of the Chamber of Commerce: " At the beginning of the eighteenth century, and during the
" greater part of the first half of it, the habits and style of living of the

---

[1] Autobiography, pp. 75, 76.   [2] Ibid. p. 63.

"citizens were of a moderate and frugal cast. The dwelling-houses of
"the higher classes contained in general only one public room. About
"the year 1735 several individuals built houses to be occupied solely
"by themselves, in place of dwelling on a floor entering from a common
"stair, as they hitherto had done. This change, however, proceeded
"very slowly, and up to the year 1755 or 1760 very few of these single
"houses had been built. The living was simple—a few plain dishes
"and these all put on the table at once. The first instance of a dinner
"of two courses was about the year 1786, when Mrs. Andrew Stirling
"of Drumpellier made this change, and she justified herself against the
"charge of introducing a more extravagant style of living by saying
"that she had only divided her dinner and had put no more dishes on
"her table than before. After dinner the husband went to his place
"of business, and in the evening to a club in a public house, where, with
"little expense, he enjoyed himself till nine o'clock. The dinner hour
"was early. Down to 1770 it was two o'clock; after that it came to
"three, and not till about 1818 did it reach six o'clock. The lady
"gave tea in her own bed-room receiving there the visits of her female
"friends, and a great deal of intercourse of this kind was kept up, the
"gentlemen seldom making their appearance at these parties. After
"the year 1740 the intercourse of society was chiefly by evening parties,
"never exceeding twelve or fourteen persons who were invited to tea
"and supper. They met at four, and after tea played cards till nine,
"when they supped. The gentlemen did not go away with the ladies
"after supper, but continued to sit with the landlord, drinking punch to
"a very late hour. The people were in general religious, and parti-
"cularly strict in their observance of the Sabbath—some of them indeed
"to an extent that was considered by others to be extravagant. There
"were families who did not sweep or dust the house, nor make the
"beds, nor allow any food to be cooked or dressed on Sunday; and
"there were some who opened only as much of the shutters of their
"windows as would serve to enable the inmates to move up and down
"or an individual to sit at the opening to read."[1]

At this period profane swearing among the higher classes of citizens
was considered a gentlemanly qualification. Dissipation at entertainments was dignified with the appellation of hospitality, and he who did
not send his guests from his house in a state of intoxication was con-

---

[1] Notes by Dugald Bannatyne, Esq., quoted in Statistical Account, vol. vi. p. 231.

sidered unfit to entertain genteel company.[1] But it must be recollected that if the drinking at these entertainments was hard the " bouts" were comparatively rare, and there was probably much less drunk during a year at that time than there is now, when every day, both at lunch and dinner as well as at evening parties, wine is so freely used. Certainly in those days the abstinence of young people from stimulants was in marked contrast to the habits of our own day, when mere boys and girls, at late dinners and late dances, are found consuming an amount of stimulants which would not have been tolerated in the time of their grandfathers.

EDUCATION—AMUSEMENTS—FAIRS.

If the Glasgow people were content with moderate house accommodation they were always liberal in providing instruction for their children. In few places indeed was more regard paid to education than in Glasgow. The magistrates bestowed on that subject a large amount of their attention, and they showed also a laudable desire to advance the social condition of the citizens by encouraging the settlement in the town of skilled artificers. The council records contain some curious entries on these subjects, although the ideas of the magistrates and the presbytery on some points were somewhat peculiar. In regard to education, for example, it did not appear to be considered that free trade in schools would tend to the advancement of education. In the beginning of the seventeenth century (1604) we find the Presbytery of Glasgow complaining of "a plurality of schools: they consider the school taught " by John Buchanan, and the Grammar School quite sufficient." Some thirty years after this the town council, proceeding on the same principle of restriction, "statut and ordainit that na mae Inglische Scooles be "keipt or haldin within this burghe heireftir but four onlie with ane "wrytting schooll."[2] And a few years afterwards a poor woman who had ventured to become a teacher without official permission, is thus summarily disposed of by the town council: "The same day appoynts "the Baillies to discharge [inhibit] the womane that hes tackine vpe "an schole in the heid of the Salt Mercatt at hir awin hande."[3] But a

---

[1] Principal Macfarlan, Statistical Account, vol. vi. p. 232.   [2] 9th Feb. 1639.   [3] 20th Feb. 1658.

difference appears to have been made between "Inglische Schooles" and a lower order of institutions called "Scots Schooles." Two years after the date of the last-mentioned minute there is an order of the council " to tak up the names of all persounes men or weomen who keepes " Scots Schooles within the toune and to report."[1] And at a subsequent meeting no less than fourteen individuals—eight of them being females —are "permittit to keep and hold "Scots Schooles, they *and their* " *spouses, if they ony have*, keiping and attending the ordinances within " the samyne."[2]

In those days young girls of all classes learned to spin. In every well-ordered house there was a spinning-wheel, and early in the eighteenth century a school to teach the art was established in Glasgow. In 1728 there is a minute of council approving of a contract betwixt the magistrates and Susannah Smith, relict of the minister of Cardross, whereby " the said Susannah Smith is nominate Mistress of the public school " erected in this city for teaching girls to spin flax into fine yarn fitt for " making threed or cambrick, upon an encouragement of £30 sterling " annually granted by the Commissioners and Trustees for improving " fisheries and manufactories in Scotland." And two years afterwards there is a payment of £60 " for spinning wheels and chack-wheels and " chack-reels to the girls in the spinning school."[3]

As regards other professions no one was permitted to practise in Glasgow without the special license of the magistrates, and, in some cases, not until they had shown evidence of their skill. On one occasion, in 1569, a house painter applies for permission to practise his craft. In his supplication he sets forth that " he hes skill in washing and pynting " of housses, that ther is but one the lyk within the samyn brughe, " and not ane vthir in all the wast of Scotland," and that his occupation is " rather ane science nor ane craft."[4] The permission is granted. On another occasion one James Corss, a native of the city, represents to the magistrates that having " studied the knowledge of mathematicks, and " obtained ane competent knowledge thairin and vthir sciences thairto " belonging, being naturallie adicted thairto from his infancie," he desires to take up a school in the city " for teaching of theis airtes and sciences " *in the vulgar native tongue* quhilk hes not been done formerlie in this " kingdome for want of encuragments thereto, and the tyes of birth and

[1] 20th October, 1660.   [2] 14th Nov. 1663.
[3] 24th Sept. 1731.   [4] 1st Oct. 1659.

" educatioune press him to mak the first proposels thereof to this his native
" toune." Such an appeal was not to be resisted, and the magistrates grant
the license, and " promiss heirby to him their best encuragments."[1]

In 1677 liberty is granted to an " Architector" to " exerce his employ-
" ment and calling in architectorie and measonrie;" but on this occasion
the permission is only granted on certain "consideratiounes," and it is
limited to a period ending at Candlemas, 1680.

In 1674 the citizens were favoured by the residence among them of
a certain " Mistres Cumyng mistres of maners;" but this lady, finding
that she was not sufficiently appreciated, threatened to leave the town,
a calamity which the magistrates thought would prove so " prejudiciall to
" this place, and in particular to theis who hes young weomen to breid
" therin," that they undertook to pay her " ane hundreth marks yeirlie in
" all tyme coming to pay her houss maill so long as shoe keepes a school
" and teaches childerin as formerlie."[2]   Some thirty years afterwards
a charge appears in the city accounts of a pension paid " to a school-
" mistress for teaching young gentlewomen."

In 1674 the magistrates, with an equal regard to the advantage of the
inhabitants in the matter of creature comforts, appointed one Michael
Leiper to be made a burgess gratis, " and to be keeped frie of quartering
" and localitie, for his better encuradgment to tak ane guid hous for serv-
" ing the leidges as ane commoune coock within the same."[3]   This trade
appears to have thriven, as some seventeen years afterwards we find
" Margaret Hamiltone Widow" applying for leave " to keep ane common
" cookrie within this burgh," and offering to pay a premium of " fiftie merks
" Scots to the toune" for the permission.   Her request is granted, and
she is appointed " to have the freedome as ane burgess and gild brothers
" relict during her lifetyme as a widow."[4]   In the same spirit we find
a grant of twenty pounds (20*s.*) made " to James Robesoune baxter for
" helping him to build ane oven to baik plack pyes in, as also the sowme
" of 20 punds Scots to buy him ane laid of wheat to encurradge him to
" baik guid breid."[5]   The plack—equivalent to the groat—was a piece of
money coined in *billon*, a debased white metal, and was of the value of
twopence Scots.

Cookery was more studied in Glasgow in the last century by the
better classes than it is in our more refined times, and it was not thought

[1] 13th Aug. 1660.   [2] 20th June, 1674.   [3] 27th Sept. 1674.
[4] 23d May, 1691.   [5] 30th Dec. 1679.

infra dig. in a lady to know how her husband's dinner should be dressed. We get some insight as to this from a minute of council in 1740 "anent "the petition given in by James Lochead teacher of cookery." It sets forth that the applicant, "being regularly educated by his Majesty's "cooks, under whom he served in the Art of Cookery, pastry, confection-"ery, candying, preserving, and pickling, and of making milks, creams, "seyllabubs, gellies, soups, and broaths of all sorts, and also taught to "dress and order a table, and to make bills of fare for entertainments of "all kinds; and that of late he has successfully taught severall young "ladies, to their own and their parents satisfaction, and that for instruc-"tion of his scholars he is obliged to provide, on his own charge, flesh, "fowles, fish, spiceries, and severall other ingredients, but when dresst lye "on his hand for want of sale, by which he is a loser, and will be obliged "to lay aside his teaching unless he be assisted in carrying it on." He therefore appeals to the magistrates for aid. The plea was allowed, and a grant is made to him of £10 sterling yearly during the magistrates' pleasure.[1]

On another occasion a teacher of dancing applies for permission to exercise his art; but this was a matter in regard to which the magistrates —looking probably to the state of morals at the time—thought that more caution was required, and accordingly leave is given only "under the pro-"visions and conditions underwritten." These are, "that he shall behave "himself soberly, teach at seasonable hours, keep no balls, and that he "shall so order his teaching that ther shall be noe promiscuous dancing "of young men and young women together, bot that each sex shall be "taught by themselves, and that the one sex shall be dismissed and be "out of his house before the other enter therin: And, if he transgress in "any of these poynts the Magistrats to putt him out of this burgh."[2]

The teaching of music was in early times liberally encouraged in Glasgow, and the magistrates in this were only continuing what had been the uniform practice of the Church in ante-Reformation times. From the time that the Gregorian Chant first found its way into Great Britain, in the seventh century, it was taught gratuitously to the poor in connection with our collegiate churches and monasteries and other religious houses. The clergy were thus the masters of the "Sang scuiles."[3] One of these schools, as we have seen, was attached to the collegiate church of St. Mary

---

[1] 8th May, 1740.   [2] 11th November, 1700.
[3] Dauny, Dissertation on Scottish Melodies.

and St. Anne in the Trongate. After the Reformation the government pursued the same policy. In 1579 an act was passed by the Scottish parliament ordering that " Sang schools" be provided in all burghs for the instruction of the youth in music, and the magistrates of Glasgow appear to have been very forward to act on this order. There are repeated minutes in the burgh records on the subject, and they appear to have been always careful to inquire into the competency of the teachers. On one occasion, in the early part of the seventeenth century, they found a qualified professor in the person of one James Sanderis, and for his better encouragement they granted him a monopoly. Their minute bears that they had agreed with Sanderis " to instruct the haill bairnes within " this burghe that is put to his schole, musik for ten schillings ilk quarter " to himself, and fortie pennes to his man; and thairfoir the said provest " and baillies discharges all other sangsters within this burghe to teach " musik in tyme coming during thair will allenarlie."[1]

The plan of monopoly, however, appears to have failed, and forty years afterwards we find the city without any music master. A minute of council of 14th August, 1668, bears that the magistrates " taking to " their consideratioune that this citie is altogether destitute of ane musitian " for instructing the youth in the airt of musick, and seing its the earnest " desyre of manie honest men that ane able musitiane be tryed out and " brought to this place for that effect, and seing the Bischop is willing to " bestow yeirlie upon such a persone ane hundreth punds scots for the " mans better encouragement who is to be brought here, Its concludit that " the toune pay him yeirlie thrie hundreth and fyftie marks and that to " conteinew dureing the counsells will and pleasour."[2] This, however, appears to have failed to attract a proper teacher, and twenty years afterwards we find the town still in search of one. In 1691 a " Mr. Lewis de " France, musitian," applied, and with him the magistrates concluded an arrangement. The minute of council bears that Mr. Lewis had " very " willinglie condescended to teach the inhabitants music and to take only " fourtein shilling per moneth (1s. 2d. sterling) for ane hour in the day " from these that comes to the schooll," and to teach for nothing such of the poor as the magistrates shall appoint. And for " his encouradge- " ment" it was provided that he should receive 100 pounds Scots yearly (£8, 6s. 8d.), and that no other should be allowed to teach music.

Still the taste for music languished, and concerts were rare. " There

---

[1] 15th July, 1626.　　　　　[2] 14th August, 1669.

"never was but one concert during the two winters I was at Glasgow,"
writes Dr. Carlyle, speaking of the years 1744–45, "and that was given
" by Walter Scott, Esq., of Harden, who was himself an eminent per-
" former on the violin, and his band of assistants consisted of two
" dancing-school fiddlers and the town-waits."[1]

While the magistrates were not slow to enforce justice and repress
immorality, they were always ready to encourage the legitimate pastimes
of the people. Horse-racing was a very innocent thing in those days
compared with what it afterwards became, and there were not only races
at Glasgow, but the magistrates encouraged them by giving cups. In
the early part of the seventeenth century we find an order in the burgh
records which "ordainis the Horss Raiss to be proclamit to the xxv
" day of May instant and the cours to be maid."[2] Forty years later one
of the minutes directs "that Glasgow raice be keeped in maner as is set
" doune and contained in the diurnall, and recommends to the Provest
" to cause provyde what is necessar to be made for that effect."[3] And
then follows an order for the payment of "ane hundreth punds (£8, 6s. 8d.)
" deburst to the goldsmith in part payment of the coups he is making
" to the toune for the raice."[4] Ten years later there occurs an order
that "a proclamatioune be sent throw the toune that ther is a foot raice
" to be run thrys about the New Grein on the xxii of this instant, that
" who desyres to run may be admitted, and that he who wines sall have
" twentie shilling starling."[5]

Another favourite amusement of the Glasgow people was foot-ball—
a game for which their Green was well adapted. This game was prohibited by the old acts of Parliament, as it was thought to interfere with
the practice of archery. But James IV. was fond of it, and notwithstanding the law, he often indulged in it himself. It was certainly
encouraged and promoted by the magistrates of Glasgow, who always
provided the foot-balls; and the burgh minutes, from the very earliest
times of which there is any record, contain notices on the subject. From
one of these, in 1575, we learn that the price of a foot-ball was twopence.[6]
From another in the beginning of the seventeenth century we learn that
there was "gifen upon the xxviii day of Feb. 1609 to John Neill, cor-
" doner, younger, for fute ballis to the toune at fasterins evin conforme
" to the ald use xxvi[s.] viii[d.]"

---

[1] Autobiography, p. 75. [2] 14th May, 1625. [3] 8th March, 1665.
[4] 27th April, 1665. [5] 3d April, 1675. [6] Burgh Accounts, 6th March, 1575.

While thus encouraging innocent recreation, the magistrates were ready to suppress among the young men of the city, amusements which they considered of a more questionable tendency. In this spirit we find them, on a complaint by the university, restricting the use of billiard tables. One of the minutes of council bears that on a "complent being "made be the Principall and Masters of the Colledge that some per- "sones keeps Bulzard Tables to the prejudice of the young men, their "scholars, frequenting the same neir the Colledge, quhen they sould be "att their books"—particularly by a person, not named, living in Mil- ton's land—"its concludit that he be discharged to keep the same and "that no Bulzard Board be keiped betwixt the Wynd heid and the "Croce."[1]

From another of the council minutes we learn that, besides these private "bulzard boards," games and plays were provided for the amuse- ment of the people in the houses of the publicans or vintners. Unlicensed places we would call them, and they fell under the same category then, only that the magistrates, instead of using means to suppress them, in- terfered for their protection. At that time no theatrical representations or plays of any kind were permitted by law, unless sanctioned by an officer appointed by the crown, called *Magister Ludorum*, the Master of the Revels; and towards the end of the seventeenth century we find this functionary, or rather two individuals—for it appears to have been at that time a collegiate charge—interdicting the publicans from having "revels" in their houses without the requisite license. In these circum- stances the magistrates came to the rescue, and the matter is thus disposed of by a minute of council, dated 5th June, 1682: "The same day ordains "the provost to have a warrand for two hundred and forty pounds Scots "payed to Edward and James Fountains, masters of the Revels, for "descharging the Vintnors in toune of the charges of horning given them "for keeping games or playes of quhatsomever kynd in their housis, and "for frieing them of the lyke in time coming during their gift"—that is, during the time that the two masters had a gift of the office. In con- nection with these functionaries, I may mention that one of the favours bestowed on Glasgow at the Revolution was the appointment by royal warrant of one of the citizens, "William MacLean son of Charles "MacLean merchant in Glasgow, to be our sole Magister Ludorum, "commonly called Master of the Revels, in our Kingdom of Scotland."

[1] 31st January, 1679.

The office fell into desuetude in the reign of George I., I think; but it had existed for a long time previously, and in the books of Lyon King of Arms are to be found the armorial insignia appropriate to the functionary, viz., "Argent a lady rysing of a cloude in yᵉ nombril point, "ritchlie apparelled; on her head a garland of ivye, holding in her right "hand a poniziard crowned: in yᵉ left a vizard, proper; standing under "a vale or canopie azur, garnished or: in base a thistle vert."

In providing for the amusements of the people, the magistrates—if they erred in the alienation of the commons—appear to have been forward in promoting the health and recreation of the citizens, by providing public parks for their use. In this respect, indeed, they showed, at an early period, the same public spirit and liberality which their successors have been showing in later times—and this too, sometimes, when the funds of the corporation could not very well afford it. The first park which belonged to the city was a portion of what came to be called the Laigh Green. At what time it was acquired is not known, but it was probably included in the lands originally belonging to the see, and embraced in the Notitia of David. This portion did not extend to more than twenty acres. From time to time other portions were purchased by the magistrates, till it amounts now to more than a hundred acres. To meet the price of one of the portions of the Laigh Green, formerly called the Linen Haugh, which was acquired in 1662, the magistrates were obliged to sell some of their feu-duties, and that at a very low price —only seventeen years' purchase. The westmost portion of the Laigh Green was called the Skinners' Green, from its being used by the tanners for drying their hides. It was separated from the rest of the Green by the Molendinar Burn. On part of the Skinners' Green the slaughterhouse was, as I have already mentioned, erected afterwards, with an inclosure for cattle. The remaining portions of the Green subsequently acquired consisted of the lands of Kinclaith and others. The portion called the Fleshers' Haugh, consisting of twenty-six acres, was acquired in 1792 at the price of £4000. The Green was bounded on the north by a wall, within which was a walk and a row of fine trees. A portion of the Green, including this walk, was, in 1819, taken to form Great Hamilton Street and Monteith Row.

The "old Green," called in the early charters the *Commune Viridarium Glasguense*, and afterwards "the Doucatt green," from there being a dovecot on it, was part of the common lands of the city, and consisted of the ground by the river side from the old bridge to Jamaica Street, and included a small island in the stream, which at low water was joined to the mainland. This island is shown in Blaeu's map.[1] The old Green was a pleasant grassy lawn, and in the end of the last century and the beginning of the present it formed the principal promenade of the citizens.[2] But it was not retained as a public park, and from its position, indeed, it could hardly have been so. The magistrates took possession of it, and disposed of it to various parties; but, with a prudent foresight, they stipulated that if the ground should ever be required for public purposes it might be reclaimed at the prices paid for it. Of this reserved right the magistrates afterwards availed themselves, and the portion of the ground next the river is now occupied by quays and wharfs.

In connection with the amusements of the people I may refer to those periodical pageants of the different Trades which in early times were common in the burghs of England, and of Scotland also, at least in the royal burghs. In a volume of the fourteenth century, belonging to the corporation of York, there are numerous entries relating to such pageants in that city. They occurred at the feast of Corpus Christi, on the Thursday after Trinity Sunday, and they were remarkable for the numbers who took part in them, and for their gorgeousness and the large sums expended in getting them up. In the volume referred to some of the notices relate to complaints made to the "Chamber of "Counsell" against individuals who carried on certain trades in the city, and yet refused to contribute to the expenses incurred by these trades in the pageants, and these complaints are followed by orders of the chamber on the defaulters obliging them to contribute.[3] In the same way, in the Scottish burghs, the magistrates appear to have not only permitted and encouraged, but enforced and regulated similar pageants. They were accompanied by music and banners, and the masques supported the character of some scriptural or classical person, or age, or event. A very early notice occurs in the burgh records of Aberdeen, by which the magistrates prescribe to each trade the fancy characters which it is to contribute to these pageants. It is as follows:—"Thir craftes "vnderwritten sall fynd yerly in the offerand of our Lady at Candelmas "thir personnes vnderwritten: that is to say The littistaris [dyers] sal

---

[1] See p. 115. [2] *Glasgow Past and Present*, vol. iii. p. 542.
[3] First Report on Historical MSS. p. 109.

"fynd the Empriour and twa doctoures; the Smiths and Hammermen
"sal fynd the three kingis of Culane; the talzoures sal find Our lady
"Sancte Bride, Sancte Helene, and Joseph; the skynnaris sal fynd two
"bischops and four angeles," and so on through all the trades—each, in
addition to the personated characters, being enjoined to provide "als
"mony honeste squiares as thai may."[1] A hundred years later, we find
from the same records that the custom was still observed, and the
magistrates give very special directions on the subject, enjoining "the
"craftismen of this burgh in thair best array to keipe and decoir the
"processioun on Corpus Cristi dais and Candelmas day als honorabillye
"as they can, every craft with thair awin baner with the armes of thair
"craft thairin"—following in all this, as the order bears, "the auld lova-
"bill consuetudis and rytt of this burgh, and the nobill burgh of Edin-
"burgh, of the quhilkis rite and consuetude the provest has gotin copy in
"write." And then follows the order of the procession and the particular
characters which each trade is to provide.[2]

Whether similar pageants occurred in Glasgow I do not know.
There are no notices of them in our burgh records, but there may have
been such, as our records do not go so far back as those of Aberdeen
which I have been quoting. It is not at all improbable that a procession
which occasionally took place in Glasgow at a later time, and the last of
which occurred within the memory of some still living, may have been
a relic of these mediæval displays. I refer to the processions of king
Crispin, pageants got up by the Cordiners, with banners and masques
and music, in a very gorgeous style. They took place at intervals—
sometimes alone, and sometimes in combination with the other trades.
The last was, I think, of this character. It occurred at the time of the
passing of the first Reform Bill, and attracted great attention, king
Crispin being splendidly arrayed in royal robes. There have been, since
then, many occasions on which the crafts went through the town in procession, accompanied by banners and bands of music, but the peculiar
pageants of the middle ages, if they ever existed in Glasgow, have
become there, as in all the other burghs of Scotland, things of the past.

I have already referred to the fairs held in Glasgow. In early times
they must have been very insignificant, even though "French gloves"
were to be had at them; but in later times they became of considerable
importance, and were largely resorted to. In early times, if the first

---

[1] Burgh Records of Aberdeen, 5th Sept. 1442.   [2] Ibid. 22d May, 1531.

day of the fair fell upon a Sunday, it appears to have been held on that day all the same; but after the Reformation the magistrates (in 1577) issued a proclamation prohibiting this, and forbidding the opening of booths and selling of merchandise on a day on which "na mercatt aucht "to be keipit."[1]   In such a case, as we learn from a subsequent minute, the first day of the fair was held on the preceding Saturday.[2]   The fair began on the 7th of July, and continued for eight days, and during that period, as I have already mentioned, no one frequenting the fair could be taken for debt, nor could a runaway serf be seized by his master during "the peace of the fair."   The proclamation of the fair was an important ceremony, and in Glasgow it continued to be made till at least the early part of the eighteenth century—probably till a later period. One of the burgh minutes in 1581 is interesting as containing the form of this proclamation.   It is as follows: "The quhilk day the peace of the "fair wes proclamit be David Coittes, mair of fee, vpone the Greyne, and "be Richard Tod toun officiare vpon the croce, efter the forme and "tenour vnderwritten: Forasmekle as this day is the sext of Julij quhilk "is the fair evin of Glasgow, and the morne the fair day, quhilk contine- "wis the space of aucht dayis, thairfore I inhibit and forbiddis straitlie "in our Souerane Lordis name, and in name and behaulfe of ane noble "and potent lord Esme erle of Lennox, lord Darnlie and Obinze etc. "prouest, and baillie of the baronie, and in name of the baillies of this "toun, that nane of our Souerane Lordis legis cumand to this fair, re- "paring thairin, or gangand thairfra, do ony hurt or trublens ane to ane "vther for auld dett or new dett, auld feid or new feid, bot leif peaceablie, "and vse thair merchandice and eschange vnder Goddis pece and our "Souerane Lordis protectioun, vnder all hiest pane and charge that may "be impvt to thame doand in the contrare, and to be callit and accusit "for breking the kingis Maiesteis pece and trublance of his hienes mer- "catt To the quhilk proclamatioun the officiares reqvirit witnessis viz "David Lindsay elder, Thomas Cloggie, Mungo Wilsoun, and Niniane "Drew."[3]

As a precaution against "breking the pece"—and in all probability not an unnecessary one—certain of the citizens were appointed "to keip "the fair," and for that purpose to be duly armed.   Thus at a meeting of the town council held on 6th July, 1574, "being the fair even," the magistrates issued an order for "every booth halder to have in readiness

---

[1] Burgh Records, 6th July, 1577.   [2] 3d July, 1605.   [3] Ibid. 6th July, 1581.

"within the booth ane halbert, jack, and steel bonnet, for eschewing of "sic inconveniences as may happen, conform to the auld statut made "theranent." This was in accordance with an act of the Scottish parliament which required that every yeoman or burgess possessed of twenty pounds in goods have a good doublet of fence, or a habergeon, with an iron hat, a bow, and a sheaf of arrows, a sword, a buckler, and a knife. Those possessed of only ten pounds were to have a bow and a sheaf, with a sword and knife.[1] Again, in the beginning of the following century, we find an order by the magistrates "that tuentie of the merchand rank, "togidder with tua of ilk craft, be electit and chosin, at the discretioune "and optioune of their deikinis, for keiping of the fair of this burgh, "Setterday nixt, quhilk is the fair eivin of the said burgh, and hauldin "as the fair day becaus of the Sabbothe day, and that with corslat and "pik."[2] And in the following year "it is ordanit that xij merchandis, "and tuelf of craftis nameit and warneit, attend on the sereff the tyme of "the fair with sword halbert and steilbonnet."[3]

M'Ure says that in his day the fair was proclaimed or "fenced" within an inclosure or garden where the convent of the Greyfriars stood, "at a place they call Craignaught." This place, otherwise written Craignathe, Craignache, and Craigmak, is mentioned in the old burgh records as a place where the magistrates met on the occasions when the fair was to be proclaimed. Thus, under date 6th July, 1580, there is this minute: "The quhilk daye the Court fensit be the baillies at Craigmak, and "thaireftir callit the sute roll, and proclamit the fair." And in all the subsequent minutes of council down to 1607, when the fair is ordered to be proclaimed, it is at a court held at Craignac or Craignaught, although in the same years the ordinary meetings of the council are held in other places; for example, in 1574 the ordinary meetings are held "in the "Blackfrier Kirk," and in 1575 "in the tolbuytht of Glasgw." M'Ure says he does not know what "Craignaught" means. Mr. Macvean, in his reprint of M'Ure's work, says that in recently digging a foundation there was found in the locality a whinstone rock, which it is probable in former times appeared above the surface, and that this rock may have given rise to the name. This conjecture receives confirmation from the peculiar terms of one of the old burgh minutes (6th July, 1607), which bears that the fair was proclaimed at "the heid court of Craignache "*haldin vpone the Craig thairof* by the thrie balleis and accompaneit

---

[1] Act. Parl. Scot. vol. ii. pp. 18, 132.　　[2] Burgh Records, 3d July, 1605.　　[3] 28th June, 1606.

"with the Counsell of the said bruch and deikins thairof." It would appear from this that the ceremony of the proclamation was at that time made from a "craig" or rock within the inclosure referred to. How it came originally to be proclaimed there I do not know.

The fair was held at first at the Cross at the head of the High Street. Afterwards, and for a long time, it was held at the foot of Stockwell, and latterly at the foot of the Saltmarket. There are some still living who must recollect the large numbers of cattle and horses which crowded the Stockwell and streets adjacent on the Wednesday of the fair, to the inconvenience and sometimes the danger of passengers, any thoroughfare being next to impossible. Indeed, till the establishment of the Cattle Market in Grahame Square, the Stockwell, which was then the chief entrance to Glasgow from the south, was the only place in the city where a regular cattle market was held; and the "Brig-end" was the rendez-vous of all country servants coming for hire.[1] In our day the fair of Glasgow is more noted for the inhabitants leaving the city than for crowds congregating in it.

POLICE, WATER SUPPLY, &c.

In the state of the streets and other matters of police the contrast between the present and former state of things is very remarkable. Till towards the end of the eighteenth century none of the streets in Glasgow were causewayed, and from all accounts they must have been in a state of great disrepair. In 1577 the magistrates appointed "a calsaye maker" for two years,[2] and to meet the expense imposed on the inhabitants a tax of two hundred pounds—£16, 13s. 4d. It would appear, however, that no one of sufficient skill could be had in the city, and there is an entry in the burgh records in the following year authorizing "a calsaye maker" to be brought from Dundee. It was not till 1662 that the street from the West Port to St. Enoch Square was causewayed. Before that time St. Enoch's Burn was an open limpid stream running across the highway, unspanned by any bridge, and in that year the magistrates appointed "ane hand-"some little brige with ane pen to be put over St Tenowes burne, and that "the casay be brought in therfra to the West Port; and recommends to

---

[1] Glasgow and its Clubs, by Dr. Strang, 3d edit. p. 228.   [2] 19th November, 1577.

" the Mr of Wark to send for the calsay layer in Rutherglen to do the
" work."[1]

Till so late as 1780 there was no foot-pavement on the south side of
the Trongate, and the street was not lighted.　The inhabitants had at
night to find their way by means of their own "bouets" or hand-lamps
when there was no moonlight.　In that year the magistrates agreed to
put up nine lamps on the south side of the Trongate, between the Tron
Church Steeple and Stockwell Street, on condition that the proprietors
along that line would lay a foot-pavement similar to that which had been
formed on the opposite side.　The absence of lamps in a town then so
small as Glasgow is less remarkable when we know that till near the end
of the seventeenth century the streets of London remained unlighted.　In
the last year of the reign of Charles II. a projector named Heming obtained letters patent confirming to him for a term of years the exclusive
right of lighting the metropolis.　After all, what he undertook was merely
to place a light before every tenth door on moonless nights—that is, one
night in three—from the beginning of October to the 25th of March, and
only from six o'clock till midnight.　This accommodation, scanty as it
was, was hailed as something wonderful, and the projector was over-
whelmed with applause.[2]

Not till the beginning of the present century was there any regular
police force in Glasgow.　At an early period a watch, such as it was, had
been instituted, but it does not appear to have been very efficient.　The
first notice on the subject in the burgh records occurs towards the middle
of the seventeenth century, when the council "ordains ane watche to be
" keepit neightlie heireftir" from six o'clock at night till five in the morning.[3]　And in the following year there is an order appointing one of the
citizens to keep watch at each port from seven in the morning till ten at
night.[4]　These orders appear to have received little attention, and in 1659
there occurs the following minute: " The same day for preventing of the
" great hurt and damage in the futur quhairof sundrie inhabitants hes
" fand the smart heirtofoir throw the breking of thair houssis and buithes
" be thiefes: it is therfor heirby statute and ordained that ane watch be
" keipit nightly heirefter, *to be set ilk night be the baillies* in dew tyme,
" vicissim, to consist of sik ane convenient number as they sall think
" meet."　This is ordained to be made known "be touk of drum," and

[1] 28th June, 1662.　　　　　　　　[2] Angliæ Metropolis, 1690, § 17.
[3] 2d March, 1644.　　　　　　　　[4] 20th Dec. 1645.

every man, or a substitute, is ordered to come out under a penalty.[1] This service appears to have been for a long time performed cheerfully by all the citizens, including those of the better classes. In the diary of Mr. Brown, already referred to—a Glasgow merchant in prosperous circumstances, and who amassed a considerable fortune—there occurs under date 7th December, 1745, this entry: "Read the fourteenth chapter of "first Corinthians and prayed; then went to keep the city guard at ten "o'clock at night, where I continued till near four in the morning, when "I went to bed."[2] This was at the time when the rebel army was expected, and within a few days afterwards it entered the city with Prince Charles at its head.

But towards the end of the eighteenth century the magistrates made some efforts to establish a more efficient system of watching. About 1788 they created a small police force, for which in the following year a sum of £135, 2s. was paid to Richard Marshall, for himself as superintendent and for his officers. This force appears to have been armed, and it no doubt assisted the citizens in their watch and ward, but it was found necessary to introduce among the citizens themselves a more exact system. A notice was accordingly published bearing that, "in con-"sequence of the great extent and populousness of the city," it was necessary to establish "a night guard and patrol in order to watch and "guard the streets." The town was accordingly divided into four districts, and all the male citizens, above the age of eighteen and under sixty, whose yearly rents amounted to £3 sterling or above, in rotation, to the number of thirty-six every night, were appointed to mount guard, and to continue on patrol during the night—those claiming exemption being obliged to pay two shillings and sixpence for a substitute.[3] This arrangement continued to the end of the century. It was not till 1800 that the police force of the city came to be regulated by statutory enactments.

Until near the end of the last century there was not a common sewer in the city. The first was constructed in 1790, and by 1819 the number of streets which contained common sewers was only forty-five.

So late as 1777 the total force employed by the magistrates in cleaning the streets was two men. It was only by a minute of council in the end of that year that they enacted that "a third person should be

---

[1] 3d Dec. 1659.   [2] Diary of George Brown, printed for private circulation, p. 41.
[3] 2d Dec. 1790.

"employed along with the said two men." So badly kept were the streets and roads that till far on in the present century, ladies almost universally used pattens when walking out.

Previous to 1817 the streets were seldom watered. In exceptionally dry and sultry weather, when this was done, it was effected by men *with watering cans*. In the year mentioned the present mode of watering by means of carts was introduced. It was the invention of Mr. Black, the superintendent of fire-engines.

As to the general water supply of the city there is nothing in our burgh records to show that there was ever any scarcity, but it could at no time have been very abundant. Of course, the supply was, till a comparatively recent period, derived entirely from wells, but of these there were a considerable number for the size of the city. M'Ure, writing in 1736, says: "There is plenty of water, there being sweet water wells in "several closses of the toun, besides sixteen public wells which serves the "city night and day as need requires."[1] For the ordinary wants of the inhabitants, as then understood, these were no doubt sufficient; but in those days there were no baths or other conveniences, such as we now consider so indispensable. Some few families had private wells, but as a rule the inhabitants had to resort to the wells in the public streets; and it was an everyday sight—morning and evening—to see these wells surrounded by housewives and maid-servants, with their "stoups" set down in rows, waiting their turn to be served. On Saturdays there was an extra pressure, as a supply required to be provided on that day for the Sunday. One of the most noted of these old wells, and the one which finds earliest mention in the old charters, was the Deanside or Meadow well, the water of which was so prized that the Friars Preachers, as I have already had occasion to mention, had a charter authorizing them to conduct it into their convent. Another was Bogle's well, in regard to which there is a minute of the town council "that Bogillis well should be assayed "for bringing and convoying the water of the same to the Hie street "according to the right the town hes therof," and the magistrates are recommended to arrange for having this done "by conduits of lead." There was another, an open draw-well, at the Barras yett, near the port of that name at the foot of Saltmarket. It is mentioned in a minute of council in 1664, which ordains that "in respect of the heighting of the "calsay at the Barrazet the well there be heightit twa stones higher round

---

[1] History, p. 144.

"about, for preservation of childerin falling therin."[1] Opposite the old Black Bull Inn in Trongate was another open draw-well, afterwards covered in, which was famous in the palmy days of cold punch, and which is alluded to in *Cyril Thornton* as "the west port well."[2] On ordinary occasions this favourite well was surrounded by large numbers of the town's people waiting a supply. There was also an old well on the banks of the Molendinar Burn, near the Necropolis bridge. It was called the "Minister's" or "Priest's Well." Farther down on the east bank of the burn was the "Lady Well." In early times there was also a well at the present Cross. There was another "at the Vennell," which appears to have been, like the one in Trongate, a draw-well, as there is a minute of council in 1656 arranging with John Scott, millwright, to "rewle and "governe" this well and "the new well in Trongait," he undertaking to uphold them "in cogis and rungis, the toun vphalding all ganging greth "quhan athir it weiris or breckis." There was another well on the Green, the Arns Well, so called from the arn or alder trees which were planted beside it; and there were various others. There were thirty in all, besides a few private wells. Among these last one of the finest in the city was within the precincts of the mansion in Jamaica Street belonging to Mr. Black of Claremont, which was taken down in 1849.

In 1776 the magistrates had under consideration the necessity of obtaining a larger supply, and in that year "the Treasurer is ordained "to pay to Dr. Irvine £8, 8s. for his trouble in searching round Glasgow "for water to be brought into the city." In 1804 Mr. Harley constructed in what is now West Nile Street an extensive tank or reservoir, into which he led water from springs in his lands of Willowbank, and he carted it through the streets in barrels for sale at the rate of a halfpenny for each "stoup." This water was much in demand, and Mr. Harley made a considerable sum by it. It was not till 1806 that any effectual attempt was made to introduce a general supply. In that year the Glasgow Water Works Company was projected, and afterwards, in 1808, the Cranstonhill Water Works, and by these companies the city was for a long time fairly supplied. In 1846 the supply was increased by the establishment of the Gorbals Gravitation Water Company. Ultimately the corporation took the matter into its own hands, with the result that at present no city in the world is better supplied with water than Glasgow is. During the year 1877 the average daily supply intro-

---

[1] 18th June, 1664.   [2] Dr. Buchanan's Reminiscences.

S

duced into the city amounted to the enormous quantity of thirty-three millions seven hundred thousand gallons; and as the population supplied was 730,000, this gives an amount of more than forty gallons per head each day for every man, woman, and child in the city.

In 1776 the magistrates enacted a scale of charges for porters. For carrying a letter or parcel any distance not exceeding half the length of the city the charge was to be a halfpenny, and to any place not exceeding a mile from the Cross a penny. For a back load from the Cross to the Broomielaw the allowance was twopence. For an hour's work the porter was to have threepence, and for each hour afterwards a penny.

The carters had been dealt with by an earlier edict. In 1655 the magistrates, "takeing to their consideratioune the great and exorbitant "pryces takine be the kairters within the brughe serving about the "water of Clyd," enacted that only the following rates should be charged —I state them in sterling money:—From the Broomielaw to the Trongate, Gallowgate, and Saltmarket, twopence; from the Broomielaw to any part betwixt the Cross and the College, twopence three farthings; and from the Broomielaw to above the College, to the Wynd Head, and to "the fardest place in the towne," fourpence.[1]

Hackney-coaches are said to have been introduced in Glasgow in the middle of the seventeenth century, but if so they disappeared again. Under date 15th March, 1673, the council "refers to the provest, and to "thame he pleases to tak with him, to settle and agrie with ane coach- "man for serving the toune with haikna coaches the best way they can." What came of this does not appear, but for a long time there were few if any coaches in Glasgow, either private or for hire. Dr. Carlyle, writing of the year 1744, says "there were then neither post chaises "nor hackney coaches in the town."[2] Some sedan chairs were to be had for hire, and a few were kept by gentlewomen of the better classes. From an account preserved of the household expenses of Thomas Hutcheson, one of the founders of the Hospital, who lived, as already mentioned, "in a house at the Cross," we know that his lady possessed a sedan chair—one of the items being "for dressing ane siddan with "thrie losanes of frenshe glass, 12*s.*," that is, one shilling sterling. These chairs continued to be let for hire till after the middle of the present century. In 1817, according to Mr. Cleland, there were then

---

[1] Minute of Council, 17th Feb. 1655.　　　[2] Autobiography, p. 75.

eighteen so let, but only one was kept in the city for private use. This was by a lady in George Street.[1]

In the beginning of the seventeenth century the town maintained a horse post between Edinburgh and Glasgow, but this was soon abandoned, and after the middle of the century there was for some time only a foot post between the two cities. In 1663 there is a minute appointing John Fergusone to this office, and fixing his wages at three pounds Scots—five shillings, "and to receive a penny sterling for ilk "letter he receaves and als much for ilk letter hamewards."[2] It is interesting to see a penny postage thus established in Glasgow more than two hundred years ago. In 1667 the general postage rate in Scotland was for a single letter not exceeding one sheet of paper, for any distance not exceeding forty miles, twopence; and for a double letter, fourpence. The post to Edinburgh went at first only once a week. Towards the end of the century an attempt was made by "the "trading merchands" to obtain a post three times a week, but with what result does not appear. A horse post was again established, but not for some time after the beginning of the eighteenth century. In the year 1688, indeed, the only horse posts in Scotland were those between Berwick and Edinburgh, and thence to Portpatrick for the Irish mail. All other places were supplied by foot posts or runners.[3]

From a notice in the *Glasgow Mercury* of 13th November, 1782, it appears that letters for London, despatched from the post-office in Glasgow on Saturdays, did not arrive in London till the morning of the following Thursday. At this time the post-office was in Prince's Street, then called Gibson's Wynd, and it consisted of three apartments. The front one measured about twelve feet square, and the two behind were mere pigeon-holes, not more than ten feet by six, one of these being the private room of the postmaster. The letter box fronted the street, and the place for delivery of letters was a small hole broken through the wall into the close, which was then a common thoroughfare entry to King Street.[4] In 1787 the entire staff of the post-office in Glasgow consisted of five, of whom two were letter-carriers. In the same year the complement of the custom-house was two individuals.

There was no stage-coach between Glasgow and Edinburgh till late in the seventeenth century, and none to London for a long time after-

---

[1] Abridgment of Annals of Glasgow, p. 430.   [2] 31st Oct. 1663.
[3] Short Account of Scotland; London, 1702.   [4] Glasgow Past and Present, vol. ii. p. 104.

wards. In 1678 the magistrates contracted with "Wm. Hoome mer-
"chand in Edinburge," to set up "ane sufficient strong coach to run
"betwext Edinburgh and Glasgow to be drawn by sax able horses; to
"leave Edinburgh ilk monday morning and return again (God willing)
"ilk Saturday night the passengers to have the liberty of taking a
"cloak-bag to receive their clothes linens and sick like; the burgesses of
"Glasgow always to have the preference of the coach. The fare to be
"£4, 16s. Scots (8s.) in summer and £5, 8s. Scots (9s.) in winter, and
"the said Wm. Hoome to have a sallerie of 200 merks (£11, 3s.) a year
"for five years."[1] Of this "sallerie" he received two years' payment in
advance. How the project succeeded does not appear. Probably it
was a failure, as in 1743 a proposal was submitted to the magistrates by
one John Walker "for erecting a stage coach betwixt Edinburgh and
"Glasgow, to set out twice a week from Glasgow to Edinburgh, and
"the coach or lando to contain six passengers, with six sufficient horses,
"for twenty weeks in summer, and the rest of the year once a week—
"each passenger to pay 10s. sterling and to be entitled to 14 pund
"weight of baggage, and the toun to insure to him that 200 of his
"tickets shall be sold here each year."[2] The proposal was remitted to
a committee, with what result does not appear. Thirty years afterwards[3] Patrick Heron, vintner at the Black Bull, advertises "that there
"sets out from his house, and from Mrs. Gibsons Inn Grassmarket
"Edinburgh, a stage coach to go to Edinburgh by Falkirk and to reach
"Edinburgh that evening, and to run it from Glasgow upon Mondays
"Wednesdays and Fridays, and from Edinburgh on Tuesdays Thurs-
"days and Saturdays."

To London there was, till a comparatively recent date, no stage-coach
from Glasgow. The first which ran from Edinburgh was started about
the middle of the eighteenth century. In 1755 the proprietor announced
that "it is now altered to a new genteel two end glass machine hung on
"steel springs," and that it would accomplish the journey in ten days in
summer and twelve in winter—a contrast to our day, when several trains
start from each city daily, and accomplish the journey in about ten
hours.

Till after the middle of the seventeenth century there was only one
grave-digger for the whole city, and until a period still later there was no
Register of mortality. It was not till 1670 that the magistrates ordered

---

[1] Burgh Records, 29th July, 1678.   [2] Ibid. 15th October, 1743.   [3] January, 1776.

"that ane register be keepit of all persones *who happens to deceas* within
"this burgh." Samwell Burss was appointed registrar, at a weekly salary
of forty shillings Scots—3*s.* 4*d.*[1]

The first mention of fire insurance in the burgh records occurs in
1726, and the notice is interesting. The magistrates, "considering that
" there is an agreement signed by several of the heritors within the
" burgh for a mutual insurance of tenements and houses by losses by
" fire, do agree that the towns corner house at the cross be likeways
" insured."[2]

The first regular assessment for the support of the poor in Glasgow
was made in 1638. The order to keep the poor off the street at the time
of the meeting of the Assembly had proved a great success, and the
magistrates determined to make perpetual what had only been intended
as a temporary measure. Their minute bears that the magistrates,
" understanding the great and comendable ordour that was keepit within
" this brught the tyme of last general assemblie, be retciring of the poor
" off the calsay, and susteining of them in their awin houses, to the grait
" credit of the citie and contentment of all strangeris resorting heir for
" the tyme; and seeing the same is both godlie and honest, thairfoir
" they have statut and ordanit that the poor be keepit and sustenit in
" thair houses as they are now at this present, and the inhabitants of this
" burght to be stentit to that effect, and this day aucht days ilk counseller
" to propose his best overtour what way it can be best accomplishit."[3]
At subsequent meetings the mode of assessment was arranged, and in
the following year there is an order that "intimatioun be made be sound
" of drum to certifie all personis wha comes not to pay thair contributioun
" at the ringing of the bell, as sall be appoyntit to that effect, sall be
" poynded for the double, and thair names oppinlie publisched in the
" kirks who refuses to doe the samyn."[4]

After this two individuals were appointed whose duty it was "to keip
" the beggars aff the casy," each of them to carry a staff "having the
" tounes armes therupon."[5] This order is repeated, but apparently
without effect, as more stringent orders on the subject are issued. A
distinction is made, however, between the common beggars who are
strangers, and those who are "weill knowne to have bein borne within
" the towne." The latter are to be tolerated, but, "to the effect they

" may be the better knowne, appoynts ane badge with the tounes armes
" thereon to be maid and given to each one who is suffered to begg."

The first general hospital for the poor was erected in Clyde Street
in 1735. It was standing within the recollection of many now living,
who must remember it as a very shabby old building, although M'Ure
describes it as " of modern fashion " and so grand that " nothing of that
" kind at Rome or Venice comes up to its magnificence." I have mentioned elsewhere the prices of the provisions furnished to its inmates.
They appear to have been kept in considerable comfort—being supplied,
not only with the necessaries of life but with tobacco and snuff, verifying
the statement in the first report, published by the directors in 1742, that
" the poor in general are as really relieved from the distresses of poverty
" as if they were persons of wealth." And yet the cost of living of each
inmate in that year—including lunatics—was only about 1s. 3½d. per
week, or £3, 8s. 5d. per annum. The total number of inmates was 227.
The total cost of maintaining the hospital for the year was £787, 11s. 3d.
and there was " gained by manufactory," £40, 5s. 11d.

There are now three great poor-houses connected with Glasgow—the
Barony, the City, and that of Govan. In these the average cost of the
paupers per head is more than 5s. 9d. per week, and for lunatics 10s. 6d.
each per week; and the total cost of the three institutions for the year is
considerably upwards of £150,000.

LITERARY HISTORY.

As to the state of Old Glasgow in respect of literature there is not
much to record. I have already given a few instances of grants by the
magistrates for the encouragement of authors, and a few other notices of
our local literature may be interesting.

There was no press in Glasgow till near the middle of the seventeenth century. Printing was first introduced there by George Anderson,
who came to the city by special invitation of the magistrates in 1638.
The earliest recorded notice on the subject is contained in the following
minute of the town council: "4 January 1640 Ordäines the thesaurare
" to pay to George Andersone printer ane hundrethe pundis [£5] in sat-
" isfactioun to him of the superplus he disbursit in transporting of his

" geir to this brughe by [besides] the ten dollouris he gave of him befor
" to that effect, and als in satisfactioun to him of his haill bygane fiallis
" fra Whitsonday in anno 1638 to Martinmas last." And in the following
year, 1641, there is an entry in the treasurer's accounts: " Item to George
" Andersone, printer, his yeiris pensioune lxvj lib. xiij*s.* iiij*d.*" This
pension the corporation afterwards agreed to continue " to his relict and
" his bairnes swa long as they continow in prenting in the toune." Anderson was succeeded by his son Andrew, who continued printing in
Glasgow till 1661, when he went to Edinburgh. His successor was
Robert Sanders, who styled himself " Printer to the city," and who was
for many years the only printer in the west of Scotland. I have already
noticed the Almanacks printed by him in 1667 and subsequent years.
The first copy of the Scriptures printed in Glasgow was a New Testament
printed by Sanders in 1666. In 1671, when engaged in printing another
edition of the New Testament, he was opposed by his predecessor
Andrew Anderson, who had obtained the appointment of his Majesty's
sole printer for Scotland, and who bribed the workmen to desert Sanders.
This oppressive action was brought before the privy council, which decided that Sanders should be allowed to finish his book, and that every
printer in Scotland had an equal right with his Majesty's to print the
New Testament and Psalm Book, in the letter commonly called English
Roman. In 1680 the heir of Anderson complained to the privy council
that Sanders had vended Bibles printed in and imported from Holland,
and that he had reprinted several works in divinity, contrary to privilege.
This charge having been established against Sanders, by his own confession, he was ordained to deliver to Anderson the books so printed,
but no other penalty was inflicted. He ultimately acquired by purchase
a share of the royal patent, and having brought workmen and materials
from Holland he printed several works in a creditable style.[1] Sanders
became wealthy, and bequeathed some valuable property to the
Merchants' House. He died about 1696, leaving his establishment to
his son Robert. The latter, among other works, printed in 1720 an
edition of the Pilgrim's Progress with coarse but spirited woodcuts.

Printing was now and for some years afterwards at the lowest state
in Glasgow. No one appears to have been employed by the printers
for the sole purpose of correcting the press, and the low wages given
to pressmen, with the badness of the machines, tended to retard im-

[1] Dr. Lees' Memorial, App. pp. 46, 131.

provement. A paper was presented to the Faculty in 1713, entitled "Proposals for erecting a Booksellers shop, and a printing press within "the University of Glasgow," in which it is stated that people were "obliged to go to Edinburgh in order to gett one sheet right printed." Two years afterwards "Donald Govane younger, merchant in Glasgow "and printer," was appointed printer to the university for seven years. By the contract the university became bound "to ffurnish for the use of "the said Donald two chambers within the Colledge to wit numbers "twenty four and thirtie, with a sellar for coalls, and a garret in the "steeple for drying his papers or roumes."[1]

In 1718 the art of type-making was introduced in Glasgow by James Duncan. The types were of his own manufacture, rudely cut and badly proportioned. He is well known as the typographer of M'Ure's History. In this book, which is very badly printed, he is styled "Printer to the "City." His shop was in the Saltmarket, near Gibson's Wynd. In 1740 we find Robert Urie and Company printing in the Gallowgate, and during the following year they executed several works for Robert Foulis. They also printed the *Glasgow Journal*, which had been begun by Andrew Stalker in 1741.

Another printer deserves special notice—Dugald Graham, poet and bellman as well as printer. In the rebellion of 1745 Dugald had followed the contending armies in the capacity of pedlar or suttler, and he has left us a graphic, though rather coarse, rhyming chronicle of that stirring time. This work ran through many editions, and Sir Walter Scott at one time thought of printing a correct copy from the original edition in order to present it as his contribution to the Maitland Club, because, to use Sir Walter's words, "it really contained some traits and "circumstances of manners worth preserving."[2] Dugald afterwards took to printing, and from his press there issued the celebrated Glasgow chapbooks, so dear to the book-collector of our day, and of many of which he was the author. While thus employed the office of bellman became vacant, and Dugald applied for and obtained it.

In connection with printing may be noticed a minute in the burgh records in the beginning of the seventeenth century, which is interesting not only from its reference to the publication, under government authority, of the body of laws known as the Regiam Majestatem, but as

[1] Glasgow Papers, Maitland Club, pp. 5, 120.
[2] Letter by Sir Walter Scott to the late Dr. Strang. Glasgow and its Clubs, p. 91.

showing the low state of the city finances at that time. The expense of printing these ancient statutes had been ordered to be provided by an assessment on all the Scottish burghs. The share to be paid by Glasgow was fixed at one hundred pounds Scots—only £8, 6s. 8d.; but so poor was the corporation that they were unable to provide the amount, and being threatened with "horning" they had to borrow the money "fra "William Burn merchand burgess."[1]

But the press of Glasgow obtained a European reputation by the skill and enterprise of Robert Foulis and his brother Andrew—the former born in 1707 and the latter five years afterwards. After visiting England and the Continent, and having acquired a considerable knowledge of books, they settled in Glasgow, where, in 1741, Robert began business as a bookseller. The first production of his press appeared in the following year, and in 1743 he was appointed printer to the university. The works which issued from this celebrated press—particularly the folio editions of the Iliad and Odyssey and of Milton's Poems, and other splendid works —have never been surpassed in beauty of typography or correctness of printing. The folio *Iliad*, as a Greek book, is considered one of the finest classics ever produced at any press.

Robert Foulis was an early member of the Literary Society established in Glasgow, and Andrew joined it soon afterwards. At the meetings of this society Adam Smith read his valuable essays; and Dr. Hutchison, Dr. Reid, Dr. Black, and Dr. Moir read papers and took part in the proceedings. Both Robert Foulis and Andrew delivered discourses on the fine arts and on various other subjects.

But the Foulises did not confine themselves to printing. To them Glasgow is indebted for the establishment of its first School of Art. About 1753 they established an academy for painting, engraving, modelling, and drawing, and some of the most interesting views which we possess of the city, as it was in the middle of the eighteenth century, were drawn and engraved in this academy. The university allowed them the use of what became afterwards part of the Library in the buildings in the High Street, as an exhibition room for their pictures, and of several other rooms for their students; and three Glasgow merchants, with a view to the promotion of art, became partners in the undertaking. These were Mr. Campbell of Clathic, Mr. Glassford of Dugaldston, and Mr. Archibald Ingram. In a letter written by Robert Foulis in 1763 to

---

[1] Minute of Council, 25th Feb. 1609.

Mr. Yorke, he says: "The Academy is now coming into a state of toler-
" able maturity. We have modelling, engraving, original history painting,
" and portrait painting—all in a reputable degree of perfection. In the
" morning our more advanced students sketch historical subjects from
" Plutarch's Lives and other ancient books. The day is employed in
" painting and engraving, and by the younger scholars in drawing. In
" the evening they draw three days a week after a model, and other three
" after casts of plaister from the antique."

The annexed illustration, which is copied from one of the engravings
executed in the academy, represents a portion of the library of the
college occupied by the studio of the Foulises. Like the view of the
fore court, it is interesting as showing the costume of the time, and the
prominent figure in cocked hat and flowing gown represents, in all
probability, one of the proud tobacco lords already referred to, who, in
scarlet cloaks, paced their privileged walk in the Trongate.

Besides these and other engravings, the pupils of the academy
executed many paintings, including copies of celebrated works of art.
Among these last was one which Robert Foulis, in a letter written in
1753, describes as a copy of "the most celebrated picture in Scotland,
" namely, Daniel in the den of lions—the size of life, which the Duke of
" Hamilton generously offered us the liberty of copying." In the same
letter Robert Foulis says: "The copy was finished a few days ago, and
" placed up in the Duke's gallery on his birthday, and I have been as-
" sured by many that were present that it gave universal satisfaction to
" a great number of nobility and gentry who were present."[1] I refer
specially to this work because in the view previously given of the inner
court of the college,[2] it will be recognized in the picture suspended on
the steeple over the bust of Zachary Boyd.

I may mention, in passing, that as the university provided accommodation in their own buildings for the special use of Robert Foulis, so to
its credit it accorded afterwards a similar favour to James Watt, when he
was prevented by the incorporation of Hammermen from carrying on
his important experiments in any other premises within the city.

But latterly matters did not prosper with the Foulises. The academy
was broken up in 1770, and after the death of Andrew the stock of pictures and engravings was sold at a very inadequate price. On the death
of Robert in 1776, their affairs were found to be in a state of insolvency,

---

[1] Literary Hist. of Glasgow (Maitland Club), p. 85.   [2] Ante, p. 126.

THE FOULIS' ACADEMY OF THE FINE ARTS

IN THE FORE HALL, GLASGOW COLLEGE

FROM A RARE PRINT, AFTER A DESIGN BY DAVID ALLAN, R.A.

and they were finally wound up in 1781 by Robert Chapman, printer, and James Duncan, bookseller in Glasgow.[1] Andrew left a son of the same name, by whom the printing business was for some time continued. Among other works from his press was the beautiful quarto edition of the Gentle Shepherd, published in 1788 by David Allan, with illustrations designed and engraved by himself "in the manner called aqua " tinta, a late invention."

Of the history of printing in Glasgow after this, and the very high position which it has achieved in our own day, I need not speak.

In the old catalogue, which has been preserved, of the books belonging to the Cathedral, one is stated to be in the hands of the binder, whose name is given—Richard Arr. This was probably the first bookbinder in Glasgow. His prefix of *dominus* shows him to have been a churchman.

The first Directory published in Glasgow was compiled and printed by John Tait in 1783. Its title is, "John Taits Directory for the city of " Glasgow, villages of Anderston, Calton and Gorbals; also for the towns " of Paisley, Greenock, Port Glasgow and Kilmarnock." The list for the last-named town is omitted, "the publisher not having received the " Kilmarnock list in proper time." Jones' Directory appeared in 1787. It was printed "for the Editor by John Mennons." The editor apologizes for the list of names not being so full as he wished, having found, he says, "a great backwardness in receiving an explicit answer " from a number of persons in trade, for reasons best known to them- " selves."

Till a comparatively recent period there was no newspaper printed in Glasgow. Even after the middle of the seventeenth century the means of obtaining intelligence were very scanty, and the magistrates appear to have seldom or never seen a London paper. The first step taken to remedy this dearth of intelligence is recorded in a minute of the town council of 5th September, 1657, which "appoynts Johne Flym- " ing to wryt to his man wha lyes at London to send hom for the tounes " use weiklie ane diurnall." Previous to this the magistrates were supplied with weekly intelligence by one of their counsel or law agents in Edinburgh—Mr. John Nicoll.

Some twenty years afterwards one "Collonell Walter Whytfoord" obtained an exclusive right from the magistrates "to sett up, to sell, top,

---

[1] Notices Illustrative of the Literary History of Glasgow (Maitland Club), p. 46.

" and vent coffee within the burgh for the space of nyneteen yeares."[1] One of his objects was to provide newspapers as well as coffee, as had been the custom in such houses in England. By an order of the Privy Council soon afterwards, however, masters of all such coffee-houses were forbidden to allow any newspaper to be read in their houses " but such " as were approved by the Officers of State."[2] What success the colonel had does not appear.

The first newspaper published in Glasgow appeared on the 14th of November, 1715, and, curiously enough, it was a penny paper. It bore for its title, " The Glasgow Courant containing the occurrences both at " Home and Abroad: Glasgow, Printed for R. T., and are to be sold at " the Printing House in the Colledge and at the Post office." It soon changed its name, however, as the fourth number appeared under the title, " The West Country Intelligence." The prospectus was as follows: " This paper is to be printed three times every week for the use of the " Country round. Any gentleman or Minister, or any other who wants " them, may have them at the Universities Printing House or at the Post " Office. It is hoped this paper will give satisfaction to the Readers and " that they will encourage it by sending Subscriptions for one year, half " year, or quarterly, to the above directed places, when they shall be " served at a most easie rate. Advertisements are to be taken in at " either the printing house in the College or Post office. The gentlemen " in the towns of Aberdeen St. Andrews Inverness, Brechen, Dundee, St. " Johnstoune, Stirling, Dumbarton, Inverary, Dumfries, Lanerk, Hamil- " ton, Irvin, Air, Kilmarnock, and Stranraer, are desired to send by post " any News they have, and especially Sea-port towns to advise what " ships come in or sail off from these parts." The " easy rate " at which the paper was to be sold was afterwards announced thus: " N.B. This " paper is not sold in retail under three halfpence, but for encouragement " to subscribers for one penny." Such was the first Glasgow newspaper. It is not known how long it was continued, but a set consisting of sixty-seven numbers is preserved in the College library. It was printed on Tuesdays, Thursdays, and Saturdays, in a small quarto form, each copy containing twelve pages. It was made up chiefly of extracts from foreign journals and the London newspapers, with private letters and occasionally poetry, but there was very little local news.[3] But the *Intelligence* did

---

[1] 11th October, 1673.   [2] Crookshanks' Hist. of Ch. of Scotland, vol. ii. p. 127.
[3] Notices and Documents illustrative of the Literary History of Glasgow (Maitland Club), p. 6.

not long survive, and for twenty-five years no newspaper was printed in Glasgow.

In July, 1741, as already mentioned, the *Glasgow Journal* was started, under the editorship of Andrew Stalker. It was well printed, but it exhibited little of the courage of journalism. During the rebellion of 1745 accounts of many of the most important events were suppressed, and at last the editor got so terrified that he retired from the management, announcing as his reason that "considering the situation of affairs, " I cannot with safety publish so as to please the generality of my " readers." His place was taken by a Mr. Urie, who continued to print in Glasgow till his death in 1771.

Some of the notices of marriages in this *Glasgow Journal* are amusing. For example: "March 24th 1746. On monday last James Dennistoun " Junr of Colgraine Esq. was married to Miss Jenny Baird *a beautiful young lady.*" "May 4th 1747 On monday last Dr. Robert Hamilton " Professor of Anatomy and Botany in the University of Glasgow was " married to Miss Mally Baird *a beautiful young lady with a handsome "fortune.*" "August 3d 1747 On monday last Mr. James Johnstone, " merchant in this place was married to Miss Peggy Newall an agreeable " young lady with £4000." But the *Journal* was not peculiar in this style of notices. It but followed the common practice of the time—the *Gentleman's Magazine* and other publications of that period being full of them. For example:—"1735 April. Mr. Wyatt a noted Quaker of " Ware to Miss Procter, who the day before stood Godmother to him at " his baptism." "June. George Grantham Esq. to Mrs. Marshall, widow. " He is her 5th husband and she his 5th wife." "January 20 Mr. Pitt " of Bethnall Green to Mrs. Cox widow, worth £5000. She is about 80 " and Mr. Pitt is her 5th husband. He is about 70 and she his third " wife. Their acquaintance commenced since new-year's-day."[1]

In 1747 the *Glasgow Courant* appeared, but it had only a short existence. The *Chronicle* was commenced in 1766; the *Mercury* in 1775, and the *Advertiser* in 1783. The *Journal, Mercury,* and *Advertiser* were for a long time the only local papers. The *Advertiser* was discontinued in 1801.

[1] Gentleman's Magazine, 1735.

VALUE OF PROPERTY.

While Glasgow was growing in wealth and importance, and the city was increasing in size, there were, I need not say, important changes in the value of property. I have already given incidentally the prices at which some properties in and near the city have been sold, but some farther notices on this subject may be interesting, as also the prices of different commodities in the early years of the city.

Although, as I have said, the houses within the burghs in Scotland were, as a rule, superior to those in the landward districts, yet for a long time they must have been of a very unsubstantial character, compared with those of the present day, and the ground on which they stood of little value. That such was the case in Glasgow is certain. So late as 1410 there is recorded a deed of sale of a tenement in the Rottenrow, with a garden and a considerable amount of land—"tenementum cum pertin- "entibus videlicet iiij caracatas terre in anteriore fronte, cum orto, "jacentes in burgo de Glasgu, in parte australi vici qui dicitur Ratonraw" for the price of five merks—*quinque marces vsuale monete Scocie.*[1] By that time the Scottish coinage had become somewhat deteriorated, and according to its then value the price of this house, with garden and land, would be little more than £2, 10s. of our money.

I should mention that it has been a common mistake to reckon Scottish money as worth only one twelfth of that of England, without reference to dates. Till 1355, however, Scottish money was equal in value to that of England. From that time, owing to successive public calamities, and the impoverishment of the kingdom, it sunk by degrees, reign after reign; but it was not till 1600 that it fell to a twelfth part only of the value of English money of the same denomination. At that point it remained, till the union of the kingdoms cancelled the Scottish coinage.

By another deed in 1434 the sub-dean of Glasgow, with consent of the bishop and chapter, sells to Thomas of Welk, burgess of the burgh of Glasgow, an acre of ground, part of the Deanside land, on the north side of the Rottenrow, for the yearly payment of "six syllingis and acht

[1] Lib. Coll. N. D. p. 237.

"penys of usuale mone of Scotland," the said Thomas being bound within a year "to byg a sufficiand tenement on the said akyr of land "and alsua to mac the half of the calse before the forfront of the said "akyr."[1] Six shillings and eightpence Scots, according to the relative value at that time, would be about three shillings of our money, and taking this at the rate of twenty-two years' purchase it gives the price of this acre of land in one of the principal streets of the burgh as only £3, 6s. English money.

Twenty years later—1454—we find a deed of sale of "a tenement "lying in the city of Glasgow on the east side of the street leading from "the Cathedral to the Market cross" at the price of twenty pounds Scots —*viginti libris vsualis monete scocie*[2]—at that time equal to only about £6. And in the following year, 1455, there occurs in the same register a deed of sale by David Smith, burgess, to Patrick Leiche, chancellor of the church of Glasgow, of a tenement on the east side of High Street, *cum cauda et orto*, extending to the Molendinar Burn, the price being ten merks, equal to about £2, 5s. only.[3]

In 1507 an acre of ground on the south side of the Drygate was let for 28s. yearly, equal to about seven shillings of our money—a high rent for that time.[4] In the same year a granary on the south side of the Gallowgate was let for four years at the yearly rent of 6s. 3d.—only 1s. 9½d.[5]

In the year 1600 George Hucheson, one of the founders of the Hospital, whose house, as I have mentioned, adjoined the old Tolbooth at the Cross, purchased a piece of ground next it from Norman Mackenzie for a stable. It is described as "sax elnes in length and the breid of "the said Norman's aune tenement." For this not inconsiderable piece of ground near the Cross of Glasgow Mr. Hucheson paid only twenty-four pounds Scots, or £2 sterling.[6] On 29th December, 1656, the college feued to David Scott two acres "in that part of the burgh of Glasgow "called the Long Croft next the Common Lone" for sixty pounds Scots yearly, and liberty of redemption on payment of one thousand pounds Scots—£83, 6s. 8d. The Common Lone afterwards became Sauchiehall Street.

These prices are, after all, not so surprising when we compare them with those at which the magistrates sold the common lands of the city.

---

[1] Lib. Coll. N. D. p. 249. [2] Reg. Episc. Glasg. p. 391. [3] Ibid. p. 392.
[4] Lib. Protocoll. No. 263. [5] Ibid. No. 340. [6] Huchesoniana, p. 25.

As late as 1750 thirteen acres of land in the Gallowmuir, including the property afterwards known as Annfield, and a large field of six acres on the opposite side of the Camlachie Road, called "the sixth part of Laigh "Gallowmuir," were sold for £250 or £16 the acre.[1]

In the *Glasgow Mercury* in 1782 there is advertised for sale a tenement on the north side of the Bridgegate, "being the tenement next but "one to the bridge." It is described as consisting of a fore-shop and dwelling-house on the ground-floor; a dwelling-house in the first story above the shop; two dwelling-houses in the second story; a dwelling-house in the garret with two back cellars, and a dwelling-house above them. The rental is "about £10," and the whole property is offered at the price of £65.

Of the great rise in the value of land at a later date I have already given some instances. I shall mention a few others. I have referred to the sale of the lands of Stobcross by Mr. Orr to Mr. David Watson in 1776. The property contained about eighty acres, and the price paid by Mr. Watson was £4000, being at the rate of £50 per acre. I pass over intermediate changes in the proprietorship, but between 1844 and 1870 sixty acres of these lands were sold at prices which amounted in all to upwards of £240,000, and if the remaining twenty acres were sold at no higher price than 25s. per square yard the whole lands which were sold in 1776 for £4000 will have realized upwards of three hundred and sixty thousand pounds, or ninety times the price paid a hundred years ago. But portions of Stobcross have been sold at prices far above twenty-five shillings the square yard.

The estate of Yorkhill, now becoming part of the city, but in the beginning of the century far away in the country, was acquired by Mr. Gilbert in different portions between 1813 and 1823. The total extent was 104 acres, and the price which he paid amounted in all to £19,440. Previous to 1866 there were feued of this estate about forty-four acres, at feu-duties which, taken at the low rate of twenty-two years' purchase, represent a capital sum of, in round numbers, £220,000; and assuming that the remainder—upwards of sixty acres—brings no more than twenty-five shillings the square yard—a moderate estimate—this property will have realized upwards of six hundred thousand pounds.

The lands of Kelvinbank, in the same neighbourhood, consisting of about twelve acres, were purchased in 1792 by Mr. Wilson—the uncle

---

[1] Desultory Sketches, by John Buchanan, Esq., LL.D. p. 697.

of Mr. Rae Wilson, on whom Hood has conferred an unenviable noto-
riety—for £1000. They were sold by Rae Wilson to the Trades House
in 1846 for £20,000, and the Trades House has since re-sold them for
£80,000.

In 1790 Hutcheson's Hospital advertised their ground in Gorbals,
now so valuable, to be feued at the rate of eight guineas the acre, equal
to a yearly payment of less than a halfpenny the square yard.

In 1754 a portion of Kelvingrove which now constitutes the West
End Park, consisting of something more than twelve acres, was sold by
Mr. Campbell of Blythswood to Mr. John Wotherspoon, for the sum of
1090 pounds Scots—about £90 sterling—and an annual payment of
sixteen bolls of corn of eight stones the boll. The highest price of oats
at that time was £6, 8s. Scots the boll—about 10s. 6d. sterling—which
gives as the total annual payment eight guineas, being at twenty-five
years' purchase equal to a capital sum of £210. The price therefore of
these twelve acres of ground—not of annual payment, but the entire
price—was only £300—less than a penny farthing the square yard. In
1803 Mr. John Pattison, who was then proprietor of Kelvingrove, acquired from Mr. Campbell of Blythswood an additional portion of ground,
part of "Woodsidehill," consisting of upwards of twelve acres. By that
time the value of land had increased considerably, but still the price was
only an annual feu-duty of £64, 9s. 4½d. This at twenty-five years'
purchase gives as the whole price only about £1600—less than £134 the
acre. For these two portions, consisting of about twenty-five acres, the
city in 1852 paid £30,000—about five shillings the square yard. Two
years afterwards, having set apart for building a portion of the ground
forming a continuation of Claremont Terrace, the magistrates feued that
portion at the very moderate price of £1, 7s. 6d. the square yard—equal
to £6650 the acre. At this rate the price of the 24 acres, which cost less
than £1900, would amount in round numbers to £160,000.

Moore Park, a property of 37 acres lying between the Govan and
Paisley Roads, three miles from the Cross of Glasgow, was purchased by
Mr. Alston so late as 1822 for £6500. Less than a half of it—about
sixteen acres—was recently sold to the Glasgow and South Western
Railway Company for £30,000.

The lands of Gilmourhill and Donaldshill were purchased by Mr.
Bogle in the beginning of the present century for £8500. In 1865 they
were sold to the College for £81,000.

T

About the year 1770 the College sold to John M'Auslan, a nursery-
man, twelve acres of the lands of Provanside, lying towards the head of
Buchanan Street and eastward to John Street—now in the heart of the
city—for a yearly feu-duty of only £37—little more than £800 for the
twelve acres.   In 1772 four acres of ground situated on both sides of
Stirling's Road, not far from the Cathedral, were sold for an annual
payment of £12, 12s. 1d.—little more than £260.   The increase in value
of these two properties must be enormous.

In 1782 "the Point House and land adjoining the ferry [at the mouth
"of the Kelvin] with the ferry boats" were advertised to be sold.   The
extent of land was, I understand, about three acres, and the whole property was offered at the upset price of £400.   It was subsequently sold
in lots at prices which, on the average, represent a total of about £14,000.
In the Maryhill district and other parts of Glasgow the rise in the value
of ground has been equally striking.

PRICES OF COMMODITIES AND LABOUR.

Few materials remain for ascertaining the comparative value of
provisions and other articles in Glasgow in very early times.   In the
Chartulary of Glasgow there is preserved a deed of obligation granted
by Richard de Cralein in 1304 in settlement of a claim for ten merks
alleged to have been due by him to the chapter of Glasgow.   The
chapter had taken legal proceedings against him, and the claim was
settled by compromise—Richard undertaking by the deed to deliver to
the chapter ten chalders of corn—*scx celdras frumenti boni mundi et
pacabilis*—in satisfaction of the debt.[1]   Scots money was at that time
at par.   Ten merks accordingly were equal to £6, 13s. 4d. of our
money, and if that amount was paid for six chalders it would make
the price of a boll of corn less than seventeenpence.   But as the settlement was the result of a compromise we may assume that the grain
accepted in satisfaction of the debt was, in marketable value, less than
that sum.

In the thirteenth century Alexander III. had come under an obligation to the Friars Preachers in Glasgow to find them in food for one

---

[1] Reg. Epis. Glasg. p. 217.

day in every week. In the year 1252 the king—for what reason or on what principle does not appear—transferred this obligation to the burgh of Dunbarton, and by letters-patent in that year he issued his commands, "prepositis suis de Dunbretan," to pay ten pounds yearly to the friars from the rents of that burgh in lieu of the king's provision.[1] The money payment into which the king's obligation was so commuted was thus equal to less than two shillings for one day in every week, which appears to have been sufficient to find the whole convent in a day's food.

In 1301, when Edward I. was in Glasgow, the accounts of his wardrobe show that he paid to the Friars Preachers six shillings for three days' entertainment of himself and his retinue. In the same reign—if we take as a criterion the commutation in money exigible in fines for certain crimes—the value of a cow was four shillings.

In the Fragmenta Collecta[2] there is an old burgh law providing that no "browster wife" sell the gallon of ale, from Pasch to the feast of St. Michael, dearer than two pennies; nor from the feast of St. Michael to the feast of Pasch, dearer than one penny. The date of this law is not known, and therefore we do not know what was the value of a penny Scots at the time. If it was as early as the thirteenth century it was at par, but it deteriorated very rapidly after that.

There is a statute of the Church of Glasgow in the early part of the fifteenth century (*c.* 1425) which provides that the six deacons and archdeacons assisting in the office of the mass at the high altar on great festivals are to be entertained by the canon on duty, getting from him their *esculenta et poculenta* of the day, *secundum hujus ecclesiæ veterem consuetudinem*, or, in the option of the canon, he might pay them eighteenpence each—about eightpence of our money—for their daily expenses. About the same date (1430), when Bishop Cameron founded so many new prebends, the annual provision of the vicar in each of five churches was fixed at twenty merks—less than £6 sterling. In 1480 the stipends of the vicars of the choir, which had previously been five pounds, were augmented to ten pounds Scots, to be paid by the prebendary in whose stall he ministered—the increase being due no doubt to the depreciation in the value of money, as ten pounds Scots was then equal to less than £3. Besides this allowance, however, the vicars possessed certain "common goods," with "houses, buildings, and

[1] Lib. Coll. N. D. p. 150.   [2] No. 42.

"lands." These they surrendered to the sub-dean in 1507, on condition that he should pay to each of them ten merks yearly, either from the common good or from his own benefice, and apply the remainder of their common good to the building and repairing of their houses.[1] Ten merks was at that time less than £2 of our money. In 1508 the price of a boll of oatmeal in Nithsdale and Annandale was fixed by the commissary of that district at 20s. Scots—at that time equal to about 5s. of our money.[2]

But till far on in the fifteenth century we have, from the absence of authentic records, few materials for ascertaining the general prices of commodities and labour in Glasgow. In England the materials are more abundant, and it may be interesting to notice some of these, as we may obtain from them an approximation to prices in Scotland—the latter being probably in most cases lower.

In a conveyance of land in Wallingford in the reign of Henry III. (circa 1220), part of the yearly reddendo is "one pair of white gloves, "value one halfpenny, at Easter."[3] In a taxation of the town of Bridport, in 1319, a cow is valued at seven shillings; a horse at twelve shillings, another horse ten shillings; and two hogs two shillings each.[4] In the same accounts we find that "a pipe of wine" cost the corporation 2½ merks (£1, 13s. 4d.), and a gallon of wine fourpence.[5] In the accounts of Merton College, Oxford, in 1315, the price paid for an ox for the plough is 13s. 6½d.; two sheep are sold for thirteen pence each, and two bacon hogs for a shilling each.[6] In the proctor's roll of the same college, a few years later (1346), there is paid for seven chickens fivepence farthing; for three geese, tenpence halfpenny; for two lbs. of figs, threepence; and for two lbs. of rice flour, twopence.[7]

In one of these old college accounts an item occurs of a different kind, sufficiently interesting to deserve notice. "A bad copy of Horace "bought for the boys" cost a halfpenny. It was a manuscript of course, and would, no doubt, command a very different price in our day.

Of other articles we find from the same college accounts that a pair of shoes to the warden cost, in 1329, fourpence. In 1305 the price of a pair of shoes in Feversham was threepence. A new wheelbarrow cost sevenpence.[8] In the following century (1449) the nuns of Radegunda

---

[1] Lib. Protocollorum, No. 234.   [2] Ibid. No. 361.
[3] Sixth Report on Historical Documents, p. 582.   [4] Second Report on Hist. Doc. p. 492.
[5] Ibid. p. 490.   [6] Ibid. p. 563.   [7] Ibid. p. 547.   [8] Ibid. p. 549.

paid for a horse bought at a fair nine shillings and sixpence—for another horse four shillings; for a cow, 6s. 8d.; for a lamb, sixpence; for a sheep, sixpence; and for thirty-two pullets, three shillings—little more than a penny each. For a pair of shoes they paid sevenpence; for a pair of boots to a shepherd, eightpence; for a dozen and a half of trenchers, fourpence; for a pair of bellows, sixpence halfpenny; for linen cloth, twopence the ell.[1] In 1326 an acre of growing hay was bought in Oxfordshire for ten shillings; and the charge for reaping it, by the piece, is ninepence. In the accounts of Queen's College, Oxford, in 1341, we find paid for twelve hens twopence each; and for 240 eggs, twelvepence—a penny for twenty.[2] About the same period, in certain old accounts of the Manor of Monksleigh, in Devonshire, we find that, in 1363, twenty-nine shillings was paid for a bull and three cows; 12d. for "one mutton," 12d. for four geese, and 22½d. for fifteen hens. Thirty years later (1393) a stack of wheat is mentioned in the same accounts as sold for 22s. 4d.; and 43 sheep, 3 "hoggesters," and 39 lambs cost 60s. for the whole lot.[3]

The prices paid for services and labour in these old times appear wonderfully small, when compared with those which prevail in our own day. In the accounts of Queen's College, in the twenty-seventh year of Edward I. (1299), we find that the stipend of "Robert the priest" for half a year was 16s. 8d. Another priest received for the same period only ten shillings. The wages of a cook and brewer for six months was four shillings. The "Priest's groom" for the same period received three shillings. A laundress for "washing the clothes of the house for "that time" (six months) received only fourpence; and a carpenter for two days' work had fourpence "and his victuals." It is to be hoped that the laundress also received her victuals. A slater for three weeks' work was paid sixpence a week and his food. Four years later (1303) a carter received for his yearly wage five shillings and a penny; a ploughman for the winter was paid two shillings; a shepherd for a year, five shillings; a cowherd for the same period, three shillings; and a swineherd for the whole year, one shilling. These were, no doubt, serfs, who were both housed and fed by their masters. There is a payment of 3s. 6d. to forty-two women for an entire day's work cutting stubble—a penny each; and a barber for "shaving all the household for one year" is paid eight-

---

[1] Second Report on Hist. Doc. p. 119.   [2] Ibid. p. 568.
[3] Fifth Report on Hist. Doc. p. 370.

pence. A dairymaid gets one pair of shoes at the cost of sixpence, "because she had no wages," but a woman brought to help her in the dairy and in "milking the ewes" during the summer and autumn, is paid by the piece, *ad tasciam*, two shillings.[1] In the accounts of the Hospital of St. John at Winchester there is an entry, in 1315, of wages paid to Adam atte Corrsyre of "15s. 2d. for the year, at one halfpenny "per day."[2] Even more than a century later the rate of wages was low. In the accounts at Radegunda, already referred to, we find in 1449 a payment to Simon Maydwell of ninepence for six days' work; to Katherine Rolffe, to hoe in the garden for four days, 4½d. For skilled labour the rates were higher. To a man making and mending horse collars for five days there is paid 1s. 10d., and to a man pruning the vines the nuns paid for two days' work twelvepence.[3]

There are preserved in Scotland no such early records as those of the old English colleges and municipal corporations, but in the accounts of the Lord High Treasurer, recently printed, we have some interesting information as to Scotland, which may enable us to form some estimate of what were prices in Glasgow towards the end of the fifteenth century. The price of horses varied very much, and some appear to have been sold at very low sums. For a horse to a trumpeter in 1489 the price—I give the amount in English money—was only twelve shillings. In 1491 another horse was bought at the same price. Horses bought for the king in 1489 cost from £1 to forty shillings each. Two horses, a black and a gray, of superior quality, cost for the two about £12; while in 1496 a horse bought for one of the royal grooms cost less than eight shillings.

In Aberdeen, in 1577, the magistrates fixed the hire of a horse for leading peats or other fuel at "xiid. ilk day"—being three halfpence of English money—"witht mannis meit and horss meit, and to haff four "gang ilk day."[4]

According to the accounts of the Lord High Treasurer, shoes, homemade, cost usually, towards the end of the fifteenth century, fourpence the pair. The price of a pair of French shoes was about one shilling and fourpence. Boots were expensive: they cost six shillings the pair. Of other items, we find that in 1473 there was paid " to a skynnare in Strive- " ling for a dusane of gluffis (gloves) to the Quene " less than two shillings.

---

[1] Accounts of Queen's College, Sixth Report on Hist. Doc. pp. 558, 559.
[2] Sixth Report on Hist. Doc. p. 597.   [3] Second Report on Hist. MSS. pp. 119, 120.
[4] Records of Burgh of Aberdeen, 10th July, 1577.

A hundred haddocks cost tenpence. The price of a cow was seven shillings. The wages of labourers and seamen were less than fourpence a day. Indeed, fourpence a day was reckoned not bad wages in Scotland for a tradesman even towards the middle of the eighteenth century. So late as 1748 the magistrates of Dunbarton enacted that tailors working out of their own house should be allowed only fourpence a day (with diet), and if they declined to work when required, or asked a higher wage, they were subjected in heavy penalties.[1]

Writing in 1598 as to travelling charges, Fynes Moryson says a horse might be had for " two shillings the first day and eightpence the day till " he be brought home, and the horse-letters used to send a footman to " bring back the horse." The traveller, he adds, "shall pay at the common " table about sixpence for his supper or dinner and shall have his bed " free."[2] These sums are stated in English money.

But prices varied very much in different places, and in Edinburgh, especially during the sitting of Parliament, they were comparatively high. In the account of the household expenses of Ludovick duke of Lennox, when commissioner to Parliament in 1607, one of the charges is thirteen-pence halfpenny for a partridge.[3] They were cheaper in Inverness at a later date. Captain Burt says he could buy a partridge there "for a " penny or less."[4] This was in the early part of the eighteenth century.

In 1559 the magistrates of Ayr ordered that "guid and sufficient " corne" be sold for "ten penneys the peck," and hay to be sold at "aucht " pennys the stane."[5] According to the value of money at that time this would be about one-fifth of these sums of our money. In Renfrewshire the price of "the best hay" in 1722 was twopence the stone.[6] Between 1710 and 1728 the price of horses in the same county averaged £3, 19s. 2d., the highest price being £8, which was considered exceptionally high. A leg of mutton was sold for ninepence, and a side of beef for 7s. 9d. In 1726 the average price of a cow in Renfrewshire was £1, 6s. 9d. and of a sheep five shillings.[7] The prices in Glasgow would probably be higher, but not much.

When the Laird of Macintosh attended parliament in 1681 he charged to the county as "depursements for the shire of Inverness":—"for 52 " sitting days in Parliament and 16 days comeing and goeing at £5 scotts

---

[1] Irving's History of Dunbartonshire, p. 249.   [2] Itinerary, 1617.
[3] Miscellany of Maitland Club, vol. i. p. 159.   [4] Letters, vol. i. p. 146.
[5] Memorabilia, p. 6.   [6] Judicial Records of Renfrewshire, p. 332.   [7] Ibid. p. 338.

"per day £340"—that is, 8s. 4d. a day of our money—a liberal allowance for these times.　For "ane consultatioun with the "Lord Advocat" he paid £3 sterling, showing that fees to counsel were at that date high in proportion to the price of provisions.[1]　It was not so in England in the latter part of the fifteenth century.　In the churchwarden's accounts of St. Margaret's, Westminster, in 1476, there is a payment " to Roger Fylpott " learned in the law, for his counsel giving, 3s. 8d. with fourpence for his " dinner."[2]

Of prices in Glasgow early in the seventeenth century we have some examples in a list of the property or articles of executry given up, in 1632, on the death of Mrs. Hutcheson, wife of one of the founders of the Hospital. Among other items there are " three kye ane stirk and ane calf estimate " to 44 pounds scots"—that is, £3, 13s. 4d. for the five animals.　Fourteen bolls of bere " standing in the barne at Partick," are valued " with the " fodder" at £6, 13s. 4d. scots per boll—a trifle over eleven shillings.　A quantity of "mashlock oats" are valued, with the straw, at £5, 6s. 8d. scots the boll—less that nine shillings.[3]

In the old Town's Hospital accounts of 1737, to which I have already referred, shoes for the inmates are charged a fraction over two shillings the pair.　For fresh beef the price paid was less than twopence the pound; for eggs less than twopence the dozen; for barley seven-eighths of a penny the pound; for pease, 7½d. the peck; for butter, 4s. 10d. the stone; for sweet milk, a fraction less than twopence the scots pint; for sour milk, a halfpenny the pint.　Candles were dearer; they were nearly fivepence the pound.　Oatmeal was in old times almost always disproportionately dear. In 1737 it was upwards of ten shillings the boll.[4]　And it was higher in the preceding century.　In 1645, at the time when the magistrates were employing the town's people " to caste up the trinche about the citie," the the price of a boll of meal was 13s. 4d. of our money.

Of the expense of living of the students in the College in the beginning of the eighteenth century, we get some information from a minute of agreement between the principal and professors and Alexander Eagle, a cook.　It would appear that the English students required a provision to be made for their diet of a better kind than the Scotsmen were contented with.　Accordingly by this agreement, which is dated in 1711, Eagle undertakes " to furnish with dyet all Englishmen that shall desyre

---

[1] Scottish Legal Antiquities, p. 152.　　[2] Hallam's Middle Ages, 2d edit. vol. iii. p. 452.
[3] Huchesoniana, by Laurence Hill, Esq., p. 19.　　[4] Report of Town's Hospital of Glasgow, 1742.

" to dyet within the Colledge during the continuance of this session, three
" tymes a day with meat and drink, and with such changes of dyet as is
" mentioned in a paper apart—the said Englishmen, and each of them to
" be dyeted, paying to the said Alexander three pounds sterling for each
" three months dyet, and so proportionally." The cook was also to be
allowed " the benefite of the Colledge kitchen brewhouse and ovens and
" whole outincills therein."[1] This is eightpence a day for three meals.

The articles in which there appear to have been the greatest fluctu-
ations in prices in Glasgow are oatmeal and wheat, and the price there
often differed considerably from that in neighbouring counties. This,
however, may, to some extent, be accounted for by the difference in the
measure, for there appears to have been no fixed standard. In 1692 the
College of Glasgow had under consideration " the diverse debates between
" the Colledge and severall of the gentry who pay their tithes to the col-
" ledge, anent the measure of the boll," and it ended by the university re-
solving that a measure be made for itself, and that in all leases of the
college lands it should be stipulated that grain payments be made according to that measure.[2] The same practice was followed by many of the
neighbouring landowners. For example, in a lease of the lands of Wood-
head by Sir James Hamilton of Rosehall to Mr. Baird, an ancestor of the
Gartsherrie family, in 1745, a portion of the rent is made payable " in
" good and sufficient oatmeal with the weight and measure of Woodhall."[3]
It was the same in England from a very early period. In a lease of lands
in Rye, in the twenty-fifth year of King Henry VI. (1447), mention is
made of certain quantities of grain " mesuride by the mesure of Rye."[4]
And the same absence of a fixed standard prevailed in other measures
than those of grain. There is a curious illustration of this in the contract
between Mr. George Hutcheson and the builder of his house at Partick.
It provides that a certain part of the house is to be made of the measure
of " three futtis and ane half, *of the said Georges awin fute.*"[5]

Of the wages paid to masons in Glasgow in the beginning of the
seventeenth century we have an example from the same contract. Mr.
Hutcheson was to provide the stone and lime, and the wood for the scaffolding: all the rest of the mason work was to be executed by the contractor. The house was of considerable size, yet the whole sum to be paid

[1] Munimenta, vol. iii. p. 550.   [2] Ibid. vol. ii. p. 364.
[3] The Bairds of Gartsherrie: their Origin and History.   Glasgow: Privately printed, 1875.
[4] Fifth Report on Historical Records, p. 500.
[5] The Story of Partick Castle, by Laurence Hill, Esq., p. 34.

to the contractor, " himself, his servands and borrowmen," was only 530 merks Scots, " to wit 430 merkis yrof for ye work, and 100 merkis in satis- " factioun of all morning and eftirnoines drinks, disjoynes, sondayes meitt " at onlaying of lyntalls, or ony othir thing can be cravit fra the said george " in any sorte." Five hundred and thirty merkis Scots in 1611, when the contract was made, was less than £30.

Of the prices of labour in the neighbourhood of Glasgow, fifty years later, we have some information from the records of the town council of Rutherglen, which contain various statutes on the subject. One of these, in the year 1660, bears to have been passed to provide a remedy " to those " abuses and grievances concerning the excessive pryces of fies and waidges " introduced of late in tymes of plentie by the covetousness, idleness, and " other corrupt practices of some evil affected servands and workmen." For this purpose it orders that " dureing the scarsnes of money and cheap- " nes of victwall" no more than certain fees and wages be taken. Among these are the following:—" A commone able man servand for all sorts of " husbandrie is to have termly for fie and bounteth ten punds scots " (16*s.* 8*d.*) with a paire of dowble solled shooes and a pair of hoise and " no more. A able woman servand for all necessarie worke ten merks " (11*s.* 1½*d.*) with a pair of shooes, ane ell of lining in winter, and ane ell " of playding in Sommer; A lass or young made fowr punds scots (6*s.* 8*d.*) " with a paire of shooes termly and no more; The harvest fee of an able " man shierer is not to exceed eight punds (13*s.* 4*d.*) and a peck of meill " with meit and drink; and if he be hired by days, half a merk (about " 6¾*d.*) and twa mailles for ilk dayes work; And the able woman shierer " is not to exceed sex punds (10*s.*) and a peck of meill with meit and " drink, or fyve schilling (5*d.*) and twa mailles for ilk day." " Commone " workmen or laborers," *and tailors*, are to have 3½*d.* a day " and their " dyet," and no more.[1]

Throughout the Highlands prices were much less than in the Low country. Even in Inverness, although it was a garrison town, Captain Burt, who was stationed there about a hundred and sixty years ago, says: " Mutton and beef are about a penny a pound. Salmon, which was at the " same price, is by a late legislation of the magistrates, raised to two pence " a pound, *which is thought by many to be an exorbitant price.* A fowl may " be had at market for two pence or two pence halfpenny." But these last were "so lean they are good for little."[2] As regards the salmon,

---

[1] Burgh Records of Rutherglen quoted in Ure's History, p. 65. [2] Burt's Letters, vol. i. p. 126

prices in Glasgow were as low as in Inverness. They were sometimes sold, as I have already mentioned, at a penny the pound. We are familiar with the story told of the domestic servants in Glasgow, who stipulated that they should not be obliged to eat this now costly fish on more than a certain number of days in the week, and it was the same in Inverness. Captain Burt writes that in his time " the menial servants who are not at " board wages will not make a meal upon salmon if they can get any thing " else to eat."[1] The same writer, referring to the still lower price of provisions in Inverness at an earlier date, says: " I have been told by some " old people that at the time of the Revolution General Mackay was ac- " customed to dine at one of the public houses, where he was served with " great variety, and paid only two shillings and six pence scots, that " is two pence halfpenny for his ordinary."[2] Wages were low in proportion. In Burt's time many servant girls, he tells us, had for wages only " three half crowns a year each, and a peck of oatmeal for a week's diet, " and happy she that can get the skimming of a pot to mix with her oat- " meal for better commons. To this allowance is added a pair of shoes " or two, for sundays when they go to the kirk."[3]

In looking at these old accounts, in England as well as in Scotland, we cannot fail to be struck in particular with the very low prices at which horses and cattle could be purchased, but this is in a great measure to be accounted for by the wretched state of the breeds and the difficulty of finding proper provender for them. Captain Burt refers to this. The horses in Inverness, he says, were very poor and small, and it was difficult to find the means of feeding them. He mentions that in one year he knew of nearly two hundred horses dying of mere want. He tells of an officer, newly arrived in Inverness, who observing the miserable state of the horses there, and that his own would cost him more for their keep than his pay would afford, had them shot—preferring, as he said, to do this rather than by selling them " to let them fall into the " hands of such keepers."[4] This prepares us to accept a statement by Major which otherwise it would be difficult to believe. Writing of a period about the beginning of the sixteenth century, he describes some of the Highlanders as possessing many cattle and horses, of which last, he says, two or three hundred, wild and unbroken, would be brought by one Highlander to Perth or Dundee and sold for two francs each.

Again, in regard to what appears to us as the very low wages paid in

---

[1] Burt's Letters, vol. i. p. 126.　　[2] Ibid. p. 133.　　[3] Ibid. p. 96.　　[4] Ibid. p. 82.

early times, we are too apt to overlook the relative value of commodities. Mr. Hallam, speaking of his own time (1784), observes that "the labouring " classes, especially those engaged in agriculture, were better provided " with the means of subsistence in the reign of Edward III. or of Henry " VI. than they are at present. In the fourteenth century a harvest man " had fourpence a day, which enabled him in a week to buy a comb of " wheat; but to buy a comb of wheat now, a man must work ten or " twelve days. So under Henry VI., if meat was at a farthing and a " half the pound, which I suppose was about the truth, a labourer earning " threepence a day, or eighteenpence in the week, could buy a bushel of " wheat at six shillings the quarter, and twenty-four pounds of meat for " his family. A labourer at present, earning twelve shillings a week, can " only buy half a bushel of wheat at eighty shillings the quarter, and " twelve pounds of meat at sevenpence."[1] A still greater contrast is presented in the prices of the necessaries of life in our own day.

There are other considerations which we must bear in mind, when we read of prices in the olden time. In the reign of Edward I. £20 would be the rental of a considerable estate. An income of £10 or £20 was reckoned in England a competence for a gentleman; and a knight who possessed £150 per annum was considered extremely rich. Even so late as the reign of Henry VIII. the rent of a considerable farm was no more than £3 or £4 a year. Latimer, preaching before the king, said in his homely style, "My father was a yeoman and had no lands of his own; " only he had a farm of three or four pounds a year at the utmost, and " thereupon he held so much land as kept half a dozen men. He had a " walk for a hundred sheep, and my mother milked thirty kine." This would be towards the middle of the fifteenth century.

In Glasgow, as throughout Scotland, such incomes would, in those days, go still farther. Of course, it must also be kept in mind that in the early times the people were comparatively free from taxation, and that the expenditure of those in the position of gentlemen and knights was lessened by the service of their villains or serfs. It must likewise be remembered that the soil had fewer persons to support. So late as 1377 the entire population of England did not exceed two million three hundred thousand.[2]

[1] Middle Ages, vol. iii. p. 453.   [2] Ibid. p. 456.

CONTRAST BETWEEN FORMER AND PRESENT CONDITION OF THE CITY.

In bringing these notices to a close it may be interesting to mention a few prominent points in which the Glasgow of to-day differs from the city of the last century. The contrast will be found very striking.

In 1779 the population was less than 43,000. Including its connected suburbs it now exceeds 780,000.

We do not know what the rental of the city was in the last century, but it must have been very small. In 1878–79 it amounted, in round numbers, to £3,400,000, and of this the increase within the previous twenty-five years was more than £2,000,000.

A hundred years ago the river was almost in a state of nature. It was fordable on foot at Dunbuck—twelve miles below Glasgow—and only small gabbarts could come to the Broomielaw. Now, ships drawing 24 feet of water come up to the harbour.

In 1770 the revenue of the Clyde Trust amounted to £147. In 1887 it amounted to £288,000. Up to 1885 the Trust had expended on the river, and works connected with it, £10,300,000.

A century ago shipbuilding on the Clyde was practically unknown. For the seven years ending with 1877 the tonnage of all the vessels built in the United Kingdom amounted to 3,220,000, and of this there was built on the Clyde no less than 1,360,000. In the seven following years the tonnage of the vessels built on the Clyde amounted to 1,943,339 tons, making, for the fourteen years ending with 1884, a total tonnage built of over 3,300,000.

Of the increase in commerce I shall mention only two items. In the middle of the last century a "small apartment" in Bell Street sufficed as a manufactory for all the sugar imported into the Clyde. In one year—1878—the imports of this article amounted to 250,000 tons.

A hundred years ago a very small quantity of tea was imported into Glasgow, and a few boxes must have sufficed for the yearly supply of the few families of the better classes who used it—the ladies being almost the only consumers. In 1875 duty was paid on more than six million pounds of tea imported into Glasgow.

Equally striking is the contrast in matters of police. So late as 1777 the total force employed by the magistrates in cleaning the streets and removing refuse was two men. For the year 1887–88 the ordinary expenditure of the Cleansing Department, including interest, amounted in round numbers to £74,000.

Towards the middle of the eighteenth century two individuals contracted with the magistrates "to keep up maintain and uphold the "whole causeys of the public streets, wynds, vennels, lanes, high ways "and roads, within and about this city and territories thereof." They undertook to do this for fifteen years, for a sum equal to a yearly payment of £66 per annum.[1] Of the expenditure of the Corporation in this department previous to 1856 I have no note. The total amount expended in permanent pavior work for the thirty-one years from that year to 1887 was upwards of £491,000—on an average about £16,000 per annum—and this was exclusive of all outlay on maintenance and repair. The outlay, for maintenance and repair alone, of streets and sewers for one year (1887) was £42,000. All this is exclusive of the expenditure for similar purposes in the burghs which form the suburban part of the city.

Till so late as 1780 there was not a lamp in the city. In that year the magistrates resolved to put up *nine* on the south side of the Trongate. At present there are more than 40,500 lamps lighted by the corporation in the streets, courts, and stairs of the city. This is exclusive of upwards of 730 lamps lighted by the Clyde Trustees at the harbours and docks; and it is also exclusive of those lighted in the suburbs, which, although really part of the city, are under separate municipal management. Altogether there must be more than fifty thousand lamps lighted every night in the city and suburbs and at the harbours.

In 1788 the magistrates established their first paid police force, and the expenditure in the following year, for the superintendent and his officers, was £135. The other incidental expenses must have been small. For 1886–87 the ordinary expenditure, being the cost of the force for that year, including police office, fiscal, stipendiary magistrate, &c., was upwards of £96,600. In 1878 there was paid in this department, in salaries and wages alone, exclusive of clothing to the force and various other charges, upwards of £60,000. This also was exclusive of the expense of the separate police expenditure in the suburbs.

---

[1] Burgh Records, 7th March, 1728.

As regards the post-office the change has been great over the whole kingdom, but nowhere has it been greater than in Glasgow. In 1787 the post-office was situated in Princes Street, then called Gibson's Wynd, and consisted of three very small rooms, the yearly rent of which was £8; and the whole staff at that time amounted to five individuals. In 1887, at the palatial establishment in George Square (to which there is now about to be added the extensive premises of the old Athenæum, formerly the Assembly Rooms), the staff employed amounts to upwards of 1400, besides over 200 employed at the subordinate offices. We have no account of the number of letters dealt with weekly in 1787. It must have been very small. At present it amounts to two millions five hundred thousand weekly. Even so late as 1855 the revenue of the post-office was little over £59,000. In 1887 it amounted to £336,000—the yearly expenditure being £107,000.

Previous to 1806 the only supply of water to the city was from some wells in the streets and closes, with a small quantity supplied from barrels carted through the streets by Mr. Harley and sold at a halfpenny for each "stoup." At present the quantity delivered daily to a population of 785,000 is forty-one millions seven hundred thousand gallons of water, of the finest quality, at a cost of one penny for 400 gallons.

In 1844, when the Corporation administered only the Common Good, the municipal revenue was £15,300. In 1885 the yearly revenue, including the police, water, parks, tramways, markets, and other trusts, was £1,186,000.

But I need not pursue this. In all other matters the contrast between the old city and the Glasgow of to-day is equally remarkable.

As to the city itself an inhabitant of the last century could not recognize it. Apart from its extension, a large part of the old town has entirely disappeared, and in what remains startling changes have been made. Beautiful parks have been formed at a great cost. Dingy old buildings have given way to palatial erections. Up to 1814 the Council Chambers, the Civil and Justiciary Courts, and the offices of the Corporation found accommodation within the buildings of the old Tolbooth at the Cross. Now the entire east side of George Square, with a large part of the streets on each side, is occupied by Municipal buildings of a very beautiful design, which have been erected at a cost of upwards of half a million sterling. Another magnificent building has been erected on Gilmourhill for the accommodation of the University at a large cost.

The improvements in the city have been going on since the beginning of the century with wonderful rapidity, but the changes, besides those mentioned, which have taken place within the last eighteen years are very remarkable. During that short time three and a half miles of new streets have been formed, many of the old ones have been widened and altered, and whole streets of houses have been swept away. The whole of the upper part of the High Street, including the "Bell-of-the-Brae," with its primitive and picturesque houses, has been removed, the gradient of the street has been reduced, and a large open space—Cathedral Square—has been formed at the top. The east end of Rottenrow is gone, with large portions of Drygate. Farther down, on the west side, there are many changes. Bell Street has been widened, and nearly all the north side of it pulled down. On the east side of High Street the whole of the extensive area between the College and Græme Street—with all the narrow closes and vennels which ran eastward from it—has been swept away. The old College has disappeared. An important part of its front now forms a gateway and lodge to the new College; and at the old site, and in what were but yesterday the quiet haunts of students, the scream of the railway whistle is now heard. Almost the whole of the east side of Saltmarket, with its unhealthy closes, has been pulled down. On both sides of Trongate many objectionable buildings and unwholesome passages—places which bore the worst character, and which defied police and sanitary supervision—have been annihilated. A great part of both sides of the Gallowgate, and large extents of street in Gorbals and Calton, besides many other parts of the old city, have been remodelled, or entirely swept away—the old buildings being, in many instances, replaced by structures which would have struck with amazement an inhabitant of fifty years ago. Ill-ventilated, overcrowded, and filthy, these old places had become to a large extent the hot-beds of disease and the resorts of criminals. By their removal the picturesque has in many cases suffered no doubt, but in a moral and sanitary point of view the action of the City Improvement Trustees—by whom these great changes have been effected—has conferred a lasting boon on the inhabitants.

So much cannot be said of those who preceded the Improvement Trustees. Nothing could excuse their destruction of historical monuments. The demolition of the Castle of Glasgow, in order that its materials might be used to build an inn in the Gallowgate, was an act of vandalism which only found its counterpart in the crime of those

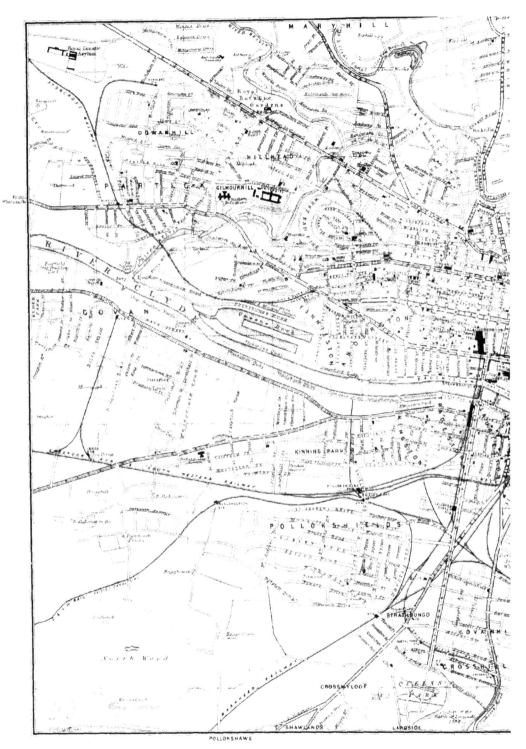

POLLOKSHAWS

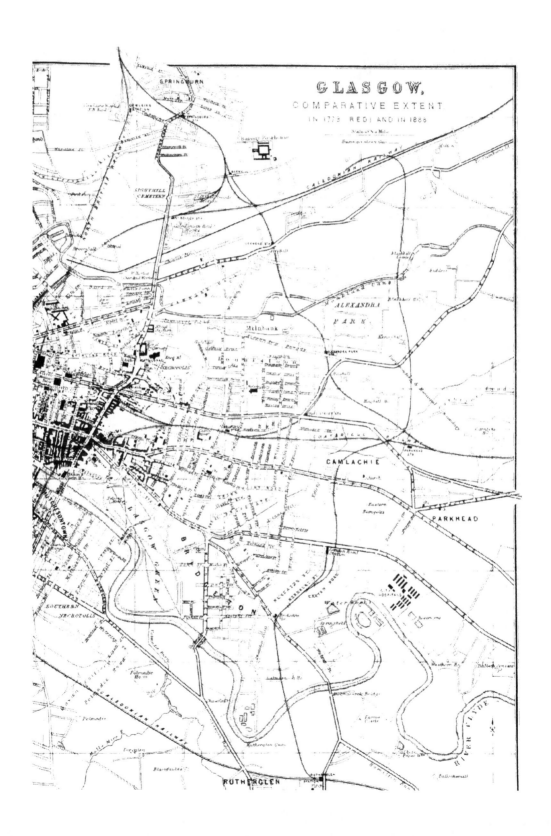

who mutilated the Cathedral, by pulling down the Western Tower and the Consistory House.

Of the extension of the city within a century nothing that I have written can convey any adequate idea. It will be better understood from the annexed map. As engraved it shows Glasgow as it is. The portion coloured red shows its entire extent in 1773.

U

APPENDIX.

Since the publication of the first edition, I have been indebted to the Rev. F. Cuthbert Wood, Father-guardian of the Franciscan Friary in Glasgow, for the following particulars relating to the Grey Friars. They were principally obtained, he informs me, from a MS. in Blair's College, entitled *Monasticon Mariani Brockii Ord. S. Benedicti Ratisbonæ*.

The Friars Minor—a branch of the Franciscans or Grey Friars— came into Glasgow from Edinburgh in the year 1449, at the instance of Bishop William Turnbull, who had been two years before promoted to the see of Glasgow. The Friars were at first lodged in a private house in or near the High Street, where, for a period of twenty-six years, they were supported by Thomas Forsyth, a Canon of the Cathedral, and afterwards Rector of Glasgow, and Rector of the University. Under the episcopate of Bishop John Laing, this private residence was in the year 1476 superseded by a regular Friary, confirmed by a bull of Sixtus IV., dated Kal: December 1476. The buildings extended down the wynd, which came to be called by their name; and the bishop assisted their patron, the canon, in erecting a church and cloister, which were consecrated in honour of the Virgin on the ninth Sunday after Pentecost, 1477. It was one of the brethren of this order—F. James Muirhead— who was sent by Bishop Turnbull to Rome in 1451, to be the bearer of the bull by Pope Nicholas V. for the foundation of the University of Glasgow. The first professor of philosophy in the College became after- wards a Franciscan, and died in the Glasgow Friary. The Friars were expelled from their possessions in 1560, and their house and church were ransacked by the troops under the Duke of Chatelherault and the Earl of Argyll. After a lapse of more than three hundred years they were re-established in premises on the south side of the river in 1869, the same year in which the operations of the City Improvement Trustees swept away certain old buildings in the Grey Friars Wynd, which were believed to be a remnant of their ancient friary.

Brown in his *History of Glasgow*[1] mentions a tradition that after the

[1] Vol. i. page 19.

expulsion of the Friars their convent was used as the bishop's prison and guard house, and that here was the scene of the sufferings of Father Ogilvie the Jesuit, in the beginning of the seventeenth century. But I find no authority for this. There is no evidence that the old convent was ever used as a prison, and at all events we know from the *Relatio*, written by Ogilvie himself and published within three months after his death, as well as from other documents, that the only places in which he was imprisoned were the Archiepiscopal Palace and the old Tolbooth at the Cross. His trial, as we know from Pitcairn, took place at the latter, and he was executed at the cross—called in the contemporary account, the *Forum* (or market-place)—having been led from the Court-house direct to the scaffold. The execution took place on a Tuesday, 10th March, 1615, at four o'clock in the afternoon, and he was buried in the ground set apart for malefactors on the north side of the Cathedral.

INDEX.

THE END.

9 781241 321789